4520

$48.

D0948391

BIOLOGY AND GEOLOGY OF CORAL REEFS

VOLUME III: Biology 2

CONTRIBUTORS

Albert H. Banner

A. J. Bruce

H. Robert Bustard

Ann M. Cameron

Ailsa M. Clark

Robert Endean

F. R. Fosberg

Barry Goldman

Harold Heatwole

Jiro Kikkawa

Wendell K. Patton

Frank Hamilton Talbot

BIOLOGY
AND GEOLOGY
OF CORAL REEFS

EDITED BY

O. A. JONES

Department of Geology
University of Queensland
St. Lucia, Brisbane
Queensland, Australia

R. ENDEAN

Department of Zoology
University of Queensland
St. Lucia, Brisbane
Queensland, Australia

VOLUME III: Biology 2

ACADEMIC PRESS   New York   San Francisco   London   1976

A Subsidiary of Harcourt Brace Jovanovich, Publishers

ACADEMIC PRESS, INC.
111 Fifth Avenue, New York, New York 10003

United Kingdom Edition published by
ACADEMIC PRESS, INC. (LONDON) LTD.
24/28 Oval Road, London NW1

Library of Congress Cataloging in Publication Data

Jones, Owen Arthur.
    Biology and geology of coral reefs.

    Includes bibliographies.
    CONTENTS: v. 1.   Geology 1.–v. 2.   Biology 1.–
v. 3.   Biology 2.
    1.   Coral reef biology–Collected works.   2.   Coral
reefs and islands–Collected works.   I.   Endean, R.,
joint author.   II.   Title.
QH95.8.J66   574.909′4′2   72-84368
ISBN 0–12–389603–7 (v.3)

PRINTED IN THE UNITED STATES OF AMERICA

To the Great Barrier Reef Committee, its office-bearers and its many members who have worked unremittingly for fifty years to further our knowledge of the Great Barrier Reef; and to the memory of geologist Professor H. C. Richards, one of its founders, and biologist Professor E. J. Goddard, an early enthusiastic supporter

CONTENTS

1. Animal Associates of Living Reef Corals

Wendell K. Patton

2. Shrimps and Prawns of Coral Reefs, with Special Reference to Commensalism

A. J. Bruce

7.   Destruction and Recovery of Coral Reef Communities

Robert Endean

8.   Coral Island Vegetation

F. R. Fosberg

9.   The Birds of the Great Barrier Reef

Jiro Kikkawa

10.   Turtles of Coral Reefs and Coral Islands

H. Robert Bustard

11.   The Ecology and Biogeography of Coral Cays

Harold Heatwole

LIST OF CONTRIBUTORS

Numbers in parentheses indicate the pages on which the authors' contributions begin.

ALBERT H. BANNER, Department of Zoology, University of Hawaii, Honolulu, Hawaii (177)

A. J. BRUCE, East African Marine Fisheries Research Organization, Mombasa, Kenya, Africa (37)

H. ROBERT BUSTARD,* Research School of Biological Sciences, Australian National University, Canberra, Australia (343)

ANN M. CAMERON, Department of Zoology, University of Queensland, St. Lucia, Brisbane, Queensland, Australia (155)

AILSA M. CLARK, British Museum (Natural History), London, England (95)

ROBERT ENDEAN, Department of Zoology, University of Queensland, St. Lucia, Brisbane, Queensland, Australia (215)

F. R. FOSBERG, Botany Department, Natural History Museum, Smithsonian Institution, Washington, D.C. (255)

BARRY GOLDMAN,† School of Biological Sciences, Macquarie University, Sydney, Australia (125)

HAROLD HEATWOLE, Department of Zoology, University of New England, Armidale, N.S.W., Australia (369)

JIRO KIKKAWA, Department of Zoology, University of Queensland, St. Lucia, Brisbane, Queensland, Australia (279)

WENDELL K. PATTON, Department of Zoology, Ohio Wesleyan University, Delaware, Ohio (1)

FRANK HAMILTON TALBOT, The Australian Museum, Sydney, Australia (125)

* Present address: Airlie Brae, Alyth, Perthshire, Scotland.
† Present address: School of Natural Resources, University of the South Pacific, Suva, Fiji.

GENERAL PREFACE

This four-volume work (two volumes covering geological and two biological topics) originated from an article on The Great Barrier Reefs of Australia written by the editors and published in the November 1967 issue of *Science Journal.* The prime aim of this treatise is to publish in one source as many as possible of the major advances made in the diverse facets of coral reef problems, advances scattered in a multitude of papers and published in a variety of journals.

Initially a one-volume work was projected, but the wealth of material available led to this four-volume treatise. Two contain chapters on aspects of geomorphology, tectonics, sedimentology, hydrology, and radiometric chronology relevant to coral reefs, and two accommodate articles on pertinent biological topics.

The task of organizing the contributions by some forty-one authors (situated in eight different countries) on forty-six different topics proved a formidable one. We wish to thank the contributors, all of whom have been as cooperative as their teaching and/or other commitments permitted.

We feel that the material presented in these volumes demonstrates that many major advances in our knowledge have been made in recent years. We realize that the treatment of the topics covered is not complete and that in many cases new problems have been brought to light. It is our hope that the volumes will provide a powerful stimulus to further work on all aspects of coral reefs.

The editors, of course, accept overall responsibility for all four volumes. Dr. Jones is mainly responsible for the editing of the two geology volumes; Dr. Endean for that of the two biology volumes.

O. A. JONES
R. ENDEAN

PREFACE TO VOLUME III: BIOLOGY 2

Coral reefs are famed for their biotic complexity. It is therefore not surprising that the topics studied by coral reef biologists are many and varied. A selection of these topics was presented in the preceding volume of this treatise and another is presented here. Clearly, it is not possible to cover all the major facets of coral reef biology in these two volumes. Rather, it is our intention to provide information that will enable the general biologist to assess the present status of research in a number of the major fields embraced by modern coral reef biology. At the same time, it is hoped that as a result of bringing together contributions dealing with a variety of topics and written from different vantage points some cross-fertilization of ideas will occur that will benefit those workers actively involved in research in coral reef biology. Also, it is hoped that some of the exciting new developments revealed in these volumes will stimulate increasing numbers of students to study the biota of coral reefs.

It is of interest that nine of the twelve authors who have contributed to this volume have carried out at least some of their research at Heron Island and adjacent reefs in the Capricorn Group at the southern end of the largest and most diverse coral reef ecosystem known. The Great Barrier Reef Committee, to which these volumes are dedicated, was responsible for establishing a research station at Heron Island in 1953. Erection of the station has provided hundreds of scientists with easy access to flourishing coral reefs, with basic facilities for studying these reefs and their fauna and flora, and with the opportunity of comparing and contrasting such with those of other areas in which they have worked.

The station at Heron Island joined a distinguished company of stations established since the beginning of this century. From them has emanated, especially during the last forty years, a steady stream of important papers on many and varied aspects of coral reef biology. Nevertheless, it is essential that the number of research stations in coralliferous areas be rapidly increased so that baseline data can be obtained before current and projected human activities in tropical areas inevitably modify biotic assemblages found there.

The great species diversity exhibited by the biota of coral reefs has for long attracted the attention of biologists. In Chapter 1 of this volume Dr. Wendell K. Patton gives a stimulating account of the great variety of animals that are permanently or temporarily associated with living corals despite the formidable nematocyst batteries possessed by corals. Some of the associations, particularly those between crustaceans and corals, are highly specific. In Chapter 2 Dr. A. J. Bruce describes some of the remarkable specializations undergone by some of the shrimps and prawns permanently associated with living corals. He points out that these associations augment the number of biological niches available for colonization, thereby contributing to the biotic complexity of coral reefs.

There do not appear to be any records of symbiotic associations between corals and the echinoderms, a conspicuous group of marine animals perhaps best known taxonomically of all marine groups. In Chapter 3 Ailsa Clark provides a valuable account of the appearance and distribution of coral reef echinoderms and discusses their biogeography.

Among the most conspicuous inhabitants of coral reefs are the fishes. The diversity, abundance, distribution, and feeding relationships of coral reef fishes are reviewed by Dr. Barry Goldman and Dr. Frank Hamilton Talbot in Chapter 4. The important role played by fishes in the energetics of the coral reef system is emphasized.

In Chapter 5 Dr. Ann M. Cameron discusses the high incidence of toxic fishes in coral reef waters. She introduces the interesting view that toxicity has helped such fishes become site-attached, and that this, in turn, has contributed to the high species diversity shown by coral reef fishes. Fishes that contain toxic material responsible for the disease ciguatera pose a significant medical problem in coral reef areas. Dr. Albert H. Banner provides, in Chapter 6, a fascinating account of the many problems posed by ciguatera, particularly those relating to the origin and transmission of ciguatoxin as well as those relating to its detection, pharmacology, and chemistry.

Natural and man-induced destruction of coral reef communities and the rate, manner, and extent of recovery from such destruction are discussed in Chapter 7 by Dr. Robert Endean. It is pointed out that international action is required if catastrophic destruction of coral reef systems as a result of human activities is to be avoided. As noted by Dr. F. R. Fosberg, the vegetation of coral islands has already been profoundly affected by human activities. In Chapter 8 he describes the remarkable range of types of vegetation that will grow on the limestone substratum provided by coral islands.

Coral cays provide important nesting and breeding sites for large numbers of sea birds. In Chapter 9 Dr. Jiro Kikkawa provides distributional data on the birds of the Great Barrier Reef region and an interesting account of the behavior and evolution of island populations of sea birds.

Sea turtles also use coral islands as breeding sites. In Chapter 10 Dr. H. Robert Bustard presents a valuable account of the general biology of these marine reptiles. Reference to the amazing migrations undergone by some species is given. Again, the need for international action to conserve remaining turtle stocks is emphasized.

In Chapter 11 Dr. Harold Heatwole stresses the unique features of coral island communities and discusses the factors that influence the numbers and types of organisms found on coral islands. The ways in which coral islands are colonized by animals and plants make interesting reading.

We are indebted to Marilyn McCorry for assistance with the indexing of this volume.

R. Endean
O. A. Jones

CONTENTS OF PREVIOUS VOLUMES

1

ANIMAL ASSOCIATES OF LIVING REEF CORALS

Wendell K. Patton

I. Introduction

The zooxanthellae-containing Madreporaria or Scleractinia, known as reef or hermatypic corals, play a variety of roles in the coral reef ecosystem. The living corals provide food for fish and other predators (Hiatt and Strasburg, 1960; Robertson, 1970) and may release significant amounts of organic matter as coral mucus (Johannes, 1967). In addition, as will be seen below, living reef corals provide a habitat for a variety of temporary and permanent residents. The dead coral skeletons are important contributors to the coral reef framework and to the sediment within and around the reef (reviewed by Stoddart, 1969). Coral skeletons also provide hiding places for small animals and a substrate to

1

which corals, algae, and a wide variety of sessile and burrowing organisms may attach. Overgrown and tunneled pieces of coral, in turn, provide habitats for still other species.

The fauna inhabiting a given living coral is generally poorer in individuals and species than that of an equally sized piece of overgrown, dead coral skeleton. The species that do occur on living coral are often quite specialized for this mode of life. Many are found only on certain families or genera so that the total fauna of coral-associated animals is actually very rich. Gerlach (1960) and Morton and Challis (1969) have drawn attention to the coral head as a community and have briefly discussed the types of organisms occurring within it. This chapter attempts a more detailed summary of the associates of reef corals and a consideration of some of the interactions that may exist between corals and their inhabitants. It is based on a review of the literature combined with personal observations made primarily at Heron Island, Australia, but also at other localities in the Indo-Pacific and in the Caribbean.

When the word symbiosis is employed, it will be used in its broad sense as a general term for the "living together" of unlike organisms, without any implications as to nutrition or effect on the host. Parasitism and commensalism are used as subdivisions indicating the nutritional relationship between the species. Thus, a parasite is a symbiont deriving energy from living host tissues, whereas a commensal is a symbiont obtaining energy from other sources (Patton, 1967b).

II. The Coral-Associated Animals

This section will review the animals found with living reef corals. Emphasis is placed on the obligatory symbionts, although some wandering predators and casual associates are included, and on the species that have been investigated most thoroughly. No attempt has been made to include all reports of animals found with coral although some, mainly recent, host records are given. In cases where the locality is not mentioned, it can be assumed to be Indo-Pacific. An important group of coral associates, the Decapoda Natantia, is dealt with by Bruce (this volume, Chapter 2) and has largely been omitted from the following discussion. The numerous species collected by McCloskey (1970) from eight colonies of the hermatypic coral *Oculina arbuscula* in North and South Carolina are not included as none was found exclusively on living coral, and the great majority of individuals and species inhabited the dead base of the colony or burrows within it.

A. Meiofauna

The smaller associates of living coral are, as would be expected, least known taxonomically and biologically, but may be quite numerous. When pieces of living coral are observed under a dissecting microscope, ciliated protozoans and small flatworms may be seen moving over the coral surface. On an Indonesian reef, Boschma (1936, p. 19) noticed "multitudes of small brown flatworms on colonies of *Merulina* and *Montipora*, which covered the greater part of the surface of these corals." In the Maldive Islands, Gerlach (1960) collected nematodes from living corals but found them to be the same species as those from dead coral, algae, or Alcyonaria.

Recent work, primarily in the Indian Ocean, has shown that Indo-Pacific hermatypic corals have a well-developed fauna of symbiotic cyclopoid copepods (Humes, 1960, 1962a,b, 1973; Humes and Frost, 1964; Humes and Ho, 1967, 1968a,b; Humes and Stock, 1972, 1973; Stock and Humes, 1969; Stock, 1966). Many more species and genera will undoubtedly be discovered as more host corals and localities are examined. At present, these copepods all seem to be obligate symbionts and many appear to be specific to a given genus of coral. They can be removed from the host by rinsing the coral in 5% ethanol in seawater, crushing the coral, and examining the debris or, most satisfactorily, by leaving the coral in the dilute alcohol for 7–14 hours and then examining the sediment in the container (Humes, 1962a,b).

Both highly modified and relatively unmodified copepods are found living with corals. The latter types (Fig. 1A) belong primarily to the family Lichomolgidae and occur on the external surface of the coral. I had an opportunity to observe a species of this group that increased in numbers and became very common on several pieces of the faviid coral *Goniastrea* that were maintained for a month in a laboratory aquarium. The copepods had white markings on their bodies and the females bore white egg sacs, making both sexes quite conspicuous against the brown coral tissue. Individual copepods remained bent over the coral tissue and motionless for long periods of time, resembling pieces of sand that had settled on the coral surface. They changed position periodically by means of a short burst of rapid, but erratic swimming, following which they again became motionless. Such behavior is clearly advantageous since a slowly moving animal of similar conspicuous coloration would be easily recognized by visually orienting predators. When copepods were removed from the host for two days and then returned, they attached to the host at once and there was a great increase in the

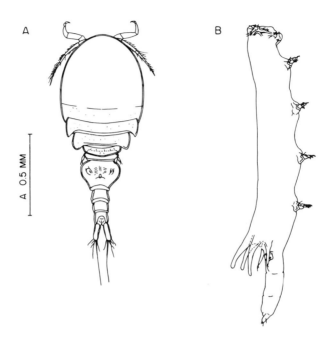

Fig. 1. Coral-associated copepods. (A) "Unmodified" type found on external surface of coral. *Lichomolgus campulus*, female, dorsal view. From Humes and Ho (1968a). (B) "Transformed" type found within coral polyps. *Xarifia lamellispinosa*, female, lateral view. From Humes and Ho (1968b).

movement of the digestive tract, suggesting that host tissue was being ingested. Specimens of two species of *Favia* were placed in the same aquarium, but despite the fact that they belonged to the same family as *Goniastrea,* the copepods did not become established on them and disappeared with the death of the *Goniastrea* fragments.

The highly modified or transformed copepods have a wormlike form (Fig. 1B) and are generally unable to swim. Only a small percentage of the specimens that eventually appear are found when the coral is initially rinsed in the 5% alcohol. This indicates that they chiefly occur inside the coral polyps and are gradually affected by the alcohol and stimulated to climb out. These species include representatives of several copepod families, with the majority of species described to date belonging to the family Xarifiidae. Gerlach (in Humes, 1960) observed specimens of a species of *Xarifia* crawl over the surface of a *Pocillopora* colony in caterpillar fashion and move in and out of the coral polyps, tearing the host tissue as they did so.

Marcus and Masry (1970) have observed a black, harpacticoid cope-pod moving with a rolling motion over the surface of a *Stylophora* colony collected in the Gulf of Eilat. The animals were never seen to leave the coral and swim freely in the water, although the population appeared to transfer suddenly from the *Stylophora* to a *Pocillopora* colony in the same tank.

A number of mysid crustaceans of the genus *Heteromysis* live in associ-ation with other invertebrates. Several species have been found in the washings of various corals, or have been netted in their vicinity, and may well be commensals (Tattersall, 1967; Pillai, 1968).

B. PORIFERA

Sponges and reef corals interact in a variety of ways. Boring sponges of the family Clionidae are found in calcareous substrates including dead and living corals and inhabit cavities that they excavate by remov-ing small chips of $CaCO_3$. Goreau and Hartman (1963) have found them to be important in the destruction of reef corals below 30 m on the forereef slope in Jamaica. The point of attachment of the coral to the substrate is eroded, causing the coral to break off and fall into deeper water where it is covered and killed by sediment. On the other hand, large nonboring sponges attached to such colonies often hold the corals in place after their point of attachment has been eroded away. Boring sponges enter Jamaican corals at exposed dead portions of the colony and may make extensive burrows throughout the skeleton. The living coral polyps do not appear to be harmed by the activities of the sponge nor does the sponge obtain any nourishment from the coral tissue (Goreau and Hartman, 1963). In the Maldives, Gardiner (1903) found that living pieces of the branching coral *Pocillopora* had a network of *Cliona* filaments extending throughout the skeleton. *Cliona* filaments did not occur in dead or decaying portions of coral and gen-erally seemed to die with the coral that they inhabited, suggesting a nutritional relationship between the sponge and the living coral.

The Caribbean sponges *Siphonodictyon coralliphagum* and *Siphono-dictyon cacharouense* excavate cavities within the skeleton of massive corals and produce chimneys that extend through and above the coral surface (Rützler, 1971). They definitely attack living coral and lead to at least localized death of the polyps.

Most Jamaican boring sponges inhabit a variety of calcareous sub-strates, with only one of the nine species found inhabiting *Acropora cervicornis* being possibly restricted to that coral. The growth form shown by the coral is, however, important in determining the distribution of sponge species, as sponges forming large excavations occur most often in massive corals, whereas the species that contain zooxanthellae are found inhabiting well-illuminated substrates (Pang, 1973).

An interesting facultative, but mutually beneficial, relationship between the common West Indian sponge *Mycale laevis* and various flattened reef corals on the forereef slope of Jamaica has been described by Goreau and Hartman (1966). The sponge grows on the under surface of the coral causing it to form upturned peripheral folds above the sponge oscules. The sponge benefits by having a continually expanding substrate on which to grow, while the presence of *Mycale* on the under surface of the coral shields it from attack by boring sponges.

C. SIPUNCULIDA AND POLYCHAETA

These two groups are common in dead coral and important in its destruction, but occur less frequently with living coral.

A mutually beneficial association exists between the spinunculid *Aspidosiphon corallicola* and the unattached hermatypic coral *Heteropsammia michelini*. These animals inhabit soft substrata and have been studied by several workers, most recently by Goreau and Yonge (1968). The initial stage of the association involves a sipunculid inhabiting an empty gastropod shell. The coral planula settles on the shell and the coral gradually grows over and encloses it, but maintains an opening around the worm. The worm is thus provided with a living shelter into which it may retreat. The association is apparently obligatory for the coral. It is provided with protection from being buried and transport to areas of fresh sediment on which it may feed (Goreau and Yonge, 1968).

The tubes of polychaetes can be found growing out of or lying on the surface of colonies of living coral. New tube is deposited as the coral grows, which may give the misleading impression that the worm has burrowed into the coral (Yonge, 1963). Best known are the serpulids of the genus *Spirobranchus*. Typically the branchial crown has a bright but highly variable coloration. The genus occurs singly on living coral heads in the Barbados (Marsden, 1960) and inhabits *Porites* and faviid mounds in the Solomon Islands (Morton and Challis, 1969), whereas on the reef flat at Heron Island, Great Barrier Reef, it is commonly seen growing out of the thick branches of *Acropora brueggemanni* (Fig. 2). Although *Spirobranchus* is not found exclusively on living coral, it appears that some species settle preferentially upon it.

In the Caribbean the omnivorous amphinomid polychaete *Hermodice*

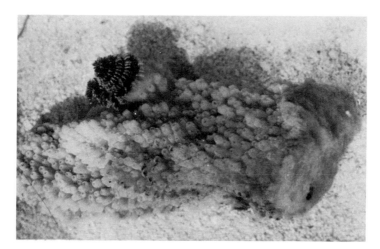

Fig. 2. The serpulid polychaete *Spirobranchus* showing the extension of the tube through a branch of *Acropora brueggemanni.*

carunculata has been observed feeding on *Porites* and other corals. The worm hides during the brightest part of the day, emerging to feed during conditions of reduced light. The buccal region is everted for several minutes over a section of living coral. The coral tissue is then sucked into the gut exposing the coral skeleton and the process is repeated (Marsden, 1962, 1963; Glynn, 1963). Barbados specimens feed primarily on the zooanthid *Palythoa* and secondarily on *Porites* species (Ott and Lewis, 1972).

D. GASTROPODA

The prosobranch gastropods associated with reef corals range from wandering predators to sedentary inhabitants of a single colony and have been throughly reviewed by Robertson (1970). Three families whose members feed exclusively on cnidarians have representatives that feed on corals. Among the Architectonicidae, Hawaiian specimens of *Philippia* (*Psilazis*) *radiata* are found buried in sand or rubble near a *Porites* colony during the day and at night emerge and feed on the coral polyps. The proboscis is unusually long and slender and bears the mouth and radula at its tip (Robertson *et al.*, 1970). Among the Epitoniidae, three species of *Epitonium* are known from the solitary coral *Fungia* and two from the ahermatypic, but reef-dwelling, *Tubastrea*. In a study of *Epitonium ulu* in Hawaii, Bosch (1965) found that the stomachs of specimens kept in the dark with *Fungia* contained coral tissue, including nematocysts and zooxanthellae. The snails avoided light and were restricted to the tentacle-free, peripheral and under surfaces of their hosts. Populations of *E. ulu* increased rapidly in laboratory tanks since the snail was able to grow from the larval stage to a mature adult within the remarkably short period of three weeks. The family Ovulidae is mainly associated with alcyonarians, but contains *Jenneria pustulata*, which lives and feeds on hard corals in the eastern Pacific. It seems to prefer the coral *Pocillopora* on which it feeds nocturnally. It is the most important predator on *Pocillopora* in the Pearl Islands of Panama and may account for the destruction of 25% of the annual growth of this coral (Glynn *et al.*, 1972).

In Jamaica the snail *Calliostoma javanicum* of the typically herbivorous family Trochidae has been observed to feed on the coral *Agaricia* (Miller, 1972). In the primarily free-living family Muricidae, several species are occasionally found on living coral and at least one, *Drupa cornus*, definitely feeds on it (Robertson, 1970; Taylor, 1971). Fankboner (in Robertson, 1970) found this species consistently on *Pocillopora* and *Porites*, where it fed nocturnally on coral tissue by digesting it externally with salivary secretions. The unusually large mucus production of the snail and the cuticularized proboscis may provide protection from coral nematocysts.

The family Coralliophilidae is apparently derived from the Muricidae, is found exclusively in association with cnidarians, and contains the most modified of all the prosobranch coral-associates. Its members lack jaws and a radula, but have a strongly muscular pharynx, and seem to feed suctorially. The coral-dwelling species of *Coralliophila* have globular shells and are somewhat sedentary. In the Caribbean *C. caribaea* occurs chiefly on gorgonians but on corals, zoanthids, and actinarians as well, while *C. abbreviata* is more common on corals but also inhabits other anthozoans (Robertson, 1970; Miller, 1972). Ward (1965) has studied the behavior and anatomy of feeding in *C. abbreviata* in the Barbados, where it is found in clusters on massive colonies of *Montastrea annularis*. When an individual is placed on a new host, it moves to the boundary of dead and living coral and eventually extends its slender proboscis into an adjacent coral polyp. Ward believes that the coral epidermis is penetrated chemically by a secretion of the salivary glands and that material is withdrawn by a pumping action within the proboscis. Stomach contents consist of mucus, zooxanthellae, nematocysts, and green algae. Feeding occurs during both day and night and is partly responsible for the destruction of the host coral (Ward, 1965). Miller (1972) observed the proboscis of *Coralliophila* being inserted in the coral epidermis and also into the oral openings of individual polyps. Ott and Lewis (1972) only rarely observed the direct removal of coral tissue and found that the dead coral areas inhabited by *C. abbreviata* specimens at the base of 14 *Montastrea* colonies did not increase measurably over a six-month period. In the Indo-Pacific, *Coralliophila violacea* occurs on *Porites* and *Goniopora* of the family Poritidae while *Coralliophila erosa* has been collected from *Acropora* and *Montipora* of the family Acroporidae (Maes, 1967; Morton and Challis, 1969; Robertson, 1970).

In the Indo-Pacific genus *Quoyula*, the shell is somewhat flattened and limpetlike and is permanently attached on the living portion of the coral, inducing a scar on the underlying skeleton. It probably consists of a single variable species, *Q. monodonta*, and has been found mainly on corals of the family Pocilloporidae, but also on *Montipora* and *Porites* (Robertson, 1970).

Three genera and four species of the Coralliophilidae are found within the skeletons of living Indo-Pacific corals, chiefly members of the family Faviidae. *Leptoconchus globulosus*, *L. cummingii*, and *Magilopsis lamarckii* are found apex down within burrows in the coral with the siphons extending to a small aperture at the surface. The aperture is generally lined with calcareous material secreted by the siphons, while the lower portion of the burrow usually contains soft muddy deposits presumably composed of coral fragments (Soliman, 1969). Soliman believes that the snails burrow upward by a rocking movement of the shell, thus preventing the aperture from being closed by newly deposited coral. The most highly modified member of the family Coralliophilidae is *Magilus antiquus*. This species does not burrow. As the small initial shell is enclosed and then passed by coral growth, the snail secretes an irregular tubelike extension of the shell into which it moves. This structure extends to the coral surface and increases in length as the coral grows. *Magilus antiquus* is known from *Goniastrea*, *Leptoria*, and perhaps *Platygyra*; all are members of the family Faviidae (Demond, 1957; Robertson, 1970).

Two other gastropod groups, the vermetids and the nudibranchs, have representatives that occur with coral. Vermetid tubes are frequently surrounded by living coral in the same manner as are tubes of serpulid worms. The vermetid survives the death of the coral and the association is clearly not obligatory. In view of the numerous and often highly specific feeding associations that exist between nudibranch gastropods and sessile marine invertebrates, the number of species that has been reported to feed on reef corals is less than might be expected. Species of the genus *Phyllidia* have been observed on *Acropora* (Vicente, in Robertson, 1970; Miller, 1969), while four species of the aeolid genus *Phestilla* inhabit various living corals (Harris, in Robertson, 1970). *Phestilla melanobrachia* feeds on several dendrophyllid corals including the hermatypic genus *Turbinaria* and incorporates host pigment into its own tissues. *Phestilla sibogae* inhabits *Porites.* The veliger larvae of the former species must feed during their planktonic life whereas those of the latter species do not. The larvae of both species require the presence of a host in order for metamorphosis to occur (Harris, 1971). In *P. sibogae, Porites* mucus contains the metamorphosis inducing factor (Hadfield and Karlson, 1969). Both of the above species are unusual among the aeolid nudibranchs that feed on cnidarian tissue in that they do not store host nematatocycts. Instead, the tips of the ceratae contain secretory glands that function in defense against predators (Harris, 1970).

E. PELECYPODA

Although more species are found on dead coral, quite a few bivalves seem capable of attachment to living coral. A few recent Indo-Pacific examples are the following: family Arcidae—*Barbatia complanata,* in pockets in living massive corals at Raroia Atoll (Morrison, 1954); family Pteriidae—*Electroma alacorvi,* attached to *Acropora* and *Pocillopora* at Cocos-Keeling (Maes, 1967); family Pinnidae—*Streptopinna saccata,* growing between branches of *Goniopora* at Mahé in the Seychelles (Taylor, 1968); family Pectinidae—*Chlamys dringi* and *Gloriapallium pallium,* "attached within branching coral" at Mahé (Taylor, 1968); and *Coralichylamys acroporicola* (? = *Chlamys madreporarum*) partially surrounded by *Acropora* at Heron Island (Woolacott, 1955). The scallop *Pedum spondyloideum* is restricted to living coral and has been studied in detail by Yonge (1967). In Rabaul harbor it was common on massive species of *Porites,* where it was attached by byssus threads to the bottom of crevices formed by the growth of the coral around the animal. At Bermuda, in the Atlantic, the small arcid *Barbatia domingensis* occurs most frequently attached to the undersurface of living corals, but is also found on rocks. It shows no preference for any coral species, but does prefer crevices in the coral or burrows formed by other organisms (Bretsky, 1967).

The well-known date mussels of the genus *Lithophaga* (family Mytilidae) burrow into calcareous substrates, including limestone and dead and living coral. They are elongate and tubular, resembling the pit of a date, and are attached to the inside of their burrows by byssus threads. Some, but not all, species are capable of rotation within the burrow. Calcareous fragments derived from burrowing activities may form a granular layer on the anterior and posterior shell surfaces. Three species restricted to living corals of certain genera have been studied by Gohar and Soliman (1963a) and reviewed by Soliman (1969). The shells of these species are weaker than those of mytilids burrowing in dead coral. The presence of a *Lithophaga* within a piece of living coral is generally revealed by a dumbbell-shaped aperture on the coral surface. This reflects the growth of the coral around the excurrent and the slightly larger incurrent siphons of the mussel.

The rock-dwelling *L. lithophaga* burrows anteriorly into calcareous rock with the aid of a neutral mucoprotein with calcium binding properties, secreted by the pallial gland (Jaccarini *et al.*, 1968). Chemical assistance with burrowing seems to be characteristic of the genus (Turner and Boss, 1962; Yonge, in Goreau *et al.*, 1969). Gardiner (1903) states that entrance into a living coral can only occur through a dead portion of the colony. In contrast to this view, Soliman (1969) suggests that the association between date mussels and living corals originates by the settlement of a young *Lithophaga* on the living coral surface. Coral will be gradually deposited around the mussel which will then burrow outward, maintaining contact with the exterior. Burrowing is sporadic and its extent depends on the degree to which the host deposits skeleton around the siphons. Pasty deposits accumulate in the bottoms of the burrows. Soliman (1969) further believes that burrowing in these species is primarily mechanical and is accomplished by abrading the hard calcareous deposits on the posterior surface of the valves against the coral skeleton.

The most intimate association between bivalve and reef coral yet found is that of the mytilid *Fungiacava eilatensis* and various monostomatous corals of the family Fungiidae recently discovered and investigated by Goreau *et al.* (1969, 1970, 1972). The results of these excellent studies can only be briefly summarized. *Fungiacava* is unusual in many ways (Fig. 3). The shell is extremely thin and is completely covered by an extension of the mantle. It lies within a cavity of the host skeleton whose close fit to the shape of the mussel is maintained as the animal grows by the selective absorbtion and secretion of $CaCO_3$. The enlarged inhalant siphon opens into the host coelenteron, rather than to the exterior as in *Lithophaga*. The gills are large but the labial palps are reduced. The foot is extended actively through the side or end of the siphon, and appears to have a sensory function and play an active role

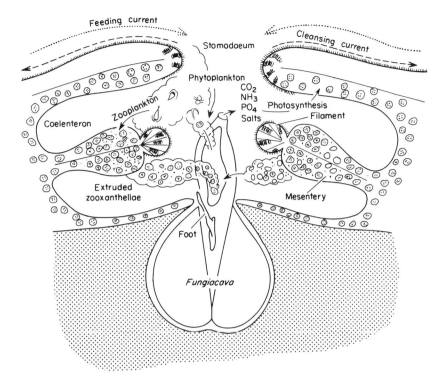

Fig. 3. Diagram of the coral *Fungia* containing the bivalve *Fungiacava*, showing the movement of materials into the host and the symbiont. From Goreau *et al.* (1970).

in feeding. *Fungiacava* is believed to feed on phytoplankton and on zooxanthellae and other material found in the host coelenteron.

F. CIRRIPEDIA

There is considerable literature dealing with the sessile barnacles associated with living reef corals. The generic placement of certain coral-inhabiting species varies widely; the terminology given in the recent revision by Ross and Newman (1973) is followed here. A compilation of host records by Kolosvary (1951) lists several free-living species that are "accidental settlers" on living coral and seven species of *Balanus* (subgenus *Armatobalanus*) that have an affinity for coral. In *Balanus* (*Armatobalanus*) *durhami*, which inhabits *Porites* in the Gulf of California, the entire barnacle except for the pedal opening is covered by coral skeleton and there is a fracture zone between the coral covering the wall plates and that covering the basis (Zullo, 1961). This species grows both in the normal balanid manner by the lengthening of the wall plates and by upward growth of the basal plate (Newman and Ladd, 1974).

The subfamily Pyrgomatinae of the family Balanidae contains 33 species of obligatory coral associates all of which show some fusion of the six wall plates found in typical balanids. This group has commonly been divided into two genera (or subgenera): *Creusia* for those with four wall plates and *Pyrgoma* for the geologically more recent forms with the wall plates fused into a single shell. Ross and Newman (1973) have reexamined the subfamily and conclude that the group is polyphyletic and contains ten genera, nine of which inhabit corals. The single-shelled condition has evolved independently on several occasions. Both in Tanabe Bay, Japan and in the Palau Islands, Hiro (1936, 1938) found that, in general, varieties of the supposedly less highly evolved types with four wall plates showed less host specificity than did the species with a completely fused shell. All coral inhabiting species have a cup-shaped calcareous basal plate and grow mainly by the elongation of the sides of this plate rather than by adding new material to the bottom of the wall plates in the manner of most free-living balanids. Since coral skelton adheres to the sides of the barnacle, upward movement of the wall plates could only occur if the attached coral skeleton could be broken free from the rest of the colony. Growth by addition to the outer margin of the cup-shaped basis, however, permits the rim of the cup to grow, keeping pace with the growth of the surrounding coral. In some species the coral skeleton grows over a portion of the wall and is fractured by the upward growth of the edge of the basal plate, whereas in other species the barnacle seems to inhibit the deposition of coral skeleton around the margin of the shell (Ross and Newman, 1973; Newman and Ladd, 1974). Hiro (1936, 1938) noted that pyrgomatine barnacles could be divided into a small-sized and a large-sized group. The small-sized species are found in corals that grow mainly in a horizontal direction, and have a shallow, cup-shaped base and a conical shell extending above the coral surface (Fig. 4A). The large-sized species inhabit corals that grow radially outward. They have thicker shells and a cylindrical base which grows outward as the coral grows (Fig. 4B), maintaining the aperture at the same level as the coral surface.

Since these barnacles are surrounded by living coral, it would seem to be possible for the barnacle to absorb energy-containing molecules from the host or for other types of exchange to take place, although such exchange has not yet been demonstrated. Some species bear tubes

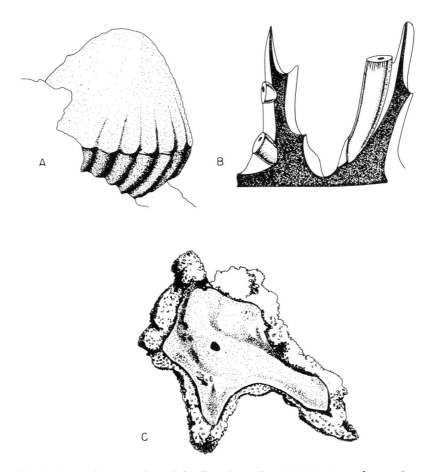

Fig. 4. External views of coral-dwelling barnacles. (A) *Boscia anglicum,* showing shallow base and conical shell. From Ross and Newman (1969). (B) *Savignium crenatum,* showing cylindrical base that grows in response to surrounding coral growth. From Hiro (1938). (C) View from above the parasitic barnacle, *Hoekia monticulariae.* From Ross and Newman (1969). (Not drawn to the same scale.)

in the walls or pores in the basal plate (Ross and Newman 1973; Utinomi, 1967), whereas Moyse (1971) suggests that the suture line between basis and wall that is covered by coral tissue in a number of species is a likely site for the diffusion of solutes into the barnacle. Ross and Newman (1973) believe that a more important function of such openings is to permit the barnacle to exercise physiological control over the deposition of coral skeleton.

The most modified of all the Pyrgomatinae is *Hoekia monticulariae* (Fig. 4C), which inhabits the coral *Hydnophora* and is unusual in having a minute aperture and an irregular stellate shell (Annandale, 1924; Hiro, 1936). The significance of these peculiarities has been elucidated by Ross and Newman (1969) who studied specimens from the Indian Ocean and found that coral tissue was growing completely over the barnacle. The large stomach of the barnacle contained macerated tissue and undischarged nematocysts. There is but one pair of cirri, which are not suitable for filter feeding (Fig. 5B), and the mouth parts are modified. *Hoekia monticulariae* is entirely parasitic and feeds on host tissue that grows over and down into the aperture. [Such a transition is not completely unique, as the pedunculate barnacle *Lepas anserifera* has been reported feeding on *Physalia* tentacles (Jones, 1968).]

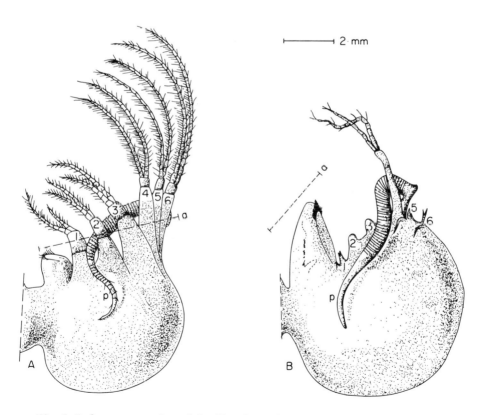

Fig. 5. Body structure of coral-dwelling barnacles. (A) *Boscia anglicum.* (B) The parasitic barnacle *Hoekia monticulariae.* a, Relative size of aperture; l, labrum enclosing mouth parts; p, penis; 1, 2, 3, 4, 5, 6, cirri. From Ross and Newman (1969).

Other types of barnacle are also known to inhabit corals. The pedunculate *Lithotrya* is a common burrower in calcareous substrates, including coral (Sewell, 1926), whereas acrothoracican barnacles inhabit a variety of calcareous substrates, with three species of the genus *Berndtia* occurring in living coral (Tomlinson, 1969).

G. DECAPOD CRUSTACEA

In the Indo-Pacific a variety of small crabs and shrimp is generally found between the branches of living pocilloporid and acroporid corals (Patton, 1966, 1974). Although less diverse, decapods are also found on corals of other families and on Atlantic corals. Although some species are facultative symbionts or merely wanderers onto the living coral, many are obligatory symbionts showing a variety of morphological adaptations and usually being specific to a given coral family. The majority of associations seem to have originated with small species that fed on sediment settling on the coral, and on the mucus secreted by the coral to remove the sediment. This mode of feeding is still widespread, although certain species have evolved other modes of nutrition or greater dependence on host mucus. The species that move freely about the colony will be dealt with separately from those that are sedentary and cause modification of the host skeleton.

1. Mobile Forms

The shrimps associated with corals are discussed in detail in Chapter 2 on commensal Natantia by Bruce and will only be mentioned briefly. The subfamily Pontoniinae of the family Palaemonidae contains numerous coral-associated species that vary from agile facultative associates to highly modified and host-specific obligate symbionts. Bruce (1969, 1972) has discussed the evolution of the coral-inhabiting genera and reviewed the occurrence of the various species on different species of coral. A few additional coral-associated species are found in the families Alpheidae and Hippolytidae. In several of the shrimp species it is usual for a given coral colony to contain only a single male–female pair.

The brachyuran family Xanthidae is abundantly represented on coral reefs. For example, of the 112 species of Brachyura reported from Eniwetok by Garth (1964), 63 belonged to this one family. Most species are fairly small, and quite a few inhabit living coral. Some of these species may use the coral colony only for shelter, whereas others clearly feed on sediment that settles within it (Patton, 1974). As Borradaile (1902) has noted, there is an interesting modification of the walking

legs, which, although not restricted to the coral-dwelling xanthids, is
very common among them. The terminal joint (dactyl) has a flange
on its posterior margin that fits over the flattened margin of the preceding
segment (propodus). This arrangement means that the dactyl cannot
be twisted from its socket if the crab is pulled anteriorly or posteriorly.
It also permits the dactyl to be held firmly at a right angle to the
propodus, forming a hook that can be placed around a coral branch.
A crab can often be provoked into leaving the coral, but an attempt
to pry one loose will usually result in the removal of the legs from
the body, or the crab being broken in two.

In the Indo-Pacific the species of *Cymo* and *Domecia* occur primarily
on living coral and show distinct host preferences. Thus *C. andreossyi*
and *D. hispida* are found on pocilloporid corals whereas *C. melanodacty-
lus*, *C. deplanatus*, and *D. glabra* are found on *Acropora* (Garth, 1964;
Patton, 1966). In the Atlantic *D. acanthophora* is found on *Acropora*
and other corals. This species is most unusual among xanthids in that
it makes filtering motions with its second maxillipeds, which contain
rows of paddle-shaped distal spines. Strands of coral mucus are rejected
and *D. acanthophora* evidently feeds in large part on "organic aggregate"
particles that it removes from the surrounding water (Patton, 1967a).

The subfamily Trapeziinae contains xanthids with a smooth, shiny,
and often brightly colored carapace and is composed of three genera:
Trapezia occurs typically on pocilloporid corals; *Tetralia* on *Acropora*;
and *Quadrella* on soft corals and gorgonians. *Trapezia* and *Tetralia* are
very characteristic inhabitants of their respective corals, and seem well
adapted to their environment. They can hold onto the coral tightly with
their walking legs, but can also move around in the branches with considerable speed and agility. The dactyls of the walking legs have tips
that are broad and blunt. As Borradaile (1902) has suggested, this is
clearly an adaption to the hard, unyielding coral surface since *Quadrella*
has the usual sharply pointed dactyls. Knudsen (1967) has observed
two species of *Trapezia* collecting and eating coral mucus and suggests
that the various setae and spines on the dactyls of the walking legs
have evolved in connection with the induction and transfer of host mucus
secretions.

The division of *Trapezia* and *Tetralia* into species is complicated by
the fact that morphologically similar specimens possess markedly different color patterns (Ortmann, 1897; Patton, 1966). These color forms
are certainly distinct species because both members of a pair always
belong to the same form. Serène (1971) has published a provisional
key to the species of *Trapezia*.

As in several of the commensal shrimps, pair formation is characteristic of *Trapezia* and *Tetralia*. At Heron Island *Trapezia areolata* and the forms of *Tetralia glaberrima* inhabiting open *Acropora* colonies almost invariably occur as a single pair per colony. In *Trapezia cymodoce,* however, a given *Pocillopora* colony often contains a single largest pair plus a variety of distinctly smaller individuals. Preston (1973) has studied the distribution of five species of *Trapezia* inhabiting *Pocillopora meandrina* var. *nobilis* in Hawaii. As a result of intraspecific aggressive interactions, each coral colony typically contained only a single adult pair of a given species. Interaction between species was less intense, as colonies often contained more than one species, although potential competition between certain species was reduced by a preference for hosts of different sizes. At Heron Island, there is also a niche division based on host size, with the smaller *T. areolata* occurring most commonly on the smaller colonies of *Pocillopora damicornis* (Patton, 1974). The ease of movement between the coral branches plays a part in determining whether or not the entire colony will be maintained as a territory. In several instances I have collected closely branched platelike colonies of *Acropora* that contained several pairs of a small form of *T. glaberrima* spaced a few centimeters apart around the periphery of the coral. More open colonies contain only a single male–female pair.

Several brachyuran crabs of the family Majidae are found with living *Pocillopora* in the eastern Pacific (Garth, 1946; Crane, 1947). Spider crabs are known to be obligate symbionts of other anthozoans, and it could be expected that some may be restricted to living corals. In the Caribbean the majid *Mithrax sculptus* is abundant among the branches of *Porites furcata* and feeds nocturnally on the expanded polyps. These are clipped off with the sharp edges of the spoonlike tips of the chelipeds (Glynn, 1963).

The anomuran crabs of the families Galatheidae and Porcellanidae are common under blocks of dead coral, but in the Singapore region at least, several species appear to be obligate symbionts of living coral (Johnson, 1970), and on the Pacific coast of Panama, porcellanids are regularly found on living *Pocillopora* colonies. In the Panamanian region, the hermit crabs *Trizopagurus magnificus* and *Aniculus elegans* feed on *Pocillopora* tissue that they remove by scraping the tips of branches with their chelipeds (Glynn *et al.,* 1972).

2. *Species That Modify the Coral Skeleton*

Several species of decapod remain in one position on the surface of the living coral long enough for the coral skeleton to grow around it, producing a space in which the animal lives. The degree to which the coral skeleton is modified varies from slight to very considerable.

In two species the coral surrounds the animal imprisoning it in a cyst or gall within the coral skeleton. One of these is a seldom collected, highly modified pontoniin shrimp *Paratypton siebenrocki* whose habitat has been recently described by Bruce (1969). The species lives in pairs inside a two-chambered cyst within various species of *Acropora*. The cyst is incorporated into the body of an *Acropora* branch with two small (1.5 mm diameter) openings to the surface. The internal surface of the cyst is covered with a green algal film. *Paratypton siebenrocki* appears to feed on plankton.

The other cyst-inhabiting decapod is the aptly named gall-crab, *Hapalocarcinus marsupialis*. This species is common on three genera of pocilloporid corals and occurs from the Red Sea across to the eastern Pacific. Thanks to the excellent paper of Potts (1915), it has become quite a well-known animal. The adult female is only slightly larger than a pea, with a soft exoskeleton and appendages. As in other members of the family Hapalocarcinidae, the abdomen of the female is much enlarged and contains lateral extensions that fold inward forming a pouch that shelters the developing eggs. The formation and structure of the gall varies with the type of host coral (Potts, 1915; Hiro, 1937). On *P. damicornis*, a young female crab settles at the tip of a branch which is itself beginning to branch into two parts. These branches now broaden and grow upward forming a small cavity for the juvenile crab. New small branches are produced that flatten and coalesce. They grow above the crab, forming an enlarged second stage gall in which the adult female crab will live. At a certain distance above the crab, the sides of the gall come together and fuse in several places closing the gall except for a number of small apertures through which water may pass. The coral may grow above and around the gall so that, except for the apertures and a slight thickening of the coral branch, the gall will be quite inconspicuous.

In *Seriatopora*, whose branches are only a few millimeters in diameter, the crab settles lower down in the colony. It induces the branches around it to produce both flattened extensions and additional branches that together form the gall. In the species of *Stylophora*, gall production usually occurs at the tip of a branch. This genus shows less branching than *P. damicornis* and, as Hiro (1937) has noted, a developing gall often has the appearance of a pair of cymbals (Figure 6A). On the flat-topped, massive branches of *Pocillopora eydouxi*, the crab settles on the top of the branch at right angles to the long axis. As the coral

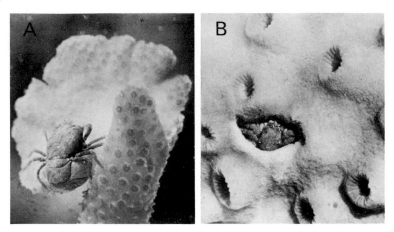

Fig. 6. Hapalocarcinid crabs. (A) *Hapalocarcinus marsupialis* female in an opened gall in the coral *Stylophora pistillata.* (B) *Pseudocryptocheirus viridis* in the coral *Turbinaria.* Carapace width of crabs: A, 5.5 mm; B, 3.0 mm.

grows upward, a gall is formed without the massive deformation of the coral seen in other host species.

The coral tissue within the gall lacks zooxanthellae but is still alive, although both the soft parts and the corallites are considerably modified (Potts, 1915; Hiro, 1937). Semper (1881) suggested that gall formation was caused by the crab's respiratory current and was merely another manifestation of the effect that water currents have on the form of coral skeletons. Potts also felt that the respiratory current was of paramount importance. A stronger current that has been overlooked by previous authors is created by the periodic flicking of the exopods of the first and second maxillipeds. All four exopods may beat together or only those of a single side or a single appendage. Whether water currents alone are involved in gall formation remains to be determined. The production of many small branches and totally atypical flattened branches is certainly suggestive of direct chemical interference with skeleton formation.

The mouthparts of *Hapalocarcinus* are quite different from those of free-living crabs and according to Potts (1915) the female probably feeds on small plankton that it separates from the water with the fringes of setae on the mouthparts. However, I have noticed that specimens on opened galls frequently pick at the underlying coral tissue with their chelae and transfer material to the mouthparts.

Males of *H. marsupialis* are much smaller than females and until recently few had been found. They were thought to be free-living and short-lived (Hiro, 1937). Fize (1956), however, discovered that males are not uncommon and inhabit small open galls that may be overlooked or mistaken for young female-containing galls. The female is presumably fertilized prior to the closing of her gall and, in the manner of a queen bee, is able to store viable sperm for a considerable length of time.

There is a single record (Henderson, 1906) of another hapalocarcinid being enclosed within living branching coral. *Cryptocheirus dimorphus* is reported to live in pairs within cylindrical cavities in *Acropora* that constrict toward the mouth preventing the exit of the larger female.

Twenty-five additional species of hapalocarcinid are currently recognized (Serène, 1967). Of these, two are known from Atlantic corals (Verrill, 1908; Monod, 1956), one from the east Pacific (Garth and Hopkins, 1968), and 23 from the Indo-Pacific. This last figure is due largely to the monographic study of Vietnamese hapalocarcinids by Fize and Serène (1957). These species inhabit open cavities on the surface of a wide variety of corals, although most individual species seem to inhabit only a single coral family. The cavities range from "dens" raised above the surface of the coral to cylindrical pits extending down into the skeleton to shallow depressions between polyps to spaces within large polyps in which the crab is nearly covered by folds of coral tissue. Males and females inhabit separate cavities. Cavity formation is evidently initiated by the crab remaining in one place on the coral until the underlying tissue is killed. In the normal process of coral growth, new skeleton will be deposited around the crab. The cavity thus formed will take the crab's shape and is usually crescent-shaped, oval, or circular. The shape of the cavity is characteristic of the species and depends on the size of the legs, the shape of the carapace, and the position the crab takes on the coral. The depth that the cavity may attain depends on whether the crab lies across the main direction of coral growth. *Pseudocryptocheirus viridis* (Fig. 6B) inhabits very shallow pits between the corallites of *Turbinaria* because the host is a foliaceous coral that grows mainly by lateral extension of the coral sheet. On the other hand, *Cryptocheirus coralliodytes* living on faviid corals that grow upward at a rate of a centimeter or so a year may inhabit cavities that are ten centimeters deep. Hapalocarcinid crabs are small, whereas most of the hosts have large, soft polyps. This fact probably explains the retention of the sharp dactyl on the walking legs rather than the evolution of blunt dactyls as seen in the much larger species of *Trapezia* and *Tetralia*.

Cryptocheirus coralliodytes is common on Indo-Pacific faviid corals and has been studied by both Potts (1915) and Hiro (1937). It inhabits cylindrical pits of varying depth and has the anterior third of the cara-pace bent forward at an angle, forming an operculum that blocks the entrance to the pit. The crab can move up and down the length of the pit, but is usually found near the surface and often with the anterior part extending slightly above it (Semper, 1881). Hiro (1937) inferred, from the great variation in pit depth that exists and the fairly close correspondence between crab diameter and pit diameter, that the crabs leave their pits at the time of molting and either enter new corallites and form new pits or locate vacant pits of a suitable diameter. An individual pit could thus be occupied by a succession of crabs, and the depth of the pit gives no information about crab longevity.

At Puerto Rico in the Caribbean, the xanthid crab D. acanthophora is a facultative cavity former. On the openly branched Acropora prolifera and A. cervicornis, it is found grasping a branch in the manner of the mobile crabs listed above, whereas on A. palmata, it modifies the forma-tion of coral skeleton. Acropora palmata shows fine branching at the periphery of the colony, but as the colony increases in size the spaces between these branches are filled in, forming a solid plate of coral. A young specimen of D. acanthophora occupies a space between the peripheral branches and remains there as new skeleton is deposited around it, leaving the crab inhabiting various types of pits and crevices within the coral skeleton. There is evidently considerable movement of crabs around the coral as cavities from which crabs are removed are readily occupied by new individuals (Patton, 1967a). As was men-tioned above, D. acanthophora has modified second maxillipeds that are used in suspension feeding.

H. ECHINODERMATA

I do not know of any record of a symbiotic associations between echinoderms and living corals. The starfish Acanthaster planci is, of course, a well-known coral predator, whereas ophiuroids are often com-mon in the dead basal regions of living coral colonies.

I. PISCES

Fish and living reef corals interact in numerous ways. In the Indo-Pacific several types of fish feed directly on living coral either biting off individual polyps, scraping the coral surface, or biting off the tips of coral branches (Hiatt and Strasburg, 1960). In the West Indies, fish do not seem to eat corals in significant amounts (Randall, 1967). Many species of small fish dart into branching corals when disturbed, while quite a few species sleep within the coral branches. The bases of coral heads are used as a spawning location. Occasionally oval scars were seen on the outside of living *Acropora* branches at Heron Island. These contained a tuft of algae and appeared to be maintained as spawning sites. On the reef flat at Heron Island the blenny *Petroscirtes grammistes* is frequently found inhabiting holes in the larger colonies of living massive corals. The majority of these holes are clearly the result of an initial breakage of the tissue layer by *C. coralliodytes* or another hapalocarcinid crab. Although the coral initially grows around the crab at the normal rate, eventually a broad depression is formed around the crab's hole. The crab eventually dies and with the continued outward growth of the coral a larger hole is formed that is a few centimeters in diameter and may extend several centimeters into the skeleton, thus creating a home for the blenny. On Puerto Rican reefs, I have seen small fish of the genus *Coralliozetus* inhabiting small holes within living *A. palmata* colonies.

In the Indo-Pacific, open, loosely branched colonies of living coral such as *Acropora pulchra* frequently harbor a cluster of small fish hovering above and around it. A member of this community is the black and white banded humbug, *Dascyllus aruanus*. It feeds on both zooplankton and material from the living and dead coral surfaces and when disturbed sinks down between the coral branches (Hiatt and Strasburg, 1960). In a study of the behavior of this fish on the reef flat at Heron Island, Sale (1971) has found evidence of habitat conditioning, as juvenile fish from *P. damicornis* tended to prefer this species when given a choice, while juveniles of the same size from *A. pulchra* moved preferentially to this coral. Individuals of *D. aruanus* sleep within crevices in the coral and were found to remain in the vicinity of a given colony over periods as long as seven months (Sale, 1970).

The closely branched Indo-Pacific corals such as some species of the genus *Acropora* and the family Pocilloporidae harbor young of several species and occasional wanderers, but also three genera that seldom leave the coral head. In the Marshall Islands two species of *Caracanthus* are commonly found living between the branches of *Acropora* colonies in areas subject to strong wave action (Schultz, 1966). *Caracanthus* has spine-bearing gill covers that can be extended, wedging the animal between the coral branches (Hiatt and Strasburg, 1960; Eibl-Eibesfeldt, 1965). At Heron Island, the gobies *Paragobiodon* and *Gobiodon* are obligatory symbionts of living coral and may well spend their adult life within a given colony. The black, orange-headed *P. echinocephalus* lives in pairs or small groups within colonies of *P. damicornis*. Specimens attach themselves to the walls of aquaria with an adhesive disc formed by the pelvic fins and presumably can attach themselves equally firmly to their host coral. A green species of *Paragobiodon* lives in groups within the pocilloporid coral *Seriatopora hystrix*. On reefs off North Queensland, Tyler (1971) found the dark form of *Paragobiodon* on the pocilloporid *Stylophora* pistillata and a pale form on S. *hystrix*. Several species of *Gobiodon* inhabit a number of closely branched species of *Acropora*. This genus is more compressed laterally than is *Paragobiodon* and the pelvic fins are much smaller, but still form a small suction cup. Usually only a single pair of a single species is found in a given colony. During an exceptionally low tide, I have observed a pair of *Gobiodon* remaining within an *Acropora* colony at a North Queensland reef even though they were about ten centimeters above the water level. Schultz (1948) found G. *citrinus* associated with a cluster of eggs attached to an algal patch. This patch was at the base of a branch near the center of an *Acropora* colony and was surrounded by a raised lip of living coral. A few of the colonies that I have seen containing *Gobiodon* had similar algal patches within them, although the great majority did not. Tyler (1971) found that a single pair of a *Gobiodon* was present on a given coral colony to the exclusion of other pairs of the same species. The various fish species did not seem to prefer certain species of *Acropora*, while G. *ceramensis* occurred on both *Acropora* and *Stylophora*, showing that the genus is not completely specific to one family of coral. From a study of stomach contents, Hiatt and Strasburg (1960) concluded that *Paragobiodon* and *Gobiodon* are highly carnivorous and feed on small invertebrates inhabiting their coral colony. *Gobiodon* also takes material drifting into the colony since fish eggs were found in two individuals, whereas Schlichter (1968) observed specimens take pieces of mussel tissue that had been allowed to drift onto their host. The stomachs of five specimens of *Paragobiodon* from Heron Island contained zooxanthellae and coral tissue, showing that this species is at least partially parasitic on the tissues of its host (Patton, 1974).

III. Interactions between Living Corals and Their Associates

Although many more species remain to be discovered, it is already apparent that associations with coral have evolved on hundreds of occasions, and there seems little doubt but that corals exceed all other invertebrate groups in the diversity of forms and number of species to which they play host. Much of this diversity is, of course, due to the way in which corals dominate many reef environments, leading to strong selection favoring animals that can utilize this resource. Also important must be the fact that living corals offer potential symbionts not only food, but also shelter and a hard substrate, thus permitting a greater diversity in symbiotic modes of life than do many other types of host. Once an association has been initiated on whatever basis, then the stage is set for its refinement and modification. Thus we have the mobile predatory gastropods giving rise to the benign, advanced coralliophillids imbedded within the coral skeleton and the plankton-feeding pyrgomatine barnacles giving rise to the coral-eating *H. monticulariae* (see Fig. 5A,B).

Possible ways in which a coral associate could be affected by its host are given in Table I and four areas of interaction are discussed further in the following sections. The type of environment that a symbiont faces will be greatly influenced by its own size, by the feeding methods of the host, and by whether the coral polyps are small and numerous or large and fleshy.

TABLE I

POTENTIAL INTERACTIONS BETWEEN CORALS AND THEIR INHABITANTS

Coral feature	Possible positive effects on coral associate	Possible negative effects on coral associate
Nematocysts and feeding mechanisms	Protect established symbionts from predators, parasites, and fouling organisms	Could kill symbionts or their larval stages attempting to settle
Coral tissue	Food; source of materials that might deter predators	Enzymes from mesenterial filaments could destroy symbiont stages
Coral mucus	Food source	Could entangle and remove larval stages
Plankton caught by coral	Food source	
Sediment settling on coral	Food source	
Zooxanthellae and cells expelled by coral	Food source	
Dissolved material released by coral	Food source ?	?
Coral skeleton	Firm substrate to settle on; coral growth provides support and protection; branching skeletons provide shelter	Symbiont overgrown and killed by growth of skeleton

A. Food Habits

Potential food sources for coral associates are given in Table II, together with a summary of the food habits of various species.

Most coral barnacles and bivalves retain their basic plankton-feeding mode of life. Provided they can cope with its growth, such sedentary suspension feeders should find living coral to be an excellent habitat. They are raised above the sediment, and the surrounding coral protects them against crowding by other species and overgrowth by fouling organisms. The most modified bivalve, *F. eilatensis*, has become depen-

TABLE II

UTILIZATION OF FOOD SOURCES BY CORAL-ASSOCIATED ANIMALS

Possible energy source	Coral associate utilizing that energy source
Food collected away from host	Possibly three shrimp species (Patton, 1974)
Food collected from water near host	
Plankton	Most barnacles and bivalves; the gall crab *Hapalocarcinus* (Potts, 1915); some fish— *Dascyllus* (Salc, 1970), *Gobiodon* and *Paragobiodon* (Hiatt and Strasburg, 1960)
Organic aggregates	Crab *Domecia acanthophora* (Patton, 1967a)
Dissolved organic matter	?
Sediment settling on the coral	Many mobile decapods (Patton, 1974)
Food derived from the host	
Food material collected by the coral	Bivalve *Fungiacava* (Goreau *et al.*, 1970)
Coral tissue	Several gastropods, (review by Robertson, 1970); several types of Indo-Pacific fish (Hiatt and Strasburg, 1960); the annelid *Hermodice carunculata* (Marsden, 1962); the barnacle *Hoekia monticulariae* (Ross and Newman, 1969); the spider crab *Mithrax sculptus* (Glynn, 1963); the modified copepod *Xarifia* (Gerlach, 1960); the coral dwelling goby *Paragobiodon* (Patton, 1974).
Coral mucus	Crabs *Trapezia ferrunginea* form *ferrunginea* and *T. f.* form *areolata* (Knudsen, 1967); other mobile decapods (Patton, 1974); *Fungiacava* (Goreau *et al.*, 1970)
Zooxanthellae and debris extruded by the coral	*Fungiacava* (Goreau *et al.*, 1970)
Dissolved organic matter released by the coral	?
Other coral-associated organisms	?

dent on its host for food. The siphons never extend outside the living coral but instead open into the host coelenteron. The contents of the *Fungia* coelenteron and the *Fungiacava* gut are similar, consisting of mucus, particulate matter collected by the coral, and zooxanthellae, nematocysts, and cell debris extruded by the mesenterial filaments, although the bivalve also feeds on phytoplankton drawn into the coelenteron (Goreau *et al.*, 1970).

Reef sediment is continually being suspended and redeposited. Living corals receive their share of this material and thus sediment is a likely food source for coral symbionts. The mobile crabs and shrimp found on coral seem to feed in large part on sediment, with several species of shrimp having combs of setae that are used in gathering it. The nutritive value of this material is shown by the fact that while the flagellar currents of most corals carry sediment off the colony, those of several species carry it into the polyps (Yonge, 1930; Abe, 1938). During its movement across the coral, the sediment is concentrated in certain pathways that would seem to be prime locations for deposit-feeding symbionts. [McCloskey (1970) has suggested that the branch structure decreases the velocity of water flow through colonies of branching coral and so increases the amount of sediment deposited within them.]

There are several products released by living corals that may be significant in symbiont nutrition but whose importance cannot yet be assessed. Corals secrete mucus as an aid in removing sediment that settles upon them and so coral-dwelling animals that feed on deposit also ingest greater or lesser amounts of coral mucus. From this may have evolved the situation in two species of *Trapezia* where, in the absence of sedimentation, the crabs scratch the coral with the tips of their walking legs. This induces the production of mucus that is then eaten (Knudsen, 1967). Corals may release quite large amounts of organic matter as mucus (Johannes, 1967) and this could prove to be an important energy source for the animals inhabiting coral.

Excess zooxanthellae are continually being extruded from the mesenterial excretory zone of corals (Goreau *et al.*, 1970) and could be eaten by coral associates. To date, only *Fungiacava* has been shown to ingest zooxanthellae and discarded cell debris. No coral-associated animal has yet been demonstrated to utilize dissolved organic matter produced by its host, although it may be expected that this will eventually be shown, since many species have tissue lying in intimate contact with that of the coral. [The large copepod *Antheacheres duebeni*, which inhabits galls in the sea anemone *Bolocera* in Norwegian waters, lacks a digestive tract and evidently absorbs nourishment by diffusion through its body wall (Vader, 1970), as do certain of the copepods inhabiting the coelenteron of alcyonarians (Bouligand, 1966).]

B. CORAL FEEDING AND DEFENSE MECHANISMS

The role of host feeding and defense mechanisms in the evolution of coral associations is quite uncertain and no doubt varies widely between types of corals and groups of potential symbionts. Clionid boring sponges, for example, can only enter the coral at its dead base (Goreau and Hartman, 1963). And yet, at least by comparison with sea anemones, most corals appear relatively benign. Many small free-living fish sleep within branching corals while quite a variety of fish and invertebrates are occasionally found on or within living coral without appearing to suffer any ill effects. Many kinds of animals are known to feed on coral tissue (Robertson, 1970) and although structural adaptations that could be associated with this diet have been suggested in some cases, the fact that feeding on coral has evolved so often could indicate that it is not a particularly difficult food to handle. Harris (1970) has found that two species of *Phestilla* feeding on the corals *Dendrophyllia* and *Porites* differ from most of the coelenterate-feeding aeolid nudibranchs in that they do not transfer host nematocysts to the ceratae on their dorsal surface. *Phestilla* could perhaps be primitive, but in the absence of any evidence in this regard, there is a strong possibility that the nematocysts of these two corals do not provide adequate protection against fish predators and thus selection has favored the evolution of defensive secretions rather than the storage of nematocysts.

For the smaller symbionts, however, and for the postlarval stages of the larger species, the nematocysts and feeding behavior of living coral would appear to represent a considerable hazard. The work of Yonge (1930), Abe (1938), and others has shown that a wide variety of corals are able to capture and ingest members of the zooplankton. Coles (1969) found that three Caribbean coral species belonging to two families are able to ingest *Artemia* nauplii in amounts equivalent to several times that required for their respiration. The coral nematocysts are presumably of major importance in capturing prey animals and no doubt prevent certain potential symbionts from settling on certain corals. Yet symbiotic animals are found on and within coral polyps and many coral associations must be initiated by small, recently postplanktonic individuals. For example, most barnacles inhabiting *Galaxea* are found within coral calices (Gravier, 1911), indicating that the barnacle cyprids settle directly on a living coral polyp. Moyse (1971) observed cyprids of the pyrgomatine barnacle *Boscia anglicum* attaching to the epithelium of the ahermatypic coral *Caryophyllia smithi*. Why are these stages not killed by the nematocysts and ingested by the coral?

The gland cells of the coral's mesenterial filaments can secrete a potent protein-digesting enzyme (Yonge and Nicholls, 1930). This could affect not only copepods and *Fungiacava* living within the polyps, but also external species, since in many corals the mesenterial filaments can extend from the polyps. These filaments can wrap around food items and digest them externally (Yonge, 1930), and can dissolve tissues on adjacent corals belonging to certain different species (Lang, 1973).

The mucus secretions and flagellar currents of the coral epithelial cells constitute a third type of host defense that would tend to entangle and carry away small animals. In fact, Gerlach (1960) found far fewer meiofaunal organisms on *Acropora* than on the pocilloporid corals, and suggests that this may be correlated with the fact that *Acropora* secretes more mucus.

Since copepods are found on and in living coral and since postlarval stages do grow into adults, it is obvious that at least some symbiont individuals successfully overcome any problems presented by their own particular hosts. The literature contains a number of observations and suggestions indicating ways in which this might be accomplished. Gohar and Soliman (1963b) found that veliger larvae of the symbiotic gastropod *L. cumingii* remained undisturbed for several days among the expanded polyps of the host coral *Cyphastrea*. This observation suggests that the veligers are somehow immune from the action of nematocysts and other host defenses. The postlarvae of the Atlantic coral-feeding gastropod *Philippia krebsii* are too large to be ingested by the small polyps of *Porites*, a possible normal host. They are, however, caught and swallowed by the large-polyped, abnormal host, *Astrangia danae*. The postlarvae of *P. krebsii* responded to contact with *Astrangia* by withdrawing the foot and expelling mucus. They did not seem to be seriously injured by *Astrangia* nematocysts, and could occasionally survive being swallowed (Robertson *et al.*, 1970). The larva of the burrowing sponge, *Siphonodictyon*, contains a large amount of mucus that could protect it during settlement or perhaps even kill coral tissue (Rützler, 1971). Mucus secretion thus seems to be a likely major defense against nematocysts. See also Salvini-Plawen (1972).

On a completely different tack, Schlichter (1968, 1970) and Martin (1968), in working on sea anemones, have suggested that symbionts achieve protection through host molecules absorbed on to their body surfaces. The anemone would then not recognize the symbionts as being foreign objects and there would be no nematocyst discharge or feeding behavior. If true, this mechanism could easily apply to coral symbionts. Postlarval stages might then be expected to approach and withdraw from their hosts until they had absorbed enough host substances so that they no longer elicited a response from the coral.

C. GROWTH OF CORAL SKELETON

Deposition of new skeletal material is a characteristic of living corals, although the rate of deposition can vary greatly with the size of the colony and between parts of the same colony (Motoda, 1940; Goreau, 1963). It has long been known that skeleton deposition can respond markedly to differences in the external environment. In particular, the amount of wave action and illumination influence the growth form that will be assumed by a given colony.

In a similar manner the presence of organisms on or in a coral can alter skeleton growth. Coralla frequently contain bumps, depressions, or other irregularities due to present or past responses to other organisms. The type and degree of alteration seem to vary considerably between different types of coral. In Puerto Rico A. palmata produces living coral-lite-free coenosteum around areas inhabited by the xanthid crab D. acanthophora (Patton, 1967a), and Acropora, in general, tends to respond to the continued presence of a foreign object by a reduction in number of corallites on the adjacent coenosteum. In Galaxea fascicularis, however, Gravier (1911) found a proliferation of new corallites around a damaged area. The extent of coral modification depends on whether or not the foreign object lies across a region of active coral growth. This is shown clearly in the case of D. acanthophora, which may inhabit a pit on the side of a plate of A. palmata, a hole extending through it, or a crevice dividing the plate in two (Patton, 1967a). Attached corals overgrow their substrate to varying degrees and a number of species will deposit skeleton along other structures with which they come in contact. Thus cylindrical tubes of P. damicornis are sometimes seen surrounding the tubes of vermetids or serpulid worms. Acropora palmata does not normally produce vertical branches and when found they generally contain tufts of algae extending throughout their length. There is little doubt that these branches represent the response of the coral to algae that somehow settled upon it (Patton, 1967a). The galls of Hapalocarcinus (Fig. 6A) provide what is probably the most striking example of novel coral growth induced by the presence of another organism.

Gravier (1911) and Otter (1937) have suggested that overgrowth

by coral and subsequent death may be a frequent fate for sedentary
coral-associated animals. The remains of barnacles, date clams, hapalocarcinid holes, etc., can be found within coral skeletons, but there is
no way of knowing whether the overgrowth by the coral followed or
preceded the death of the symbiont. In general, deposition of a coral
skeleton does not seem to occur against a resistance of any substance.
Most of the sessile symbionts have structures that extend above the
coral surface and either by growth, burrowing, or simply changing position can maintain these structures above the surrounding coral. The
siphons of the date clam *Lithophaga* extend to the surface and are
surrounded by coral, producing a characteristic dumbbell-shaped opening. Among the coralliophilid gastropods living within corals, *M. lamarckii* and the *Leptoconchus* species have siphons extending to the surface,
whereas *M. antiquus* deposits a vermiform shell that keeps pace with
coral growth and becomes a new lodging for the animal. In the barnacles
of the subfamily Pyrgomatinae, the walls of the basal plate grow, keeping
pace with the growth of the corallum and maintain the shell at or above
the level of the surrounding coral (Fig. 4A,B). Ross and Newman (1973)
believe that in many cases the barnacles can suppress the deposition
of surrounding coral skeleton. In *Balanus* (*Hexacreusia*) *durhami* the
shell is almost covered by coral skeleton. However, the basal plate of
the barnacle can be extended despite this constraint and a fracture zone
exists between the coral covering the shell plates and that surrounding
the basal plate (Zullo, 1961). In *H. marsupialis* the water currents
created by the female crab apparently prevent the sides of the gall
from fusing completely together.

Several species of symbiont not only tolerate coral growth but are
absolutely dependent on it. The females of *Hapalocarcinus* provide the
most obvious example. *Cryptocheirus coralliodytes* relies on coral growth
to produce the cylindrical pit into which the elongated body of the
female extends. Coral is deposited to a greater or lesser degree around
most other hapalocarcinids, but it is doubtful whether this is essential
to their development. Baluk and Radwanski (1967) have suggested that
growth of the basal plate in the pyrgomatine coral barnacles occurs
only in response to growth of the adjacent coral. If so, these animals
would require coral growth in order to reach maturity. The date clams
and coralliophilid gastropods found within living coral skeletons may
provide additional examples of a complete dependence on coral growth.
Soliman (1969) believes that the young stages of these animals settle
initially on the live coral surface. When the coral surrounds them, they
burrow outward creating a space within which they can grow.

D. Effect of Coral Associates on Their Host

The coral-associated animals profit from the coral by obtaining a place to live and, in some cases, food, protection, and other benefits. How is the survival of the corals affected by the various associations? Predators on coral, most notably the crown-of-thorns starfish (*A. planci*), have an obvious deleterious effect. In the case of the symbionts, the effect of most species would seem to be nil or slightly negative, although there are cases of apparent benefit.

Date clams (*Lithophaga*) are not infrequent inhabitants of the branching coral *P. damicornis* at Heron Island. Major branches containing clams break more easily than do uninfected ones and it is likely that continued growth or unusual wave action will lead to breakage of the infected branches. A similar effect could result from the presence of worm tubes, barnacles, etc. The existence of the symbiont prevents normal skeleton deposition and thus weakens the skeleton, despite the fact that there may be no burrowing whatsoever. Another equally important effect of these animals is that they break the continuity of living coral tissue and so provide a point of entry into the skeleton for bacteria and boring algae and sponges. They also provide a point of attachment for algae that may then extend over living portions of the coral.

An interesting case of a symbiont possibly benefitting the host involves the highly modified mussel *Fungiacava* that lives within suspension-feeding fungiid corals (Goreau *et al.*, 1970). The fact that an infected coral contains a herbivore means that nutrients tied up in ingested phytoplankton and excreted zooxanthellae are no longer lost to the coral but will eventually be released by the mussel into the coelenteron. They will thus be made aviailable for the production of more symbiotic algae some of which in turn will be released as food for the *Fungiacava*. These interactions are shown diagrammatically in Fig. 3.

The deposit-feeding crustaceans that inhabit living branching corals would be expected to eat sediment settling within the coral and thus benefit their host by retarding the death of the basal branches. The fish and crustacean symbionts probably benefit the coral by ingesting some of the larval stages of boring and sedentary organisms that attempt to settle on it. Pearson and Endean (1969) noticed that crabs inhabiting *P. damicornis* nipped at the tube feet of *Acanthaster* that crawled over their colony, and suggest this as a possible explanation for the survival of colonies of this coral in areas infested by the starfish. Independently, Weber and Woodhead (1970) observed the associates of Fijian corals bite the tube feet of *Acanthaster* that attacked their colony. This was done by crabs and the fish *D. aruanus* inhabiting a *Stylophora* colony while *Acropora* colonies were defended by another small fish, *Acantho-chromis polyacanthus.*

Acknowledgment

Drs. A. G. Humes, A. Ross, and B. R. Wilson have kindly reviewed draft versions of the sections on copepods, barnacles, and bivalves, respectively, while Dr. M. Keenleyside has reviewed the entire manuscript. The helpful comments of these individuals are much appreciated. The authors concerned and the Harvard University Press, the University of Hawaii Press, and the Zoological Society of London kindly gave permission to use their published illustrations. The original version of this paper was written while I was on sabbatical leave in Australia. I am most grateful to the Department of Zoology, University of Queensland and to the Great Barrier Reef Committee for making space available to me at Brisbane and Heron Island.

References

Abe, N. (1938). *Palao Trop. Biol. Sta. Stud.* 1, 469.
Annandale, N. (1924). *Mem. Indian Mus.* 8, 61.
Baluk, W., and Radwanski, A. (1967). *Acta Paleontol. Pol.* 12, 457.
Borradaile, L. A. (1902). *In* "The Fauna and Geography of the Maldive and Laccadive Archipelagoes" (J. S. Gardiner, ed.), Vol. I, pp. 237–271. Cambridge Univ. Press, London and New York.
Bosch, H. F. (1965). *Pac. Sci.* 19, 267.
Boschma, H. (1936). *Snellius-Exped.* 6, 1.
Bouligand, Y. (1966). *In* "The Cnidaria and Their Evolution" (W. J. Rees, ed.), pp. 267–307. Academic Press, New York.
Bretsky, S. S. (1967). *Postilla* No. 108, p. 1.
Bruce, A. J. (1969). *Crustaceana* 17, 171.
Bruce, A. J. (1972). *Proc. Symp. Corals Coral Reefs, 1969* pp. 399–418.
Coles, S. L. (1969). *Limnol. Oceanogr.* 14, 949.
Crane, J. (1947). *Zoologica (New York)* 32, 69.
Demond, J. (1957). *Pac. Sci.* 11, 275.
Eibl-Eibesfeldt, I. (1965). "Land of a Thousand Atolls." MacGibbon & Kee, London.
Fize, A. (1956). *Inst. Oceanogr. Nhatrang, Viet-Nam Contr.* 22, 1.
Fize, A., and Serène, R. (1957). *Arch. Mus. Hist. Natur. Paris* [7] 5, 3.
Gardiner, J. S. (1903). *In* "The Fauna and Geography of the Maldive and Laccadive Archipelagoes" (J. S. Gardiner, ed.), Vol. I, pp. 313–346. Cambridge Univ. Press, London and New York.
Garth, J. S. (1946). *Allan Hancock Pac. Exped.* 5, 341.
Garth, J. S. (1964). *Micronesica* 1, 137.
Garth, J. S., and Hopkins, T. S. (1968). *Bull. Soc. Calif. Acad. Sci.* 67, 40.
Gerlach, S. (1960). *Zool. Anz., Suppl.* 23, 356.
Glynn, P. W. (1963). *Ass. Isl. Mar. Lab. Caribb., 4th Meet.* p. 16.
Glynn, P. W., Stewart, R. H., and McCosker, J. E. (1972). *Geol. Rundsch.* 61, 483.

Gohar, H. A. F., and Soliman, G. N. (1963a). *Publ. Mar. Biol. Sta. Ghardaqa* **12**, 65.

Gohar, H. A. F., and Soliman, G. N. (1963b). *Publ. Mar. Biol. Sta. Ghardaqa* **12**, 99.

Goreau, T. F. (1963). *Ann. N.Y. Acad. Sci.* **109**, 127.

Goreau, T. F., and Hartman, W. D. (1963). *In* "Mechanisms of Hard Tissue Destruction," Publ. No. 75, pp. 25–54. Amer. Ass. Advan. Sci., Washington, D.C.

Goreau, T. F., and Hartman, W. D. (1966). *Science* **151**, 343.

Goreau, T. F., and Yonge, C. M. (1968). *Nature (London)* **217**, 421.

Goreau, T. F., Goreau, N. I., Soot-Ryen, T., and Yonge, C. M. (1969). *J. Zool.* **158**, 171.

Goreau, T. F., Goreau, N. I., Yonge, C. M., and Neumann, Y. (1970). *J. Zool.* **160**, 159.

Goreau, T. F., Goreau, N. I., and Yonge, C. M. (1972). *J. Zool.* **166**, 55.

Gravier, C. (1911). *C. R. Acad. Sci.* **152**, 210.

Hadfield, M. G., and Karlson, R. H. (1969). *Amer. Zool.* **9**, 1122.

Harris, L. G. (1970). *Amer. Malacol. Union Annu. Rep.* p. 67.

Harris, L. G. (1971). *In* "Aspects of the Biology of Symbiosis" (T. C. Cheng, ed.), pp. 77–90. Univ. Park Press, Baltimore, Maryland.

Henderson, J. R. (1906). *Ann. Mag. Natur. Hist.* [7] **18**, 211.

Hiatt, R. W., and Strasburg, D. W. (1960). *Ecol. Monogr.* **30**, 65.

Hiro, F. (1936). *Rec. Oceanogr. Works Jap.* **7**, 45.

Hiro, F. (1937). *Palao Trop. Biol. Sta. Stud.* **1**, 137.

Hiro, F. (1938). *Palao Trop. Biol. Sta. Stud.* **1**, 391.

Humes, A. G. (1960). *Kiel. Meeresforsch.* **16**, 229.

Humes, A. G. (1962a). *Crustaceana* **4**, 47.

Humes, A. G. (1962b). *Bull. Mus. Comp. Zool., Harvard Univ.* **128**, 35.

Humes, A. G. (1973). *Zool. Anz.* **190**, 312.

Humes, A. G., and Frost, B. W. (1964). *Cah. Oceanogr.* **6**, 131.

Humes, A. G., and Ho, J. S. (1967). *Proc. U.S. Nat. Mus.* **122**, (3586), 1.

Humes, A. G., and Ho, J. S. (1968a). *Bull. Mus. Comp. Zool., Harvard Univ.* **136**, 353.

Humes, A. G., and Ho, J. S. (1968b). *Bull. Mus. Comp. Zool., Harvard Univ.* **136**, 415.

Humes, A. G., and Stock, J. H. (1972). *Bull. Zool. Mus., Univ. Amsterdam* **2**, 121.

Humes, A. G., and Stock, J. H. (1973). *Smithson. Contrib. Zool.* **127**, 1.

Jaccarini, E., Bannister, W. H., and Micallef, H. (1968). *J. Zool.* **154**, 397.

Johannes, R. E. (1967). *Limnol. Oceanogr.* **12**, 189.

Johnson, D. S. (1970). *Bull. Nat. Mus. Singapore* No. 35, p. 1.

Jones, E. C. (1968). *Crustaceana* **14**, 312.

Knudsen, J. S. (1967). *Pac. Sci.* **21**, 51.

Kolosvary, G. (1951). *Acta Biol. (Budapest)* **2**, 291.

Lang, J. (1973). *Bull. Mar. Sci.* **23**, 260.

McCloskey, L. R. (1970). *Int. Rev. Gesamten Hydrobiol.* **55**, 13.

Maes, V. O. (1967). *Proc. Acad. Natur. Sci. Philadelphia* **119**, 93.

Marcus, A., and Masry, C. (1970). *Isr. J. Zool.* **19**, 169.

Marsden, J. R. (1960). *Can. J. Zool.* **38**, 989.

Marsden, J. R. (1962). *Nature (London)* **193**, 598.

Marsden, J. R. (1963). *Can. J. Zool.* **41**, 165.

Martin, E. J. (1968). *Comp. Biochem. Physiol.* **25**, 169.
Miller, A. C. (1972). *Atoll Res. Bull.* **152**, 3.
Miller, M. C. (1969). *Phil. Trans. Roy. Soc. London, Ser. B* **255**, 541.
Monod, T. (1956). *Mem. Inst. Fr. Afr. Noire* **45**, 1.
Morrison, J. P. E. (1954). *Atoll Res. Bull.* **34**, 1.
Morton, J. E., and Challis, D. A. (1969). *Phil. Trans. Roy. Soc. London, Ser. B* **255**, 459.
Motoda, S. (1940). *Palao Trop. Biol. Sta. Stud.* **2**, 1.
Moyse, J. (1971). *In* "Fourth European Marine Biology Symposium" (D. J. Crisp, ed.), pp. 125–141. Cambridge Univ. Press, London and New York.
Newman, W. A., and Ladd, H. S. (1974). *Verh. Naturforsch. Ges. Basel* **84**, 381.
Ortmann, A. (1897). *Zool. Jahrb., Abt. Syst., Oekol. Georgr. Tiere* **10**, 201.
Ott, B., and Lewis, J. B. (1972). *Can. J. Zool.* **50**, 1651.
Otter, G. W. (1937). *Sci. Rep. Gt. Barrier Reef Exped.* **1**, 323.
Pang, R. K. (1973). *Bull. Mar. Sci.* **23**, 227.
Patton, W. K. (1966). *Crustaceana* **10**, 271.
Patton, W. K. (1967a). *Biol. Bull.* **132**, 56.
Patton, W. K. (1967b). *Proc. Symp. Crustacea, Mar. Biol. Assoc. India* **3**, 1228.
Patton, W. K. (1974). *In* "Symbiosis in the Sea" (W. B. Vernberg, ed.), pp. 219–243. Univ. of South Carolina Press, Columbia.
Pearson, R. G., and Endean, R. (1969). *Fish. Notes, Dep. Harbours Mar., Queensl., Aust.* **3**, 27.
Pillai, N. K. (1968). *J. Bombay Natur. Hist. Soc.* **65**, 47.
Potts, F. A. (1915). *Carnegie Inst. Wash., Pap. Dep. Mar. Biol.* **8**, 33.
Preston, E. M. (1973). *Ecology* **54**, 469.
Randall, J. E. (1967). *Stud. Trop. Oceanogr.* **5**, 665.
Robertson, R. (1970). *Pac. Sci.* **24**, 43.
Robertson, R., Scheltema, R. S., and Adams, F. W. (1970). *Pac. Sci.* **24**, 55.
Ross, A., and Newman, W. A. (1969). *Pac. Sci.* **23**, 252.
Ross, A., and Newman, W. A. (1973). *Trans. San Diego Soc. Natur. Hist.* **17**, 137.
Rützler, K. (1971). *Smithson. Contrib. Zool.* **77**, 1.
Sale, P. F. (1970). *Aust. Nat. Hist.* **16**, 362.
Sale, P. F. (1971). *Anim. Behav.* **19**, 251.
Salvini–Plawen, L. (1972). *Cah. Biol. Mar.* **13**, 385.
Schlichter, D. (1968). *Z. Tierpsychol.* **25**, 933.
Schlichter, D. (1970). *Naturwissenschaften* **57**, 312.
Schultz, L. P. (1948). *Smithson. Inst., Annu. Rep.* p. 301.
Schultz, L. P. (1966). *U.S., Nat. Mus., Bull.* **202**, 43.
Semper, K. (1881). "Animal Life as Affected by the Natural Conditions of Existence." Appleton, New York.
Serène, R. (1967). *Proc. Symp. Crustacea, Mar. Biol. Ass. India* **1**, 395.
Serène, R. (1971). *J. Mar. Biol. Ass. India* **11**, 126.
Sewell, R. B. S. (1926). *Rec. Indian Mus.* **28**, 269.
Soliman, G. N. (1969). *Amer. Zool.* **9**, 887.
Stock, J. H. (1966). *Beaufortia* **13**, 145.
Stock, J. H., and Humes, A. G. (1969). *Crustaceana* **16**, 57.
Stoddart, D. R. (1969). *Biol. Rev. Cambridge Phil. Soc.* **44**, 433.
Tattersall, O. S. (1967). *Trans. Zool. Soc. London* **31**, 157.
Taylor, J. D. (1968). *Phil. Trans. Roy. Soc. London, Ser. B* **254**, 129.
Taylor, J. D. (1971). *Symp. Zool. Soc. London* **28**, 501.
Tomlinson, J. T. (1969). *U.S., Nat. Mus., Bull.* **296**, 1.

Turner, R. D., and Boss, K. J. (1962). *Johnsonia* **4**, 81.

Tyler, J. C. (1971). *Proc. Acad. Natur. Sci. Philadelphia* **123**, 1.

Utinomi, H. (1967). *Publ. Seto Mar. Biol. Lab.* **15**, 199.

Vader, W. (1970). *Sarsia* **43**, 99.

Verrill, A. E. (1908). *Trans. Conn. Acad. Arts Sci.* **13**, 299.

Ward, J. (1965). *Can. J. Zool.* **43**, 447.

Weber, J. N., and Woodhead, P. M. J. (1970). *Mar. Biol.* **6**, 12.

Woolacott, L. (1955). *Proc. Roy. Soc. N.S.W.* p. 79.

Yonge, C. M. (1967). *Proc. Malacol. Soc. London* **37**, 311.

Yonge, C. M. (1930). *Sci. Rep. Gt. Barrier Reef Exped.* **1**, 13.

Yonge, C. M. (1963). *In* "Mechanisms of Hard Tissue Destruction," Publ. No. 75, pp. 1–24. Amer. Ass. Advan. Sci., Washington, D.C.

Yonge, C. M., and Nicholls, A. G. (1930). *Sci. Rep Gt. Barrier Reef Exped.* **1**, 59.

Zullo, V. A. (1961). *Veliger* **4**, 71.

2

SHRIMPS AND PRAWNS OF CORAL REEFS, WITH SPECIAL REFERENCE TO COMMENSALISM

A. J. Bruce

I. Introduction

The Decapoda Natantia occur in great variety in the warm waters of shallow tropical seas and the greatest diversity of species is probably to be found on the well-developed coral reefs of the Indo-West Pacific region. Their abundance is generally not obvious to the skin diver or scuba diver swimming among the corals. Indeed, the small size of many of these species renders them unlikely to be noticed unless specially searched for but a few species, such as the brightly colored white, red, and blue *Stenopus hispidus* (Olivier), can be observed readily. The majority of species escapes detection as a result of being cryptically colored, or transparent, or because they conceal themselves in the complex structure of the reef, often in intimate associations with other animals.

Early studies on the tropical shrimp fauna usually provided few ecological data. Dana (1852) described the brilliantly colored *Oedipus superbus* and *Oedipus gramineus* (Fig. 1) from living corals at Tongatabu and Fiji but he also reported that the shrimps swim freely. Subsequently, these species, now placed in the genus *Coralliocaris* Stimpson, have invariably been found in association with scleractinian corals. Peters (1852) reported on the new genus *Conchodytes*, the two species of which were found to occur in pearl shells and giant clams, respectively. Later, Stimpson (1860) reported the presence, also in a tridacnid, of

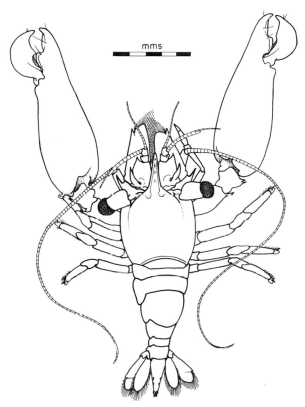

Fig. 1. Coralliocaris graminea (Dana), male; Mazizini, Zanzibar.

Pontonia maculata, a species of uncertain identity but probably synonymous with *Anchistus miersi* (De Man). He also confirmed the occurrence
of *Coralliocaris superba* and *Coralliocaris graminea* in corals and re
corded the presence of *Coralliocaris lamellirostris* and *Harpilius depressus* [now *Jocaste lucina* (Nobili) and *Harpiliopsis depressus*
(Stimpson) respectively] in other corals. The first records of the habitats
of tropical shrimps showed, therefore, that they were associated with
corals or bivalve mollusks. In his revision of the Pontoniidae, Borradaile
(1898a) reported the association of *Periclimenes parasiticus* with a starfish *Linckia* sp. The papers of Kemp (1914, 1916, 1922, 1925) reported
the presence and associations of many species in Indian waters, as did
the Siboga Expedition monograph on the Pontoniinae (Holthuis, 1952)
for Indonesian waters. Gradually, more and more reports have appeared
that indicate the widespread occurrence of associations between shrimps

and a wide range of marine invertebrates. Several families of shrimps are now known to live in special associations and the range of types of partners has been greatly extended and now includes even fishes.

General aspects of commensalism have been detailed by Caullery (1952) and, more recently, by Henry (1966). The decapod crustaceans have attracted little attention in these works but Balss (1956) has provided a more detailed account. Patton (1967) has given a broad general account of commensalism in Crustacea and Gotto (1969) has provided an outline of variations on the commensal theme illustrated with many examples taken from the Crustacea.

New collecting methods have enabled more precise data upon the various associations to be obtained and gradually the specificity of the associations has become apparent. It is probable that many of the shallow water species of tropical marine shrimps, whose habitats are still poorly known, will eventually be found to live in associations with other animals. The common use of scuba apparatus now provides a more satisfactory method of collecting specimens for such investigations, at the same time enabling precise ecological data that cannot be obtained from a trawl or dredge haul to be gathered.

The ecological niches occupied by the shallow water coral reef shrimps appear to be closely similar in the different tropical zoogeographical regions. In this report examples are selected primarily from the reefs of the Indo-West Pacific and, in particular, from the subfamily Pontoniinae of the Palaemonidae, which exhibits a particularly wide range of commensal associations.

II. The Major Shrimp Habitats of the Coral Reef

A. SEAWARD SLOPE

Abundant growth of corals occurs in the upper parts of this zone and these corals may be expected to contain a variety of shrimp associates. However, very few collections of shrimps have been made in this region.

B. ALGAL CREST

In general, few shrimps have been found in this region. However, the crest is frequently honeycombed with small passages, and deep pools are often present. The fauna of these passages and pools have been little studied. Shrimps such as *Brachycarpus biunguiculatus* (Lucas) and *Leander urocaridella* Holthuis may be characteristic of these habitats. Small stenopids, such as *Odontozona,* are frequent in this zone.

C. Reef Flat

Again, few shrimps appear to occur in this region, especially in the parts that dry out at low tide. In the deeper parts, particularly where slabs of dead coral in small pools of shallow water are abundant, a variety of free-living shrimps may be found. Particularly characteristic of this habitat are shrimps of the genera *Hippolysmata* (Hippolytidae) and *Athanas* (Alpheidae). In the larger pools, sponges, corals, bivalve mollusks, asteroids, and echinoids are generally common and all have associated commensals. Also common in this habitat are free-living shrimps of the family Gnathophyllidae and the stenopids *Micropros- thema* Stimpson and *Odontozona* Holthuis. Browsing pontoniinid shrimps, such as *Periclimenes petitthouarsi* (Audouin) (Fig. 2), and

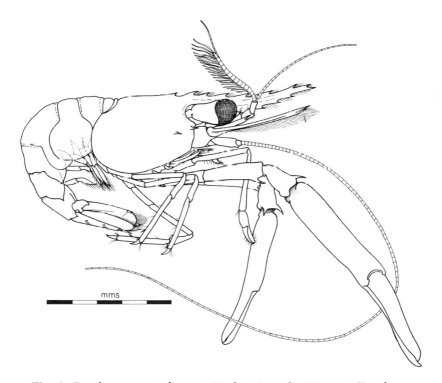

mms

Fig. 2. *Periclimenes petitthouarsi* (Audouin), male; Mazizini, Zanzibar.

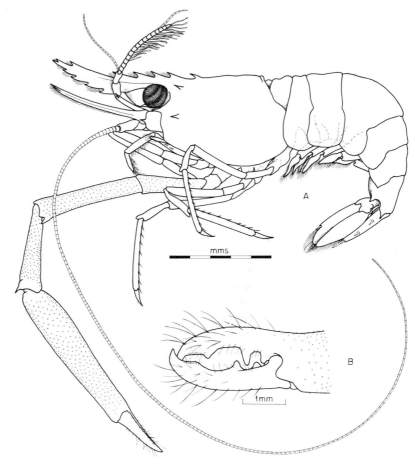

Fig. 3. (A) *Periclimenes elegans* (Paulson), male; Mombasa Island, Kenya and
(B) fingers of second pereiopod of *P. elegans*.

also predatory species, such as *Periclimenes elegans* (Paulson) (Fig.
3), are particularly common in this region.

D. Sea Grass Banks

Sheltered regions of the reef flat generally support extensive areas
of turtlegrasses. Numerous shrimps live in burrows among the roots of
these plants. Free-living species of the genus *Alpheus* (Alpheidae) are
abundant, while a variety of species of the family Hippolytidae, such
as *Hippolyte, Latreutes, Thor, Angasia,* and *Saron* spp., is to be found
among the leaves. The fauna of the Madagascar beds has recently been

reported on by Ledoyer (1968). In this region large numbers of fan shells, often with shrimps inside, are commonly found, together with many starfish, holothurians, and urchins. Also conspicuous are the nocturnally active species of *Processa.*

E. CORAL SAND BOTTOMS

Between coral heads or patch reefs, or interspersed with patches of *Thalassia,* large and small areas of coral sand are usually common. In burrows in the sand is a variety of shrimps including species of the penaeid genus *Metapenaeopsis* Bouvier as well as carideans of the genera *Leptochela* (Pasiphaeidae) and *Pontophilus* (Crangonidae).

F. LAGOON SLOPE

In the more sheltered water of lagoons an abundant growth of coral is again found, together with numerous alcyonarians, sponges, and a wide variety of echinoderms and mollusks, all of which may contain associated commensal shrimps. Free-living species of shrimps are also abundant around the bases of live corals or under slabs of dead coral. Shrimps of the genus *Rhynchocinetes* (Rhynchocinetidae) especially are found in this region.

G. LAGOON FLOOR

Generally composed of fine coral sand, this region supports a fauna of alcyonarians, gorgonians, and pennatulaceans not found on the higher parts. The echinoderm fauna also appears characteristic and all support a fauna of shrimp associates that are not found in the intertidal zone.

Each major habitat offers only a limited number of niches for the free-living shrimp species. By living in association with another animal the range of niches is greatly increased for the commensal species. Each niche occupied appears to have resulted in increased speciation with special adaptations to the niche, thereby reinforcing the great diversity of species already found on the coral reef. The niches occupied by the shrimps include representatives of most of the marine invertebrate phyla with attached or sessile species of more than minute size, as well as a few that are mobile and even a few fishes (Gerlach, 1960).

III. Commensalism

Although the shrimp associates of other marine invertebrates are frequently referred to as "commensals," in almost all cases nothing is known about the trophic relationship with the host animal. It can safely be assumed that a wide variety of such relationships are involved. These will range from predatory or parasitic links—such as a shrimp that lives on a coral and eats bits of its tentacles (a parasite, or a predator?)— through varying degrees of commensal dependence, to states where the association is only of a protective nature and no nutritional link is involved. As these relationships have been little studied and are poorly understood at present, it is preferable to refer to the animals as associates rather than as commensals.

IV. The Criteria for Shrimp–Host Associations

The criteria for deciding if one animal is an associate of another have been given by Garth (in press) and may be summarized as: (1) the association with the living host is constant and free-living individuals do not normally occur, (2) all stages of postlarval life are present in or on the host; and (3) adult breeding individuals occur in or on the host, generally in pairs.

In general, the association between shrimp commensals and their host animals is constant and the shrimps are not found away from their host unless disturbed, for example by collecting activities involving the use of fish poisons. If disturbed or removed from their hosts, the shrimps usually return immediately, if this is possible. Occasionally, abnormalities in host selection may occur but these usually involve only isolated, sub-adult individuals. For example, I have collected from an alcyonarian, a single small specimen of *Periclimenes brevicarpalis* (Schenkel), a well-known, widely distributed, Indo-West Pacific shrimp that is normally associated with giant anemones. Similarly, a juvenile of *C. graminea*, almost always found on *Acropora* corals, has been found on a small colony of *Stylophora* and Lanchester (1901) has reported *Anchistus custos* (Forskål), which is usually found in bivalves of the genus *Pinna*, from the mantle cavity of a large gastropod. These instances must stem from failure of the planktonic postlarva to postpone settlement beyond a certain duration and its adoption of the most suitable host available in the immediate vicinity.

The whole postlarval life is passed in association with the host. Juveniles are naturally much smaller than adults and are also much less heavily pigmented. In a number of species, such as *Periclimenes soror* Nobili, they are almost completely transparent. Careful examination of the host animals, particularly coelenterates, will usually provide numbers of small juveniles, even as small as postlarvae. Specimens may be found with characteristic color patterns, presumably representing those of the last planktonic stages, that are lost after settling in the host animals. However, the juvenile stages of the species found in bivalve mollusks seem comparatively rare.

The constant presence of breeding adults is the best indication that the shrimps under study are obligatory associates of another animal. In a number of host animals, particularly bivalve mollusks and tunicates, each host is normally occupied by a single male and female shrimp. In small corals and other coelenterates, only a single pair is frequently present but, as the size of the host coelenterate increases, so may the number, and also the variety of associates increase. In bivalve mollusks the presence of more than one species of associate has only occasionally been reported.

V. Host Specificity

Considerable variation in the degree of host specificity is shown by different shrimps. Throughout their entire distribution some species are known from only a single host. In these cases the distribution of the shrimp may be considered to be controlled by the distribution of its host, although the shrimp does not always occur throughout the full range of the host. As examples, the pontoniinid shrimps *Anapontonia denticauda* Bruce, *Ischnopontonia lophos* (Barnard), and *Platycaris latirostris* Holthuis, as well as the alpheid *Racilius compressus* Paulson, are all obligatory associates of the oculinid coral *Galaxea fascicularis* L., and a large colony of this coral occasionally contains specimens of all four species. The closely related coral *Galaxea flavus* (Dana), which is frequently present in the same habitat, has never yielded a single specimen of any of these species despite considerable searching. The different species of other coral-inhabiting genera of shrimps, such as *Coralliocaris, Jocaste,* or *Harpiliopsis,* may be found in several species of corals but specific associations appear to exist at the generic level in these cases. *Coralliocaris* and *Jocaste* are associates mainly of *Acropora,* and *Harpiliopsis* of *Pocillopora.* Finally, some coral associates, such as *Periclimenes diversipes* Kemp, show a low degree of specificity in host selection and may be found in association with a wide variety of corals belonging to several families.

So far there have been no studies carried out to ascertain whether any attractive factor is released by the host animal. The high degree of host specificity shown by some shrimps makes it seem highly probable that some host factor does exert an initial attraction on the settling postlarva. Once the association is established, the behavior of the shrimp is sufficient to maintain the association. The presence in corals of shrimps of a wide range of size indicates that the host has remained attractive over a prolonged period.

The host specificity of decapod crustaceans in branching coral has been discussed by Patton (1966), Bruce (1972a), and Garth (in press). Hipeau-Jacquotte has provided some quantitative data on the associations of Madagascar Pontoniinae with bivalves (Jacquotte, 1964; Hipeau-Jacquotte, 1967). Much additional collecting with careful attention to the accurate identification of host animals will be required before a comprehensive picture of the specificity of these associations becomes available.

VI. Adaptations of Shrimps to Their Hosts, as Shown by the Pontoniinae

The shrimps of the subfamily Pontoniinae exhibit a particularly wide range of morphological modifications in their basic body plan, many of which are paralleled in other shrimp families, such as the Alpheidae and Gnathophyllidae in particular, and to a lesser extent the Disciadidae and Hippolytidae. Many of these variations must be considered adaptations to life as associates of their various hosts and are generally not found in free-living shrimps.

The basic body structure of a pontoniinid shrimp may be typified by such species as *Palaemonella rotumana* (Borradaile) and *P. elegans* (Fig. 3). These are both active, free-living species, the former a micropredator and the latter well able to prey upon other shrimps about half its own size. These species have a slenderly built body, with a well-developed, strongly toothed rostrum, and with slender elongated pereiopods. The ambulatory pereiopods are provided with a slender, simple dactylus. All ranges of variation exist between these unspecialized species and the most highly modified genera, all of which, as far as is known, are not free-living. The variations found may be illustrated by comparison with these unmodified species.

VII. Morphological Adaptations

A. Changes in Basic Body Shape as Adaptations to Niche Occupied

1. Adaptations to Small Niches

Many of the species with commensal habits are very small; for example, the coral commensal *Fennera chacei* Holthuis is fully adult at a total length of 4–6 mm (Bruce, 1965).

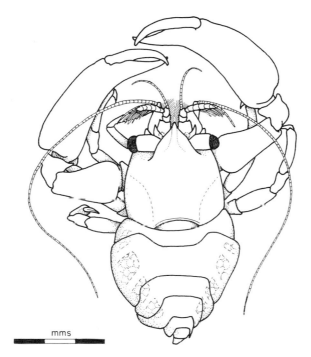

Fig. 4. *Platycaris latirostris* Holthuis, female; Ras Iwatine, Kenya.

2. Adaptations to Narrow Spaces

a. The body may be strongly flattened or depressed, as is found in *Platycaris* (Fig. 4), which lives inactively among the corallites of *G. fascicularis,* or as is exhibited by *Chernocaris,* which is found in the greatly flattened bivalve, *Placuna* (Bruce, 1966b; Johnson, 1967).

b. The body may be strongly compressed. This feature is well shown by *Ischnopontonia* (Fig. 5), which is active among corallites of *G. fascicularis.* [An even more extreme example is the alpheid shrimp *R. compressus,* found occupying the same niche (Barnard, 1958).]

3. Adaptations to Tubular Spaces

Species adapted to such spaces occur mainly in the channels of sponges, a favorite habitat for several genera of shrimp.

a. The body is vermiform. This modification is shown by some species of *Onycocaris* and *Typton,* which have a relatively small thoracic region and an elongated subcylindrical abdomen.

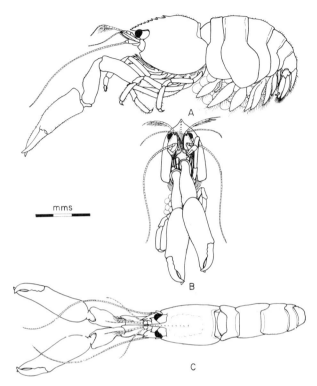

mms

Fig. 5. *Ischnopontonia lophos* (Barnard), female; Ras Iwatine, Mombasa. (A)
Lateral aspect; (B) frontal aspect; and (C) dorsal aspect.

4. Adaptations to Confined Spaces

a. The body is greatly swollen. Shrimps with swollen bodies occur
noticeably in *Conchodytes* spp., found living inside bivalve mollusks
where there still is often considerable room for movement [e.g., *Conchodytes biunguiculatus* (Paulson) in *Pinna* spp.].

b. The body is subglobular. This extreme stage is shown only by
Paratypton (Fig. 6), which occupies a very small cystlike chamber in
Acropora corals where very little free movement is possible (Bruce,
1969a).

5. Adaptations to Exposed Situations

Such adaptations are relatively few in the Pontoniinae, as most species
are cryptic in their habits and are not found in exposed situations.

a. The body is greatly elongated. The two genera, *Tuleariocaris* and

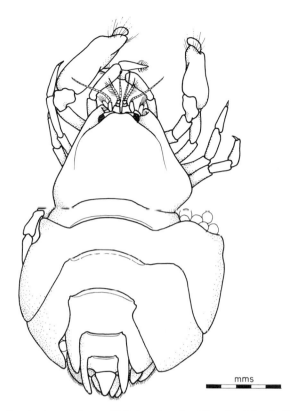

Fig. 6. Paratypton siebenrocki Balss, female; Chumbe Island, Zanzibar.

Stegopontonia (Fig. 7), illustrate the extremes to which this feature can be developed. Both genera are found on the long spines of diademid sea urchins.

B. Loss of Spines and Processes as Adaptations
   to Free Movement on or within Host

1. Rostral Modifications

   a. Reduction of rostral teeth. Normally, about seven teeth are present on the dorsal border of the rostrum. In many commensal species the number is reduced, as in *Periclimenes zanzibaricus* Bruce, or the size may be reduced, as in *A. miersi*. In many cases reduction is complete and the rostrum is toothless as exemplified by *Stegopontonia* (Fig. 7), *Parapontonia*, or *A. custos*.

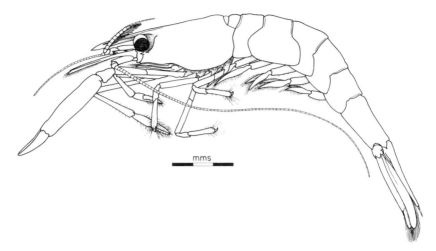

Fig. 7. *Stegopontonia commensalis* Nobili, male; Anse Étoile, Mahé, Seychelle Islands.

b. Reduction of rostral lamina. In unmodified species the rostrum generally distinctly exceeds the antennular peduncle and, in some free-living species, such as *Periclimenes tenuipes* Borradaile, it is greatly elongated. Many commensal species show a decrease in the size of the rostrum. All stages are shown in *Periclimenaeus,* ranging from a normally well-developed rostrum to a short process that fails to exceed the eyes. In *Onycocaris* the rostrum is greatly reduced and more or less rudimentary and in *Paratypton* it is absent.

2. Reduction of Carapace Spines or Processes

In many of the unspecialized species of *Periclimenes* (Figs. 2 and 3) and in *Palaemonella,* the carapace bears its full complement of supraorbital, antennal, and hepatic spines. No branchiostegal or pterygostomial spines are present. Varying combinations of presence and absence of these spines are present in the different genera, showing an increased tendency to absence in the species living in confined spaces.

a. Absence of supraorbital spines. This is of common occurrence in the various commensal genera, particularly those such as *Jocaste* and *Coralliocaris* found living in association with scleractinian corals.

b. Mobility of hepatic spine. This feature is found rarely in the Pontoniinae. It is characteristic of the genus *Paranchistus* and the relative size of the spine appears to decrease with the growth of the shrimp. Mobility in this case probably precedes the complete loss of the spine.

c. Loss of hepatic spine. This occurs frequently in commensal genera associated with sponges, corals, mollusks, or tunicates, e.g., *Thaumastocaris* (Fig. 8), *Vir* (Fig. 9), *Anchistus*, and *Pontonia*.

d. Loss of antennal spine. This occurs less frequently than the loss of the above mentioned spines, but is found in such genera as *Platycaris* (Fig. 4) or *Waldola*.

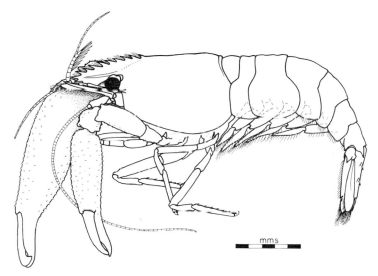

Fig. 8. Thaumastocaris streptopus Kemp, male; Bawi Island, Zanzibar.

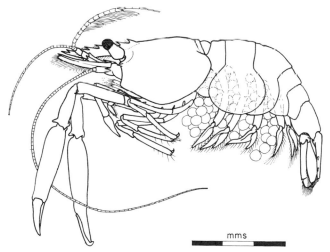

Fig. 9. Vir orientalis (Dana), female; Victoria Harbour, Mahé, Seychelle Islands.

e. Reduction of inferior orbital angle. Although generally distinct in most genera, the inferior orbital angle is obsolescent in some genera such as *Pontonia* and absent in others, such as *Onycocaris* and *Platycaris*.

3. Reduction of Abdominal Spines

a. Posterior ventral processes of pleura. In free-living species and in some commensal species living in fairly unconfined circumstances (for example, *Dasycaris* on pennatulaceans or antipatharians), the posterior ventral angles of the pleura of the fourth and fifth abdominal segments and the posterior and posterior ventral angles of the sixth segment are acutely produced. In most of the commensal species found in association with sponges (*Onycocaris*), corals (*Coralliocaris*), mollusks (*Anchistus*), echinoderms (*Pontoniopsis*) (Fig. 10), or tunicates (*Dasella*), these angles are blunt or rounded and not produced.

b. Reduction of telson spines. Normally two pairs of well-developed spines are present on the dorsal aspect of the telson and a further three pairs are present along the posterior margin. These spines may undergo marked reduction in size (*P. brevicarpalis* and *A. custos*), although they are rarely absent. In *Paratypton* the dorsal spines are minute and in *Anapontonia* they are absent (Bruce, 1967a, 1969a).

4. Reduction of Spines on Appendages

a. On antennae. The distolateral angle of the basal segment of the antennular peduncle is generally provided with an acute tooth. In

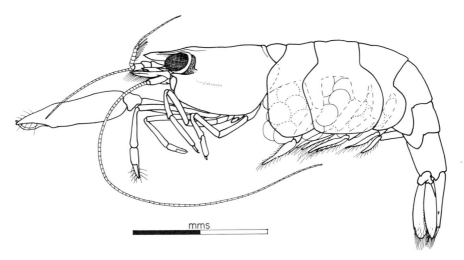

Fig. 10. *Pontoniopsis comanthi* Borradaile, female; Chango Island, Zanzibar.

sponge-inhabiting species this tooth is often markedly reduced or even absent. Similar changes are also found in the spine at the lateral aspect of the basicerite and in the distolateral spine of the scaphocerite, for example, in many species of *Periclimenaeus* and *Onycocaris*. In *Typton*, the whole scaphocerite is greatly reduced, forming only a small lamella. Similar changes are also found in the coral-gall-inhabiting shrimp *Paratypton* (Fig. 6) (Bruce, 1969a).

b. On pereiopods. The first pereiopods are generally without spines but in most free-living species acute spines are present on the distal borders of the merus and carpus of the second pereiopods. In commensal species these spines are frequently reduced or replaced by rounded lobes. This is especially noticeable in species found in confined spaces such as those belonging to the genera *Anchistus*, *Paranchistus*, and *Conchodytes*, which live in molluscan hosts.

c. On uropods. The lateral border of the exopod usually terminates in an acute tooth, with a large mobile spine on its medial side. The tooth and spine undergo considerable reduction in many of the more cryptic species, the tooth being lost and the spine being only very small; e.g., *A. miersi*.

C. Adaptations to the Maintenance of the Association with the Host

Such adaptations generally represent specializations of a wide variety found in the appendages that often appear to be the converse of those mentioned above as assisting free movement of the shrimp. The reduction of some spines to assist free movement may be found to occur simultaneously in some shrimps with increased development of other spines to prevent separation of the shrimp from its host.

1. General Streamlining

This is virtually the same as adaptation to an exposed situation as discussed in Section A,4, when referring to species found living on sea urchin spines [*Stegopontonia* (Fig. 7) and *Tuleariocaris*].

2. Modification of Scaphocerite

The distolateral process may be much enlarged. This modification is found in some coral-inhabiting species such as *Anapontonia* and *Ischnopontonia* (Fig. 5), and in some sponge inhabitants, particularly *Anchistioides*. In these the lateral abduction of the scaphocerite has been observed to have a jamming effect on the sides of the cavity occupied.

3. Modifications of the Second Pereiopods

Adaptations of these appendages for the maintenance of an association appear to be very infrequent. In *Hamodactylus boschmai* Holthuis the tip of the dactylus is enlarged and hook-shaped and is used to hold the limb in contact with the host, very much in the same fashion as the hooked dactylus of an ambulatory pereiopod.

4. Adaptations of Ambulatory Pereiopods

These are most noticeable in the dactylus, where a very wide range of modifications is found to occur (Fig. 11). Many of these modifications are highly specific in nature and probably closely correlated with the morphology of the host. There is a general tendency for the development

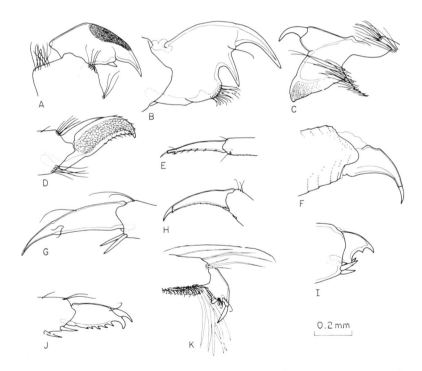

Fig. 11. Dactyls of ambulatory pereiopods. (A) *Anchistus miersi* (De Man); (B) *Conchodytes tridacnae* Peters; (C) *Jocaste japonica* (Ortmann); (D) *Harpiliopsis beaupresi* (Audouin); (E) *Periclimenes attenuatus* Bruce; (F) *Periclimenes consobrinus* (De Man), propodal setae omitted, (G) *Periclimenes petitthouarsi* (Audouin); (H) *Periclimenaeus arabicus* (Calman), holotype; (I) *Periclimenaeus tridentatus* (Miers), holotype, (J) *Pontonia anachoreta* Kemp; and (K) *Stegopontonia commensalis* Nobili.

of a short stout limb, rather than a long slender one as found in free-living species (Fig. 11G).

a. Dactylar modifications. *i.* Development of a stout, hooked dactylus. This is one of the commonest modifications and occurs independently in various genera associated with a variety of hosts. Thus it is found in *Anapontonia* and *Ischnopontonia,* which are associated with corals, and in *Pontonides,* which is associated with antipatharians and pennatulaceans.

ii. Development of additional dactylar spinulations. (a) Single accessory spine. A simple spine is frequently found at the distal ventral margin of the corpus of the dactylus, at the base of the unguis. It is particularly common in commensal species of the genus *Periclimenes* (Fig. 11E) but is more strongly developed in genera such as *Thaumastocaris,* some *Periclimenaeus,* and some *Conchodytes* (Fig. 11B) and also occurs in *Parapontonia* and *Pontoniopsis,* which are associated with crinoids. (b) Accessory spine and spinules. These are found frequently in the sponge inhabiting genera, *Periclimenaeus* (Fig. 11H) and *Onycocaris,* in which a wide range of specific modifications occur. An interesting modification is found in several species of *Pontonia* (Fig. 11J) each of which has an elongated dactylus with a row of numerous small hooklike spines along the ventral border. It seems likely that the variations are related to the sizes of the pharyngeal stigmata of their tunicate hosts.

iii. Development of dactylar carinae. This development appears to occur only in the coral-associated genus *Harpiliopsis* (Fig. 11D), in which a well-developed lateral carina is present on the outer side of the particularly stout dactylus.

iv. Development of a simple basal dactylar process. This feature appears to be present in different forms in unrelated genera. The functions of each type are probably quite distinct. (a) An unarmed basal process. This is found in genera such as *Fennera,* which occur on pocilloporid corals. In this genus the dactylus is capable of a great degree of extension, reaching perpendicular to the propod. It probably acts as a fulcrum when the propod is adducted, causing the tip of the dactyus to press into the host's tissues. A similar dactylus is found in the tunicate associate *Dasella.* (b) As a support for accessory spines. This situation may occur in some species of the genus *Conchodytes* (Fig. 11B) and also in the genus *Chernocaris,* all found in bivalve mollusks. The modifications occurring here may be related to the size of the branchial lamellae.

v. Development of an ungulate basal process. This is found only in the species of the coral-associated genera *Coralliocaris* and *Jocaste* (Fig. 11C) and the echinoid-associated *Tuleariocaris.* In *Coralliocaris* the tip of the hoof-shaped process is often minutely acute and is the only part in contact with the host, the reduced corpus and unguis projecting freely.

In addition to the major variations outlined above, many minor modifications, often found only in individual species, occur throughout the Pontoniinae. Most of these are presumably adaptations to each particular host but detailed functions in most cases have not been studied and so remain obscure. Variations that are worth mentioning include the articulated unguis found in some species of *Periclimenaeus* and the scooped dorsal surface of the dactylus in some species of *Anchistus*.

b. Propodal modifications. Much variation of a minor nature occurs in the spinulation of the ventral border of the free-living *Periclimenes* as well as the commensal *Periclimenaeus*. Most of the commensal genera lack spines in this situation or, at the most, bear only a few small spines at the distal end. Only one special modification, the subchelate propod, has been noticed. In *Periclimenes galene* Holthuis the distal end of the propod is broadened and strongly spinose. The strong dactylus can be fully flexed to oppose these spines and is used for grasping the branches of the hydroid host.

c. Modifications of the caudal fan. Numerous minor variations are again found in the spinulation of the telson and uropods, but are generally only of specific importance. In a few genera important modifications have been developed that greatly facilitate attachment to the host.

d. Modifications to the telson. *i.* Enlargement of dorsal spines. In some species of *Pontonia* and particularly in *Periclimenaeus,* the two pairs of dorsal spines are greatly enlarged and erectile. In *Periclimenaeus* the caudal fan is normally carried flexed beneath the abdomen. In this position erection of the dorsal spines will tend to resist any attempt to draw the shrimp from its sponge channel.

ii. Enlargement of posterior spines. This has been noticed in *Fennera,* whose spines can probably be flexed ventrally to dig into the host's tissues.

iii. Development of posterior telson hooks. Such a development is known only in the genus *Hamopontonia,* in which distinct posterior telson spines are lacking and are replaced by a pair of large, ventrally curved, hooklike processes. These can probably be pressed into the host tissues on flexion of the abdomen (Bruce, 1970a).

e. Modifications of the uropods. Modifications in the lateral border of the exopod of the uropod are relatively uncommon but are found in coral- and sponge-inhabiting genera. *i.* Increased spinulation of exopod. This is found only in a few species of the genus *Periclimenaeus* and may take the form of a series of numerous small serrations of the lateral border or a row of small mobile spines.

ii. Specialized jamming mechanisms. These are known only in two genera, *Ischnopontonia* and *Anapontonia,* which inhabit the narrow spaces between the corallites of *G. fascicularis.* In the former genus the distal mobile spine is greatly enlarged, curved, hooklike, and fixed. In the latter genus the distolateral border of the exopod bears a series of large, anteriorly directed, hooklike processes. Abduction of the uropod will clearly have the effect of jamming the caudal fan in position between the adjacent corallites, in much the same way as is done with the scaphocerite (Bruce, 1966c, 1967a).

D. MORPHOLOGICAL ADAPTATIONS OF FEEDING MECHANISMS

The shrimps of the subfamily Pontoniinae must be adapted to utilizing a wide range of foodstuffs, although very little is known about this aspect of their life. Predatory species clearly require a different mechanism from those that may behave as cleaners or that may utilize a finely divided source of food derived from their host. The variety of habits is reflected in the numerous modifications found in the mouthparts and associated appendages of the shrimps. Even at intrageneric levels, numerous small differences may be found among closely related species living in association with related hosts (Bruce, 1971).

In the unspecialized genera, such as *Palaemonella,* the oral appendages closely resemble those of the *Palaemoniinae,* as exemplified by the genera *Palaemon* or *Macrobranchium* (Bruce, 1970c).

1. Modifications of the Oral Appendages

a. Mandibular modifications. In almost all genera of the Pontoniinae, the mandibular palp has been lost. It is retained only in the relatively unspecialized genera *Palaemonella, Vir, Eupontonia,* and in one species of *Periclimenes.* The significance of the loss is not apparent, but may be associated with the adoption of a soft diet or of one consisting of finely divided particles. The molar process is particularly robust in some of the more actively predatory species such as *P. elegans,* in which strong teeth are present. In these species the incisor process is also usually stout, with 3–4 acute teeth distally. In the commensal species either the molar process or the incisor process may be greatly reduced and in some species of *Typton,* the incisor process may be completely absent. The reduction of the molar processes suggests that these species have a diet of soft food that does not require grinding. Reduction of the molar process is well shown by the genus *Metapontonia,* found on fungiid corals, in which it is reduced to a small acute process. The opposite extreme can be found in the sponge-associated genus *Anchistioides,* in which the molar process is broadly expanded distally and possesses very large, strong, blunt teeth. Expansion of the incisor process occurs in species such as *Periclimenes ceratophthalmus* Borradaile, which has large teeth distally, whereas in others, numerous small teeth are present, as in several species of *Periclimenaeus.* Also, in a few species small denticles are present along the medial border of the process, e.g., *Periclimenes indicus* (Kemp) and *Pontonia okai* Kemp.

   b. Maxillary modifications. The maxillae conform mainly with a common pattern although there is much variation in minor details. In the first maxillae the laciniae vary considerably in broadness and spinulation from species to species. In the second maxillae a wide range of variation in the degree of suppression of the basal endite is found. In a few genera, such as *Anapontonia* and *Metapontonia,* the basal endite is completely absent whereas, in others, it is broadly expanded, as for example in *Conchodytes.* Many unilobed or bilobed intermediate stages also occur in different genera (Kubo, 1940).

   c. Maxilliped modifications. The maxillipeds show considerable structural variation in both endopods and exopods. The former may be elongated and slender, or short and stout. In some genera, they are broadly expanded and almost opercular. The predatory species, in particular, have long slender endopods. The exopods are of particular interest. In the predatory species they closely resemble those of other Caridea. Several variations occur in commensal species. In the majority of commensal species the exopod is relatively feebly developed, slender, narrow, subcylindrical, with only 4–5 plumose setae at the distal extremity. In some genera, particularly one group associated with corals (*Philarius, Harpiliopsis, Jocaste,* and *Coralliocaris*) and another with echinoids (*Tuleariocaris* and *Stegopontonia*), the exopods are well developed, robust, and broadened, with a large number of plumose setae along the sides of the distal half. They are probably an important component of the feeding mechanism. In other genera, particularly those associated with coelenterates, all degrees of reduction of the exopod of the third maxilliped occur. In a few genera, the exopod of the second may also be completely absent, e.g., *Paratypton.*

2. Modifications of the Fourth Thoracic Sternite

   In the unspecialized genera *Palaemonella, Eupontonia,* and *Vir,* and in predatory species of the genus *Periclimenes,* the fourth thoracic sternite bears a long, slender, fingerlike median process. This process does not appear to be present in any of the commensal genera, although it does occur in three species of *Periclimenes* that are found in association with corals (*P. lutescens* auct., *P. consobrinus* De Man, and *P. amymone* De Man). It would appear that the function of this process is to act as a "backstop" to the oral region, preventing the escape of prey backwards between the bases of the pereiopods. In the commensal genera the fourth thoracic sternite usually bears only a low ridge, often with a small median notch. The species of *Periclimenes* mentioned above may possibly be highly specific coral predators rather than commensals. No information is available on their feeding habits but the feces of *P. amymone* appear to contain zooxanthellae.

3. Modifications of the First Pereiopods

These appendages are invariably chelate and are particularly concerned with the transference of food to the mouthparts. Their function has been studied only in one species, *A. custos*, by Johnson and Liang (1966). Numerous modifications occur, all probably related to the food consumed and with all types of intermediate stages of development.

a. Chela with spatulate or subspatulate fingers. Chelae of this type are conspicuously developed in browsing species of *Periclimenes* (*P. petitthouarsi, P. spiniferus* De Man, *P. denticulatus* Nobili, and *P. sibogae* Holthuis). They also occur in some asteroid associates, such as *P. soror* and *P. noverca* Kemp and some species associated with bivalves, e.g., *Paranchistus biunguiculatus* (Borradaile). In most cases, the cutting edges are finely denticulate.

b. Fingers elongated and palm shortened. This arrangement is found in the genus *Stegopontonia* but not in the related *Tuleariocaris*. The fingers in this genus appear to have a scissorlike action.

c. Palm elongated and fingers shortened. In *Periclimenaeus* and *Onycocaris*, which are genera found in sponges, several species have a chela with a long, slender, tapering palm possessing only a very small pair of fingers at the end. This arrangement would appear to be an adaptation for picking at very small particles.

d. Canaliculation of palm. This modification is found only in the shrimp *A. custos*. The dorsal and ventral edges of the palm of the chela are expanded, curved medially, and fringed with long setae, forming a deep channel along the palm. Johnson and Liang (1966) have reported that the chela is used to sweep up mucus and food from the host's gills, so that they accumulate in the palmar groove and are then transferred to the mouthparts.

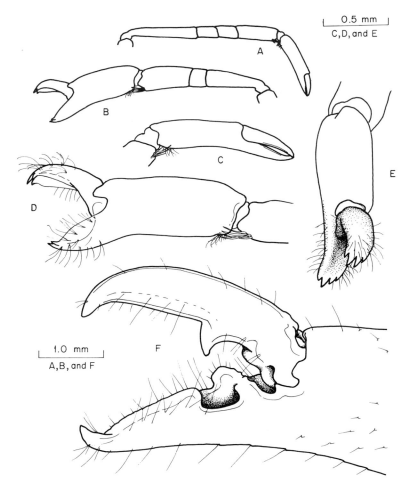

Fig. 12. *Thaumastocaris streptopus* Kemp, male; Wasin Island, Kenya. (A) Minor first pereiopod; (B) major first pereiopod; (C) chela of minor first pereiopod; (D) chela of major first pereiopod; and (E) fingers of major second pereiopod.

e. Asymmetry of chelae. In *Thaumastocaris* (Fig. 12) the chelae are of different types on each side of the body, a feature not found in any other pontoniinid shrimp. The minor chela is slender with long, slender, tapering fingers. In the major chela, which is probably used for some specialized feeding process, the fingers are short and broad, subspatulate, and with strongly multidentate tips.

f. Segmentation of carpus. Such segmentation is of common occurrence in the pereiopods of shrimps of many families. It is found in only one pontoniinid shrimp, *Thaumastocaris streptopus* Kemp (Fig. 12), which occurs in sponges. Presumably its function is to increase the flexibility of the limb. It is surprising that this modification is not of more frequent occurrence in the Pontoniinae in view of the restricted spaces in which some of them live.

4. Modifications of the Second Pereiopods

These appendages are generally the most conspicuous features in the shrimps and are primarily concerned with attack and defense. In many genera the pair of chelae are almost identical on each side or differ only slightly in size. In some genera, however, the two chelae are often of completely different types, one usually very much larger.

a. Predatory modifications. In the highly predatory species of *Periclimenes*, such as *P. grandis* (Stimpson) and *P. elegans* (Fig. 3A) and related species, the fingers of the subequal chelae of the second pereiopods show increased development of the strong teeth arming the cutting edges of the fingers that must assist in seizing and holding their prey. These teeth are less well developed in the micropredatory species, such as *P. rotumana* and *Periclimenes seychellensis* Borradaile.

b. Food gathering modifications. Some genera, such as *Jocaste*, have one second pereiopod modified to form a small scoop, which may assist in food gathering. Similar modifications may be found in some species of *Periclimenes* (*P. diversipes* or *P. kempi* Bruce) or may occur in both chelae as in *Propontonia* and *Cavicheles*.

c. Extreme specializations. In *Tuleariocaris* the minor second pereiopod is very feebly developed when compared with the major one and bears only a minute chela. *Stegopontonia* shows similar but less marked changes. One species of *Periclimenes*, *P. attenuatus* Bruce, also shows very great differentiation in the size and shape of its chelae, as does *Pontoniopsis comanthi* Borradaile (Fig. 10). In the former the minor chela has fingers resembling a small pair of forceps that may be used for picking up small particles of food. All species are associated either with echinoids or crinoids.

E. DEFENSIVE MODIFICATIONS

1. Modifications of the Second Pereiopods

As mentioned above, the chelae of the second pereiopods are the main means of defense. In the species that inhabit exposed niches, such as the branches of corals, these pereiopods are often greatly enlarged, usually symmetrically, as in *Coralliocaris* and *Harpiliopsis*, but unilater-

ally in *Jocaste*. In species such as *Periclimenaeus* and *Onycocaris* that
live in channels in sponges, the chelae also are often enlarged and may
almost fill the lumen of the canal. In *Onycocaris* both chelae are generally
symmetrically enlarged and when held side-by-side form a barrier in
front of the body of the shrimp.

In *Periclimenaeus* the chelae are markedly asymmetrical and often
the larger chela is big enough to occlude the channel in which the
shrimp is living. In a few species the chela is also covered with small
tubercles or even spines, which would have a further deterrent effect.

2. Sound Producing Mechanisms

The sound producing capabilities of the alpheid shrimps, particularly
Alpheus and *Synalpheus,* are well known. The ability of the pontoniinid
shrimps to produce sound in the field has been largely ignored. *Coralliocaris graminea* is probably one of the best producers of snapping noises
on coral reefs. Whereas the shrimps of the genera *Alpheus* and *Synalpheus* have only one large chela modified for sound production, in
C. graminea both chelae of the second pereiopods are able to produce
sound. When disturbed, the fingers of the chelae are alternately rapidly
snapped shut and emit bursts of sharp reports. Unlike *Alpheus* and
Synalpheus, the pit and hammer mechanism is reversed and the molar
process is on the fixed finger and not the dactylus (Fig. 13). Most
species of *Periclimenaeus* have a mechanism similar to *Alpheus* spp.
(with the molar process on the dactylus) and are also able to produce
a sudden snapping noise. The close resemblance of the sound producing
mechanisms in these shrimps is an interesting example of convergent
evolution, as it is the first pair of pereiopods that produce sound in
the alpheids and the second in the pontoniinids. A different mechanism
is found in *P. petitthouarsi* and *P. spiniferus,* which are also able to
produce loud snapping noises. In these species the fingers of the major
chela are provided with opposing pits on the cutting edges. When the
shrimp is threatened, the fingers are held open and their sudden closure
produces a sharp report (Fig. 14). Species of *Coralliocaris* such as *C.
superba* lack the pit and hammer mechanism found in *C. graminea*
but are still able to produce a distinct snap. Other shrimps that are
able to produce distinct snaps are *Thaumastocaris, Harpiliopsis, Jocaste,*
and *Onycocaris.* The sound produced is quite loud in the case of the
first two genera but much less so in the second two. In these genera
there is no conspicuous sound producing mechanism. In *Thaumastocaris,*
immediately in front of the hinge of the fingers, a small fossa is present

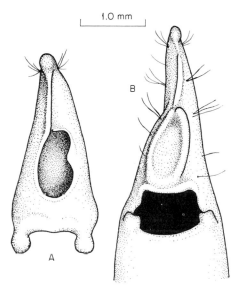

Fig. 13. Sound producing mechanism of *Coralliocaris graminea* (Dana). (A) Dactylus and (B) fixed finger.

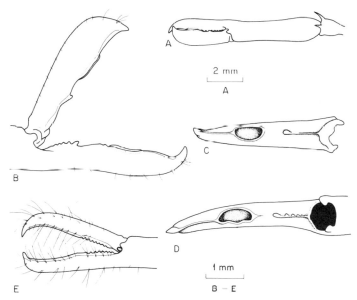

Fig. 14. *Periclimenes petitthouarsi* (Audouin), Male; Mazizini, Zanzibar. (A) Chela of major second pereiopod; (B) fingers of chela of major second pereiopod; (C) occlusal aspect of dactylus of major second pereiopod; (D) occlusal aspect of fixed finger of chela of major second pereiopod; and (E) fingers of minor second pereiopod.

on the pollex with a small, opposing, strongly reinforced swelling on the base of the dactylus (Fig. 12E). These may function in the same way as the sound producing mechanism in *C. graminea*. Alternatively, the sound producing mechanism may have evolved from the strong dactylar tooth that opposes a deep fossa on the fixed finger.

VIII. Feeding Methods

Very few observations have been made on the feeding methods of commensal shrimps. The behavior of *A. custos* has been studied by Johnson and Liang (1966) who reported that the shrimp holds onto the edge of the gill lamella of the host *Pinna* with the ambulatory pereiopods, while the surface of the gill is scraped with the specially modified chelae of the first pereiopods, which also convey food collected to the mouthparts. It would appear, therefore, that *A. custos* is a true commensal.

Some observations have been made on *Coralliocaris* sp. that indicate that a different feeding method may be employed in this genus. It has been noted above that the exopods of the maxillipeds are particularly well developed in this genus and also in some related genera. Observations of live specimens in a seawater suspension of yeast cells clearly show that strong currents converging on the oral region of the shrimp are set up. In *C. graminea* the exopods of either the right or the left side were vibrated very rapidly in short bursts of about 6–8 seconds. This activity resulted in a strong current converging from the left anterior side of the shrimp and leaving laterally on the right side, or posteriorly on the left when the left side maxillipeds were used (Fig. 15B,C). The converse arrangement occured when exopods of the right side were vibrated. Changes from left to right side use of the exopods were frequent and irregular. In *C. superba* a similar function of the exopods was also observed but in this species the exopods of both sides functioned together, producing a strong current from the front of the shrimp (Fig. 15D). The normal respiratory current is slow and does not involve the use of the maxillipeds, being produced by slow undulations of the scaphognathite. The inhalant current enters around the posterior margins of the branchiostegite and the exhalant current leaves from beneath the pterygostomial angle of the branchiostegite (Fig. 15A). Although not confirmed by observation, it is probable that the strong currents produced by the exopods of the maxillipeds, which do not appear to enter the branchial chambers, carry planktonic food that is extracted by the mouthparts (Fig. 16). This has not been possible to observe. It should be noted

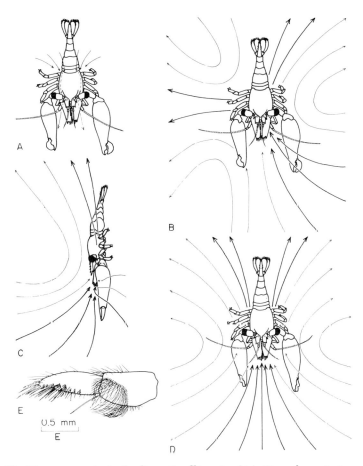

Fig. 15. Water currents in feeding *Coralliocaris*. (A) Normal respiratory current in *C. graminea* (Dana); (B) maxillipedal current in *C. graminea* (Dana), caused by exopods of left side only, in dorsal view; (C) same, in lateral view; (D) maxillipedal current in *C. superba* (Dana) caused by exopods of left and right sides; and (E) setal "basket" on penultimate segment of third maxilliped in *C. graminea* (Dana).

that both *C. graminea* and *C. superba* have a specialized basketlike arrangement of finely plumose setae on the distal dorsal aspect of the carpus of the third maxilliped (Fig. 15E), a feature that is absent from the majority of pontoniinid shrimps. It is possible that these setae may retain food particles brought by the maxillipedal current. The stomach of the specimen used in the preparation of Fig. 16 was full of very finely divided opalescent, cottony material of unidentified origin, but

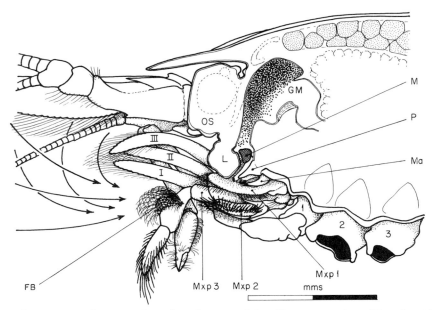

Fig. 16. Sagittal section through oral region of *Coralliocaris graminea* (Dana), with maxillipedal currents indicated. FB, food bolus in maxillipedal "basket"; GM, gastric mill; L, labrum; M, molar process of mandible; Ma, maxillula; OS, ophthalmic somite; P, paragnath; Mxp 1–3, first to third maxillipeds; I–III, exopods of first to third maxillipeds; 1–3, coxae of first to third pereiopods.

a small quantity of similar material was also present in the basket on the carpus of the third maxilliped. The contents of the basket are probably removed by the dactylus of the second maxilliped, which is densely spinose along its medial border, and transferred to the maxillae. Unlike those of *A. custos,* the first pereiopods were not observed to participate in the feeding mechanism, but the cleaning setae on the palm are particularly numerous and well developed and could possibly be used in the transfer of food from the third maxilliped to the mouth.

IX. General Behavioral Adaptations

The general behavior of tropical shrimps has been little studied and, in general, only casual observations upon isolated species are available. It is clear that the behavior of the shrimps is most important in maintaining the association with the host but the general behavior of the commensal species closely resembles that of free-living Caridea and it is probable that the photophobic and thigmotactic responses of noncommensal shrimps have been an important factor in the evolution of commensal habits.

A. REACTIONS TO LIGHT

1. Avoidance

It has been noticed, particularly in species of *Periclimenes* found in association with asteroids (e.g., *P. soror* and *P. noverca* Kemp), that they tend to avoid light and move onto the oral surface of their host, which is normally applied to the substratum. If the host is inverted, the shrimps then move onto the aboral surface.

2. Indifference

Many commensal shrimps show no avoidance to daylight and remain on their hosts in full sunlight. This is particularly noticeable in *P. brevicarpalis,* which is often completely exposed to full sunlight on the discs of its host anemones, *Stoichactis* spp., Other species, such as *Tuleariocaris* and *Stegopontonia* spp., living on the spines of diademid urchins must also be fully exposed to strong sunlight at times.

B. MOVEMENTS

Most of the commensal species of shrimp are sluggish in their movements and, once they have adopted their various characteristic positions, move around relatively little.

1. Characteristic Attitudes

Many species adopt characteristic attitudes when on their hosts. Thus *Coralliocaris* sp. are, by day, usually attached to the inner branches of the host in a head down position with the chelae of the second pair of pereiopods hanging in front of them. *Platycaris* adopts a similar head down attitude, but the chelae are crossed transversely in front of the head. *Harpiliopsis* spp., are usually found head downward also but the merocarpal joint of the second pereiopods is flexed so that the chelae lie alongside the anterior carapace. The stick-insectlike attitude adopted by the Bermudan anemone associate *Periclimenes anthophilus* Holthuis and Eibl-Eibesfeldt, which clasps the host's tentacles with its fourth pair of pereiopods, has been described by Holthius and Eibl-Eibesfeldt (1964).

2. Characteristic Positions

In the coral-inhabiting species belonging to the Pontoniinae and Alpheidae, many species occupy characteristic positions on the host. The following examples are given: *Periclimenes amymone* is found on the outermost branches. *Jocaste* spp. occur on the outer branches of corals but not at the extremities of the branches. *Periclimenes lutescens* and *P. consobrinus* occur on the intermediate sections of branches and *Coralliocaris* and *Harpiliopsis* on the bases of branches. *Philarius* spp. occur in the basal grooves and channels of *Acropora* and *Synalpheus charon* (Heller) and *Alpheus lottini* Guerin are found in those of the Pocilloporidae. It is very likely that other commensal shrimps found on other coelenterates or echinoderms have preferences of a similar nature. Some records of species found in bivalves report the presence of shrimps in the hypobranchial chamber of tridacnids, but Johnson and Liang (1966) have reported that the shrimp *A. custos* is usually found on the gill lamella of *Pinna*. In giant clams, in particular, it is especially difficult to observe the undisturbed position and activities of the commensal shrimps.

3. Characteristic Motions

It can be observed readily that aquarium specimens of *P. brevicarpalis* maintain almost continuous side to side twisting movements of the abdomen. At times, the cephalothorax is also similarly rotated. This activity is maintained whether the shrimp is associated with the host or not. Its function is obscure but it has the effect of making the eye spots on the caudal fan very conspicuous. In the Bermudan species *P. anthophilus* Holthuis and Eibl-Eibesfeldt, found on anemones, similar movements have been reported by Holthuis and Eibl-Eibesfeldt (1964). Similar movements have also been noted in *Thor amboinensis* (De Man), an associate of anemones, which possesses large white spots on the body. However, similar movements also occur in the free-living *Gnathophyllum americanum*, which has a barred pattern and is without eyespots.

4. Nocturnal Migrations

a. Local. In *C. graminea* and *C. superba*, which are found on the inner bases of coral branches by day, activity is much increased at night. The individuals move around considerably more than they do by day and they are also found on the outer parts of the coral branches. Such activities may well be associated with a plankton diet as suggested above.

b. General. Swarming of *Anchistioides antiguensis* (Schmitt) at night in association with the new moon period has been reported by Wheeler (1944) but this behavior has not been reported in any other commensal species. These swarms are possibly associated with mating.

5. *Swimming*

Probably all commensal species can swim well but rarely do so unless disturbed and forced to leave their host. When this occurs they generally return to the host almost immediately, after swimming only a very short distance. In some species, such as *Jocaste* spp., these swimming movements are extremely rapid but in others, such as *Periclimenaeus* spp., swimming is more leisurely, and in *Onycocaris* spp., distinctly labored. In *Paratypton* the male is able to swim well but the female appears extremely clumsy when swimming. In those genera that have large chelae on the second pereiopods, these are folded backward so as to lie beneath the body when swimming. An interesting adaptation is found in the swimming habits of the echinoid commensals *Tuleariocaris* spp., which, when disturbed, will swim between spines maintaining a head down position, similar to that described for the fish *Aeoliscus* which occurs in a similar niche (Davenport, 1955).

6. *Cleaning Behavior*

This particular aspect of commensalism has recently attracted considerable attention, largely due to the increased use of scuba equipment. Most observations have been concerned with fishes, but cleaning behavior has also been observed to be engaged in by representatives of three families of shrimps. These observations have been made mostly in tropical American waters and the occurrence of similar behavior in the Indo-West Pacific region is based on very few reports. However, cleaning behavior does appear to be a feature specially associated with tropical waters and is of rare occurrence elsewhere. The species of shrimps known to behave as fish cleaners are listed below (Limbaugh *et al.*, 1961):

1. *Periclimenes pedersoni* Chase and *P. yucatanicus* (Ives) (Pontoniinae)
2. *Hippolysmata grabhami* Gordon and *H. californica* Stimpson (Hippolytidae)
3. *Stenopus hispidus* (Olivier) and *S. scutellatus* Rankin (Stenopodidae)

Of these shrimps, only *S. hispidus* is known to occur in the Indo-West Pacific region* and fish cleaning does not seem to be an important aspect

* *Hippolysmata grabhami*, now transferred to *Lysmata*, has since been recorded from its Indo-West Pacific region (Bruce, 1974).

of its behavior, judging from the paucity of reports. It is interesting to note that both the species of *Periclimenes* are associated with anemones and have characteristic color patterns. However, no records of cleaning behavior have been reported although one species, *P. brevicarpalis*, is extremely common and well known. In addition to cleaning fish, *H. californica* has also been reported to clean the spiny lobster *Panulirus interruptus* Randall.

In the case of *P. pedersoni* the antennal flagella are white and have been considered to be particularly important in attracting fish to the shrimp, which vigorously waves its antennae. White antennal flagellae are also very conspicuous in *S. hispidus* but have not been reported in the Indo-West Pacific species of *Periclimenes* that are associated with anemones, in which they are usually transparent. White antennal flagellae are found only rarely in the Indo-West Pacific fauna, although another conspicuous example is provided by the spiny lobster *Panulirus versicolor* (Latr.).

7. Reactions to Tide Level Changes

Many of the intertidal hosts are exposed during the periods of low water, particularly during spring tides. During these periods shrimps such as *Coralliocaris* and *Jocaste* spp. remain attached to the branches of their *Acropora* hosts, near to their bases, and do not desert their hosts to seek shelter in the water. *Periclimenes brevicarpalis*, usually found on the upper surface of the disc of giant anemones, migrates onto the lower side of the disc during the period of exposure.

X. Color Adaptations

The shrimps of coral reefs are frequently of striking coloration, often with elaborate multicolored patterns. In their natural habitat, most species are quite inconspicuous, even when removed from their particular niche. The types of coloration may be divided into two categories.

A. PATTERNS BLENDING WITH BACKGROUNDS

1. Cryptic Patterns

Most of the shrimps that live in exposed situations are cryptically colored and closely resemble the host on which they live. This type of adaptation is particularly noticeable in the species that live on echinoid spines, e.g., *Stegopontonia* and *Tuleariocaris* spp., which are of a very dark purple color, almost black, with a narrow lateral line of white.

In these genera some of the purple pigment is deposited in the cuticle and is lost on molting. Other shrimps that resemble their host are some species of *Dasycaris* and *Pontonides* which are found on *Cirripathes*. These are transparent with transverse bands of yellow, that exactly match the color of the host's polyps.

2. Disruptive Patterns

Shrimps of the genera *Harpiliopsis* and *Jocaste,* living on the more peripheral branches of corals, are largely transparent but heavily speckled with dark brown or black spots or streaks. When immersed in water this pattern renders the shrimps quite difficult to see. The shrimp *P. spiniferus,* a browser, but often found on live or dead corals, is similarly largely transparent but heavily speckled with red, white, and blue. This coloration enables it to blend inconspicuously with a sand or pebble background, although it is quite conspicuous when isolated from its habitat.

3. Transparent Patterns

A few shrimps have lost almost all chromatophores and developed a glassy transparency of their body tissues. A few are almost invisible in clear water and are noticeable mainly by the disturbance they create or by the movement of the cornea, which is still deeply pigmented. Shrimps of the genera *Periclimenes* (*P. diversipes, P. kempi,* and *P. inornatus* Kemp), *Propontonia,* and *Anchistioides* are noteworthy for the high degree of transparency developed. *Anchistioides* occurs in sponges and the others associate with coelenterates. The predatory species of *Periclimenes* are also highly transparent or with a freely disruptive color pattern.

B. Patterns Contrasting with Backgrounds

1. "Irrelevant" Patterns

Species of shrimp that live in well-protected niches may have color patterns that render them very conspicuous when removed from their hosts. The coral shrimps *C. graminea* and *C. superba* live deep among the branches of their hosts and appear relatively well protected. The former species is a brilliant green and the body of the latter is a striking porcelain white. Owing to the protection offered by their niche, it is probable that their bright colors do not subject them to any marked disadvantages. Many of the shrimps that live in bivalve mollusks also have color patterns that do not appear related to their hosts. For example,

Anchistus demani Kemp and *A. miersi* are basically transparent with
large bright red and blue dots, respectively.

2. Signal Patterns

Although this term is used for the color patterns of certain very conspicuously colored shrimps, the significance of the signals is unknown.
An example is provided by the shrimp *P. brevicarpalis*, which is one
of the commonest Indo-West Pacific commensals found on *Stoichactis*
spp. from East Africa to Hawaii. It is largely transparent but the ovary,
the dorsal aspect of the eyestalk, the dorsum of the third abdominal
segment, the pleura of the first three abdominal segments, and the anterior half of the caudal fan are all intensely white. The pereiopods are
conspicuously ringed with blue. The tips of the caudal fan are orange-
yellow, ringed with blue. The function of these markings is obscure.
They may represent a form of warning coloration. Under aquarium conditions and separated from their hosts, this species has rarely been mo-
lested by fish when other shrimps of similar size have been eaten. The
markings on the tips of the uropods form negative eyespots. It has also
been noted that, under aquarium conditions, fish such as *Dasyllus
aruanus* when deprived of their natural cleaners will incite *P. brevicarpalis* to "clean" them, although with little response. Those species of
Periclimenes that are known to be cleaners (*P. pedersoni* and *P. yucatanicus*) also have well-developed caudal eyespots (Limbaugh *et al.*, 1961)
as do several other species of *Periclimenes* that are not yet known to
be cleaners [e.g., *P. aesopius* (Bate), *P. tosaensis* Kubo, *P. anthophilus*,
and *P. holthuisi* Bruce]. Like *P. brevicarpalis* and *P. pedersoni*, both
P. anthophilus and *P. holthuisi* are also associated with anemones.

One interesting anomaly concerning color patterns is of note. *Periclimenes imperator* Bruce is a large and brightly colored shrimp, mainly
red with a broad white dorsal stripe down the length of the body,
that is generally found in the large red and white nudibranch *Hexa-
branchus marginatus*. In this situation it is quite inconspicuous, blending
well with its host's color pattern. Not infrequently, small specimens of
the shrimp, still with the red and white pattern, may be found on the
dull olive-brown holothurians *Stichopus chloronotus* or *S. variegatus*,
where they are extremely conspicuous. So far no adult shrimps of this
species have been found in association with the holothurians.

Nonpontoniinid shrimps found in coral reefs also frequently possess
striking color patterns. The well-known cleaner *S. hispidus* is always
conspicuous with its red and white pattern and long white antennae.
The gnathophyllid shrimps *Hymenocera picta* Dana, white with large

pink and blue patches, and *G. americanum* Guerin, yellow with transverse black or dark brown bands, seem to be largely ignored by fish under aquarium conditions, which again suggests that their patterns may have a warning significance.

3. Nocturnal Color Changes

Many species change their color at night. This is particularly noticeable in the dark purple-black species found in association with echinoderms, e.g., *P. soror*, *P. zanzibaricus* Bruce, and *Tuleariocaris zanzibarica* Bruce. At night these become a pale pink, although in *T. zanzibarica* the tips of the rostrum, antennae, chelae, and the sixth abdominal segment and caudal fan remain dark purple. In contrast, one species, *Eupontonia noctalbata* Bruce, which is transparent by day, becomes white at night. However, several species, such as *C. graminea* and *C. superba* do not change their coloration at night.

XI. Reproductive Adaptations

A. CYCLICAL ADAPTATIONS

1. In tropical regions where coral reefs are found shrimps appear to breed throughout the year, although there are no precise reports upon this aspect of their lives. The absence of any clearly defined breeding season is indicated by examination of field collections that show that virtually all adult females carry eggs, or that the ova have recently hatched. In the Pontoniinae, the female molts very soon after the ova have hatched—generally the same night, since hatching usually occurs in the early part of the night. Mating occurs at once, and usually a fresh batch of eggs is laid immediately. In females carrying ova on the point of hatching, the ovary is usually readily visible and greatly enlarged. A continuous supply of planktonic larvae throughout the year will enable the larvae to be distributed through the widest possible variety of water currents.

2. Just as there is no well-defined annual breeding cycle, there similarly does not appear to be any precise link between reproductive and lunar cycles. Adult females in field collections are found to have the ova at all stages of development, so that hatching will occur at all stages of the tidal cycle from spring to neap tides.

3. Precise observations on the time and duration of hatching of reef shrimps are not available but in the course of keeping ovigerous females of numerous genera in the laboratory to obtain early larval stages, it has been found that hatching generally commences in the early part

of the night, usually about 10–11 P.M. Hatching of eggs at such times will allow dispersal of the larvae during darkness when predation is probably at a lower level than during daylight, when sight-feeding predators will be more active. In *Alpheus microstylus* (Bate), which carries a very large number of ova, hatching is spread over several days but is suspended during the day.

B. VARIATIONS IN FECUNDITY

1. Increased numbers of ova are found in incarcerated species. The ovary in most free-living pontoniinid and palaemonid shrimps is confined to the thoracic region. The ova when laid vary little in size in the different genera and species, usually having a maximum diameter of 0.4–0.6 mm. In many of the commensal species the ovary is greatly enlarged and extends well into the abdominal region. This is particularly noticeable in the transparent shrimps *Periclimenaeus* and *Onycocaris*, which are associated with sponges, and in *Typton* the ovary may even extend into the sixth abdominal segment. The size of the ova being relatively constant, these species with extra large ovaries produce larger numbers of ova at a given size. Also, in these species the pleura and rami of the pleopods are often enlarged so as to enclose the ova in a protective marsupium. Relatively increased numbers of ova are found most noticeably in species that live in semienclosed niches, e.g., the genera *Anchistus* and *Paranchistus* found in bivalve mollusks, or *Paratypton* in its coral cyst. In a particular niche, such as is provided by the coral G. *fascicularis*, the sedentary species *Platycaris latirostris* carries a relatively larger number of ova than the similarly sized, but active, *Ischnopontonia lophos*. Clearly the production of large numbers of ova in sedentary or incarcerated species enables the maximum dispersion of the larvae to be obtained. Few details are available concerning the number of ova carried by tropical shrimps but a few examples will suffice to illustrate the range of variation. *Fennera chacei*, one of the smallest species, with a carapace length of 1.1 mm, carries only nine ova. *Metapontonia fungiacola* Bruce, with a carapace length of 2.10 mm carries 11 ova. Average sized species, such as *I. lophos* (Barnard), carry from 40–266 ova, with a mean value of 156. *Conchodytes meleagrinae* Peters has been found with 479 ova, and *C. tridacnae* Peters with 725, at carapace lengths of 10.0 and 9.1 mm, respectively. *Paratypton siebenrocki* Balss, at a carapace length of 3.1 mm, carried 1278 ova—a very large number for its size. The largest number so far found was on a specimen of *T. streptopus* Kemp, which, at a carapace length of 9.0 mm carried 2114 ova. For

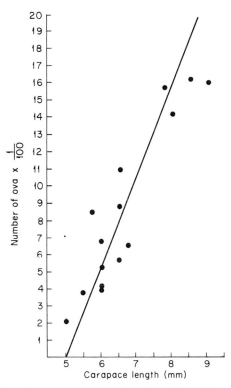

Fig. 17. Relationship between carapace length and number of eggs produced in *Thaumastocaris streptopus* Kemp, Stn. 136, Wasin Island, Kenya, October 7, 1971.

comparison with *Paratypton*, a specimen of *T. streptopus* with a carapace length of 5.0 mm carried only 217 ova. The range of variation in number of ova carried by females of this species from a single collection is illustrated on the graph (Fig. 17).

2. Decreased numbers of ova and abbreviated larval development. In the coral reef caridean fauna, abbreviated larval development is of rare occurrence. It has been shown to occur in some species of the genus *Synalpheus* [e.g., *S. goodei* Coutière (Gurney, 1949) and *S. brooksi* Coutière (Dobkin, 1965)] and also occurs in *R. compressus* (personal observation). In the Pontoniinae only a single example of abbreviated larval development, *Pontonia minuta* Baker, the host of which is as yet unidentified (Bruce, 1972b), is known. In this species the ovum is 1.55 mm in diameter and the pereiopods and pleopods of the larva are well developed immediately before hatching. If the molt to the

postlarval stage occurs shortly after hatching from the egg, or if the larval stages are completely suppressed, then the juvenile shrimp would be able to colonize the parent's host readily, without any intervening planktonic stage. This would have considerable survival value in situations where the host animals were naturally very rare since the chances of larval wastage through failure to locate a suitable host would thereby be greatly reduced. The host of *Racilius* is the coral *G. fascicularis*, which often forms extensive colonies that could easily accommodate the newly hatched juveniles. In the shrimps with abbreviated larval development the number of ova is greatly reduced and their relative size is increased. Dobkin (1965) has given the name of pseudolarvae to these nonswimming larval forms.

XII. Dispersal

A. PLANKTONIC LARVAL DISTRIBUTION

As mentioned above, most of the coral reef shrimps have small ova that develop into small planktonic larvae that are distributed away from their parents by water currents. The duration of larval life is unknown and the distances travelled may vary considerably according to local circumstances. Most of the common Indo-West Pacific species have achieved a very wide distribution in that region and commonly extend from East Africa to Hawaii. It is probable that many of the supposedly rare species will be found to have similar distributions when more material becomes available for study.

B. HOST DISTRIBUTION

Clearly, in many of the species that are obligate commensals the distribution of the shrimps will be dependent on the distribution of the host. Enough information is not yet available to establish whether certain species have a more limited distribution than their hosts. Some adaptability may compensate for differences in host distribution; for example, *Hamodactylus noumeae* Bruce occurs on gorgonians in the Pacific Ocean, but on alcyonarians in the Indian Ocean.

C. SETTLEMENT

The presence of very small postlarvae on the hosts favored by adults indicates that settlement occurs at the end of the planktonic larval phase in many of the commensal species. These are most readily observed in the branching coral communities. Often the postlarvae may show a markedly different chromatophore pattern from that found in the juveniles, that is probably persistent from their planktonic phase and which may indicate that settlement has occurred during the previous night as it is soon lost. The survival of the postlarvae of commensal species probably also depends upon their being able to settle upon an appropriate host. This event may be determined by specific chemical interaction, but there is as yet no evidence for the existence of any attractive host factor. The juveniles are generally more transparent than some fully grown specimens and are usually difficult to find on this account. After careful searching they can generally be found among the shrimps associated with sponges, coelenterates, and echinoderms but seem to be unusually infrequent in the shrimps associated with bivalve hosts. Examination of large numbers of *Tridacna* spp. for the presence of *A. miersi* and *A. demani,* for example, has revealed that the material collected consists almost entirely of adult pairs or very well grown specimens, and only very rarely has a juvenile been found.

XIII. The Range of Host–Animal Types

Host animals that harbor shrimp associates are found in all phyla including large marine animals. Shrimps are generally not found in association with small animals and usually the host animal is many times the size of the shrimp associate. A diagrammatic representation of the distribution of hosts on a typical East African fringing reef is given in Fig. 18.

A. Porifera

Sponges are frequently hosts for a variety of alpheid and pontoniinid shrimps, as well as some hippolytids and *Discias.* Several species may often be found in a single host. Large sponges, especially those species that are honeycombed with small passages, often contain numbers of shrimps. In contrast, sometimes the host may be just large enough to form a small thin-walled sac enclosing a pair of shrimps. Many apparently suitable sponges fail to attract any shrimps and sponges of a slimy nature are particularly avoided.

B. Coelenterata

The Coelenterata attract a wider variety of shrimp associates than any other phylum, the majority of which are found on anthozoan coelen-

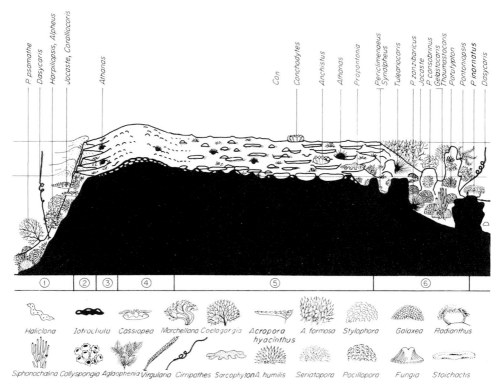

Fig. 18. Schematic representation of the distribution of shrimp commensals and their hosts on a typical East African fringing reef and lagoon. 1, Outer reef slope;

terates. So far, only two species of shrimps are definitely known to be associated with hydroids, the pontoniinid *P. galene* Holthuis and the hippolytid *H. commensalis* Kemp. Similarly, few associates of jellyfish are known. *Periclimenes holthuisi* has been observed recently on jellyfish on the sea floor (Bruce, 1972c) and the hippolytid *Latreutes anoplonyx* Kemp has been reported several times to be associated with jellyfish (Hayashi and Miyake, 1968). In contrast, several genera and numerous species are found associated with the Anthozoa, particularly scleractinians and alcyonarians. Of the six orders of the Alcyonaria, all except the Stolonifera and Coenothecalia have provided examples of associated shrimps. In the Zoantharia, no shrimps have yet been described in association with Zoanthidia or the Ceriantharia. The most remarkable example is found in the case of *P. siebenrocki* which causes the formation of cystlike cavities in corals of the genus *Acropora*. The pair of shrimps

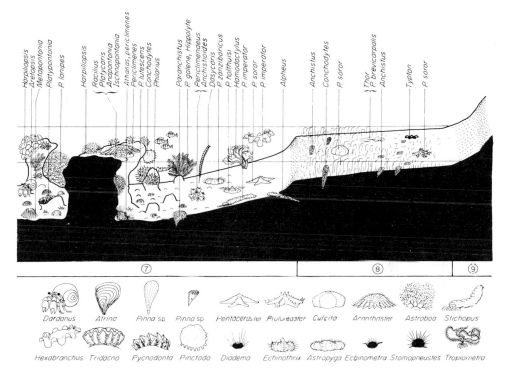

Fig. 18 (*continued*). 2, groove and spur zone; 3, outer reef slope; 4, algal crest; 5, inner reef flat; 6, lagoon slope; 7, lagoon floor; 8, sea grass flats; 9, sand beach.

is completely enclosed in a small chamber with only a few minute apertures (Bruce, 1969a).

C. ANNELIDA

This phylum has provided few definite examples of association with shrimps and the single reported example of the association between alpheid shrimps of the genera *Salmoneus* and *Eurynome* requires further investigation (Edmondson, 1946). The repeated association of two animals in the same habitat need not necessarily indicate any commensal relationship.

D. MOLLUSCA

Associations between shrimps and mollusks are almost confined to the Pontoniinae and the Lamellibranchiata. Only a few out of the large number of lamellibranch families have so far been found to harbor shrimps and the families that are involved in general are those which occupy relatively exposed positions. The only report of a shrimp being found in a burrowing bivalve is the record by Rumphius (1705) of a small shrimp in *Tapes litterata* L. The identity of this shrimp, presumably a pontoniinid, is still unknown. The majority of the hosts are firmly fixed to the substrate but some shrimps are found in mobile hosts. Thus *Conchodytes nipponensis* (De Haan) and *Anchistus pectinis* Kemp are found in members of the Pectiinidae, which swim freely when disturbed. There appear to be no special adaptations that prevent shrimps being carried out of their host by the water currents produced during swimming.

The most noteworthy association between shrimps and gastropods is found in *P. imperator* and the nudibranch *H. marginatus,* which is freely mobile and frequently free-swimming (Bruce, 1967a). The host is generally a bright red color, with yellow-white markings and the shrimp is beautifully patterned in similar colors. *Periclimenes imperator* has also been found in association with other genera of nudibranchs (P. Castro, personal communication). The only other gastropods reported to have associated shrimps are *Haliotis,* in which a species of the alpheid genus *Betaeus* inhabits the mantle cavity and *Strombus galeatus* Swainson from the mantle cavity of which the only known specimen of the American shrimp *Pontonia chimaera* Holthuis was obtained (Holthuis, 1951).

E. CRUSTACEA

Only a single example is so far known of a shrimp being a commensal of another crustacean. The large pagurids of the genus *Dardanus* may be found sharing their gastropod shell with the alpheid shrimp *Aretopsis amabilis* De Man (Lewinsohn, 1969; Bruce, 1969c). The role of the shrimps in their association has not been investigated but it seems possible that they may be fecal feeders, as has been suggested for the mysid *Heteromysis harpax* Hilgendorf, which is found in the same habitat (Tattersall, 1967).

F. ECHINODERMATA

The shallow water tropical echinoderms are frequently found to have associated shrimps. The coral reef-inhabiting species of the Asteroidea and Echinoidea have so far provided the majority of records but crinoids are also frequently found with associated shrimps. The ophiuroids, generally so common under dead coral blocks, have not been found to have any commensal shrimps except in the case of the large basket-stars of the family Gorgonocephalidae. In the Indo-West Pacific these large ophiuroids frequently contain large numbers of the shrimp *Periclimenes lanipes* Kemp and, in American waters, *Periclimenes perryae* Chace is similarly associated. Genera have evolved that are found only in association with echinoids and crinoids, but not with the asteroids, holothuroids, or ophiuroids, which are mainly associated with species of the genus *Periclimenes*. Some species have been recorded from the cloaca of holothurians (Chopra, 1931).

G. Ascidiacea

Relatively few species of shrimp are found in association with tunicates and generally only with the larger species of solitary ascidians, where various species of the genus *Pontonia* are the best known and are found living in the pharyngeal cavity of the host. The masses formed by colonial tunicates may also sometimes provide shelter for shrimps of the genus *Periclimenaeus*, which can be found in small cavities in the center of the common tunic rather than in the common cloaca.

H. Pisces

Two distinct types of relationship are found between shrimps and fishes. The cleaner association differs from the other associations mentioned above in that it is transient, different fishes of a wide variety presenting themselves for treatment by the cleaner shrimp and then departing. It is probable that the shrimps are not fully dependent upon the fish for their food supply and are capable of feeding independently by predatation or scavenging. The cleaner relationship does appear to be of definite value to the fish and to be therefore an example of true commensalism or mutualism (Limbaugh, 1961; Limbaugh et al., 1961; Feder, 1966). In the second type of association, between gobies and shrimps of the genus *Alpheus*, the association appears permanent and the shrimp, being the excavator of the burrow, is the host rather than the commensal (Kalk, 1958; Luther, 1958; Miya and Miyake, 1969).

XIV. The Extent of Commensalism in the Tropical Marine Decapoda Natantia

Only a single report of commensalism has been recorded in the Penaeidea. In 1898, Borradaile (1898b) described from Fiji the prawn *Metapenaeus commensalis*, which was said to have been living in the stomodaeum of a giant anemone. The only specimen was subsequently

TABLE I
General Distribution of Tropical Shallow-Water Shrimp Species

Family	Genus		Total no. of species	Atlantic	Indo-West Pacific	East Pacific	Commensal habits	Free-living habits	Remarks	References
Pasiphaeidae	Leptochela	Stimpson, 1860	7–8	3	4–5	1		+		
Disciadidae	Discias	Rathbun, 1902	4	2	1	1	+		D. exul associated with sponges	Bruce, 1970b
Rhynchocinetidae	Rhynchocinetes	H. Milne Edwards, 1837	8	1	5	2		+	Possibly some species are coral associates	
Palaemonidae										
1. Palaemoninae 4 genera	Brachycarpus	Bate, 1888	2	2	1	1		+	B. biunguiculatus Lucas circumtropical	
	Leander	Desmarest, 1849	3	1	3	1		+	L. tenuicornis Say circumtropical	
	Leandrites	Holthuis, 1952	3		3			+		
	Palaemon	Weber, 1795	26	4	9	3		+	Probably all free-living	
2. Pontoniinae 41 genera	Palaemonella	Dana, 1852	8	1	5	2	+	+	P. potsi (Borr.) associated with crinoids	Bruce, 1970c
	Vir	Holthuis, 1952	1		1		+		Associated with pociloporid corals	
	Eupontonia	Bruce, 1971	1		1			+	Apparently free-living	
	Periclimenes	Costa, 1884	114	21	87	3	+	+	Most species are known commensals (see Fig. 21)	
	Philarius	Holthuis, 1952	4		4		+	?	Acroporid coral associates	
	Hamopontonia	Bruce, 1970	1		1		+		One sp. possibly free-living	Bruce, 1967b
	Ischnopontonia	Bruce, 1966	1		1		+		Associated with faviid corals	
	Anapontonia	Bruce, 1966	1		1		+		Associated with G. fascicularis L.	
	Metapontonia	Bruce, 1967	1		1		+		Associated with G. fascicularis L.	
	Paratypton	Balss, 1914	1		1		+		Associated with fungiid corals; Cyst-forming in Acropora spp.	Bruce, 1969a

Genus	Authority					+	Remarks	Reference
Platycaris	Holthuis, 1952	1		1		+	Associated with *G. fascicularis* L.	Bruce, 1965
Fennera	Holthuis, 1951	1		1	1	+	Associated with pocilloporid corals	Bruce, 1966a
Caricheles	Holthuis, 1952	1		1		+	Associated with *Acropora* spp.	
Coralliocaris	Stimpson, 1860	7		7		+	*Acropora* associates	Patton, 1966
Jocaste	Holthuis, 1952	2		2		+	*Acropora* associates	Bruce, 1969b; Patton, 1966
Harpiliopsis	Borradaile, 1917	3		3	1	+	Pocilloporid coral hosts	Holthuis, 1951
Dasycaris	Kemp, 1922	4		4		+	Various coelenterate associations	
Mesopontonia	Bruce, 1967	1		1		+	Associated with gorgonians	
Hamodactylus	Holthuis, 1952	3		3		+	Gorgonian and alcyonarian hosts	Bruce, 1970d
Waldola	Holthuis, 1951	1		1	1	+	Probably coelenterate commensal but host unknown	
Pontonides	Borradaile, 1917	2		2		+	Antipatharian and gorgonian hosts	Patton, 1963
Neopontonides	Holthuis, 1951	2			1	+	Gorgonian hosts	
Veleronia	Holthuis, 1951	2			2	+	Gorgonian hosts	
Lipkebe	Chace, 1969	1				+	Probably a coelenterate commensal but host unknown	
Thaumastocaris	Kemp, 1922	1		1		+	Found in shallow-water sponges	
Periclimenaeus	Borradaile, 1915	45	33	33	3	+	Mainly associated with sponges, a few with tunicates	
Onycocaris	Nobili, 1904	9		9		+	All found in association with sponges	
Typton	Costa, 1844	11	6	3	3	+	Probably all associated with sponges	Fujino and Miyake, 1969
Araiopontonia	Fujino and Miyake, 1970	1		1		+	Host unknown, probably a crinoid	
Parapontonia	Bruce, 1968	1		1		+	Associated with crinoids	Bruce, 1968

TABLE I (Continued)

Family	Genus	Total no. of species	Atlantic	Indo-West Pacific	East Pacific	Commensal habits	Free-living habits	Remarks	References
Palaemonidae (Pontoniinae)	Pontoniopsis Borradaile, 1915	1		1		+		Associated with crinoids	
	Stegopontonia Nobili, 1906	1		1		+		Associated with diadematid echinoids	
	Tuleariocaris Jacquotte, 1965; Bruce, 1967a	3	1	2		+		Associated with diadematid echinoids	
	Dasella Lebour, 1945	1		1		+		Tunicate hosts	
	Pontonia Latreille, 1829	20	5	8	7	+		Lamellibranch or tunicate hosts	
	Paranchistus Holthuis, 1952	4		4		+		Lamellibranch hosts	Jacquotte, 1964; Hipeau-Jacquotte, 1967
	Anchistus Borradaile, 1898	5		5		+		Lamellibranch hosts	Jacquotte, 1964; Hipeau-Jacquotte, 1967
	Platypontonia Bruce, 1968	2		2		+		Associated with ostreid bivalves	Hipeau-Jacquotte, 1971
	Conchodytes Peters, 1872	5		5		+		Lamellibranch hosts, occasionally holothurians	
	Chernocaris Johnson, 1967	1		1		+		Associated with Placuna sp.	
	Anchistioides Paulson, 1875	4	1	3		+		Probably all sponge associates	Bruce, 1971
Gnathophyllidae 6 genera	Gnathophyllum Latreille, 1879	6	4	1	1	+		One species associated with echinoids?	Manning, 1963
	Gnathophylloides Schmitt, 1933	2	1	2		+		Associated with echinoids	
	Pycnocaris Bruce, 1972	1		1		+		Probably associate of echinoids but host unknown	
	Levicaris Bruce, 1973	1		1		+		Associated with Heterocentrotus mammillatus	Edmondson, 1931

Genus	Author, year					+	+	Remarks	Reference
Phyllognathia	Borradaile, 1915	1		1		+		Habits unknown, probably starfish predator	
Hymenocera	Latreille, 1819	1	1	1		+		Predatory on starfish	Coutière, 1899
Pterocaris	Heller, 1862	1	1	1		+	+	Reported as associated with echinoids	
Alpheopsis	Coutière, 1897	14	11	1		+		No recorded associations	
Neoalpheopsis	Banner, 1953	2	2			+	+		
Athanas	Leach, 1814	33	26	4		+	+	A few species associated with echinoids	Banner and Banner, 1960
Athanopsis	Coutière, 1897	1	1			+		No recorded associations	
Aretopsis	De Man, 1910	1	1	1		+	+	Lives in gastropod shells occupied by dardanid hermit crabs.	Lewinsohn, 1969; Bruce, 1969c
Betaeus	Dana, 1852	10	2	3	4	+	+	*B. harfordi* reported associated with *Haliotis* and echinoids	
Parabetaeus	Coutière, 1897	1	1			+		No recorded associations	
Automate	De Man, 1883	8	4	3	1	+	+	Probably are free-living	
Salmoneus	Holthuis, 1955	15	11	4		+	+?	Some species possibly associated with annelids	Edmondson, 1946
Metabetaeus	Borradaile, 1899	2	2			+	+		
Amphibetaeus	Coutière, 1897	2	1	1		+			
Racilius	Paulson, 1875	1	1			+	+	Associated with corals of the genus *Galaxea*	Barnard, 1958
Prionalpheus	Banner and Banner, 1930	4	4			+		No recorded associations	
Alpheus	Fabricius, 1798	(200 + species)				+	+	Some commensal but mainly free-living	Patton, 1966
Batella	Holthuis, 1956	2	2			+	+		
Pomagnathus	Chace, 1937	1							
Synalpheus	Bate, 1888	(100 + species)	1			+	+	Probably all commensals	See table in Patton, 1966

Alphaeidae
18 genera
(see Fig. 20)

TABLE I (*Continued*)

Family	Genus		Total no. of species	Atlantic	Indo-West Pacific	East Pacific	Commensal habits	Free-living habits	Remarks	References
Ogyrididae	Ogyrides	Stebbing, 1914	10	6	4			+	Free-living mud burrowers	
Hippolytidae 15 genera	Saron	Thallwitz, 1891	2	2	2			+	Both species common on Indo-West Pacific reefs	Holthuis, 1947
	Ligur	Sarato, 1855	2	1	1			+		
	Alope	White, 1847	2		1			+		
	Trachycaris	Calman, 1906	1	1				+		
	Phycocaris	Kemp, 1916	1		1			+		
	Hippolyte	Leach, 1874	25	14	5	3	+	+	One known tropical commensal species only	Kemp, 1925
	Thor	Kingsley, 1878	5	1	4		+	+	1–2 coelenterate associated species	
	Gelastocaris	Kemp, 1914	1		1		+	+	Associated with sponges (*Siphonochalina* sp.)	Monod, 1969
	Latreutes	Stimpson, 1860	18		14	1	+?	+	One species possibly associated with medusae	Holthuis, 1947; Hayashi and Miyake, 1968
	Paralatreutes	Kemp, 1925	1		1			+	No recorded associations	
	Argasia	Bate, 1863	10	2	7			+		
	Mimocaris	Nobili, 1903	1		1			+		
	Merguia	Kemp, 1914	2	1	1			+		
	Lysmata	Risso, 1816	12	6	5	1	+	+	One species associated with sponges	
	Hippolysmata	Stimpson, 1860	17	6	8	2	+	+	Two "cleaner" species known from Atlantic and California	Limbaugh et al., 1961
Processidae 3 genera	Processa	Leach, 1815	35	21	14			+	Nocturnal, free-living inhabitants of marine grass beds	

Family	Genus	Author							Remarks
Pandalidae 2 genera	*Nikoides*	Paulson, 1875	5	1	4		+		
	Ambidexter	Manning and Chace, 1971	1	1			+		
	Chlorotocella	Balss, 1914	1		1		+		Semipelagic, occurs with medusae
Thalassocaridae	*Chlorocurtis*	Kemp, 1925	1		1		+		
	Thalassocaris	Stimpson, 1860	3		3		+		Habitat uncertain, one occurs in shallow- water corals
Crangonidae	*Pontophilus*	Leach, 1817	(about 45 species)				+		All free-living sand burrowers
Stenopodidae 3 genera	*Stenopus*	Latreille, 1819	4	2	3	1	+		Two "cleaner" species Limbaugh *et al.*, 1961
	Odontozona	Holthuis, 1946	4	1	3		+	+	
	Microprosthema	Stimpson, 1860	4		4	+	+		One species associated with shallow-water sponges

reported lost by De Man (1911) and there has been no confirmation
of the association since. The specimen, now referable to the genus
Metapenaeopsis, has recently been rediscovered in the Zoology Museum,
Cambridge (Dr. C. B. Goodhart, personal communication). It seems
likely that the reported association was accidental. The specimen is
synonymous with *M. borradailei* (De Man).

Among the nonpenaeid Natantia, instances of associations are common,
most noticeably in the shallow water tropical marine genera and, in
particular, the coral reef fauna. Some 210 genera of caridean and stenopo-
didean shrimps are known at present. Of these, at least 98 genera (Table
I) are represented in the shallow water tropical marine biotope. Thus,
46% of known genera occur in this zone, in contrast with the remainder
that are found in temperate, cold, deep, or freshwater habitats. Commensalism is relatively uncommon in nontropical shrimps and does not appear to have been evolved in any of the genera that occur only outside
the shallow water marine tropical zone. Some 61 genera are now known
to contain at least some commensal species, which represent 29% of
the total number of known genera. In contrast 62% of the shallow water
marine tropical genera contain species, often numerous, that are known
to have commensal associations. This clearly indicates the increased importance of such associations in the tropical marine shallow water
environment.

The richness of the Indo-West Pacific fauna is indicated by the occurrence of 91 of the 98 tropical genera (93%), which contrasts markedly
with the Atlantic tropical fauna, (41 genera; 42%) and even more with
the East Pacific fauna, (28 genera; 29%). The incidence of commensalism
in each region remains approximately comparable. In the East Pacific
region 14 genera out of 28 (50%) contain commensal species, whereas
in the Atlantic only 17 genera out of 41 (41%), but in the Indo-West
Pacific region 54 genera out of 91 (59%) are known to contain species
that live in permanent associations with other animals. Owing to the
lack of knowledge concerning the ecological roles of many species of
tropical shrimps, an analysis of the incidence of commensalism at the
species level cannot be presented but it appears that an even higher
incidence will be found to occur in the coral reef biotope, both in terms
of the numbers of species and also the number of individuals.

Commensalism is most highly developed in the families Alpheidae
and Palaemonidae, (subfamily Pontoniinae). The range of hosts and
their relationships in the two groups are compared in Figs. 19 and 20.
In Fig. 21 the range of hosts in the genus *Periclimenes* is illustrated
for more detailed comparison.

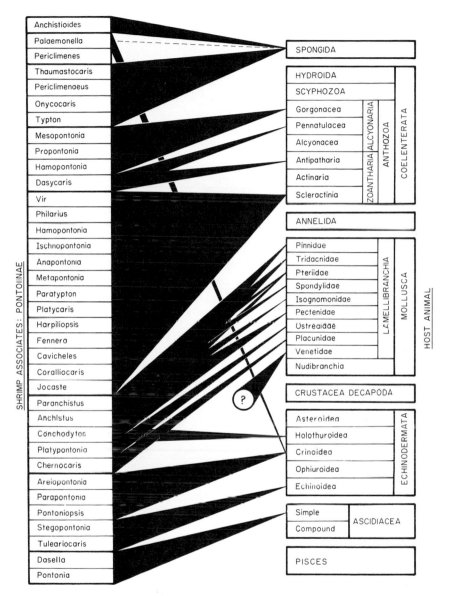

Fig. 19. The relationship of the commensal Indo-West Pacific genera of the subfamily Pontoniinae (excluding *Periclimenes*) to their host types.

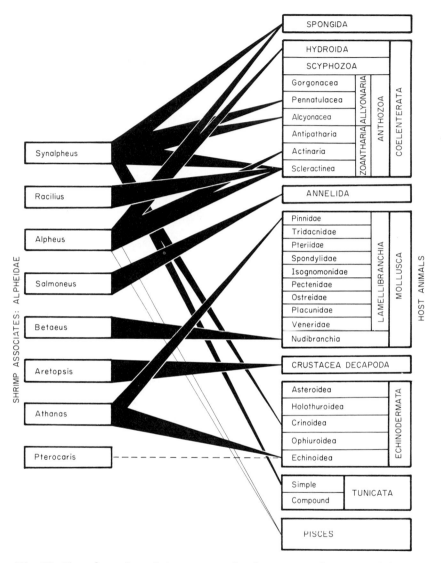

Fig. 20. The relationship of the commensal Indo-West Pacific genera of the family Alpheidae to their host types.

XV. Summary

The wide variety of families, genera, and species of shrimps and prawns that may be found on coral reefs has been outlined. Some details have been provided concerning 98 genera belonging to 13 different fami-

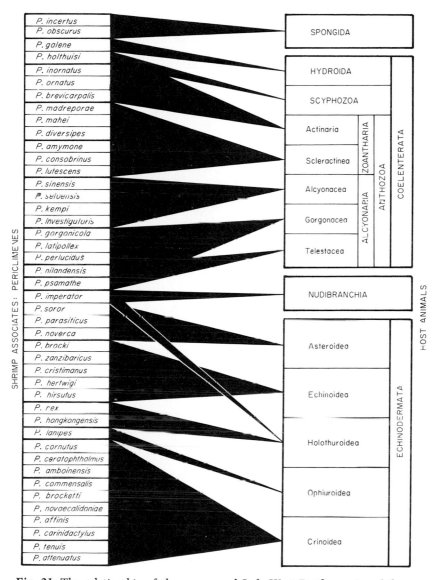

Fig. 21. The relationship of the commensal Indo-West Pacific species of the genus *Periclimenes* to their host types.

lies that may be represented in this biotope. Of these genera, 61 (62%) contain some species that live in a permanent association with another animal. The importance of this adaptation to their way of life is thereby clearly illustrated. The effect of living in these associations, which are in general highly specific in nature, is to increase greatly the number of ecological niches available for occupation without at the same time increasing the amount of competition among the occupants. Similarly, adaptation to these highly specialized niches has probably also stimulated the evolution of an equally specialized variety of predators, all adding to the fascinating complexity of the life of the coral reef habitat.

Although these associations are such a striking feature of the coral reef, they are not limited to that region. Examples are known from temperate waters, but the phenomenon seems comparatively rare there. Its occurrence in the deep sea has again been little studied owing to practical difficulties but photographs do indicate that hippolytids (?) may be associated with anemones as in shallow water and several stenopids are associated with sponges. Further study, particularly studies involving the use of scuba apparatus, will answer many of the questions about the life histories of these animals that cannot be answered by other methods. Also careful collecting methods, with attention to recorded details, especially if combined with laboratory studies, will help to fill in many of the gaps in our present knowledge.

References

Balss, H. (1956). *Bronn's Klassen* **5**, Part 1, No. 11, 1369.
Banner, A. H., and Banner, D. M. (1960). *Pac. Sci.* **14**, 129.
Barnard, K. H. (1958). *Mem. Mus. de Castro* **4**, 3.
Borradaile, L. A. (1898a). *Ann. Mag. Natur. Hist.* [7] **2**, 376.
Borradaile, L. A. (1898b). *Proc. Zool. Soc. London* pp. 1000–1015, pls. 63–65.
Bruce, A. J. (1965). *J. Mar. Biol. Ass. India* **7**, 80.
Bruce, A. J. (1966a). *Bull. Mus. Hist. Natur., Paris* **38**, 266.
Bruce, A. J. (1966b). *Crustaceana* **11**, 1.
Bruce, A. J. (1966c). *Bull. Mar. Sci.* **16**, 584.
Bruce, A. J. (1967a). *Zool. Verhand. Leiden* **87**, 1.
Bruce, A. J. (1967b). *Bull. Mus. Hist. Natur., Paris* **39**, 564.
Bruce, A. J. (1968). *Bull. Mus. Hist. Natur., Paris* **39**, 1148.
Bruce, A. J. (1969a). *Crustaceana* **17**, 171.
Bruce, A. J. (1969b). *Crustaceana* **17**, 298.
Bruce, A. J. (1969c). *J. Mar. Biol. Ass. India* **11**, 175
Bruce, A. J. (1970a). *Crustaceana* **18**, 37.
Bruce, A. J. (1970b). *Crustaceana* **18**, 315.
Bruce, A. J. (1970c). *Crustaceana* **19**, 273.
Bruce, A. J. (1970d). *J. Zool.* **160**, 537.
Bruce, A. J. (1971). *Zool. Verh. Leiden* **114**, 1.
Bruce, A. J. (1972a). *Proc. Symp. Corals and Coral Reefs, 1969, Mar. Biol. Ass. India* p. 399.
Bruce, A. J. (1972b). *Crustaceana* **23**, 65.
Bruce, A. J. (1972c). *Crustaceana* **23**, 300.

Bruce, A. J. (1974). *Crustaceana* **27**, 107.

Caullery, M. (1952). "Parasitism and Symbiosis." Sedgwick & Jackson, London.

Chopra, B. (1931). *Rec. Indian Mus.* **33**, 303.

Coutière, H. (1899). Thèses presentées à la faculté des Sciences de Paris (Ser. A 321, 1).

Dana, J. D. (1852). "Crustacea. United States Exploring Expedition During the Years, 1838, 1839, 1840, 1841, 1842, Under the Command of Charles Wilkes," Vol. 13, p. 1. U.S. Navy.

Davenport, D. (1955). *Quart. Rev. Biol.* **30**, 29.

Dobkin, S. (1965). *Bull. Mar. Sci.* **15**, 450.

Edmondson, C. H. (1931). *Occas. Pap. Bishop Mus.* **9**, 1.

Edmondson, C. H. (1946). *Spec. Publ. Bishop Mus.* **22**, 1.

Feder, H. M. (1966). *In* "Symbiosis" (S. M. Henry, ed.), Vol. 1, p. 327. Academic Press, New York.

Fujino, T., and Miyake, S. (1969). *Ohmu* **2**, 79.

Garth, J. S. (1975). *Mar. Biol. Ass. India* (in press).

Gerlach, S. A. (1960). *Zool. Anz., Suppl.* **23**, 356.

Gotto, R. V. (1969). "Marine Animals: Partnerships and Other Associations." English Univ. Press, London.

Gurney, R. (1949). *Proc. Zool. Soc. London* **119**, 293.

Hayashi, K.-I., and Miyake, S. (1968). *Publ. Seto Mar. Biol. Lab.* **16**, 11.

Henry, S. M., ed. (1966). "Symbiosis," Vol. 1. Academic Press, New York.

Hipeau-Jacquotte, R. (1967). *Rec. Trav. St. Mar. Endoume, Pap. Hors Ser., Suppl.* **6**, 153.

Hipeau-Jacquotte, R. (1971). *Crustaceana* **20**, 125.

Holthuis, L. B. (1947). *Siboga Exped. Mon.* **39a**, 1.

Holthuis, L. B. (1951). *Occas. Pap. Allan Hancock Found.* **11**, 1.

Holthuis, L. B. (1952). *Siboga Exped. Mon.* **39a[10]**, 1.

Holthuis, L. B., and Eibl-Eibesfeldt, I. (1964). *Senckenbergiana Biol.* **45**, 185.

Jacquotte, R. (1964). *Rec. Trav. St. Mar. Endoume* **29**, 59.

Jacquotte, R. (1965). *Rec. Trav. St. Mar. Endoume* **37**, 247.

Johnson, D. S. (1967). *J. Zool.* **153**, 499.

Johnson, D. S., and Liang, M. (1966). *J. Zool.* **150**, 433.

Kalk, M. (1958). *In* "A Natural History of Inhaca Island, Mocambique" (W. Macnae and M. Kalk, eds.) i–iv, 1–163, pls. 1–11. Witwatersrand Univ. Press, Johannesburg.

Kemp, S. (1914). *Rec. Indian Mus.* **10**, 81.

Kemp, S. (1916). *Rec. Indian Mus.* **12**, 385.

Kemp, S. (1922). *Rec. Indian Mus.* **24**, 113.

Kemp, S. (1925). *Rec. Indian Mus.* **27**, 249.

Kubo, I. (1940). *J. Imp. Fish. Inst.* **34**, 31.

Lanchester, W. F. (1901). *Proc. Zool. Soc. London 1901*, 534.

Ledoyer, M. (1968). *Rec. Trav. St. Mar. Endoume, Fasc. Hors. Ser., Suppl.* **8**, 63.

Lewinsohn, C. (1969). *Zool. Verh. Leiden* **104**, 1.

Limbaugh, C. (1961). *Sci. Amer.* **205**, 42.

Limbaugh, C., Pederson, H., and Chace, F. A. (1961). *Bull. Mar. Sci. Gulf Carib.* **11**, 237.

Luther, W. (1958). *Natur Volk* **88**, 141.

Man, J. G. de. (1911). *Siboga Exped. Mon.* **39a[1]**, 1.

Manning, R. B. (1963). *Crustaceana* **5**, 47.

Miya, Y., and Miyake, S. (1969). *Publ. Seto Mar. Biol. Lab.* **16**, 307.

Monod, T. (1969). *Cah. Pac.* **13**, 191.

Patton, W. K. (1963). *Amer. Zool.* **34**, 522.

Patton, W. K. (1966). *Crustaceana* **16**, 27.

Patton, W. K. (1967). *Mar. Biol. Ass. India, Proc. Symp. Crustacea 1965* Ernakulam **3**, 1128.

Peters, W. (1852). *Ber. Verh. Akad. Berlin* p. 588.

Rumphius, G. E. (1705). D'Amboinsche Rariteitkamer.

Stimpson, W. (1860). *Proc. Acad. Natur. Sci. Philadelphia* **22**, 22–48.

Tattersall, O. S. (1967). *Trans. Zool. Soc. London* **31**, 157.

Wheeler, J. F. G. (1944). *Rev. Agr. Ile Maurice* **23**, 151.

3

ECHINODERMS OF CORAL REEFS

Ailsa M. Clark

I. Introduction

Nearly 6000 species of echinoderms are currently recognized, of which just over 1000 have been recorded from the shallow waters of the Indo-West Pacific to a depth of about 20 meters within the area where reef-forming corals occur. The comparable fauna in the West Indies amounts to approximately 150 species. Fewer than ten species are common to both areas. Several of these shallow water echinoderms, particularly sea urchins, are among the most conspicuous noncolonial animals to be seen on coral reefs but surprisingly few detailed studies of the biology of individual species have yet been made, partly, perhaps, because of their lack of obvious economic importance. Little is known of the life histories and habits of even the holothurians used as *bêche-de-mer*, except in Japan where fisheries have a high priority and the main species utilized, *Stichopus japonicus*, has been studied in depth (Choe, 1963). The situation is a little better in the West Indies with regard to the common sea urchins *Eucidaris tribuloides*, *Diadema antillarum*, *Tri-*

pneustes ventricosus, Echinometra lucunter, and *Echinometra viridis,* as
well as the heart urchin *Meoma ventricosa,* examined by McPherson
(1965, 1968, 1969), Randall *et al.* (1964), Lewis (1958), and Chesher
(1969). Although on some Pacific reefs the large asteroids *Culcita, Protoreaster, Linckia laevigata,* and sometimes *Acanthaster* are conspicuous
by their size and number, until recently only isolated aspects of the
biology of tropical asteroids had been studied. Consequently, the great
Acanthaster scare of the 1960's found biologists unprepared except for
an unknowingly prophetic note on its feeding habits by the late Tom
Goreau (1964). As for the ophiuroids and crinoids, these are not obvious
in daytime on most reefs, though numerous brittle stars, especially of
the family Ophiocomidae, are almost invariably present. However, these
live mainly concealed in crevices or under coral blocks, showing themselves only when the current is suitable for feeding. A night swim over
reefs populated by the crinoids *Lamprometra* or *Heterometra* shows
a surprisingly large number of specimens belonging to these genera
fanned out on any projecting foothold of the reef and filtering food
from the current, as described by Magnus (1963, 1967) and Rutman
and Fishelson (1969). Also the dramatic basket stars (up to a meter
in diameter when extended), such as *Astroboa nuda* (see Tsurnamal and
Marder, 1966), may be found aligned on vertical faces.

A few general ecological surveys of particular reefs have been made,
notably two dealing with peripheral parts of the Indo-West Pacific area
by Edmondson (1933) on Hawaii and by Macnae and Kalk (1969)
on Inhaca Island, southern Mozambique, respectively. Ecological studies
reveal a remarkably narrow size range in most echinoderm species in
any one area. In general, the young are elusive, often epizoic and consequently little known or not reliably correlated with adults of their own
species. Yamaguchi (1973) has outlined briefly the various kinds of
development shown by Micronesian reef asteroids and is continuing
to study the postmetamorphosal development of several others as well
as *Acanthaster.* Hopefully his work may help to unravel the ontogeny
of species such as the autotomous *Linckia multifora* and the conspicuous
blue starfish *L. laevigata.* Attempts to rear these and other young starfishes in aquaria have also revealed our relative ignorance of their food
requirements and their interactions with other members of the reef fauna.

The present survey reviews our current knowledge of the biology and
recognition of the more common tropical reef echinoderms, though the
keys of Clark and Rowe (1971) or H. L. Clark (1933) for the Indo-West
Pacific and West Indies, respectively, should be consulted for proper
identification. Notes are also given on the biogeography of reef echino-

derms. The sequence here used for the five main echinoderm groups follows their approximate degree of conspicuousness on the reefs.

II. Coral Reef Echinoderms

A. Echinoidea

Probably the most obtrusive echinoderm of many tropical reefs is the long-spined echinoid *Diadema,* represented in the Indo-West Pacific mainly by the closely related *D. setosum* Leske (distinguished most easily by the red ring round its anus) and *D. savignyi* Michelin or in the West Indies by *D. antillarum* (Philippi). Although primarily nocturnal animals, the spines of numerous individuals of *Diadema* can be seen by day projecting from their shelters in crevices or under rocks or loose coral in the shallower parts of almost any reef. The highly developed light sensitivity exhibited by species of *Diadema* has been the subject of many papers, notably one written by Millott (1954). At night the diademas emerge from hiding, stilt-walking on the lower spines at an unusually fast rate for a sea urchin, and move to exposed positions where they can spread their formidable armament, the length of which varies to some extent according to the turbulence of the water in the vicinity. The maximum spine length recorded (for *D. antillarum* by Mortensen, 1940) is approximately 400 mm but Mr. Lewis, Director of the Institute of Jamaica, reports (personal communication) some specimens in a quiet lagoon protected by a hurricane beach at Pedro Cays with spines up to two feet (600 mm) in length, though the test diameter was not unusually large. Following breakdown of the beach by wave action, the diademas found in the lagoon did not have unusually long spines. A Jamaican specimen, supposedly of *Diadema,* with a horizontal test diameter of 156 mm (exceeding Mortensen's record size for *D. antillarum* by nearly 50 mm) is in the Science Museum in Kingston, Jamaica. However, following A. H. Clark's discovery off Florida of the larger diadematid *Astropyga magnifica,* it seems more likely that this is the true identity of the Jamaican specimen. Apart from the ability of *Diadema* to point its spines in the direction of a threatening shadow, their ease of penetration, their fragility (so that they break off in the wound), and their painful effect, owing to the presence of toxic material in the skin covering them, warn off many potential predators and make the space between the spines a useful shelter for several species of commensal Crustacea and small fishes. Even so, Snyder and Snyder (1970) traced a total of more than 20 species of fishes besides two helmet shells and a spiny lobster that are known to attack *Diadema*, which shows well-developed escape reactions in response to the presence of damaged sea urchins upcurrent, especially other diademas.

Echinothrix, a close relative of *Diadema*, has two widespread Indo-West Pacific species—the superficially diadema-like *E. diadema* (Linnaeus) with generally dark spines in the adult and *E. calamaris* (Pallas) in which the adults more often retain the dark and light banding shown by juveniles of all these diadematids. *Echinothrix calamaris* also differs in having verticillate primary spines that feel very rough when stroked toward the body. The long spines of *Echinothrix* rarely achieve the same relative length as those of *Diadema* and differ also in that the ambulacral ones are abruptly thinner and more needlelike than the interambulacral primary spines. A third genus of the Diadematidae, the somewhat flattened *Astropyga*, is represented in the Indo-West Pacific by *A. radiata* (Leske). This species is known from depths of two meters and beyond, whereas *A. pulvinata* (Lamarck) from the East Pacific is rarely found in depths of less than five meters and the minimum for the apparently rare West Indian *A. magnifica* A. H. Clark is 25 meters (discounting a "littoral" Brazilian *Astropyga*). Kier and Grant (1965) have observed something of the habits of *A. magnifica*. With the lesser light intensity at the depth in which it lives, it is evidently more active in the daytime than *Diadema*, though otherwise its habits and reactions are similar. Large specimens of *A. radiata* are red or brown in color and possess the blue shining iridophores commonly displayed in this family; they also have the habit of inflating the anal cone, as does *Echinothrix* (see Fechter, 1973). *Astropyga* is unusual in having the test quite flexible in larger specimens.

Another echinoid that should not be grasped with the naked hand is *Asthenosoma varium* (Grube), which has shorter spines but an even more flexible test than *Astropyga*. It belongs to the Echinothuriidae, otherwise known only from fairly deep water. Quantitively it is more venomous than the diadematids since the tips of some of the spines bear poison sacs. The diameter reaches 170 mm. However, the species is much less common, its known range being restricted to the Red Sea and from the Maldive Islands eastwards to southern Japan, the Philippines, and East Indies. Another shallow water species, *Asthenosoma intermedium* H. L. Clark, has been taken once on the Great Barrier Reef (a third species, *A. periculosum* Endean, has been taken from nearly 90 meters off southern Queensland).

Venomous in another way—because of its relatively large globiferous pedicellariae that range up to 3 mm in diameter between the gaping fangs—is the toxopneustid *Toxopneustes pileolus* (Lamarck). This species is known from the western part of the Indian Ocean (but not from the Red Sea) to Japan, Fiji, and even to New South Wales and southern Queensland, though, surprisingly, unrecorded from northern Australia. Fujiwara (1935) has recounted, from painful personal experience, the far-reaching toxic effects of being stung by several pedicellariae fastening on to the side of his finger. Another toxopneustid in which the globiferous pedicellariae compensate for their microscopic size by their vast numbers is the short-spined *Tripneustes*. There are two species, *Tripneustes gratilla* (Linnaeus) from the Indo-West Pacific and *Tripneustes ventricosus* (Lamarck) from the West Indies, where it is fished for its roes, at least in Barbados. In shallow water, individuals of *Tripneustes* shade themselves by holding up with their tube feet either flat bits of substrate or pieces of the sea grass among which they usually live, as described by Herring (1972) in a survey of distribution and feeding habits of the littoral echinoids of Zanzibar.

After the diadematids, the most abundant reef echinoids belong to the Echinometridae, notably *Echinometra* itself, represented throughout the Indo-West Pacific by *Echinometra mathaei* (de Blainville), in the West Indies by *E. lucunter* (Linnaeus) and *E. viridis* Agassiz, while *Echinometra vanbrunti* Agassiz occurs in the East Pacific. *Echinometra lucunter* and *E. mathaei,* at least, usually live in slight hollows in the coral, either natural pockets or excavations made by abrasive action of their strong sharp spines. This burrowing habit is carried even further in *Echinostrephus,* of which *E. molaris* (de Blainville) is a widespread species found throughout the whole Indo-West Pacific except for the Persian Gulf, the Philippines, and the Hawaiian Islands. *Echinostrephus* makes cylindrical pits deep enough for the whole animal with its tuft of long vertically directed upper spines to drop completely out of sight from its usual feeding perch at the top (Campbell *et al.,* 1973). Viewed from above, the test of *Echinostrephus* is circular, not ovate as it is in *Echinometra* and in *Heterocentrotus*. Like *Echinostrephus*, the genus *Heterocentrotus* is restricted to the Indo-West Pacific though both species, *H. mammillatus* (Linnaeus) and *H. trigonarius* (Lamarck), are widespread. The former species is distinguishable by the marked reduction in size of the upper ambulacral (but not interambulacral) primary spines to simulate the diminutive secondary spines. It is the massive primary spines which prompt the name of slate-pencil urchins applied to specimens of *Heterocentrotus*. The spines are very variable in shape, ranging from cylindrical to triangular in cross section and in relative length and color, ranging from red to olive green in both species. To compensate for the top-heaviness caused by the spines, *Heterocentrotus* often lives in hollows and also has a considerable massing of tube feet on the flattened lower side to assist in anchorage. This is carried even further in the almost limpetlike *Colobocentrotus,* especially *C. atratus* (Linnaeus) with its extremely short, stout, polygonal upper spines fitting closely together to form a smooth mosaiclike surface. The flattened ambital spines form a marginal fringe and the tube feet are massed below, so that the animal can hold fast on wave beaten rocky shores. *Colobocentrotus atratus* appears to have a discontinuous distribution, being recorded from East Africa and the islands of the western Indian Ocean (but not the Red Sea) and from Ceylon to the East Indies but not from the Pacific islands (except the Hawaiian Islands).

About 20 species of the family Temnopleuridae are found on various Indo-West Pacific reefs but nearly all of them are rather small and inconspicuous, such as *Temnotrema siamense* (Mortensen), which attains a test diameter of only 12 mm. However, *Temnopleurus toreumaticus* (Leske) may exceed 50 mm in diameter and *Salmacis bicolor* L. Agassiz, with spines banded red and yellow or green, can reach 100 mm. The latter has not been found in northern Australia and both are unknown in the Hawaiian Islands.

The only other family of regular echinoids to be well represented on coral reefs is the Cidaridae, characterized by massive, spaced primary spines that lose their covering skin, allowing settlement of encrusting organisms and that are ringed by small, more or less spatulate and appressed secondaries, as well as by the plated, rather than naked, peristome. *Eucidaris* is the most common genus, the small Indo-Pacific *E. metularia* (Lamarck) reaching a diameter of only about 25 mm though the Atlantic *E. tribuloides* (Lamarck) may exceed 50 mm and *E. thouarsi* (Valenciennes) from the East Pacific is reported as reaching 65 mm in the Galapagos Islands. Somewhat larger Indo-Pacific species of cidarids include the handsome *Phyllacanthus imperialis* (Lamarck), *Prionocidaris baculosa* (Lamarck) with basally spotted primary spines, and *Prionocidaris verticillata* (Lamarck), in which the spines bear successive whorls of large thorns. These are all widespread though only the last named reaches the Hawaiian Islands. *Eucidaris,* at least, has rather a furtive habit by day, living in crevices and under rocks or coral fragments, coming out at night to graze.

Of the irregular echinoids, *Echinoneus cyclostomus* Leske is doubly unusual. First, as a holectypoid it retains the sea urchin-like continuity of the tube feet series all the way from apical system to the central (though lopsided) mouth but at the same time the test is ovate in shape, though somewhat flattened, and the large periproct is ventral and posterior, not apical. The spines are fine and hairlike. Second, it is the only echinoid species found both in the West Indies (extending to Ascension Island) and throughout the Indo-West Pacific (even to Easter Island but surprisingly not on the west coast of America). It lives in coarse sand among rocks.

Other irregular echinoids have the ambital and some ventral tube feet reduced, whereas the upper ones are arranged in conspicuous "petals" radiating from the apical system. The flattened clypeasteroids have the mouth central. With the exception of a few species, such as the common West Indian *Clypeaster rosaceus* (Linnaeus), which lives on the surface of sandy, sea grass areas, most burrow out of sight. The slotted sand dollars, notably the Indo-West Pacific *Echinodiscus auritus* Leske and *Echinodiscus bisperforatus* Leske (with two slots, as the latter's name suggests) and the West Indian *Leodia*, *Mellita*, and *Encope* (with five or six slots) are particularly efficient at burying themselves; only their dead tests are found exposed or washed up on shore. The most nearly ubiquitous Indo-West Pacific clypeasteroid is *Clypeaster reticulatus* (Linnaeus) with an entire oval test, usually thickened around the edge.

Among the more common heart urchins in the Indo-West Pacific are the brissids *Metalia spatagus* (Linnaeus), *Metalia sternalis* (Lamarck), and *Brissus latecarinatus* (Leske), all with a peripetalous fasciole of ciliated spinelets looping around the petaloid area. Brissids are also common in the West Indies, notably the superb flattish *Plagiobrissus grandis* (Gmelin), exceeding 200 mm in test length, and *Meoma ventricosa* (Lamarck), which grows to 150 mm long and which has been studied in detail by Chesher (1969) and by Kier and Grant (1965), who described the distribution and habits of the echinoids found off the Florida Keys.

B. Asteroidea

The most conspicuous asteroids found in the vicinity of coral reefs belong to the Oreasteridae, a predominantly tropical family. Many of the species favor sandy substrates, often with sea-grass, though some are found on rock. The only West Indian species is *Oreaster reticulatus* (Linnaeus) but in the Indo-Pacific no less than eight genera occur. The commonest is the armless *Culcita*, resembling a slightly deflated football, with an endemic species, *C. coriacea* Müller and Troschel, in the Red Sea, *C. schmideliana* (Retzius) in the western Indian Ocean, giving way eastwards to *C. novaeguineae* Müller and Troschel. These species are very variable in color and tuberculation and the same is true of *Pentaceraster*. As many as 11 nominal species of this genus are currently recognized, though more synonymizing will probably prove necessary. The largest pentacerasters reach a diameter of about 60 cm when the arms are prolonged beyond their usual short triangular form, as in *Pentaceraster gracilis* (Lütken) recorded from northern Australia to the Bay of Bengal. *Pentaceraster mammillatus* (Audouin) is common on East African coasts but gives way to *Pentaceraster regulus* (Müller and Troschel) (with which *Pentaceraster australis* (Lütken) is probably synonymous) in the region extending from east of Ceylon into the Pacific.

Less variable in color are the two more common species of *Protoreaster*, *P. nodosus* (Linnaeus) ranging from Ceylon to the Caroline Islands and south to the New Hebrides and northern Australia and *P. lincki* (de Blainville) ranging from East Africa to the Bay of Bengal (a record from the East Indies is probably incorrect). *Protoreaster* is distinguished from *Pentaceraster* by its smooth ventral and inferomarginal plates. In *Pentaceraster* these tend to develop tubercular armament. *Protoreaster nodosus* is predominantly whitish in color on the upper surface with the massive tubercles (including one at the base of each arm) black or brown, whereas *P. lincki* is grayish in ground color on the upper surface with the tubercles (which include some laterally directed ones at the arm tips) bright red. No single oreasterid species is known to extend right through the Indo-West Pacific but this may be due to unnatural fragmentation in the taxonomic treatment they have received. Most of them grow so large that few collectors preserve any quantity of specimens and studies of variation are difficult for museum taxonomists. In contrast with these very tuberculose species, another oreasterid, *Choriaster granulosus* Lütken, is completely covered with smooth, thick, pink or orange skin and lacks any protuberances except for the adambulacral spines bordering the furrow. Once thought to be restricted to the western Pacific, it has recently been found in the Gulf of Aqaba and on the coast of Kenya.

Little has been published on the biology of any of these large starfishes but Thomassin (1975) has recently made a study of those found in Madagascar, especially *Culcita schmideliana*, which is known to feed on corals and sponges.

In contrast with the limited distributions of most oreasterids, some of the coral reef ophidiasterids, such as the three common species of *Linckia*, extend from the southwest Indian Ocean to most of the Pacific islands and one of them, *L. guildingi* Gray, is also found in the West Indies. All three have smooth cylindrical granulose arms and even the furrow spines are more or less recessed. Whereas the drab-colored *L. guildingi* has multiple subambulacral spines projecting slightly to form a herringbone pattern along the underside of its long narrow arms, *L. multifora* (Lamarck) and *L. laevigata* (Linnaeus) both have only single tuberculiform subambulacral spines isolated in the ventral granulation in a line separated from the furrow. In fact, except for shape, these two are very similar in morphological detail. Most specimens of *L. multifora* are less than 100 mm in diameter, with slender pointed arms and cryptic coloration in irregular patterns of dull colors. Their form and arm number are irregular. This is correlated with an autotomous habit, parts of single arms tearing themselves off and regenerating to form at first a comet with six more often than five arms—the new ones growing in an apparent attempt to reach equality with the original arm but apparently rarely quite achieving it. There are usually at least two madreporites in a comet, one forming on each side of the original arm. In contrast, *L. laevigata* is rarely found with an arm radius of less than 50 mm, when it is dully (though perhaps always uniformly) colored; it usually has five regular, fingerlike arms, rather stouter than those of *L. multifora,* a single madreporite, grows to an arm radius commonly of 150 mm sometimes more, and is usually a conspicuous deep blue color. However, it is not unknown in some localities (certainly in Micronesia) for a significant number of blue linckias with equal, fingerlike arms to possess two madreporites and some of them have six or even seven arms! Conversely, M. Yamaguchi (unpublished) has discovered at Guam drab, regular, five-armed linckias with single madreporites, the arm radius exceeding 200 mm and adambulacral armament of the *laevigata-multifora* type, to which it is very difficult to put a name. Cryptic linckias may be found either on sandy areas with sea-grass or in crevices of the reef but *L. laevigata* usually exposes itself on rocks or coral debris as well. In the Red Sea the only reliable records of *Linckia* are of *L. multifora.*

Other widespread but less common ophidiasterids in the Indo-West Pacific include *Dactylosaster cylindricus* (Lamarck), *Leiaster glaber* Peters and *Leiaster leachi* (Gray). In *Leiaster* the arm radius may exceed 200 mm. Both genera superficially resemble *Linckia* in the cylindrical arms but their plates are more regularly arranged and concealed (in wet specimens) by a thick slimy skin, though in *Dactylosaster* granular patches in the centers of the plates are exposed. *Ophidiaster* itself also has cylindrical arms with regular plates but these are fully granule covered with barely perceptible skin. Fourteen shallow, Indo-West Pacific species of *Ophidiaster* are known but only *O. hemprichi* Müller and

Troschel ranges as widely as from East Africa to Fiji. In none of these ophidiasterids are the two series of marginal plates at all prominent, whereas in *Nardoa* with 12 Indo-West Pacific nominal species and even more so in the somewhat flattened *Fromia* with 11 species, the marginals form a distinct border to the body. *Fromia milleporella* (Lamarck) with an arm radius up to only 30 mm is the most widespread, being found almost everywhere but at the more remote Polynesian Islands, whereas nearly all the other species of *Fromia* and of *Nardoa* are restricted to the Pacific.

Superficially ophidiasterid-like with its cylindrical arms but having a skin-covered reticulate skeleton is *Echinaster*, the type genus of a family more common outside the tropics. Apart from two endemic Australian species, there are three others more widespread in range. *Echinaster callosus* von Marenzeller ranges from East Africa to Melanesia but seems uncommon with few records. It differs from the others in its large spaced, pointed spines surrounded by inflated pustular sheaths. *Echinaster luzonicus* (Gray) from the Pacific (except Polynesia) is a fissiparous species dividing across the disc and regenerating, in contrast to *Linckia multifora,* which is simply autotomous; nevertheless the resultant individuals also commonly have more than five arms. In the Indian Ocean, *E. luzonicus* gives way to *Echinaster purpureus* (Gray), which does not appear to be fissiparous but is otherwise barely distinguishable. In the West Indies *Echinaster* is represented by several species, the commonest of which is *Echinaster sentus* (Say), also purple or red in color.

There are four monotypic families in the same order (Spinulosida) as the Echinasteridae that are all widespread in the Indo-West Pacific. These are Mithrodiidae, Metrodiridae, Valvasteridae, and Acanthasteridae. (*Acanthaster* has been discussed by Endean, 1973 in Volume II of this treatise.) *Mithrodia clavigera* (Lamarck) is an ungainly starfish with reticulated cylindrical arms slightly constricted at the base where they are liable to break and bearing some irregular large blunt spines. It has an apparently spotty distribution, being recorded from the islands of the western Indian Ocean (including the Maldives), East Africa, and the Red Sea, and from the East Indies, South China Sea, and Pacific islands but not from the Persian Gulf, from either side of the Indian subcontinent, from northern Australia, or from the Hawaiian Islands. In the last-named islands a second species occurs, *Mithrodia fisheri* Holly, with a more compact reticular skeleton than *M. clavigera* and possessing a uniform tubercular appearance. It is also known from a few other Pacific localities and has been found twice in the Seychelles recently (unpublished records). No representative of *Mithrodia* occurs in the West

Indies but *Mithrodia bradleyi* Verrill is found in the East Pacific. Of the second family, *Metrodira subulata* Gray has a more limited range from Ceylon to the Philippines and northern Australia. *Valvaster striatus* (Lamarck) (Valvasteridae) is one of those species known from Mauritius and from the Hawaiian Islands but from only a few places between. It is distinguished by the presence of relatively huge bivalved pedicellariae on most of the superomarginal plates that outline the body—an unusual feature in spinulosids where the marginals are normally inconspicuous. A second species of *Valvaster, V. spinifera* H. L. Clark, has been described from northern Australia but may prove indistinct from *V. striatus.*

Probably more common than any of the last three genera is *Asteropsis carinifera* (Lamarck) of the predominantly temperate or boreal family Asteropidae (possibly to be merged with the Poraniidae). This has a broad flat underside and arms that are triangular in cross section, with a median keel bearing spaced, conical spines similar to those fringing the margin; otherwise the surface is covered with smooth skin. *Asteropsis carinifera* extends throughout the Indo-West Pacific but has not yet been recorded from either side of India or from the Maldives, though taken in Ceylon.

Also broad and flat on the lower surface with a marked ventrolateral angle and usually very short arms are the members of the family Asterinidae. One of the most extreme is *Patiriella pseudoexigua* Dartnall (formerly included in *P. exigua,* recently restricted to nontropical localities). This is almost pentagonal in shape. Even flatter is *Asterina sarasini* (de Loriol) restricted to Indian waters. The species with the most extended range is *Asterina burtoni* Gray, with moderately short arms (the arm radius rarely exceeding 20 mm). It is usually found with five arms and a single madreporite. However, in certain parts of its range, notably in the Red Sea (and even the eastern Mediterranean—it is one of the few migrants through the Suez Canal), in the Pacific islands, and northern Australia, it is sympatric with fissiparous multirayed asterinas very similar in morphological detail. Those from the western area have been called *Asterina wega* (Müller and Troschel) and the Pacific ones *Asterina anomala* H. L. Clark but I suspect their specific distinction from *A. burtoni.*

The only asteroid to show pairing of males and females in spawning is the handsome, stellate *Archaster typicus* Müller and Troschel (family Archasteridae) with large marginal plates placed on the vertical sides of the arms. Most records of this species are from the Bay of Bengal to the Hawaiian Islands; those from the western Indian Ocean are probably mistakes for *Archaster angulatus* Müller and Troschel which has several short appressed spines at the upper end of each inferomarginal plate rather than the single one of *A. typicus. Archaster angulatus* is also known from the East Indies, the Philippines, and Fiji. In northern Australia there is an endemic species, *Archaster laevis* H. L. Clark. *Archaster* lives on sand, usually rather muddy sand. The same is true of many of the carnivorous Luidiidae and Astropectinidae, which burrow in sand, often emerging only at twilight. *Astropecten polyacanthus* Müller and Troschel with its sharp single superomarginal spines culminating proximally in a prominent spikelike pair in each interradius, is the best known and farthest ranging of these burrowers. Two multiradiate luidias, the seven-armed *Luidia savignyi* (Audouin), common in the western Indian Ocean and Red Sea but also with isolated eastern records, and *Luidia maculata* Müller and Troschel with eight arms, more common in southeast Asia, though known from East Africa, are the most widespread members of their family. Another multiradiate *Luidia, L. senegalensis* (Lamarck) with nine rays, occurs in the West Indies, though two five-armed species, *Luidia clathrata* (Say) and *Luidia alternata* (Say), are more common in Florida.

C. OPHIUROIDEA

Among the ophiuroids, the genus *Ophiocoma* is by far the best represented on coral reefs, with five species extending throughout the Indo-West Pacific. These are *O. brevipes* Peters, *O. dentata* Müller and Troschel, *O. erinaceus* Müller and Troschel, *O. pica* Müller and Troschel and the small *O. pusilla* (Brock) [records of *O. scolopendrina* (Lamarck) from the Hawaiian Islands having been rejected by Devaney (1970)]. In the Caribbean, the black *O. echinata* (Lamarck) is the counterpart of *O. erinaceus;* other common species are *O. wendti* Müller and Troschel (with synonym *O. riisei* Lütken) and *O. pumila* Lütken. The last-named extends to West Africa and has closely related species in the East Pacific (*O. alexandri* Lyman) and western Indian Ocean and Red Sea (*O. valenciae* Müller and Troschel); all three have elongated marginal disc granules and single tentacle scales on nearly all the pores. Other tropical ophiocomids rather similar to the *O. pumila* group of *Ophiocoma* but with six arms have been referred to the fissiparous nominal genus *Ophiocomella*. These are probably common throughout the tropics but are often overlooked because of their small size (rarely exceeding 4 mm disc diameter) and epizoic habit (usually in sponges). Although Atlantic specimens, under the name of *Ophiocomella ophiactoides* (H. L. Clark) are currently treated as specifically distinct from the Indo-Pacific *Ophiocomella sexradia* (Duncan), I think that they may well prove to be conspecific, just as all the Atlantic and Pacific specimens of the similarly fissiparous six-armed *Ophiactis* with two distal oral papillae are now accepted as being referable to *Ophiactis savignyi* Müller and Troschel. The absence of any *Ophiocoma* of the *pumila* group from the western Pacific militates against the possibility that this group may represent the nonfissiparous form of *Ophiocomella* and Devaney (1970) has also found some small morphological differences apart from the arm number.

Ophiocoma erinaceus and *O. scolopendrina* offer an interesting example of two morphologically similar species that differ mainly in habits. At least in the Red Sea and in Torres Strait, northern Australia, the all-black *O. erinaceus* lives below low water mark among live coral branches (especially at Eilat in the folds of the poisonous hydrozoan *Millepora* together with *O. pica,* which is also dark-colored, but with a beautiful pattern of radiating gold lines on the disc). *Ophiocoma scolopendrina,* which is always colored lighter underneath than above, lives mainly under loose pieces of coral on sandy patches, or in crevices of the reef at and above low water mark, partially emerging at some stages of the tide, as Magnus (1967) has described, to collect food with several arms by filtration or by sweeping the substrate or water surface.

A proper study of the comparative functional morphology of ophiocomas is needed to relate the structure of the arms to the method of feeding, as Fontaine (1965) has done with the temperate *Ophiocomina nigra* (one of the few nontropical members of the family). Knowledge of the function of the tentacle scales might explain why there are normally two of these on each pore in specimens of both *O. erinaceus* and *O. scolopendrina* from the western Indian Ocean, whereas at some Pacific localities, such as the Solomon Islands, there is a marked reduction to a single scale except on the basal pores in specimens otherwise indistinguishable from the western ones. This reduction seems to be carried further in *O. erinaceus* and has been distinguished nomenclatorially as *Ophiocoma schoenleini* Müller and Troschel, currently awarded only infraspecific rank.

The related genus *Ophinomastix* with sporadic uppermost arm spines vastly enlarged and disc armament spiniform is far more common on Pacific reefs than those of the Indian Ocean. Of 14 Indo-Pacific species, only three have been found in the western Indian Ocean as well as in the Pacific, though another one, *Ophiomastix annulosa* (Lamarck), extends as far west as the Maldive Islands. In recent collections in the Solomon Islands, no less than five species of *Ophiomastix* were found, namely, *O. annulosa* (Lamarck), *O. asperula* Lütken, *O. caryophyllata* Lütken, *O. luetkeni* Pfeffer, and one of uncertain identity, but only four species of *Ophiocoma* (*O. brevipes, O. dentata, O. erinaceus schoenleini,* and *O. scolopendrina*). In contrast, a collection from Zanzibar yielded only two species of *Ophiomastix* (*O. venosa* Peters and *O. caryophyllata*) but as many as seven different ophiocomas [*O. valenciae, O. pica,* and *O. wendti*: Koehler, 1907 (non-Müller and Troschel) as well as *O. brevipes, O. dentata, O. erinaceus,* and *O. scolopendrina*].

Another predominantly tropical family related to the Ophiocomidae is the Ophiodermatidae, differing mainly in having only one or two oral papillae at the apex of each jaw superficial to the teeth, rather than a cluster of papillae replacing the outer teeth as in ophiocomids. The largest known simple-armed ophiuroid belongs to this family. This ophiuroid is *Ophiarachna incrassata* (Lamarck) with disc diameter up to nearly 60 mm and a striking color pattern of green areas interspersed with brown or black reticulations on white. *Ophiarachna* has some sporadic enlarged clavate arm spines too, but in this case they are some of the lowermost ones, not the uppermost. *Ophiarachna incrassata* has been recorded from East Africa (but not from the Mascarene Islands where two endemic species are recognized) and from Ceylon to the Caroline Islands and Fiji. The other ophiodermatid genera have much shorter and more or less appressed arm spines giving a snakelike appearance to the arms. They include *Ophiarachnella* with nine shallow water species, the most widespread of which are *O. gorgonia* (Müller and Troschel) with large naked radial shields and *O. septemspinosa* (Müller and Troschel) with small rounded shields. Both species have been recorded from the southwest Indian Ocean and from Ceylon or the Maldive area eastwards to the western part of the Pacific, *O. gorgonia* extending to Fiji.

Also possessing rather snakelike arms but with naked, rather than granule covered disks, are the tropical species of the family Ophiuridae, which is better represented in colder and deeper waters. Among the commonest are *Ophiolepis cincta* Müller and Troschel, a dull-colored species of moderate size (disc diameter rarely as much as 15 mm) and the handsome, much larger, *O. superba* H. L. Clark with its bold pentaradiate disc pattern and arm bands of purple or black on light brown. *Ophiolepis* has several regular small supplementary dorsal arm plates on each arm segment; in *O. cincta* these encircle the main dorsal arm plates. Such fragmentation of the arm plating dorsally is carried further in *Ophioplocus imbricatus* (Müller and Troschel), which has a mosaic of irregular platelets all over the upper side of the arms. Both species of *Ophiolepis* named extend throughout the Indo-West Pacific (except the remoter Polynesian Islands) but *Ophioplocus* is so far unknown from the Red Sea, Persian Gulf, or Maldive Islands. Most ophiodermatids and ophiurids live under stones or coral fragments, at least during daylight. In the West Indies, *Ophiarachnella* is replaced as the common ophiodermatid by *Ophioderma* itself. In this genus genital slits are subdivided into two (i.e., four in each interradius). The four more common species are *O. appressum* (Say), *O. brevicaudum* Lütken, *O. brevispinum* (Say), and *O. cinereum* Müller and Troschel. However, *Ophiolepis* is represented by *O. elegans* Lütken and *O. paucispina* (Say), though the latter is particularly small and secretive.

More conspicuous members of the coral reef fauna belong to the very successful family Ophiotrichidae, notably *Ophiothrix* itself, a conglomerate of very variable taxa designated by a multiplicity of names, the specific limits being often uncertain. Many of these live in colder waters but the subgenera *Keystonea* (formerly *Ophiotrichoides*), *Acanthophiothrix*, and *Placophiothrix*, together with the genera *Macrophiothrix* and *Ophiogymna* are essentially reef-dwellers, especially numerous in the Pacific. *Ophiothrix* (*Acanthophiothrix*) *purpurea* von Martens, with delicate form, needlelike spines, and a purple midline on the arms, extends right through the Indo-West Pacific, as does the much coarser *Macrophiothrix demessa* (Lyman), which possesses rugose stumps on the dorsal arm plates. The range of *Macrophiothrix longipeda* (Lamarck), with arms about 20 times the disc diameter and a total span of about 30 cm, stops just short of the Hawaiian Islands. A particularly handsome species is *Ophiothrix* (*Keystonea*) *nereidina* (Lamarck), which has the mostly naked disc scales outlined in contrasting color and each arm segment marked by a transverse line (yellow or orange in life) extending on to the uppermost arm spine each side. The most striking West Indian ophiotrichid is *Ophiothrix* (*Acanthophiothrix*) *suensoni* Lütken with a ground color ranging from lavender to red and pink and an arm stripe of purple or crimson, sometimes black. The more slender ophiotrichids, such as species of *Acanthophiothrix*, have arms capable of much more downward flexure than is usual in brittle stars, a modification that helps them to cling to gorgonians or arborescent corals. The only echinoderms that may be called parasites belong to the genus *Ophiomaza*. *Ophiomaza cacaotica* Lyman lives on the discs of crinoids, stealing their food as it passes along the ambulacral grooves from the arms to the mouth. Several other members of the family have an epizoic habit, simulating some of the simple-armed euryalids that also live on gorgonians, pennatulids, and other ramifying hosts. *Ophiothela tigris* Lyman lives on branching corals but is restricted to the coast of East Africa and the Seychelles area. It is worth noting because of its unusual pigmentation, the disc being patterned with meandering blue and white lines in a pentagon framed in red that also extends along the upper sides of the arms. The other species of *Ophiothela* are smaller with disc diameter rarely exceeding 3 mm and live mostly on gorgonians. *Ophiothela danae* Verrill, a six-armed fissiparous species, ranges from southeast Africa to Palau and Fiji. This genus has no representative in the West Indies, though *Ophiothela mirabilis* Verrill occurs in the East Pacific, near Panama. On the contrary, the best-known of all fissiparous ophiuroids, the ophiactid *Ophiactis savignyi* Müller and Troschel, is tropicopolitan, being found throughout the Indo-West Pacific, the East Pacific, and on both sides of the tropical Atlantic. It is primarily epizoic in sponges but also hides in crevices of any kind. Though small, its greenish coloration with darker markings and large bare radial shields make it easily recognized among six-armed ophiuroids, though some blue species of *Ophiactis* also share this asexual form of reproduction.

The only cosmopolitan ophiuroid, the insignificant looking *Amphipholis squamata* (Delle Chiaje), lives under rocks on sand. It belongs to the Amphiuridae, most of which are burrowers in sand or mud. Their ranges are mostly narrow but *Amphioplus* (*Lymanella*) *laevis* (Lyman) has been recorded from the Red Sea to the Gilbert Islands.

The most spectacular ophiuroids, but perhaps the least often seen because of their primarily nocturnal habits are those euryalids with branching arms, the basket stars, some of which may reach a total span of as much as a meter. *Astroboa nuda* (Lyman), known from East Africa to southern Japan, has been studied in the Red Sea by Tsurnamal and Marder (1966). During daylight these animals compact themselves in places of concealment but emerge at dusk, often on to vertical parts of the reef at depths of as little as half a meter, extending their arms in a feeding net to catch small swimming prey. The common West Indian basket star, *Astrophyton muricatum* (Lamarck), has been studied by Davis (1966).

D. HOLOTHURIOIDEA

Since a general account of various aspects of the biology of tropical reef holothurians has been given by Bakus (1973) in Volume II of this treatise, only a few observations concerned mainly with recognition of the more common species are given here.

The most conspicuous and numerous holothurians of any reef are

the thick-walled, usually sausagelike, aspidochirotids, including the Holothuriidae and the Stichopodidae. All these possess short, frilly-tipped,
peltate tentacles, usually numbering about 20 or 25. Generally the sticho-
podids have well-marked ventrolateral angles and often dorsolateral ones
as well, so that *Stichopus variegatus* Semper and *S. chloronotus* Brandt
are distinctly rectangular in cross section. The latter ranges through
the whole Indo-West Pacific; in color it is dark green or even black
with the tips of the large conical projections colored red; its ventral
tube feet are arranged in three bands, the middle one widest. The
range of *S. variegatus* stops just short of the Hawaiian Islands. The
species has low projections crowned by small papillae; it is usually some
shade of brown, either patterned or plain, and grows much larger than
S. chloronotus. Semper (1868) found one about a meter long in the
Philippines. It is one of the species used as *bêche-de-mer*, which is
also true of *Thelenota ananas* (Jäger), found mainly in the Pacific and
called the "red prickly fish" because of the huge teatlike processes (sometimes two or three grouped together) that give it a shaggy appearance.
The maximum recorded length is 1200 mm [by Saville-Kent (1893)
for a specimen from northern Australia]. Some of the Holothuriidae
also have a ventrolateral demarcation but this is usually more rounded
and the shape is most often flattened cylindrical. *Holothuria (Microthele) nobilis* (Selenka), the wide-ranging "teat or mammy fish" of
commerce, has five or six large conical elevations along each side when
alive and about twelve smaller knobs on each of the two dorsal ambulacra. Several color forms exist, including black, white, piebald, or
dappled with yellow or brown. A distinctive feature is the five calcareous
"teeth" around the anus, a character shared by the genus *Actinopyga*,
of which there are several common Indo-West Pacific species. These
are *A. echinites* (Jäger) (the "red fish"), *A. lecanora* (Jäger) (the "stone
fish"), and *A. miliaris* (Quoy and Gaimard) (the "black fish"). These
are absent only from the Hawaiian and remoter Pacific Islands while
the range of *A. mauritiana* (Quoy and Gaimard) (the "surf red fish")
extends to Hawaii as well. The first three species have the ventral tube
feet in three bands but they are scattered all over the under side in
A. mauritiana, which is usually colored deep reddish-brown above and
cream or yellow below. All these *Actinopyga* species may exceed 300
mm in length when alive (undergoing 50% or more shrinkage when
preserved, as a rule). The West Indian counterpart is *A. agassizi*
(Selenka).

The species of the related genus *Bohadschia* also mostly reach a length
of 300 mm but differ from *Actinopyga* in having only groups of papillae

around the anus, not proper teeth. The most easily recognized is *Bohad-schia argus* Jäger, called the spotted or leopard fish (or even the tiger fish by some aborigines who appear to have their big cats confused), but, in fact, little valued as *bêche-de-mer*; it is marked with conspicuous "eyes" of concentric contrasting rings on a yellow-brown or gray background and ranges from the Seychelles to Tahiti. *Bohadschia marmorata* Jäger ranges from Mauritius to Fiji and is usually brownish in color, often with yellow-ochre or sometimes violet or brown in well-defined but irregular patches.

The most common Indo-West Pacific holothurian of all is the stout, black, rather inert, *Holothuria* (*Halodeima*) *atra* Jäger (the "lolly fish"), up to 600 mm long and widely used as *bêche-de-mer* (partly because of its availability) though not one of the most prized species. It contrasts with the sympatric *Holothuria* (*Mertensiothuria*) *leucospilota* Brandt, which is not used commercially, in its habit of lying exposed on open patches of sand and in shallow water often covering itself more or less completely with a coating of sand stuck on by mucus. On the other hand, *H. leucospilota* wedges itself with its posterior half strongly contracted under a rock and stretches out its front end in very attenuated form into the open, reacting when disturbed by contracting back into shelter or, if the rock is moved, by readily ejecting its sticky Cuvierian tubules. These are undeveloped in *H. atra,* though the latter species may eject its guts if provoked enough. In spite of its name, the long narrow, sausagelike *H.* (*Halodeima*) *edulis* Lesson is little used as human food. It is easily recognized by the beautiful deep pink or red underside (in life) contrasting with the dark brown, grey, or black upperside; the range is from East Africa to Fiji.

Many other aspidochirotids, such as *Holothuria* (*Thymiosycia*) *arenicola* Semper, *H.* (*T.*) *impatiens* (Forskaal), and *H.* (*T.*) *hilla* Lesson, have more secretive habits and hide under rocks. All three range right through the Indo-West Pacific and the first two are also common in the West Indies. These and many other species of *Holothuria* are not particularly distinctive in appearance and often very variable in color, being frequently black, grey, or brown. Their identity needs to be checked by examination of the microscopic calcareous spicules in their body walls.

However, a completely different kind of holothurian, *Synapta maculata* (Chamisso and Eysenhardt) is very easily recognized. It is common on most sandy shores at about low water (often where there is sea grass) almost everywhere in the Indo-West Pacific (except the Hawaiian Islands) where aspidochirotids such as *H. atra* are found. Like these, it feeds on organic matter sticking to the sand which it shovels into the mouth with its relatively large pinnate tentacles. It may reach a length of several meters but is relatively narrow and wormlike in proportions, without dorsoventral modification; the thin body wall is pouchy and mottled dark and light grey or brown and is apparently sticky to the touch, owing to its anchorlike spicules that tend to catch on any solid contact, providing friction as it crawls actively along. In the West Indies the common big synaptid is *Euapta lappa* (Müller), growing to about a meter; it hides under rocks, at least during daylight.

The only other large group of shallow water holothurians is the Dendrochirotida, characterized by relatively long, irregularly branching, bushy tentacles that are capable of entrapping live prey in mucus and that are completely retractable by introversion of the entire front end of the animal. No dendrochirotid is particularly common in the Indo-West Pacific but a fairly widespread species is *Afrocucumis africana* (Semper), ranging from East Africa to Rotuma, north of Fiji; it is found clinging to the undersides of rocks cast up on algal ridges, at least in the Seychelles (Taylor, 1968) but is found in crevices in northern Australia according to H. L. Clark (1946), who gives the color as dull purplish or nearly black. Few dendrochirotids exceed a length of about 100 mm. *Afrocucumis* has the feet scattered over the whole surface but in many other dendrochirotids such as *Cucumaria* and *Pentacta* they are restricted to the ambulacra. These two genera also have only ten tentacles whereas *Afrocucumis* has 20 of varying size. *Pentacta quadrangularis* (Troschel) is rectangular in cross section with long processes along the angles; its color ranges from pearly gray through bright yellow, red, or brown to almost black, the lower side often more colorful than the upper. It has been recorded only between Ceylon, Japan, and northern Australia. Another dendrochirotid, *Stolus buccalis* (Stimpson), ranges further west to East Africa though not found in the Pacific islands either. The latter lives in soft mud around partly buried rocks; its color varies from yellow-brown to purplish-black, with the ten tentacles darker. The tube feet are scattered all over the body surface and, if the body wall is slit open just behind the mouth, the calcareous ring around the gut is seen to be an elongated sleeve rather than the usual narrow band of most holothurians.

E. Crinoidea

A number of the commoner shallow water crinoids of coral reefs have a nocturnal habit, hiding during daylight in crevices or under projecting rocks or corals with their arms rolled up, whereas at dusk they appear in remarkable abundance on some parts of the reef and extend their arms and pinnules to catch food. Fishelson (1968) records a density of as many as 70 specimens of *Lamprometra klunzingeri* (Hartlaub) per square meter on the reef at Eilat (Gulf of Aqaba). Before nocturnal studies of reefs had been made, a false impression of the size and activity of the crinoid population existed, as shown by H. L. Clark's account of the crinoids of Mer Island in Torres Strait (Clark, 1915), in which only three of the 22 nominal species collected were said to be at all active.

The pioneer work on feeding of nocturnal tropical crinoids was done by Magnus (1963, 1967) on *Heterometra savignii* (J. Müller) which is found on sandy areas with sea grass or rocky patches in the Sudanese Red Sea. He showed that the traditional concept (derived from aquarium observations) of feather stars feeding with the arms in a radiating horizontal position is not necessarily true for all species. In feeding specimens of *Heterometra*, the usually 20 arms are held up in a vertical filtration fan across horizontal currents with half of the arms twisted through 180° so that all have the ambulacral furrows on the lee side facing away from the current. Accordingly, the species can be termed rheophilic, or current loving. *Heterometra* is a very fragmented genus with a number of apparently restricted nominal species extending to southern Japan and northern Australia but not found in the smaller Pacific island groups. Rutman and Fishelson (1969) have also studied *H. savignii* at Eilat as well as *Lamprometra klunzingeri*, which appears to replace it there at depths of less than two meters. *Lamprometra klunzingeri* may also have about 20 arms but the number is more often 25–30, or even more. The two species may further be distinguished by the enlarged second pinnules in *Lamprometra* that are often reflexed over the disc and the smaller, blunter spines on the incurled side of the cirri than in *Heterometra*. Both belong to the suborder Mariametrina, though to different families. *Lamprometra palmata* (J. Müller) replaces *L. klunzingeri* in the remaining part of the Indo-West Pacific from India eastwards but may prove specifically indistinct. Closely related to *Lamprometra* is *Stephanometra indica* (Smith), also widely distributed except in the remoter Pacific Islands and so far unrecorded between the Red Sea and the Maldive area; it has the second pinnules stiffened like spikes, probably for protection of the disc.

Rutman and Fishelson (1969) also studied the feeding of *Capillaster multiradiatus* (Linnaeus) at Eilat. This is another nocturnal, shallow water species, ranging from East Africa to the more western Pacific island groups but belongs to the Comasterina, having the mouth offset to the edge of the disc and the oral (proximal) pinnules modified terminally into comblike organs for grasping larger prey than can be trapped by the pinnular tentacles. In spite of its specific name it rarely has more than 40 arms. A much more impressive comasterid with 60–200 arms in the adult and numerous strong cirri is *Comanthus bennetti* (J. Müller), a rheophilic species that can be found perching on coral pinnacles or gorgonians in daytime at a depth of about two meters or more at some localities from the Bay of Bengal to Micronesia and Melanesia. This contrasts with a rheophobic *Comanthus, C. parvicirrus* (J. Müller), known from East Africa to southern Japan and Tonga, that wedges itself partly under flanges of coral by means of the arms, only some of which are fully utilized in feeding (Utinomi and Kogo, 1965). In the variety *timorensis* the cirri are very reduced or even absent.

In the West Indies Meyer (1973) has compared the behavior of the comasterids *Nemaster grandis* A. H. Clark with up to 40 arms, sometimes 300 mm long and many long, strong cirri, living at depths of six meters or more and *N. rubiginosa* (Pourtales), a more slender species with fewer and smaller cirri, found in shallower water. The latter has a feeding habit comparable with that of *Comanthus parvicirrus,* which wedges itself in cavities from which some of its arms radiate, whereas *N. grandis* is rheophilic like *C. bennetti* and perches on pinnacles. It shows an interesting versatility in feeding habit according to the strength of the current, adopting a radiating position of the arms when the current strength is negligible.

All the tropical crinoids so far mentioned are multiradiate but a number do have only ten arms, like the vast majority of species from colder waters. This is true of some small comasterids such as *Comatula purpurea* (J. Müller) with arm length up to only about 70 mm found in the East Indies, the Philippines, and northern Australia. The color of the ventral (upper) surface is reddish but the dorsal side may be white or yellowish with small red dots. Much more conspicuous and widespread ten-armed tropical species belong to *Tropiometra* (family Tropiometridae of the suborder Mariametrina). These include *T. afra* (Hartlaub) with arms up to 200 mm long and often all purple or all yellow in color, ranging from southern Japan to northern Australia and the smaller variable *T. carinata* (Lamarck) with arms up to about 150 mm. The second has an unusual distribution from the West Indies to South Africa and the Indian Ocean. Both species have smooth stout cirri capable of maintaining position in slightly disturbed shallow water. *Tropiometra carinata* is distinguished by keeling on the dorsal sides of the arms (at least basally). Meyer (1973) observed it on a variety of substrates, reef, beachrock, or mixed sand with rocks, whereas H. L. Clark (1917) found it on sandy areas with sea grass and coral debris. The arms may or may not form a vertical fan, according to the condition of the current.

Other ten-armed members of the Mariametrina but generally of smaller size than those just discussed belong to the Colobometridae, characterized by having paired tubercles (or spines) on the incurled face of each distal cirrus segment, affording an improved grip. The most widespread Indo-West Pacific species is *Oligometra serripinna* (P. H. Carpenter), absent only from the remoter Pacific Islands and distinguished by having the second pinnule highly modified. This pinnule is enlarged and prismatic or serrated, rather than spikelike and smooth as in the multiradiate *Stephanometra*. Like many of the other smaller feather stars, *Oligometra* can easily be provoked to swim beautifully by flailing its arms, whereas most larger species, notably the large comasterids, are much more inert.

III. Zoogeography of Coral Reef Echinoderms

A. Indo-West Pacific Species

The total numbers of species of the five echinoderm classes (or subclasses in the case of the Asterozoa) found in tropical Indo-West Pacific waters to a depth of approximately 20 meters are as follows:

Echinoidea	146
Holothurioidea	287
Stelleroidea: Asteroidea	232
Stelleroidea: Ophiuroidea	294
Crinoidea	138

These total 1027, of which 57 extend from one end of the region—the southwest Indian Ocean—to the other—the Hawaiian Islands. These 57 are listed in Table I. Some of these widespread species of echinoderms have not yet been found in certain areas within the Indo-West Pacific, notably the west and south of the Indian subcontinent and the Persian Gulf. This may be attributable to lack of suitable habitats as well as to inadequate collecting.

No crinoids extend through the region, unless *Lamprometra klunzingeri* (Hartlaub) is reduced to a subspecies of *L. palmata* (J. Müller), which I think may well prove to be advisable.

TABLE I
CORAL REEF ECHINODERMS FOUND THROUGHOUT THE
INDO-WEST PACIFIC REGION

Echinoidea
  Eucidaris metularia   *Prionocidaris verticillata*[a]
  Astropyga radiata   *Echinothrix calamaris*
  Echinothrix diadema   *Cyrtechinus verruculatus*
  Pseudoboletia indiana   *Tripneustes gratilla*
  Colobocentrotus atratus   *Echinometra mathaei*[b]
  Heterocentrotus mammillatus   *Echinoneus abnormis*
  Echinoneus cyclostomus   *Clypeaster reticulatus*[b]
  Echinocyamus crispus   *Brissopsis luzonica*[b]
  Brissus latecarinatus   *Metalia sternalis*
Holothurioidea
  Actinopyga mauritiana[b]   *Holothuria (Halodeima) atra*
  H. (Lessonothuria) pardalis[b]   *H. (Lessonothuria) verrucosa*[b]
  H. (Mertensiothuria) leucospilota[b] *H (Mertensiothuria) pervicax*
  H. (Microthele) nobilis   *H. (Platyperona) difficilis*
  H. (Semperothuria) cinerascens   *H. (Thymiosycia) arenicola*
  H. (Thymiosycia) hilla   *H. (Thymiosycia) impatiens*
  Stichopus chloronotus   *Euapta godeffroyi*
  Opheodesoma grisea
Asteroidea
  Astropecten polyacanthus   *Archaster typicus*
  Dactylosaster cylindricus   *Leiaster glaber*
  Leiaster leachi   *Linckia guildingi*
  Linckia multifora[b]   *Asteropsis carinifera*
  Asterina burtoni[b]   *Acanthaster planci*[b]
  Mithrodia fisheri[c]   *Valvaster striatus*
Ophiuroidea
  Amphipholis squamata[b]   *Ophiactis savignyi*[b]
  Macrophiothrix demessa   *Ophiothrix (Acanthophiothrix) purpurea*
  Ophiocoma brevipes   *Ophiocoma dentata*
  Ophiocoma erinaceus   *Ophiocoma pica*
  Ophiocoma pusilla   *Ophiocomella sexradia*
  Ophionereis porrecta   *Ophioplocus imbricatus*[b]
Crinoidea
  None

[a] The Hawaiian record of this species needs confirmation.

[b] Species that have been collected in the "empty quarter" between the Gulf of Oman and the southern tip of India.

[c] Prompted by unpublished records extending the range to the Seychelles Islands.

In addition to these 57 species, a further 101 range from the southwest Indian Ocean (East Africa or the mascarene islands) to some of the Pacific island groups, excepting the Hawaiian and more remote Polynesian islands. Another 266 with somewhat narrower ranges break down into the following totals:

Red Sea to Polynesia and the Hawaiian Islands	48
Maldive area and/or Ceylon to the Pacific islands except the Hawaiian Islands	58
Bay of Bengal to the Pacific islands	46
Western Pacific, except the Hawaiian Islands	104
Western Pacific, including the Hawaiian Islands	10

The whole Indo-West Pacific area can be subdivided into the following fifteen smaller areas:

Madagascar and East Africa	S.W. Indian Ocean Islands
Red Sea	S.E. Arabia (including Gulfs of Aden and Oman)
Persian Gulf	
Pakistan and W. India	Maldive, Laccadive, and Chagos Islands
Ceylon and S.E. tip of India	Bay of Bengal
Malaysia, Indonesia, and New Guinea	Philippine Islands
S. China Sea to S. Japan	North Australia
Pacific Island groups*	Hawaiian Islands

A breakdown of the species apparently endemic to these 15 areas gives the following sequence:

North Australia	147	Malaysia–Indonesia area	91
Pacific islands	46	South China Sea	29
Philippines	28	Red Sea	28
Bay of Bengal	27	S.W. Indian Ocean	22
Madagascar and East Africa	20	Hawaiian Islands	14
Persian Gulf	10	S.E. Arabia	7
Ceylon area	6	Pakistan and West India	1
Maldive area	1		

To some extent, the large number of species endemic to northern Australia must reflect the intensive studies of H. L. Clark and subsequent Australian collectors. Conversely, over 420 other species recorded from one or more areas of the western Pacific have not so far been taken in Australian waters. About 110 species are common to Australia and other parts of the Pacific. Considering the close proximity of Australia to the East Indian area (Malaysia–Indonesia), especially in the vicinity of Torres Strait, this marked distinction is surprising.

* Possibly this area can be further split by separating off Melanesia in the southwest (east to New Caledonia and the New Hebrides) but a number of species extend further east to at least Fiji. Also, Palau (the westernmost Micronesian group) could be linked rather with the Philippines.

Most of the other peripheral areas do have a significant proportion of endemic species, notably the Red Sea, which is so nearly landlocked. Its southern end is restricted further by a relatively shallow sill. Considering their small land mass (though somewhat larger reef area), the islands of the western Indian Ocean (notably the Mascarene Islands—Mauritius with Reunion and Rodrigues—which contribute 21 out of the 22 endemic species) have a remarkably distinctive fauna. Thanks to the use of Mauritius as a staging post in the days of sail by early French expeditions, it is the type locality for many of Lamarck's species and that excellent collector de Robillard provided de Loriol with a number of additional species.

A breakdown of the number of species endemic to a single area by classes (or subclasses for Stelleroidea) shows that a much higher proportion of echinoid species have a more or less extended distribution than have the other groups. Less than 30% of echinoids are restricted to a single area compared with about 35% of crinoids and 44–49% of asteroids, ophiuroids, and holothurians, respectively. It may be significant that both echinoids and crinoids have been reviewed comprehensively in the monographs of Mortensen and A. H. Clark. I think some species in the remaining groups have undergone a degree of unnatural fragmentation in their treatment by a greater variety of taxonomists with independent ideas on speciation and using uncorrelated literature.

At the family level, probably the most obvious example of restricted distribution in the shallow Indo-West Pacific fauna is that provided by the asteroid family Goniasteridae. As many as 47 species are represented, but not one of these has so far been collected in Micronesia, Melanesia, or Polynesia. The two largest genera, *Anthenea* and *Goniodiscaster*, include 30 nominal tropical species, of which 14 are endemic to Australia and only seven are found in even the eastern half of the Indian Ocean. Only one species of the family, *Stellaster equestris* (Retzius), has a wide distribution—from East Africa to the South China Sea and northern Australia.

Many of the apparently localized species of echinoderms are still known only from the type material and are clearly uncommon or so furtive in their habits as to have escaped the attention of many collectors. More intensive collecting will certainly lead to considerable modifications in the known ranges of many species, as illustrated by the fact that no less than 14 species new to the Red Sea have been found there by Israeli biologists since my survey of the fauna was published in 1967.

B. Comparison between Indo-West Pacific, East Pacific, and Tropical Atlantic Species

Although a number of deep sea species range between the Atlantic and the Pacific, only eight from shallow water are known throughout the tropics in both oceans, as follows:

Tropiometra carinata (Lamarck)   *Linckia guildingi* Gray
Amphipholis squamata (D. Chiaje)   *Ophiactis savignyi* Müller & Troschel
Echinoneus cyclostomus Leske   *Holothuria arenicola* Semper
Holothuria imitans Ludwig   *Holothuria impatiens* (Forskaal)

However, if the fissiparous *Ophiactis muelleri* Lütken and *O. modesta* Brock, on the one hand, and *Ophiocomella ophiactoides* (H. L. Clark) and *O. sexradia* (Duncan), on the other, are considered as conspecific, then two further names can be added to the list. The two nominal species of *Holothuria* marked with asterisks in Table II may also prove to be conspecific, which would make an eleventh "tropicopolitan" species. A considerable number of other Indo-West Pacific species also have close relatives in the Caribbean area and in the East Pacific, as shown in Table II. This is not an exhaustive list but includes most of the

TABLE II
Related Species Occurring in the Indo-West Pacific, East Pacific or Caribbean Areas

Indo-West Pacific	East Pacific	Caribbean
Echinaster purpureus	E. tenuispinus	E. sentus
Ophiocoma erinaceus schoenleini	O. aethiops	O. wendti
Ophiocoma valenciae	O. alexandri	O. pumila
Ophiolepis superba	O. variegata	O. elegans
Eucidaris metularia	E. thouarsi	E. tribuloides
Diadema setosum	D. mexicanum	D. antillarum
Astropyga radiata	A. pulvinata	A. magnifica
Tripneustes gratilla	T. depressus	T. ventricosus
Echinometra mathaei	E. vanbrunti	E. lucunter
Clypeaster humilis	C. rotundus	C. subdepressus
Moira stygia	M. clotho	M. atropos
Brissopsis luzonica	B. pacifica	B. elongata
Brissus latecarinatus	B. obesus	B. unicolor
Holothuria(Cystipus)rigida	H.(C.)inhabilis	H.(C.)cubana
Holothuria(Selenkothuria)moebii	H.(S.)lubrica	H.(S.)glaberrima
Holothuria(Semperothuria)cinerascens	H.(S.)languens	H.(S.)surinamensis
Holothuria(Thymiosycia)hilla	H.(T.)zihuatenensis	H.(T.)gyrifer
Chiridota hawaiiensis	C. aponocrita	C. rotifera

commoner species that have closely related counterparts in both the other areas.

Some other common tropical species are generically distinct from their closest relatives in one or both of the other two main areas. For instance, the common scutellid sand dollar, *Echinodiscus*, with three Indo-West Pacific species, is replaced on both sides of America by *Leodia, Mellita,* and *Encope*. Also there are no authenticated West Pacific records of the ophiuroid *Ophioderma*, which has multiple American species, especially on the Atlantic side, its place being taken by the numerous species of *Ophiarachnella*.

In other cases the American continent provides the dividing line. This is true of the large oreasterid starfishes. *Oreaster* itself is restricted to the Atlantic and the most closely related species from both East and West Pacific are referred to *Pentaceraster*.

Finally, a few genera common to both sides of the Pacific have no close relatives at all in the Caribbean, even at the generic level. Such a one is the heart urchin *Lovenia*, with *L. elongata* (Gray) and *L. cordiformis* Lütken, respectively, in West and East Pacific, the nearest Atlantic (indeed almost cosmopolitan) relative, *Echinocardium*, being aligned in a distinct subfamily, while the infamous *Acanthaster* is limited to both sides of the Pacific and, fortunately perhaps for the Caribbean, has no counterpart there, the family being monogeneric.

IV. Conclusions

In the last twenty years, the upsurge of a generation of diving biologists has brought a vast improvement in our knowledge of the life of macroscopic marine animals, such as echinoderms. This has been fostered in the tropics by improved facilities and accessibility, the spurs of the International Indian Ocean Year, and then the *Acanthaster* problem, which emphasized the need for basic biological work on widespread reef animals, formerly neglected. The more important studies so far include those on the light sensitivity of *Diadema*, the biology of the commoner Caribbean echinoids, and the feeding and behavior of unstalked crinoids and of some aspidochirotid holothurians, apart from those on *Acanthaster*. However, large gaps still exist, particularly in our knowledge of the early life histories of many common genera found on the reefs, as well as in their feeding habits and food, reproduction, migrations, predator–prey relations, and other aspects of their biology. Notable subjects for study include the echinoids *Asthenosoma, Stomo-*

pneustes, Toxopneustes, Heterocentrotus, Colobocentrotus, Echinodiscus, and *Laganum,* the asteroids *Linckia, Nardoa, Protoreaster, Pentaceraster, Luidia,* and *Astropecten,* ophiuroids such as *Macrophiothrix, Ophiarachnella,* and those ophiocomids so far largely ignored, as well as holothurians like *Actinopyga, Synapta,* and other apodids and *Afrocucumis* or other dendrochirotids. In addition to these more conspicuous subjects there are also many smaller ones needing attention including those which I find especially interesting, namely, the fissiparous and autotomous species of ophiuroids and asteroids with their remarkable deviations from pentamerous symmetry.

References

Bakus, G. J. (1973). *In* "Biology and Geology of Coral Reefs" (O. A. Jones and R. Endean, eds.), Vol. 2, Biol. 1, pp. 325–367. Academic Press, New York.

Balinsky, B. I. (1969). *In* "A Natural History of Inhaca Island, Moçambique" (W. Macnae and M. Kalk, eds.), pp. 96–104. Witwatersrand Univ. Press, Johannesburg.

Campbell, A. C., Dart, J. K. G., Head, S. M., and Ormond, R. F. G. (1973). *Mar. Behav. Physiol.* **2,** 155.

Chesher, R. H. (1969). *Bull. Mar. Sci.* **19,** 72.

Choe, S. (1963). "Biology of the Japanese Common Sea Cucumber *Stichopus japonicus* Selenka." Pusan National University, Pusan.

Clark, A. M. (1967). *Bull. Sea Fish. Res. Sta. Isr.* **41,** 26.

Clark, A. M., and Rowe, F. W. E. (1971). "Monograph of Shallow Water Indo-West Pacific Echinoderms." British Museum (Natural History), London.

Clark, H. L. (1915). *Carnegie Inst. Wash., Pap. Dept. Mar. Biol.* **8,** 212.

Clark, H. L. (1917). *Carnegie Inst. Wash., Publ.* **251.**

Clark, H. L. (1933). *Sci. Surv. P. R.* **16**(1).

Clark, H. L. (1946). *Carnegie Inst. Wash., Publ.* **566.**

Davis, W. P. (1966). *Bull. Mar. Sci.* **16,** 435.

Devaney, D. M. (1970). *Smithson. Contrib. Zool.* **51.**

Edmondson, C. H. (1933). *Bishop Mus. Spec. Publ.* **22.**

Endean, R. (1973). *In* "Biology and Geology of Coral Reefs" (O. A. Jones and R. Endean, eds.), Vol. 2, Biol. 1, pp. 389–437. Academic Press, New York.

Fechter, H. (1973). *Mar. Biol.* **22,** 347.

Fishelson, L. (1968). *Nature (London)* **291,** 1063.

Fontaine, A. R. (1965). *J. Mar. Biol. Ass. U.K.* **45,** 373.

Fujiwara, T. (1935). *Annot. Zool. Jap.* **15,** 62.

Goreau, T. F. (1964). *Bull. Sea Fish. Res. Sta. Isr.* **35,** 23.

Herring, P. J. (1972). *J. Natur. Hist.* **6,** 169.

Kier, P. M., and Grant, R. E. (1965). *Smithson. Misc. Collect.* **149**(6).

Lewis, J. B. (1958). *Can. J. Zool.* **36,** 607.

Macnae, W., and Kalk, M. (1969). "A Natural History of Inhaca Island, Moçambique." Witwatersrand Univ. Press, Johannesburg.

McPherson, B. F. (1965). *Bull. Mar. Sci.* **15,** 228.

McPherson, B. F. (1968). *Bull. Mar. Sci.* **18**, 400.

McPherson, B. F. (1969). *Bull. Mar. Sci.* **19**, 194.

Magnus, D. B. E. (1963). *Natur Mus.* **93**, 355.

Magnus, D. B. E. (1967). *Stud. Trop. Oceanogr.* **5**, 635.

Meyer, D. L. (1973). *Mar. Biol.* **22**, 105.

Millott, N. (1954). *Phil. Trans. Roy. Soc. London, Ser. B* **238**, 187.

Mortensen, T. (1940). "A Monograph of the Echinoidea," Vol. III, Part 1. C. A. Reitzel, Copenhagen.

Randall, J. E., Schroeder, R. E., and Starck, W. A. (1964). *Carib. J. Sci.* **4**, 421.

Rutman, J., and Fishelson, L. (1969). *Mar. Biol.* **3**, 46.

Saville-Kent, W. (1893). "The Great Barrier Reef of Australia: Its Products and Potentialities." Allen, London.

Semper, C. (1868). "Die Holothurien. Reisen im Archipel der Philippinen." Wiesbaden.

Snyder, N., and Snyder, H. (1970). *Science* **163**, 276.

Taylor, J. D. (1968). *Phil. Trans. Roy. Soc. London, Ser. B* **254**, 129.

Thomassin, D. D. (1975). *Micronesica* (in press).

Tsurnamal, M., and Marder, J, (1966). *Isr. J. Zool.* **15**, 9.

Utinomi, H., and Kogo, I. (1965). *Publ. Seto Mar. Biol. Lab.* **13**, 263.

Yamaguchi, M. (1973). *In* "Biology and Geology of Coral Reefs" (O. A. Jones and R. Endean, eds.), Vol. 2, Biol. 1, pp. 369–387. Academic Press, New York.

4

ASPECTS OF THE ECOLOGY OF CORAL REEF FISHES

Barry Goldman
and
Frank Hamilton Talbot

I. Introduction

Jordan (1971) has said that there is relatively little known about tropical forest ecosystems because of their remoteness from most universities and laboratories. This applies even more to coral reef ecosystems, although a generalized picture is beginning to emerge. This review is particularly concerned with diversity, distribution, abundance, and feeding relationships of fishes on coral reefs and we have, owing to the paucity of information in this field, referred considerably to work done by us and our collaborators on One Tree Island Reef in the Great Barrier Reef System over the last five years.

The most obvious attributes of coral reefs are their biotic complexity, their high productivity, and the fact that they are relatively closed ecosystems. There are no areas richer in fish species than flourishing coral reefs (Marshall, 1965). This also holds for a number of invertebrate groups such as crustaceans and mollusks. Within a distance of 100 m on a reef one may find thousands of individuals belonging to some hundreds of fish species, a situation unparalleled in other vertebrate groups and one not found in temperate marine conditions. On the Great Barrier Reef a single rotenone collection station on the leeward outer slopes of One Tree Reef has yielded 150 species of fishes and in the Palau Islands a similar collection yielded over 200 species (Dr. H. A. Fehlmann, personal communication).

Several workers (e.g., Sargent and Austin 1949; Gordon et al., 1971) have demonstrated that the primary production on a coral reef is exceptionally high. Coral reefs grow in shallow tropical seas exposed to a maximum of solar energy. Nutrients (in the form of salts and plankton) appear to be gradually accumulated from the surrounding areas. Coral reefs are among the most highly productive of all natural ecosystems. Energy is not stored in the form of large plant or animal standing crops, however, but the reef is characterized by a rapid energy flow through a complex, highly organized system. Coral reefs are the epitome of mature, biologically accommodated communities.

Furthermore, from both a physical and energetic point of view, reef communities are reasonably discrete from each other. The tropical waters in which coral reefs flourish are relative deserts having a poor nutrient load (Johannes et al., 1970). Because of the close dependence of the majority of coral reef fishes on their reef habitat, the distance between separate reef systems constitutes a considerable ecological barrier. Nevertheless, the majority of reef fish species cover vast distances geographically, but the breeding populations tend to be small, fragmented and, because of the sedentary, nonmigratory nature of the adults, restricted to the particular reef complex on which they live (J. H. Choat, personal communication). This discreteness of populations is not typical of the majority of open ocean and nonreef species.

Coral reef fishes are thus seen to be members of ecosystems with high productivity, rapid energy turnover, and a complex community organization with small but viable populations that are both genetically and energetically more or less discrete from those of neighboring reef systems. They live in an environment that has had a long, stable geological history (Helfrich and Townsley, 1961) and equable physical conditions.

A. DEFINITION OF CORAL REEF FISHES

With the many different geographical distributions of both fishes and hermatypic corals (probably in large measure determined by temperature tolerances) it may be argued whether it is permissible to talk of coral reef fishes as such (see Abel, 1972). We believe that the concept of "coral reef fishes" is worthwhile.

The coral reef or bioherm phenomenon has a distinct geographical cutoff point beyond which only some of the hermatypic corals can be found and then usually not in reef-building quantities. At this same point there is a marked but less distinct discontinuity in the distribution of many tropical shore fishes. Notwithstanding the fact that many of these fishes are also found in coastal habits within the tropics away from coral reef regions, there is a predominance of species whose populations are strongly correlated with the presence of coral reefs. In this paper, therefore, we use the term coral reef fishes to mean those fishes usually found to be associated with coral reefs. This is a definition with obvious looseness but it has an operational value as it embraces those species with a dependence or direct impact on the energy relations of a coral reef system.

B. METHODS AND TECHNIQUES IN THE STUDY OF CORAL REEF FISH ECOLOGY

Because most work on fishes has been concentrated on temperate species and because of the complexity of the coral reef community, relatively little is known of the ecological relationships of coral reef fishes. The bulk of temperate fish species are now taxonomically well known but, for tropical marine fishes, particularly those of the rich Indo-West Pacific region, considerable basic taxonomic work is still to be done. It is therefore still difficult to compare one region with another and different names are currently used for the same species in different areas. It is usually even difficult to determine adequately the species in one area; this applies particularly to the smaller fishes such as pomacentrids, gobiids, apogonids, anthiids, and blenniids and also to those species exhibiting marked color changes with age and sex, such as the labrids and scarids.

Technical difficulties add a further dimension to the problems of studying reef fish ecology. Collecting methods are varied—at worst they are extremely selective and at best only roughly quantitative. Visual observations have added considerable qualitative information and some quantitative data.

Coral reef fishes can be collected by spearfishing, handlining, nets, traps, poisons (such as rotenone preparations), drugs (e.g., quinaldine), and explosives, or a combination of these. All methods have some disadvantages. Spearfishing, handlining, and trapping are extremely selective as to the types of fishes collected. Nets generally foul on the coral and are difficult to use; they are also visible to the majority of fishes because of the clarity of tropical waters and setting the nets may scare away many of the larger individuals. Poisons and drugs yield numerous cryptic and burrowing species that are otherwise missed but larger individuals generally are able to swim out of the poisoned area. Explosives are quite efficient and kill fishes instantly, irrespective of size or habits. But those fishes without swim bladders, such as sharks, eels, and blennies, are hardly affected. This bias is constant, however.

Brock (1954) in Hawaii, Odum and Odum (1955) in Eniwetok, and Bardach (1959) in Bermuda have used visual censusing techniques for estimating species numbers and biomass over certain areas of reef. Randall (1963, p. 36) stated, "While this is a useful technique for some purposes, it is not desirable for more exact quantitative work. Not only is there a human error in estimating the number and sizes of fishes observed, but the more secretive fishes such as the nocturnal squirrel fishes and eels are mostly not seen by divers during daylight hours. Even the diurnal fishes can be overlooked when the reef has many crevices and caves." Certainly the relative abundance of herbivorous to carnivorous fishes obtained by Odum and Odum (1955) appears, in view of more recent work (see Section V), to be highly suspect. However, the extremely thorough visual observations on very small reef habitats by Smith and Tyler (1972, 1973a,b) in the Bahamas and Virgin Islands must be considered a useful technique.

Randall (1963) poisoned known areas of reef in the Virgin Islands after first enclosing the area with a net. The purpose of the net was to prevent dead or dying fish from escaping from the study area and to stop predators from entering. The reef topography, however, severely limits the use of nets on a reef and certainly precludes any "randomized" collections.

On One Tree Reef we have used standardized explosive charges and estimated the area of reef from which the fish were collected. This area is fairly constant and it is our opinion that for repeatable, quantitative samples of a coral reef fish fauna, standardized explosive charges yield the most reliable results (Russell *et al.*, in prep.).

Published estimates of standing crop cannot be accepted with too much reliance, as can be seen by the variation within our samples from the same habitats on One Tree Reef (Fig. 6). As fish populations are mixed and highly mobile on a local basis, this large sampling variance is expected and thus a repetition of samples is needed.

The degree of fish movement within and between reefs has been estimated by the tag-recapture studies of Randall (1961a, 1962) and Springer and McErlean (1962) as well as from visual observation of marked individuals (Winn *et al.*, 1964).

II. Diversity

A. INTRODUCTION

There are three large, main, tropical regions in the world that can be defined by the high endemism of their faunas. These are the Indo-West Pacific region, the East Pacific region, and the Atlantic region (Ekman, 1953). With regard to coral reefs, the first of these is by far the largest and has the greatest number of fish species. Even though there is a paucity of detailed knowledge of the total Indo-West Pacific coral fish fauna, it is clearly very much greater than the total fish fauna of the tropical Atlantic. Table I presents a comparison of the presently known total fish faunas of some of the major reef regions. Even though the areas of these regions are not equivalent, the central region of the

TABLE I

FISH SPECIES OCCURRING IN SEVERAL CORAL REEF REGIONS SHOWING INCREASED RICHNESS IN THE CENTRAL INDO-PACIFIC

Region (Reference)	Coral reef fish species
Bahamas (Bohlke and Chaplin, 1968)	507
Seychelles (Smith and Smith, 1963)	880
Philippines (Herre, 1953)	2177[a]
New Guinea (Munro, 1964, 1967; W. Filewood, personal communication)	1700[a]
Great Barrier Reef (Marshall, 1964)	1500
Marshall and Marianas (Schultz *et al.*, 1953, 1960, 1966)	669[a,b]
Hawaii (Gosline and Brock, 1965)	448

[a] Includes freshwater fishes.

[b] 608 species, plus 10% estimate for Gobiidae as suggested by Dr. E. Lachner (personal communicaton).

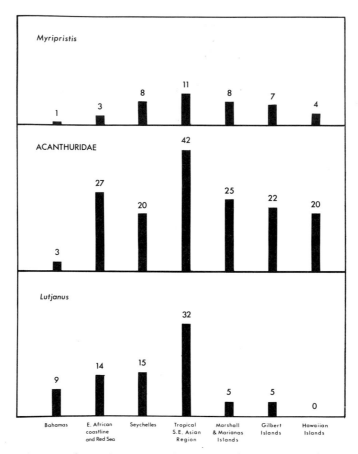

Fig. 1. Three coral reef fish groups showing trends in species richness across the Indian and Pacific Oceans and the Bahamas.

Indo-West Pacific, called by Weber and De Beaufort (1911–1953) the Indo-Australian Archipelago, is seen to be the richest area of fishes in the world. Weber and De Beaufort listed nearly 3000 species for the whole area but this number is likely to be greatly increased. As one moves east or west from this central region the number of species is reduced. Figure 1 indicates a pattern in some better known tropical families and genera (information from Randall, 1955a,b,c, 1956, 1960; Smith, 1966; Greenfield, 1968; Talbot, 1970). It is highly probable that most other fish groups will show the same pattern.

If we consider a series of single reef complexes, species numbers are found to be high but vary from region to region. At Alligator and surrounding reefs in the Florida Keys for example, 398 coral reef fish species have been recorded (Starck, 1968). In the Capricorn group at the southern end of the Great Barrier Reef system, we have now collected some 850 species, whereas from Tutia and adjacent reefs (Mafia complex) off the east coast of Africa, 244 species have been collected (Talbot, 1965). These reef systems are roughly equivalent in size.

Coral is not greatly developed into reef systems on the West African and West American coastlines. It is at present difficult to get an accurate assessment of coral reef fish species from these areas. B. Walker (in Hobson, 1968) has indicated that some 300 species of coral reef fishes are known from the tropical East Pacific but we have no comparative data for the fishes from tropical West Africa.

B. Ecological Aspects of Diversity

The basic reasons for very high species diversities of the tropics are still under discussion and this topic has been reviewed by Pianka, (1966), Sanders (1968), Margalef (1968), MacArthur (1965, 1969a), and Johnson (1970). It is likely that communities tend to diversify with time and a long and stable history without major perturbations or great temperature change, plus high productivity, lead to high diversities (Sanders, 1968; Talbot, 1970). Conditions are not greatly seasonal on coral reefs. They have high productivity and they have also had a long and stable ecological history through at least the Tertiary (Helfrich and Townsley, 1961).

Furthermore, coral reef areas include a variety of habitats such as lagoon areas, patch reefs, back-reef coral windrows, exposed outer slopes, etc. A coral reef region richer in species than another may have more species in each habitat than the other (within-habitat diversity) or there may be a fewer number of species shared between differing habitats in the one region than are shared between differing habitats in the other (between-habitat diversity).

The difference between within-habitat and between-habitat diversities can be illustrated by comparing One Tree Island reef at the southern end of the Great Barrier Reef (a southerly extension of the rich Central Indo-West Pacific region) with Tutia Reef on the East African Coast. We find that very different diversity measures for the whole reef occur. One Tree Island Reef has about two and a half times the total number of species that is found on the East African Reef. But if we compare explosive samples made on Tutia Reef (Talbot, 1965, also unpublished data) with equivalent samples from One Tree Reef they have similar numbers of species per sample. There seem to be no within-habitat diversity differences between the two regions but more species are obviously shared between samples on Tutia Reef than between samples from One Tree Reef, resulting in a lower total number of species in the Tutia Reef region. This also appears to be true for bird species from relatively impoverished Puerto Rico compared with those from the richer tropical American mainland (MacArthur et al., 1966).

The basic problem in reef fish diversity—that of species packing (Mac-Arthur, 1969b)—has still to be resolved. Obviously in a discrete system such as a coral reef, resources are finite and the total biomass is limited by primary production and energy flow rates. Thus, for the number of species to increase, energy flow pathways must be more finely partitioned and the relative biomass of each of the species populations has to decrease (by lower numbers or smaller sized individuals). But concomitant with this increase in organization is an increase in efficiency that, according to Margalef (1968), will lead to a greater biomass being supported by the same energy supply. An evolutionary feedback is thus involved. Questions remain as to how such high diversity is maintained. Chance events may be important. Coral reefs can be regarded as environmental mosaics in which vacant patches are continually and unpredictably created, because of local physical perturbations and through mortality, predation, and emigration. Given that larval dispersal and successful juvenile recruitment are also largely unpredictable (Russell et al., 1974), there is likely to be continued local variation in the sorts of species present and this may well contribute to a high overall diversity. However, questions remain, such as how small populations maintain their viability and how the increasing numbers of species avoid competition.

Numerous behavioral and physiological mechanisms have developed that may tend to increase the fecundity of reduced fish populations. Parental care of the young (e.g., some pomacentrids) and mouth breeding (e.g., the apogonids) help to decrease larval mortality, while breeding aggregations and release of gametes in the upper and turbulent water layers in the lee of a reef are thought to increase the fertilization rate and also to place the eggs and larvae out of reach of most benthic predators (Randall, 1961a; Jones, 1968).

Fishelson (1970) and Popper and Fishelson (1973) in their work on *Anthias squamipinnis* (Serranidae) and Robertson (1972), who has worked on *Labroides dimidiatus* (Labridae), have found that adult populations of these fishes may be predominantly females with only a small, but sufficient, percentage of males. Should the male sector of the population be reduced, new males are rapidly "recruited" from the female stocks by some individuals undergoing a protogynous sex reversal. Egg production is maximized by this mechanism and a greater proportion of energy is channeled into population maintenance.

The coexistence of a high number of species implies that the niche parameters are becoming more finely partitioned or that considerable overlap in resource utilization is occurring. It is possible that both these alternatives are available to a species at different life stages or in different reef areas, for example, and both strategies appear to be utilized by various elements of the fish fauna. Jones (1968), for example, recorded a considerable degree of niche separation in the surgeon fishes (Acanthuridae) of the Hawaiian and Johnston Island reefs. In considering habitat selection, foraging methods, food taken, and food handling ability in combination, all species were found to be more or less distinct. He concluded that although it might not necessarily be a continuous pressure, competition for a limited food supply has led to the evolution and maintenance of differing modes of food and space exploitation.

Choat (1969), on the other hand, found that the parrot fishes (Scaridae) of Heron Island reef have considerable overlap in their exploitation of the reef environment both in food types taken and time of feeding. Mixed schools of parrot fishes were often observed feeding together on the same algal turfs. The implication here is that other factors are acting to limit the populations of parrot fishes to levels low enough for coexistence without competition. Paine (1966) has hypothesized that this type of control could be affected by predators. The wrasses (Labridae), however, were found by Choat (1969) to have more circumscribed niches. Both spatial distribution and feeding requirements were more narrowly defined for the carnivorous labrid species, this specialization apparently being a mechanism for avoiding or minimizing competition for a limited food resource.

Choat's observations on scarids and labrids lend support to the hypothesis of Hairston *et al.* (1960) that while predators are generally resource-limited, herbivores are predator-limited. We should not exclude the possibility, however, that other factors, such as larval recruitment, juvenile mortality, and parasitism may be acting to control population sizes with results analagous to those of adult predation.

It is surprising that neither Jones (1968) nor Choat (1969) compared the scarids with the acanthurids, as both groups have apparently similar space and food requirements. Yet according to these authors the two groups have evolved different strategies—the acanthurids being apparently resource-limited whereas the scarids are predator-limited. It may, of course, be possible that the acanthurids enjoy a greater immunity from predation (owing to their tough skin and caudal lances) thus allowing populations to reach resource limitation.

III. Local Distribution of Coral Reef Fishes

A. CORAL REEF HABITATS AND ZONATION

As with most shallow water communities, zonation on coral reefs is distinctive (Wells, 1957; Maxwell, 1968; Stoddart, 1969). A typical reef is characterized by five morphologically distinct regions.

1. The off-reef floor. This is that zone immediately surrounding a coral reef.

2. The reef slopes or reef front. These may be terraced and can be divided into the following: (a) The spurs and grooves zone. This is generally less than four meters in depth. (b) The lower reef slopes that extend seaward from the spurs and grooves zone to the off-reef floor.

3. The algal rim or reef surface. This is a pavement of encrusting coralline algae that, together with the upper spurs and grooves zone, takes the full force of any wave action. The lagoonward section of the algal rim is sometimes strewn with pieces of dead coral and is usually referred to as the boulder tract.

4. The reef flat. This is on the lagoon side of the algal rim and may be further subdivided into (a) the windrows area and (b) the sand flat or microatoll zone at the edge of the lagoon.

5. The lagoon. These zones or habitats support markedly different fish communities (see Fig. 2). They are interdependant, however, and to a certain extent each zone is transitional between those on either side. The zones have been schematically illustrated, with some of their typical fish representatives, by Hiatt and Strasburg (1960), Hobson (1965), and Jones (1968).

In view of the mobility of most reef fishes and the proximity of their habitats, it is surprising to find that of the 395 species we have so far collected by quantitative samples from One Tree Island Reef, only 7% (26 species) are cosmopolitan, i.e., occurring on the reef base and windward reef slopes as well as the reef flat, the lagoon patch reefs, and the lee-ward reef slopes. Furthermore, approximately half (188 species or 49%) of all species thus collected are restricted to one or another of the five major habitats. Fifteen percent (61 species) of the One Tree fish fauna have so far been collected only outside the algal rim, while 11% (45 species) can be termed "deep water species," being restricted to depths

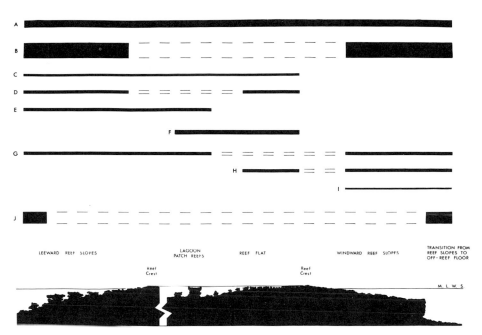

Fig. 2. Number of species shared among the various habitats across One Tree Island Reef. The width of each line is proportional to the number of species. A, Cosmopolitan (i.e., found on all major habitats)—27 species; B, found on outer reef habitats—60 species; C, found only on the leeward reef slopes, the lagoon patch reefs and the reef flat—9 species; D, found only on the leeward reef slopes and the reef flat—12 species; E, found only on the leeward reef slopes and the lagoon patch reefs—11 species; F, found on the reef flat and the lagoon patch reefs but not outside the reef—17 species; G, found on all habitats except the reef flat—11 species; H, found only on the windward side of the reef, on both the outer slopes and reef flat—11 species; I, found only on the windward reef slopes (i.e., from the upper slopes to the transition to the off-reef floor)—5 species; and J, restricted to deep water habitats (i.e., over 25 meters)—45 species.

greater than 25 meters (Fig. 2). That these reef zones are indeed supporting different fish communities is further illustrated by the differing number of species collected from each region (Fig. 3). For example, a total of only 23 species has been collected from the compacted, seaward upper slopes, whereas 124 species have been collected from the windrows area of the reef flat and 216 species have been taken from the leeward outer slopes. Figure 4 further illustrates this point in that the average number of species per explosive sample also differs among reef areas.

It can also be seen that the fish communities found in different reef areas may be very generalized in some areas (e.g., the surge channels

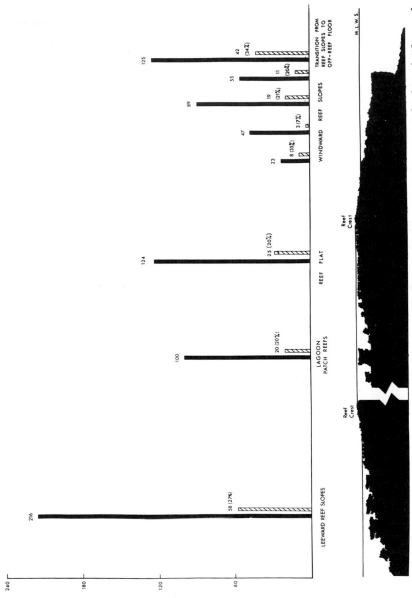

Fig. 3. Total number of species (solid lines) found in the various habitats across One Tree Island Reef. The number of species restricted to each habitat (hatched lines) are also shown with their percentage of the total number for that habitat.

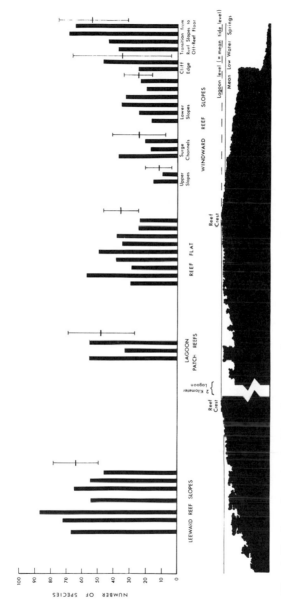

Fig. 4. Number of species in 36 explosive samples across One Tree Island Reef. The mean number of species with 95% confidence limits is also shown for each major habitat.

in the windward reef flat with only 6% of its species not found in other areas) or quite distinctive (e.g., the transition to the off-reef floor where 34% of the species are restricted to that area) in their species composition. A certain degree of habitat selection is thus discernable in the fish fauna of a coral reef and we can now state with a fair degree of certainty the types of habitat in which the majority of reef fishes are found. This is "because reef fishes are for the most part non-migratory and their environment ordinarily somewhat circumscribed" (Randall, 1963, p. 44).

There are numerous cases where behavioral requirements limit the distribution of fish species. The damsel fishes of the genus *Amphiprion*, for example, associate with the large sea anemones (Allen, 1972), some of the eleotrids live in sandy burrows and are restricted to sandy patches at the edge of the lagoon (Karplus *et al.*, 1972), and many of the nocturnally active holocentrids and apogonids require habitats with abundant overhangs and caverns for shelter during the day (Vivien, 1973).

B. DISTRIBUTION ACROSS A REEF

The amount of movement of the majority of reef fishes appears to be limited and many of the smaller species such as the gobiids, blenniids, and pomacentrids are known to maintain territories, at least for part of the year (Reese, 1964). These territories may be for feeding or reproductive purposes and are often rigorously defended against a wide variety of intruders (Salmon *et al.*, 1968; Rasa, 1969; Low, 1971; Myreburg, 1972; Vine, 1974). It is also evident that some of the larger carnivorous reef fishes maintain home ranges. Skin divers (e.g., Miss J. Booth, Great Barrier Reef, personal communication), have reported that large groupers (Serranidae) can be found in the same locality on a reef for extended periods of a year or more.

Tagging experiments in the Caribbean by Bardach (1958) and Springer and McErlean (1962) have shown that many fishes such as serranids, lutjanids, chaetodontids, and acanthurids remain in a fairly circumscribed place on a reef. Some serranids and lutjanids were recaptured at their place of release after as much as three years at large (Randall, 1961b, 1962).

Quite clearly, a great majority of the reef fishes recognizes a certain part of the reef as their normal living area but the size of this home range may vary with the type and behavior of the fish species. Some species of parrot fish (Scaridae) have home caves to which they retreat from danger or return from their feeding grounds (Winn and Bardach,

1960). They may travel considerable distances (Ogden and Buckman, 1973) and are known to use sun-compass orientation as a means of navigating over open grounds (Winn *et al.*, 1964).

The larger serranids may move freely across a particular reef and can find their way "home" when displaced (Bardach, 1958); but results from tagging chaetodontids suggest that these fishes "spend their entire lives associated with a relatively small portion of the reef environment" (Bardach, 1958, p. 143) and "their chances of relocating such a small home range, if displaced, was negligible" (Bardach, 1958, p. 142). Even schooling fishes such as some lutjanids are likely to be permanent residents of relatively small areas of a coral reef system (Potts, 1970).

Apart from the obvious territorial and home range behavior patterns, other factors that may act at limiting the distribution of reef fishes are dependence on a particular food supply (which may itself be restricted in distribution), a tendency to avoid open spaces away from shelter (Randall, 1963), especially during daylight hours, and depth limitations, among others.

C. DISTRIBUTION BETWEEN REEFS

Little is known of the reproductive behavior and life histories of most coral reef fishes (but see Randall, 1961a; Breder and Rosen, 1966). Some species do have demersal eggs and even exhibit parental care of the young, [e.g., the damsel fish *Acanthochromis polyacanthus* (see Robertson, 1973)], which tends to maintain the population in a particular locality. Even in those species that have planktonic eggs and larvae, reproductive effort may be considerably conserved by tidal movements, eddy currents, and gyres that would tend to return the recruits to their parent populations (Emery, 1972).

It is difficult to imagine how a significant gene flow can be maintained between populations as far separated as East Africa, Hawaii, and the Tuamotus, yet a great number of reef fish species are phenotypically very similar. It may be, however, that these species have achieved a considerable degree of genetic stability and that, in such a highly organized and interdependent system as a coral reef community, selection for change (cf. Ehrlich and Raven, 1969) is minimal.

Ocean current systems, water temperatures, the availability of food, and length of time a species can exist in a free swimming or drifting condition would be important factors in the dispersal of typically reef-dependent fishes. If the distance between reefs is too great, dispersion will be hindered. The Hawaiian region, for instance, is lacking many species that have not been able to cross from the central Pacific. There are, for example, no species of the genus *Lutjanus* and an almost complete lack of epinephaline serranids (Randall and Brock, 1960). The East Pacific barrier is a further example of the isolating effect of distance and factors associated with it. According to Briggs (1964), only 62 species of tropical marine shore fishes have crossed from the central Pacific via the equatorial counter current to the west coast of the Americas. Gosline (1971), however, suggests that ecological factors (such as the abundance of the initial stocks from which recruitment is taking place, or competition with previously established forms) are more important than distance per se at limiting species migrations.

D. Nocturnal Distribution

Several important papers summarize our knowledge of the nocturnal habits of coral reef fishes in nature. These include Hobson's papers (1965, 1968) for the gulf of California, and the paper of Starck and Davis (1966) for Alligator Reef, Florida, (for further references, see Collette and Talbot, 1972; and a general account is given by Schroeder, 1967). Information on nocturnal activity, because of the difficulty of study, has been very slow in accumulating but there is a fair amount of information scattered in the more recent literature. Behavior, and often distribution, is completely different between night and day for almost all reef fish species.

The typical day mode of a coral reef shows a mass of variously colored and patterned benthic feeders (Scaridae, Acanthuridae, Chaetodontidae, Labridae, and many others), schools of plankton feeders (Pomacentridae, often Atherinidae, and the genus *Caesio*), large predators cruising along the reef edge, and schools of Lutjanidae or Pomadasyidae milling slowly in their daytime resting areas.

The nocturnal mode is quite different, with only a fraction of the number of active species compared with the daytime. The overall picture is one of a sparse fauna. A number of species of apogonids move into midwater, and on the reef there are a few species of holocentrids, lutjanids, haemulonids, lethrinids, and occasional moray eels. None of the grazers (Chaetodontidae, Acanthuridae, Scaridae, and Blenniidae) seem to feed at night. In the areas studied, the lutjanids seen in day resting schools spread out singly in interreef areas hunting over sand flats and weed beds.

In two coral reefs studied intensively over a few weeks in the Caribbean (Collette and Talbot, 1972) all diurnal species had disappeared by sunset and there was then a period when the reef looked almost deserted. The nocturnal fishes became active at about civil twilight, i.e., when the center of the sun is some 6° below the horizon, which is about 20 minutes after sunset. In the morning changeover, the earliest time diurnal species appeared was civil twilight (light intensity approximately 1 foot candle) but nocturnal species were still mostly out at this time. Hobson (1972) found a similar pattern in Hawaii.

In both changeover periods there were often clear differences in onset of the alternative activity pattern in different species. Labrids, for instance, are late risers (Hobson, 1965). On Virgin Island reefs the labrid *Thallosoma bifasciatum* was the last to rise, some 20 minutes after the early rising serranid *Hypoplectrus puella* (Collette and Talbot, 1972). Domm and Domm (1973) report an invariable sequence in the pattern of changeover according to family.

Some of the diurnal species are replaced by nocturnal species ecologically. Apogonids, for example, replace some pomacentrids in midwater and also close over the reef. Daytime benthic invertebrate feeders such as the smaller serranids, labrids, balistids, and pseudochromids may be replaced at night by lutjanids and pomadasyids. All nocturnal species are predatory (Hobson, 1968; Collette and Talbot, 1972, Vivien 1973).

The large diurnal fish predators (such as the big serranids of the genera *Plectropomus*, *Epinephelus*, and *Promicrops*, the carangids, and the scomberomorids) are not so obviously replaced, although the larger lutjanids may partially fill this role. In East African coral reefs there is some evidence for different species of the genus *Sphyraena* replacing each other ecologically. Williams (1959) has found that along the edges of coral reefs and over shallow coral banks, two species, *Sphyraena barracuda* and *Sphyraena jello*, are active by day (and take lures) and two species, *Sphyraena toxeuma* and *Sphyraena genie*, at night. The latter two also have relatively larger eye diameters.

It is likely that the diurnal and nocturnal behavior of fishes is tied in with the behavior of food organisms (Vivien and Peyrot-Clausade, 1974). Many polychaetes, mollusks, and crustaceans hide during the day but are active at night, and these are important foods for most nocturnal benthic feeders. Fish feeders seem to have peaks of activity, which are very obvious on the reef, during the morning and evening changeover periods (Hobson, 1968; Collette and Talbot, 1972). Nocturnal piscivores such as the eels work through the coral reef seeking out diurnal species in their nocturnal sheltering places. Plankton feeders are active both night and day. No work has been done on the biomass of nocturnal and diurnal plankton feeders to our knowledge.

IV. Standing Crops and Productivity

A. Introduction

With the increasing demands for the exploitation of natural fish stocks, the productive potential of coral reef fishes may become more important as a food source for expanding human populations. Experience has shown the inadvisability of cropping a population without sufficient knowledge of its fecundity, turnover rate, and limiting standing crop (Hardy, 1959).

B. Biomass Estimates for Coral Reef Fish Communities

We find only five references in the literature that give reasonable estimates of the standing crops of fish populations on coral reefs (Fig. 5). Reported standing crops range from 350 kg/ha (Clark *et al.*, 1968; fringing reef in the Red Sea); to 425 kg/ha (Odum and Odum, 1955; average of zones of smaller and larger coral heads, corrected to wet weight as in Bardach, 1959); to 450 kg/ha (Bardach, 1959; patch

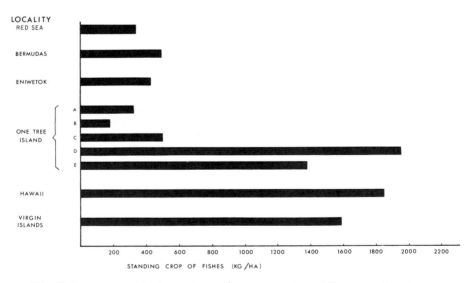

Fig. 5. Comparison of fish standing crop estimates from different coral reef regions. Red Sea (Clark *et al.*, 1968): fringing reef. Bermudas (Bardach, 1959): patch reef. Eniwetok (Odum and Odum, 1955): average of zones of smaller and larger coral heads, corrected to wet weight as in Bardach (1959). One Tree Island (Talbot and Goldman): A, reef flat; B, windward upper slopes; C, windward lower slopes; D, transition from windward reef slopes to off-reef floor; E, leeward reef slopes. Hawaii (Brock, 1954): average of two estimates from collections at Keahole Point. Virgin Islands (Randall, 1963): average of two collections from natural reefs.

reef in the Caribbean); to 1590 kg/ha (Randall, 1963; average of two collections in the Virgin Islands); to 1850 kg/ha (Brock, 1954; average of two collections at Keahole Point, Hawaii). Our own estimates of biomass at One Tree Island range from 175 kg/ha on the upper reef slopes to 1950 kg/ha at the transition between the reef and the off-reef floor. The variation in these estimates may have several causes, one of which is that the methodology is not standardized.

The structure of the habitat must affect the biomass distribution of coral reef fishes. As Randall (1963, p. 43) stated, "no matter how attractive an area might seem from the standpoint of food supply, it will not contain an appreciable number of reef fishes of moderate to large size during daylight hours unless there is enough sculpturing of the reef to provide cover." Factors affecting nocturnal distribution are less clearly understood and we have no quantitative data to indicate nocturnal biomass distributions. But for the diurnal period Randall's (1963, p. 43) statement is fully supported by results from One Tree as shown in Fig. 6 (data from Goldman and Talbot, in prep.). The greatest standing crop of fishes is found on those outside reef habitats with considerable sculpturing, whereas the lagoon back reefs, similar to the zones of smaller and larger coral heads of Eniwetok (Odum and Odum, 1955) and somewhat similar to the patch reefs of the Bermudas (Bardach, 1959), supported much smaller standing crops.

It seems reasonable to conclude at this stage that a standing crop of coral reef fishes in the order of 2000 kg/ha would be the maximum maintained by the majority of reef communities. Seasonality, time of day, and tidal cycle are variables that would also modify fish biomass distributions but their effects have yet to be quantitatively explored.

C. COMPARISONS WITH OTHER BIOMASS ESTIMATES

Fish standing crops from temperate, rocky reefs are in broad agreement with those values reported here from coral reef environments (Quast, 1968; Russell, 1971). The standing crops may be limited by factors such as water depth, input of solar energy, and available nutrients. Artificial reefs, on the other hand, may be capable of supporting boosted standing crops for a limited period. Randall (1963) found that after a little more than two years, an artificial reef he established in the Virgin Islands supported about 11 times (17,400 kg/ha) the biomass from nearby natural reefs. Similar high standing crops for artificial reefs are reported by Fast and Pagan-Font (1973) and Russell (1975).

Randall suggested that the much greater biomass associated with his artificial reefs was due to the proximity of the seagrass beds that sur-

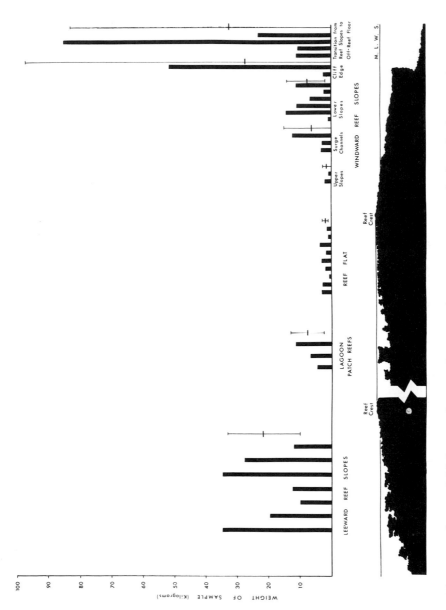

Fig. 6. Distribution of fish biomass for 36 explosive samples across One Tree Island Reef. The mean biomass per sample with 95% confidence limits is also shown for each major habitat.

rounded the reef. These beds were fed upon at night, particularly by grunts (Pomadasyidae) that sheltered on the reef by day and dominated the fish population both in numbers and in weight. Large concentrations of fish, particularly of those species using the reef for shelter and feeding elsewhere, appear to be a predominant feature of small isolated reefs, including artificial structures, in both tropical and temperate areas (Russell, 1975).

D. Productivity

Bardach (1959) appears to be the only author to give any estimate as to the productivity of coral reef fish communities. He quoted a figure of 2.2×10^5 Kcal/ha/year as the energy production by the fishes of a Bermuda reef. This he estimated as 0.0014% of the annual solar energy available, a value similar to that obtained by Hayne and Ball (1956) for a shallow freshwater lake, but considerably higher than the value Bardach quoted from Georges Bank (0.00005–0.00025%).

V. Feeding Relationships

A. Introduction

Detailed work has been done on the feeding relationships of coral reef fishes by Hiatt and Strasburg (1960) in the Marshall Islands and Randall (1967) in the West Indies [the latter also summarizes the work of Beebe and Tee-Van (1928) and other earlier workers in the area]. Bakus (1969) has published a major review of feeding in shallow marine waters. Recent work has been done in Madagascar by Vivien (1973) and in Hawaii by Hobson (1974). A picture with some clear differences between high and low latitudes is emerging. In marine shallow water in temperate and boreal regions, there are usually considerable exposed standing crops of algae dominated by brown algae of large thallus size. In contrast, tropical benthic primary producers are smaller in size and comprise greater proportions of green and red algae. On coral reefs considerable standing crops of algae are associated with the corals themselves, both symbiotically in the coral tissues (Zooxanthellae), in the skeletons underlying the living tissue, and on dead coral surfaces. Coralline algae, however, form much (possibly the bulk) of the standing crop, at least in the Indo-Pacific (Bakus, 1969), although their relative energy fixation appears to be much lower than that of corals (Marsh, 1970).

The benthic invertebrate fauna of a coral reef is obviously of considerable importance in the energy flow through a reef ecosystem (Vivien and

Peyrot-Clausade, 1974), especially in the roles of herbivores, planktivores, and detrivores. No overall information is available as to relative standing crops and energy relationships of these categories.

B. Description of Fish Feeding Categories

1. Herbivores

Phytoplankton feeders were not found by Randall (1967) in his West Indian study, nor by Hiatt and Strasburg (1960) in the Marshall Islands. This contrasts with temperate areas where phytoplankton may be the major food of some fishes with huge standing crops, for example, the genus *Sardinops* in southern Africa, as shown by Davies (1957). In the opinion of Suyehiro (1942), 6% of temperate species may consume phytoplankton.

The herbivores on coral reefs are sustained mainly by low algal turfs of filamentous and other low growing algae and by surface diatoms. Stephenson and Searles (1960) reported "intense" grazing activity on the beach rock turfs on Heron Island, Great Barrier Reef, with the fishes being the most important grazing group. Among the fish populations of a coral reef, the scarids and acanthurids are by far the most important among the herbivores although the siganids, some pomacentrids, and some salariine blennies must be considered as important members of this food category.

2. Omnivores

Although many reef fishes are omnivorous (Hiatt and Strasburg, 1960; Randall, 1967; Talbot, 1965; Vivien, 1973), the majority are substantially more herbivorous than carnivorous or vice versa. This category includes some pomacentrids, chaetodontids, pomacanthids, monocanthids, ostractiontids, tetraodontids, canthigasterids, some labrids, balistids, hemirhamphids, and leiognathids. In some areas, scarid species may feed on algae and also scrape coral (Hiatt and Strasburg, 1960, in the Marshall Islands; Talbot, 1965, in East Africa; Motoda, 1940, in the Palau Islands; and Al-Hussaini, 1947, in the Red Sea) but this was never observed by Randall (1967) in his detailed work on West Indian Reefs. Choat (1969), in an intensive study on the Great Barrier Reef, also recorded only rare coral scrapes that are usually closely adjacent to heavily grazed algal turfs. East African massive corals of the genus *Porites,* however, are often covered with scarid grazing scrapes (F. H. T., personal observation) and Bakus (1969) has also observed scarids grazing on *Porites* on the Pacific coasts of Costa Rica and Panama. Randall (1974) reports a number of observations of heavy grazing of corals by scarids in some areas of the Pacific. It is clear that in different areas with the same species of scarids this habit must vary. This does not necessarily represent a departure from a primarily herbivorous habit but it may be that the species are utilizing the algal symbionts in the coral (Choat, 1969; Randall, 1974). Alternately it has been shown that nominally herbivorous fishes may require some small amounts of animal tissue for continued growth (Menzel, 1959), and it is possible that some species of scarids occasionally take animal food. Certainly some scarids avidly feed on small fishes at explosive and rotenone collecting stations (Talbot and Goldman, 1972).

The main herbivorous fish groups are the Acanthuridae, Scaridae, Siganidae, Kyphosidae (including Girellidae), Chaetodontidae, Blennidae (some genera), and Pomacentridae (partially). Hiatt and Strasburg (1960) have pointed out that the herbivores are among the more advanced and specialized groups. It is also true that fish that feed on coelenterates, in spite of their nematocysts, are also of specialized groups, (e.g., some members of the Chaetodontidae, Diodontidae, Monacanthidae, and Scaridae). Although there are considerably fewer species of herbivores than carnivores, the diversity of plant feeding fishes is markedly higher than in temperate communities, and Choat (1969) has shown for parrot fishes (Scaridae) that there is considerable overlapping in resource utilization by these extremely similar fishes. It is likely that competitive pressures in the species-rich coral reef communities have led to selection of fishes that could directly exploit the rich energy source of primary producers (Bakus, 1969).

3. Zooplankton Feeders

Most reefs have schools of small, zooplankton-feeding fishes. These are usually clupeids (e.g., *Stolephorus, Jenkinsia, Sardinella, Harengula*), atherinids (e.g., *Atherina, Pranesus, Allanetta, Atherinomorus*), the lutjanid genus *Caesio;* and sometimes the carangids *Decapterus* and *Selar*. Huge schools of the pempherid genus *Parapriacanthus* may also be found on some Indo-Pacific reefs. Anthiids and several of the abundant pomacentrids (e.g., *Chromis, Pomacentrus*) are also zooplankton feeders. Other pomacentrids such as *Dascyllus* are particulate zooplankton feeders (Hiatt and Strasburg, 1960), feeding on lagoon plankton (Emery, 1968). Some *Pomacentrus* spp., however, would be better described as facultative omnivores, feeding equally on algae and zooplankton (B. G., personal observations).

Nocturnally the position and feeding activity of these species is taken by apogonids and holocentrids (Hobson, 1965; Vivien, 1973).

4. Carnivores

Hiatt and Strasburg (1960) have given a detailed analysis of carnivorous fishes found in the Marshall Islands, separating them into carnivores on fossorial, benthic, and midwater fauna, respectively. Their statement is true of most Indo-Pacific coral reefs and at the generic and familial level of any coral reefs. Most carnivorous fishes, with some notable exceptions, are amazingly opportunistic (Steven, 1930; Talbot, 1964) and will in general take the commonest foods available to them, i.e., "available" within size and catching limitations in their habitat. In one East African coral reef area on two separate occasions, huge quantities of a single food species covered the reefs (a penaeid prawn and a stomatopod larva, respectively), and almost every fish species sampled by explosives, from bottom dwelling serranids to pelagic sphyraenids, contained them (Talbot, 1960). Many carnivorous fishes will utilize different food organisms at different growth stadia; a feeder on small benthic invertebrates may change to large crabs and fishes as it grows, the most available (in the above sense) foods being taken.

In spite of this generalization there are some highly specialized predators. Parasite picking fishes such as *Labroides* spp. (Indo-Pacific), juvenile *Thallassoma bifasciatum* (West Indies), the goby *Elacatinus* (Randall, 1967; West Indies), and some other juvenile labrids and pomacanthids are examples. Adaptations such as elongate snouts (*Forcipiger, Gomphosus, Chelmon*) and unusually protrusible mouths (*Epibulus*) must at least lead to the possibility of taking additional kinds of prey, as must strong crushing teeth in some echidnids, labrids, sparids, and rays, for example. A most striking feeding specialization is shown by the blenny *Aspidontus taeniatus,* which mimics the cleaner fish *Labroides dimidiatus* (following both its "dancing" behavior and color pattern) but attacks the fins of the fish waiting to be cleaned (Eibl-Eibesfeldt, 1959). Shrimp and fish eggs have also been found in stomach contents of *A. taeniatus* (Randall and Randall, 1960).

Some food types are clearly unpalatable to most fishes. Among these, for instance, are the sponges and some coelenterates. There are, however, some genera of the more advanced Percomorph and Plectognath fishes that are known to feed intentionally on sponges. These include some chaetodontids, ephippids, monocanthids, canthigasterids, and ostraciontids (Menzel, 1959; Bakus, 1964; Randall and Hartman, 1968).

5. Detrivores

Few fishes are considered as feeding primarily on the detritus on coral reefs, but some blenniid species of the genera *Entomacrodus* and *Cirripectus,* as well as the Mugilidae, are so considered by Hiatt and Strasburg (1960). Recent work by Benson and Muscatine (1974) and by Gerber and Marshall (1974) suggests that detritus may be an important energy transfer from corals and algae to reef fishes.

6. Scavengers

Randall (1967) considered no special scavenger feeding category and Hiatt and Strasburg (1960) mentioned only the shark *Ginglymostoma ferrugeneum.* It is likely that any damaged or dead fishes, turtles, birds, or invertebrates would be eaten by those carnivores able to swallow them or tear pieces from them.

C. Trophic Levels and Biomass

Fishes play a vital part in the energetics of a coral reef system. Odum and Odum (1955) suggested that on a quantitative basis (using visual techniques which are suspect; see Section I,B) there was a striking preponderance of parrot fishes, surgeon fishes, damsel fishes, and butterfly fishes (i.e., mainly herbivores) compared with wrasses, groupers, and other carnivores. In contrast, other workers (Randall, 1963, 1967; Hiatt and Strasburg, 1960; Al-Hussaini, 1947; Talbot, 1965; Talbot and Goldman, 1972) have found carnivores to be the most abundant group. Bakus (1969) quoted an average of 9% omnivores, 22% herbivores, and 69% carnivores, but this includes percentage by weight as well as percentage by number of species. If one averages the figures given in his table VII (p. 331) pertaining only to percentage by weight, the proportions change to 14% omnivores, 16% herbivores, and 70% carnivores. In our work on One Tree Reef we have considered four feeding categories— planktivores, grazers (which includes grazers on both algae and coral), benthic invertebrate feeders, and piscivores; their relative proportion by biomass for the whole of One Tree Reef was 10%, 18%, 18%, and 54%, respectively. Carnivorous fishes constitute 3.4 times the biomass of grazers, but this reversal of the "traditional" biomass pyramid results from carnivorous fishes also feeding on second and third trophic level invertebrates. A true biomass pyramid will be achieved only if the whole reef fauna is considered.

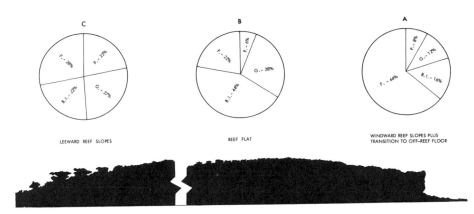

Fig. 7. Proportional abundance (of total biomass) of the four major feeding types of coral reef fishes found on the three main habitats of One Tree Island Reef (P., plankton feeders; G., grazers; B. I., benthic invertebrate feeders; F., fish feeders).

The total coral reef must be considered as a single energy system, but different reef areas have been found to have different energy sources (Goldman and Talbot, in prep.). In Fig. 7 fish samples collected by explosive charges and divided into four feeding categories by weight are shown for the three major reef areas on One Tree Reef. In the lagoon back reef (the sheltered windrow area behind the reef crest, Fig. 7b) there is a predominance of benthic invertebrate feeding fishes which comprise 44% of the total fish biomass and plankton feeders are proportionately low by weight. In samples from the outside of the pseudoatoll (both to windward and leeward of the reef, Fig. 7a and c) there is about half the proportion by weight of benthic invertebrate feeders, and two to four times that of plankton feeders. If, as found by Odum and Odum (1955), the windrow area corals rapidly remove zooplankton from the water flowing over them, this low quantity of plankton feeding fishes on the back reef is understandable. However, the greater proportion of plankton feeders in outer reef habitats may reflect the fact that it is more efficient to crop the plankton from a continuously moving current rather than picking them piecemeal from within the interstices of the coral in a back reef habitat (Davis and Birdsong, 1973). The difference in proportion of plankton feeders on the windward and leeward outer slopes of the reef may relate to the considerably greater shelter present on the leeward slopes. The high proportion of fish feeders (64%) on the windward reef slopes stems from the presence, in the deeper regions, of many large carnivorous species that are considered to be in a daytime resting phase. These fishes, notably *Plectropomus maculatus* and

Epinephalus undulostriatus, are thought to feed in other areas at night. Thus these diagrams may not be an accurate representation of fish standing crops supported by these regions.

Acknowledgment

We are indebted to Mr. B. C. Russell of The Australian Museum for criticisms and additional references.

References

Abel, E. F. (1972). *Proc. Symp. Corals and Coral Reefs, 1969, Mar. Biol. Ass. India* p. 449.

Al-Hussaini, A. H. (1947). *Publ. Biol. Sta. Ghardaqa* **5**, 1.

Allen, G. R. (1972). "The Anemonefishes: Their Classification and Biology." TFH Publ., Neptune City.

Bakus, G. J. (1964). *Allan Hancock Found. Publ., Occas. Pap.* **27**, 1.

Bakus, G. J. (1969). *Int. Rev. Gen. Exp. Zool.* **4**, 275.

Bardach, J. E. (1958). *Ecology* **39**, 139.

Bardach, J. E. (1959). *Limnol. Oceanogr.* **4**, 77.

Beebe, W., and Tee-Van, J. (1928). *Zoologica (New York)* **10**, 1.

Benson, A. A., and Muscatine, L. (1974). *Limnol. Oceanogr.* **19**, 810.

Bohlke, J. E., and Chaplin, C. C. G. (1968). "Fishes of the Bahamas and Adjacent Tropical Waters." Livingston Publ. Co., Pennsylvania.

Breder, C. M., Jr., and Rosen, D. E. (1966). "Modes of Reproduction in Fishes." Natur. Hist. Press, Garden City, New York.

Briggs, J. C. (1964). *Copeia* No. 4, p. 706.

Brock, V. E. (1954). *J. Wildl. Manage.* **18**, 297.

Choat, J. H. (1969). Ph. D. Thesis, University of Queenslands, Brisbane, Australia.

Clark, E., Ben-Tuvia, A., and Steinitz, H. (1968). *Bull. Sea Fish. Res. Stn. Haifa* **49**, 15.

Collette, B. B., and Talbot, F. H. (1972). *Bull. Nat. Hist. Mus. Los Angeles* **14**, 98.

Davies, D. H. (1957). *S. Afr., Fish., Invest. Rep.* **30**, 1.

Davis, W. P., and Birdsong, R. E. (1973). *Helgolaender Wiss. Meeresunters.* **24**, 292.

Domm, S. B., and Domm, A. J. (1973). *Pac. Sci.* **27**, 128.

Ehrlich, P. R., and Raven, P. H. (1969). *Science* **165**, 1228.

Eibl-Eibesfeldt, I. (1959). *Z. Tierpsychol.* **12**, 203.

Ekman, S. (1953). "Zoogeography of the Sea." Sidgwick & Jackson, London.

Emery, A. R. (1968). *Limnol. Oceanogr.* **13**, 293.

Emery, A. R. (1972). *Carib. J. Sci.* **12**, 121.

Fast, D. E., and Pagan-Font, F. A. (1973). *Ass. Is. Mar. Labs. Carib. 10th Meet. (Abstr.)*.

Fishelson, L. (1970). *Nature (London)* **227**, 90.

Gerber, R. P., and Marshall, N. (1974). *Limnol. Oceanogr.* **19**, 815.

Goldman, B., and Talbot, F. H. In preparation.

Gordon, D. C., Jr., Fournier, R. O., and Kransnick, G. K. (1971). *Pac. Sci.,* **25**, 228.

Gosline, W. A. (1971). *Pac. Sci.* **25**, 282.

Gosline, W. A., and Brock, V. E. (1965). "Handbook of Hawaiian Fishes." Univ. Hawaii Press, Honolulu.

Greenfield, D. W. (1968). *Syst. Zool.* **17,** 76.

Hairston, N. G., Smith, F. E., and Slobodkin, L. G. (1960). *Amer. Natur.* **94,** 421.

Hardy, A. (1959). "The Open Sea. Its Natural History," Part II. Collins, London.

Hayne, D. W., and Ball, R. C. (1956). *Limnol. Oceanogr.* **1,** 162.

Helfrich, P., and Townsley, S. J. (1961). *Proc. Pac. Sci. Congr. 10th, 1960* p. 39.

Herre, A. W. (1953). *Fish Wildl. Serv. (U.S.), Res. Rep.* **20,** 1.

Hiatt, R. W., and Strasburg, D. W. (1960). *Ecol. Monogr.,* **30,** 65.

Hobson, E. S. (1965). *Copeia* No. 3, 291.

Hobson, E. S. (1968). *Bur. Sport Fish. Wildl. (U.S.), Res. Rep.* **73,** 1.

Hobson, E. S. (1972). *U.S. Fish Wildl. Serv. Fish. Bull.* **70,** 715.

Hobson, E. S. (1974). *U.S. Fish Wildl. Serv. Fish. Bull.* **72,** 915.

Johannes, R. E., Coles, S. L., and Kuenzel, N. T. (1970). *Limnol. Oceanogr.* **15,** 579.

Johnson, R. G. (1970). *Amer. Natur.* **104,** 285.

Jones, R. S. (1968). *Micronesica* **4,** 309.

Jordan, C. F. (1971). *J. Ecol.* **59,** 127.

Karplus, I., Tsurnamal, M., and Szelp, R. (1972). *Mar. Biol.* **17,** 275.

Low, R. M. (1971). *Ecology* **52,** 648.

MacArthur, R. H. (1965). *Biol. Rev. Cambridge Phil. Soc.* **40,** 510.

MacArthur, R. H. (1969a). *Biol. J. Linn. Soc.* **1,** 19.

MacArthur, R. H. (1969b). *Proc. Nat. Acad. Sci. U.S.* **64,** 1369.

MacArthur, R. H., Recher, H., and Cody, M. (1966). *Amer. Natur.* **100,** 319.

Margalef, R. (1968). "Perspectives in Ecological Theory." Univ. of Chicago Press, Chicago, Illinois.

Marsh, J. A. (1970). *Ecology* **51,** 255.

Marshall, N. B. (1965). "The Life of Fishes." Weidenfeld & Nicholson, London.

Marshall, T. C. (1964). "Fishes of the Great Barrier Reef and Adjacent Waters of Queensland." Angus & Robertson, Sydney, Australia.

Maxwell, W. G. H. (1968). "Atlas of the Great Barrier Reef." Amer. Elsevier, New York.

Menzel, D. W. (1959). *J. Cons., Cons. Perm. Int. Explor. Mer.* **24,** 308.

Motoda, S. (1940). *Palau Trop. Biol. Stat. Stud.* **2,** 61.

Munro, I. S. R. (1964). *Papua New Guinea Agr. J.* **16,** 141.

Munro, I. S. R. (1967). "The Fishes of New Guinea." Dep. Agr. Stock Fish., Pt. Moresby, New Guinea.

Myreburg, A. A., Jr. (1972). *Behaviour* **41,** 207.

Odum, H. T., and Odum, E. P. (1955). *Ecol. Monogr.* **25,** 291.

Ogden, J. C., and Buckman, N. S. (1973). *Ecology* **54,** 589.

Paine, R. T. (1966). *Amer. Natur.* **100,** 65.

Pianka, E. R. (1966). *Amer. Natur.* **100,** 33.

Popper, D., and Fishelson, L. (1973). *J. Exp. Zool.* **184,** 409.

Potts, G. W. (1970). *J. Zool.* **161,** 223.

Quast, J. C. (1968). *Calif. Fish Game* **139,** 57.

Randall, J. E. (1955a). *Pac. Sci.* **9,** 359.

Randall, J. E. (1955b). *Pac. Sci.* **9,** 396.

Randall, J. E. (1955c). *Zoologica (New York)* **40,** 149.

Randall, J. E. (1956). *Pac. Sci.* **10,** 159.

Randall, J. E. (1960). *Pac. Sci.* 14, 267.
Randall, J. E. (1961a). *Copeia* No. 2, p. 237.
Randall, J. E. (1961b). *Proc. Gulf. Carib. Fish. Inst., 14th Annu. Sess.* p. 201.
Randall, J. E. (1962). *Proc. Gulf Carib. Fish Inst., 15th Annu. Sess.* p. 155.
Randall, J. E. (1963). *Carib. J. Sci.* 3, 31.
Randall, J. E. (1967). *Stud. Trop. Oceanogr.* 5, 665.
Randall, J. E. (1974). *Proc. Int. Coral Reef Symp. 2nd 1973, Great Barrier Reef Cte.* 1, 159.
Randall, J. E., and Brock, V. E. (1960). *Trans. Amer. Fish. Soc.* 89, 9.
Randall, J. E., and Hartman, W. D. (1968). *Mar. Biol.* 1, 216.
Randall, J. E., and Randall, H. A. (1960). *Bull. Mar. Sci. Gulf Carib.* 10, 444.
Rasa, O. A. E. (1969). *Z. Tierpsychol.* 26, 825.
Reese, E. S. (1964). *Oceanogr. Mar. Biol. Annu. Rev.* p. 455.
Robertson, D. R. (1972). *Science* 177, 1007.
Robertson, D. R. (1973). *Z. Tierpsychol.* 32, 319.
Russell, B. C. (1971). M.Sc. Thesis, University of Auckland, New Zealand.
Russell, B. C. (1975). *Helgolaender Wiss. Meersunters.* 27, 298.
Russell, B. C., Talbot, F. H., and Domm, S. (1974). *Proc. Int. Coral Symp. 2nd 1973, Great Barrier Reef, Cte.* 1, 207.
Russell, B. C., Goldman, B., and Talbot, F. H. In preparation.
Salmon, M., Winn, H. E., and Sargente, N. (1968). *Pac. Sci.* 22, 11.
Sanders, H. L. (1968). *Amer. Natur.* 102, 243.
Sargent, M. C., and Austin, T. S. (1949). *Trans. Amer. Geophys. Union* 30, 245.
Schroeder, R. E. (1967). "Something Rich and Strange." G. Allen & Unwin, London.
Schultz, L. P. *et al.* (1953). *U.S., Nat. Mus., Bull.* 202.
Schultz, L. P. *et al.* (1960). *U.S., Nat. Mus., Bull.* 202.
Schultz, L. P. *et al.* (1966). *U.S., Nat. Mus., Bull.* 202.
Smith, J. L. B. (1966). *Rhodes Univ. Ichthyol. Bull.* 32, 635.
Smith, J. L. B., and Smith, M. M. (1963). "The Fishes of Seychelles." Rhodes University, Grahamstown, South Africa.
Smith, C. L., and Tyler, J. C. (1972). *Bull. Nat. Hist. Mus. Los Angeles* 14, 125.
Smith, C. L., and Tyler, J. C. (1973a). *Amer. Mus. Nov.* (2528), 1.
Smith, C. L., and Tyler, J. C. (1973b). *Helgolaender Wiss. Meeresunters.* 24, 264.
Springer, V. C., and McErlean, A. J. (1962). *Amer. Midl. Natur.* 67, 386.
Starck, W. A. (1968). *Undersea Biol.* 1, 5.
Starck, W. A., and Davis, W. P. (1966). *Ichthyologica* 38, 313.
Stephenson, W., and Searles, R. B. (1960). *Aust. J. Mar. Freshwater Res.* 11, 241.
Steven, G. A. (1930). *J. Mar. Biol. Ass.* 16, 677.
Stoddart, D. R. (1969). *Biol. Rev. Cambridge Phil. Soc.* 44, 433.
Suyehiro, Y. (1942). *Jap. J. Zool.* 10, 1–303.
Talbot, F. H. (1960). *Ann. S. Afr. Mus.* 45, 549.
Talbot, F. H. (1964). *Trans. Roy. Soc. S. Afr.* 34, 387.
Talbot, F. H. (1965). *Proc. Zool. Soc. London.* 145, 431.
Talbot, F. H. (1970). *Rep. Aust. Acad. Sci.* 12, 43.
Talbot, F. H., and Goldman, B. (1972). *Proc. Symp. Corals and Coral Reefs, 1969 Mar. Biol. Ass. India,* p. 245.
Vine, P. J. (1974). *Mar. Biology* 24, 131.
Vivien, M. L. (1973). *Tethys (Suppl.)* 5, 221.

Vivien, M. L., and Peyrot-Clausade, M. (1974). *Proc. Int. Coral Reef Symp. 2nd 1973, Great Barrier Rf. Cte.* **1**, 179.

Weber, M., and De Beaufort, L. F. (1911–1953). "The Fishes of the Indo-Australian Archipelago," Vol. 1ff. E. J. Brill, Leiden.

Wells, J. W. (1957). *Geol. Soc. Amer., Mem.* **67**, 609.

Williams, F. (1959). *Ann. Mag. Natur. Hist.* [13] **2**, 92.

Winn, H. E., and Bardach, J. E. (1960). *Zoologica (New York)* **45**, 29.

Winn, H. E., Salmon, M., and Roberts, N. (1964). *Z. Tierpsychol.* **21**, 798.

5

TOXICITY OF CORAL REEF FISHES

Ann M. Cameron

I. Introduction

Correlated with the widespread appreciation that within coral reef systems marine species diversity reaches its maximum is the notion that toxic species are relatively more common in this environment than they are elsewhere. Data supporting this notion can be found in works by Halstead (1965, 1967, 1970), Bakus (1969, 1971), and Bakus and Green (1974). Apparently, there are factors involved that promote the elaboration of toxins by coral reef organisms belonging to many and diverse taxa (see Chapters 5 and 6 in Volume II: Biology 1 of this treatise). This contribution will attempt to define the toxicity strategies adopted by coral reef fishes and to account for differences in these strategies. In what follows, only those toxins elaborated by the fishes themselves will be involved in the discussion. Phenomena associated with ciguatera toxin (and allied toxins) are described by Banner (Chapter 6).

A biological toxin may be defined as a substance having a deleterious effect on an organism other than the one that produced it. Such toxins are distinguishable functionally by their offensive or defensive natures. Offensive toxins are exemplified by the prey-immobilizing venoms of the many species of the gastropod family Conidae and by many coelenterate venoms. Although occasions arise when these venoms function defensively, especially when the animals are disturbed by man, their primary biological role is the paralysis and/or killing of prey. Defensive toxins on the other hand, act against only those organisms posing some threat to the toxic species. As far as is known, all fish toxins are defensive in nature. It is conventional to categorize two types of fish toxins identified by the mechanisms whereby the toxic materials reach their sites of action. The first and best known type is venom. Venoms are injected into the threatening organisms and are therefore always associated with some form of puncturing device, usually dorsal and/or anal and/or ventral fin spines. It is generally believed that they are defensive against predators although this has rarely been demonstrated in the field.

The second, and less well-known type of fish toxin, has been termed crinotoxin by Halstead (1970). Crinotoxins are toxic skin secretions produced by epidermal glands, either dispersed over the body surface of the fish (the usual condition) or localized. They are never associated with any puncturing device and are therefore not injected into other organisms. Crinotoxins have been little studied but it is probable that they are defensive not only against predators but also against a range of organisms, which could include viruses, bacteria, and the generative forms of attached benthic species (Cameron and Endean, 1973); that is, it is postulated that they are antibiotic in the widest sense (see Burkholder, 1973).

It is important that both venoms and crinotoxins of fishes are elaborated by epidermal glands (Quay, 1972; Cameron and Endean, 1972a, 1973). It is the outer, protective skin barrier of fishes that has mobilized its glandular potential for the production of these toxins inimical to other forms of life. Location of an antibiotic insurance close to the surface would appear to be a strategy adopted by a wide range of coral reef organisms.

Only teleost fishes are included in this paper. It is well known that many stingrays, for example, are venomous and that several agnathans possess crinotoxins. To have included such "fishes" would have detracted from the value of the teleosts as a group within which comparisons might be made among families and species of toxic coral reef fishes.

II. Venomous Fishes

No attempt will be made to list the venomous fishes known to occur on coral reefs since there are adequate reviews from which these data can be extracted (e.g., Halstead, 1970). Instead, an attempt will be made, using representatives of several families, to determine whether venomousness is a significant feature of coral reef fish faunas. Given that the venomous condition is a predator deterrent, it must be evaluated against other defense mechanisms evoked by the threat of predation. These can be imagined to include rapid swimming, schooling, possession of pungent spines, possession of scales, and the adoption of retiring habits among and within coral formations. Several such structures and behaviors are variously combined in the majority of coral reef teleost fishes as defense mechanisms. Only relatively few coral reef teleosts, however, utilize venomousness as a defense mechanism.

As far as is known, all the venom glands of teleost fishes are derivatives and elaborations of the epidermal epithelium (Quay, 1972; Cameron and Endean, 1972a). The glands are associated with pungent spines that are variously modified for the injection process. Each spine typically has a pair of venom glands located toward its distal end and penetration of the spine is accompanied by tearing of the integumentary sheath allowing the venom to dribble into the wound. In the venomous batrachoidids (e.g., *Thalassophryne*) the venom glands are situated at the bases of the spines, which are hollow. In these fishes venom can be ejected by application of pressure to the spine bases. Only in stonefishes of the genus *Synanceia* has there developed a venom apparatus that delivers the entire contents of each venom gland in a single burst in an all-or-none fashion (Endean, 1961). Since this arrangement, together with the high toxicity of the venom itself, appears to be the ultimate in venomous specialization among teleost fishes, it is a convenient starting point.

A. FAMILY SYNANCEIIDAE

Stonefishes are scorpaenoids representing the ultimate among teleost fishes not only in venomousness but also in stationariness (Cameron, 1974). A stationary species is one that is sessile, sedentary, or site attached, possession of a home range or territory being included in the category of site attached. It injects more venom than does any other fish venom apparatus and the venom itself appears to be more potent than any other fish venom. Although the data on the venom relate principally to laboratory animals and to man, these are all vertebrates as are the potential predators of stonefishes (sharks, fishes, sea snakes) and it can be expected that the venom would affect the actual predators adversely. Of significance is the pain induced in human victims of stonefish envenomation. It is recognized as excrutiating. If the venom elicits comparable sensations in potential predators of stonefishes, the pain producing components of the venom have evident selective advantage. Unfortunately, no information is available on the deterrent effectiveness of *Synanceia* venom under natural (field) conditions. With respect to their stationariness, stonefish are sedentary, that is, they remain in the same position, on the substratum, for long periods of time. It is postulated that it was the evolution and subsequent sophistication of the venom apparatus that enabled stonefishes to exploit a stationary mode of life. Camouflage must have evolved along with the venom apparatus as the life style of these fishes became more and more bottom fixed. Detection of the stonefish by its prey species is hindered and these small prey species (fishes and crustaceans) are ingested by the stonefish when they, the prey, swim past. Hence, although stonefishes superficially seem to occur in any rubble area of reef, their distribution as individuals is undoubtedly influenced by the spatial distributions of their prey species, which are not actively searched for by the stonefish. It would appear that as the deterrent effectiveness of the venom apparatus of the evolving stonefishes became more pronounced, certain elements lost their selective advantage. Thus, the venom glands of the anal and ventral fin spines, so typical of scorpaenoids (Cameron and Endean, 1966) became nonfunctional (Endean, 1961). It is postulated that this was occasioned by the development of the digging behavior correlated with increasing sedentariness. Functional loss of those elements of the scorpaenoid venom apparatus effectively inactivated by burial attests to the sedentary mode of life of these coral reef fishes.

Concurrently, with the adoption by stonefishes of extreme sedentary habits, the scales were lost. This phenomenon of scale loss in fishes has been discussed in relation to the topic of Section III (crinotoxic fishes) by Cameron and Endean (1973) but will be elaborated on here because it seems pertinent to toxicity in coral reef fishes and to the stonefishes *Synanceia verrucosa* and *Synanceia trachynis*, in particular. Although the evolution of the stonefish venom apparatus enabled the fishes to exploit a strategy of stationariness, a point must have been reached when a compromise was made with either the degree of sedentariness or the degree of reduction of squammation. Presumably, with their overlapping integumentary pockets, the scales were prone to fouling with bottom material. This would have presented an extreme hazard as an ideal environment for potential pathogens. Possibly, this endowed scalelessness with selective advantage. Whatever the reason, the scales were lost (another adaptation increasing the necessity of remaining in one place if scales are protective against predators) and the dermis was thickened with collagen, the whole integument being adorned with tough papillae. However, as a result of the progressive loss of scales, the outer integumentary barrier of the animal became more exposed to the biota of the environment. Concurrent with scale loss, development of the venom apparatus, and adoption of sedentary habits, the toxic glandular potential of the epidermis was selected as a specialization against the biotic elements of the immediate vicinity of the integument (see Section III).

Many organisms, however, do invade the integument of stonefishes. Endean (1961) noted that the true colors of *Synanceja* (*sic*) can be seen only after removal of the algal coating and observed (1969, p. 21) "algae, detritus and small sedentary animals such as hydrozoans and polyzoans" adhering to *S. verrucosa* and *S. trachynis*. [See Eschmeyer and Rao (1973) for interpretation of the spelling of the genus *Synanceia* Bloch and Schneider.] Nematode worms and bacteria are additional components of the epifauna of *S. trachynis* (A. M. Cameron, unpublished observations). Fishelson (1973, p. 498) recorded "algae, hydrozoans, diatomeans and other organisms" contributing to the ballast accumulated by the integument of *Inimicus filamentosus* and *S. verrucosa*. Remarkably, but not uniquely among teleosts, stonefishes have the ability to slough off the outer layer of cells penetrated by the fouling organisms with the result that the accumulated ballast is discarded (Fishelson, 1973). This adaptation further attests to the extremely stationary mode of life of stonefishes.

Other coral reef synanceiid scorpaenoids of genera such as *Inimicus* and *Minous* are reputed to be venomous, but little is known of the nature of the venom apparatus in specifically coral reef forms.

B. FAMILY SCORPAENIDAE

Scorpaenids are a widespread family of carnivorous fishes and several species are usually found to occur in any coral reef system. For example, there are about 11 scorpaenid species in the waters of the Great Barrier Reef (Marshall, 1964). Since the family is not often treated in systematic reviews, there are probably many undescribed species, especially in areas remote from intensive collecting. Because no scorpaenid so far examined has lacked a venom apparatus, it can be assumed that possession of this defense mechanism is a family characteristic. The typical life style is site attachment to an area on the bottom, the fishes remaining immobile for extended periods but not being as sedentary as the stonefish *Synanceia*. An extremely interesting case of a venomous coral reef scorpaenid, *Sebastapistes bynaensis*, being mimicked by a fish of the family Serranidae, *Centrogenys vaigiensis*, was described by Whitley (1935). The mimicry is so successful (in confusing human observers) that, despite the merely superficial anatomical resemblance of the mimic to the facies of the Scorpaenidae it, the serranid mimic, has been described several times as a new species of scorpaenid. Whitley's comment (1935, p. 347) that this fish is "the *pons asinorum* of ichthyology" seems appropriate. In view of the fact that Halstead and Mitchell (1963) listed the family Serranidae among fishes reputed to be venomous, it would be interesting to know whether *C. vaigiensis* (the mimic) possesses a venom apparatus and whether the mimic actually has a life style similar to that of its model (*S. bynaensis*). That is, can the mimicry be described as Müllerian or Batesian?

A very different life style from the typical has been adopted by scorpaenid fishes of the genus *Pterois* (and closely related genera). Much has been written about *Pterois volitans*, the gorgeously colored and patterned coral reef fire fish that is a popular aquarium subject, despite its venom apparatus consisting of dorsal, anal, and ventral fin spines, each with paired venom glands. Of all venomous fishes, these are the only ones that significantly threaten intruders, the behavior being that of turning the body so that the extremely long dorsal spines are oriented toward the disturbing influence. This behavior appears to emphasize the message conveyed by the striking color pattern, which is presumably warning in nature and is atypical of scorpaenids. Although these fishes do not rest on the bottom as do other scorpaenids, they are site attached, if not territorial. Since potential predators abound in the general environment, it must be assumed that they learn to avoid *Pterois* by reception of the signals described. Again, it is the possession of a venom apparatus that has enabled these fishes to exploit a relatively stationary mode of life. Their particular refinement has been advertisement of their venomous nature, a phenomenon widespread in some groups of venomous and distasteful animals, e.g., venomous snakes and distasteful insects.

Scorpaenoids (including stonefishes) are the fishes possessing the most advanced type of venom apparatus and it is interesting that it is among the coral reef forms, rather than those of more temperate environments, that two contrasting life styles have been selected: the camouflaged sedentary type exemplified by *Synanceia* and the brilliantly advertised station-keeping type epitomized by *Pterois*.

Whereas no coral reef scorpaenid is known to be common, some temperate species of *Sebastes, Sebastodes,* and *Sebastolobus* are so common as to "constitute an important part of the offshore fishery of the Pacific coast" (of North America) according to Roche and Halstead (1972, p. 6). It is noteworthy that many of these common temperate rockfish, or rock cod as they are known, are less venomous than are the relatively less common, predominantly tropical species (Roche and Halstead, 1972).

C. Family Teuthididae

Teuthidids (or siganids as they are widely known) are very common herbivores on coral reefs and, in fact, are characteristic elements of the coral reef fish fauna of the Indo-West Pacific region, there being 10–20 species in Great Barrier Reef waters. Many species, for example *Teuthis lineatus, Teuthis oramin,* and *Teuthis chrysospilos* can be seen frequently feeding in mixed aggregations with various species of parrot fish on the reef crest and beachrock areas of sand cays of the Great Barrier Reef. In general, the schooling species are less brightly colored than are those, such as *Teuthis vulpinus,* in which site attachment is more pronounced. Teuthidids are much more common in coral reef waters than are the more stationary scorpaenids and stonefishes. Their venom apparatus, which consists of the pungent dorsal, anal, and ventral fin spines and the twin venom glands associated with each of these spines, is probably a defense mechanism against potential predation during the most vulnerable periods of the fishes' activity, e.g., when grazing or sleeping. As mentioned, grazing is often performed in company with parrot fishes and it would be interesting to know whether the parrot fishes among which the teuthidids school are afforded any protection by the presence of the venomous teuthidids. Several teuthidids are known to sleep in exposed positions, with the pungent fin spines erected (Figs. 1 and 2). This posture would enhance the deterrent effectiveness of the venom apparatus towards nocturnal predators.

Histologically, the venom glands of teuthidids are remarkably similar to those of scorpaenids. Venom granules similar to those described in

Fig. 1. Nighttime photograph of *Teuthis corallinus* asleep in exposed location on Heron Reef. The fish is approximately 150 mm in total length. Photograph courtesy of D. R. Robertson.

Fig. 2. Similar photograph of *Teuthis vulpinus*. The specimen is approximately 100 mm in total length. Photograph courtesy of D. R. Robertson.

the venom glands of the scorpaenid *Notesthes robusta* by Cameron and Endean (1966) are elaborated by the venom glands of *T. lineatus, T. oramin, T. chrysospilos,* and *T. vulpinus* (A. M. Cameron, unpublished), all of which are coral reef species. Human envenomation by teuthidids can result in severe pain.

D. FAMILY PLOTOSIDAE

The plotosid catfish *Plotosus lineatus* occurs on coral reefs of the Indo-West Pacific region frequently in great spherical shoals of juveniles, the shoals reaching the order of one meter in diameter. The species is also common in coastal (nonreef) waters from east Africa to the Indo-Australian archipelago. Both adults and juveniles possess an elaborate venom apparatus, paired glands being associated with the single dorsal spine and each of the two pectoral spines. Except when the juveniles swim in shoals, the species is typically a bottom dweller. The longitudinal yellow stripes possessed by the juveniles are very prominent and may serve as a warning. They become less pronounced as the fishes increase in size. The shoal formation of juveniles in coral reef waters is probably a defense mechanism in that potential predators are confronted with very many venomous spines at any angle of approach. It has been postulated (Knipper, 1953, 1955) that these schools of juvenile *P. lineatus* mimic the long spined echinoid *Diadema* but this is difficult to conceive for the meter-diameter schools. Magnus (1967) disagreed with Knipper's view.

Many species of catfish have been shown to be venomous (Halstead, 1970). Within the group, members of the genus *Plotosus* are recognized to possess the most specialized form of venom apparatus. The paired venom glands, although formed from the epidermis, have migrated toward the spine and form plaques of glandular tissue very closely applied to the spine. Catfishes are a major group of fresh water fishes although many are estuarine. The catfish found on coral reefs is *P. lineatus,* the one with the most sophisticated venom apparatus possessed by any member of the group.

E. FAMILY BATRACHOIDIDAE

Batrachoidids of the genera *Thalassophryne* and *Daector* are distinguished from all other fishes (as far as is known) by the possession of fin spines perforated for the passage of venom (Bean and Weed, 1910; Collette, 1966). Anatomically, this is the most highly developed venom apparatus among fishes but, if potency of venom is taken into account as well, it must be considered that the stonefishes, the grooved spines of which are so modified as to almost entirely enclose the venom glands, possess the most efficient venom apparatus among fishes. The venomous batrachoidids are confined to the Atlantic Ocean, Caribbean Sea, and East Pacific and some occur on coral reefs in these regions. None of the Indo-West Pacific batrachoidids, including such Barrier Reef forms as *Halophryne,* is venomous (Cameron and Endean, 1972b). Batrachoidids are bottom dwellers, rivaling scorpaenoids in their sedentariness and camouflage.

F. FAMILY BLENNIIDAE

"Poison-fang" blennies of the genus *Meiacanthus* are distinguished from all other fishes (as far as is known) by the possession of grooved fangs by means of which venom is injected into other organisms. There are two fangs, a canine tooth on each side of the lower jaw. A gland is situated in a depression of the dentary and in the basal portion of the groove, which is on the anterior surface of the canine (Springer and Smith-Vaniz, 1972). A milky liquid was expressed from the gland by these authors, who also studied histological preparations of the gland. They considered the granules elaborated by the secretory cells to be similar to those of the stonefish venom glands as described by Endean (1961). A toxic response was evoked by allowing *Meiacanthus nigrolineatus* to bite one of the workers but little pain was felt. In contrast, Losey (1972) felt immediate pain not unlike that of a mild bee sting in severity after being bitten by *Meiacanthus atrodorsalis.* From Springer and Smith-Vaniz's (1972) account of the complex of mimetic relationships in which *Meiacanthus* species are involved and from their experiments on predation of the models and the mimics, it is probable that the grooved canines and their associated glands are a defensive venom apparatus. Losey (1972) has also reported on this interesting mimic situation within the family Blenniidae and described experiments that indicate that the venom apparatus of *M. atrodorsalis* is probably defensive against predators. It is possible, however, that this is the unique fish venom apparatus being part of a prey catching, i.e., offensive mechanism. According to Springer and Smith-Vaniz (1972) some blenniidid mimic situations have resulted in confused human observers, and hence in incorrect identification of species involved in mimic complexes. *Meiacanthus* are tropical, reef-dwelling blennies. They usually possess refuges, that is, they are site attached and comparatively uncommon.

Additional data on the cytology and histology of the venom glands of *M. nigrolineatus* were provided by Fishelson (1974). Because they are ductless, subdivided into lobes by connective tissue septa, and function as aggregations of unicellular holocrine glands discharging their secretory products into intercellular spaces, these glands are similar to the axillary glands of the catfish *Cnidoglanis macrocephalus* as described by Cameron and Endean (1971). In view of the predominantly proteinaceous nature of gland cells that produce fish poisons and venoms (Cameron and Endean, 1973) Fishelson's (1974, p. 391) preliminary histochemical finding that mature venom cells of *M. nigrolineatus* exhibit "a strong PAS-reaction" warrants confirmation.

G. Family Acanthuridae

Many people believe that surgeon fishes are venomous but as yet there has been no demonstration of a venom apparatus in an *adult* surgeon fish. It is probable that the extreme severity of wounds inflicted on humans by the caudal spines of acanthurids has contributed to the undeserved venomous reputations of many surgeon fishes. Nonetheless, juveniles of one species, *Prionurus microlepidotus*, and acronurus larvae of another, *Acanthurus triostegus sandvicensis*, possess venomous fin spines (Tange, 1955; Randall, 1961). It would appear that venomousness in surgeon fishes is a larval and/or juvenile adaptation in some species whereas the prominent adult defensive apparatus is the caudal spines (lances).

Surgeon fishes are common coral reef herbivores. Some species, in general the more brightly colored ones, possess territories and others, less brightly colored, are schooling species.

H. Doubtful Cases

There are numerous reports scattered through a voluminous literature that members of the families Holocentridae, Parapercidae, Uranoscopidae, and others are venomous. Most of these reports are without evidence of the presence of venom glands and consideration of them must be held in abeyance until such data are collected. Many species within these families are coral reef forms.

III. Crinotoxic Fishes

This section deals with toxins elaborated in the skins of fishes but not associated in any way with any form of puncturing apparatus that could introduce them into recipient organisms. The toxins must exert their effects *in situ*, in the immediate vicinity of the fish, or in the mouths of predatory enemies. A few of these toxins are liberated from glands situated subepidermally and possessing ducts but most of them, being stored within cells of the epidermis, are released only after the epidermis has been damaged. Such damage may be caused by mechanical abrasion and also may be effected by invasion of the skin by fungal hyphae, for example, or by secondary viral or bacterial involvement.

In a survey of the literature on occurrence of skin toxins in fishes, Cameron and Endean (1973) found that a preponderance of the families with crinotoxic representatives are basically tropical, many of the species being coral reef fishes. Further, it was found that many crinotoxic fishes exhibit a stationary, often sedentary, mode of life. A positive correlation was detected between crinotoxicity and reduction of squammation. Coral reef fishes live in an environment dominated by sessile (benthic, attached) organisms, the generative forms of which face the challenge of successful settlement. Further, the water and bottom sediments are rich in potentially pathogenic microorganisms. It is postulated that scales are a disadvantage to a sedentary coral reef fish and that epidermal toxins in such fish are chemical insurance against a multitude of potential invaders. For stationary, but not sedentary, coral reef fish, crinotoxins appear to be predator deterrents. Selection of those crinotoxic fishes mentioned here has been based on availability of data and on items of apparent relevance to the coral reef environment.

A. FAMILY SYNANCEIIDAE

Stonefishes were listed first in the discussion of venomous fishes and they occupy a place of particular importance in this section on crinotoxic fishes. Duhig and Jones (1928a,b) demonstrated that the tubercles that cover the body of *Synanceia* produce a toxin. The tubercles represent epidermal glands opening on papillae, the glands having no connection whatsoever with the venom apparatus already described. Nothing is known of the functions of these skin secretions but it may be profitable to indulge in a little speculation in the hope that this will be investigated. It was noted earlier that stonefishes have lost their scales. Direct exposure of the naked integument to the environment appears to have resulted from the threat of fouling of the scale pockets with bottom material but it posed the problem of attack by pathogens other than those eliminated by removal of the integumentary pockets. There must have been selective advantage in mobilization of the glandular potential of the epidermis for production of antibiotics (*sensu lato*). It seems highly probable that the skin secretions of stonefishes will be found to be inimical to some of the potentially dangerous organisms invading the immediate environment of the fishes' integument. It appears important to keep selective advantage in perspective in this discussion. It is not necessary to conceive of the skin toxin being lethal to every organism capable of a chance encounter with the integument of the stonefish. It need convey only a slight advantage by virtue of its toxicity to even one invader species to have been selected for. The possibilities are virtually endless and activity screening should be carried out with this in mind.

B. FAMILY OSTRACIONTIDAE

Coral reef boxfishes (e.g., *Ostracion lentiginosus*) elaborate a crinotoxin that has been studied from several angles (Boylan and Scheuer, 1967; Thomson, 1964, 1968). Although the mechanism of release of the toxin from the epidermal cells has not been satisfactorily explained (cf. Thomson, 1968), its potency has been well established. One major effect of possible relevance to the fishes in their coral reef environment is the lethal one toward other fishes. It is difficult, however, considering the dilution factor in the field, to imagine how the toxin could kill potential predators. Presumably it is distasteful as well as being biologically active systemically. As with almost all of these fish crinotoxins, we are in great need of rigorous behavioral and ecological data on the real situation. It can reasonably be supposed that the lethal effect of placing *newly captured O. lentiginosus* in aquaria with other fishes was produced by release of toxin from epidermal cells damaged by capture of the boxfish. In view of the widespread occurrence of ostraciotoxin (or closely related compounds) in the family and of the prevalence of the species on coral reefs, it appears that the toxin is a specialization evoked by the prevalence of predators in the coral reef environment. Whether it is antibiotic in other ways, we need to know.

C. FAMILY GRAMMISTIDAE

All six genera of grammistids are now known to have crinotixic species (Randall *et al.*, 1971). Most of the fishes are coral reef forms. There are some data supporting the view that the toxin produced by grammistids acts as a deterrent to predators. For example, Randall (1967) examined the food habits of West Indian coral reef fishes and found no soapfishes (*Rypticus*) in the stomachs of predators. In an aquarium test, *Grammistes sexlineatus*, a coral reef species, was introduced to

a container holding a scorpaenid, *P. volitans*. After pursuing the grammistid and seizing it in its jaws, the scorpaenid expelled it and made
further expelling movements of its jaws after the prey had been rejected.
It was suggested that a lingering bad taste was being experienced by
the scorpaenid (Randall *et al.*, 1971). For a distasteful secretion to
be deterrent to a predator, it must be released by the prospective prey,
perceived by the potential predator, and the prey rejected very quickly,
before the swallowing mechanism is activated. Thus the method whereby
the toxic skin secretion is released from the glands in the skin is of
interest. Many crinotoxins appear to be released from the individual
unicellular glands which produce them by mechanical damage to the
cells. However, multicellular epidermally derived glands with structural
ducts have been described in some grammistids as the source of the
skin toxin (Randall *et al.*, 1971). In such cases it is not clear whether
the applied pressure of the predator's jaws causes release of the toxin
or whether nervously mediated muscular contraction is involved. The
latter mechanism seems unlikely in view of the lack of an enveloping
muscular sheath around the glands described by Randall *et al.* (1971).
The multicellular grammistid glands are structurally different from the
clumps of intraepidermal toxin-secreting clavate cells of the ostraciontid,
Ostracion lentiginosus, described as multicellular glands by Thomson
(1968).

D. FAMILY TETRAODONTIDAE

Puffer fishes are well known for the presence of tetrodotoxin in their
viscera and according to Halstead (1970) there are 14 crinotoxic species,
the toxin being tetrodotoxin or something similar chemically. However,
in only one species has the glandular source of the toxin been located
in the integumentary epidermis. The family as a whole is tropical to
warm-temperate basically in distribution and many species are coral
reef forms.

E. FAMILIES LABRIDAE AND SCARIDAE

Wrasses (Labridae) and parrot fish (Scaridae) are abundant coral
reef fishes of closely related families, each family represented by many
species. For example, in the waters of Heron Reef, Capricorn Group,
Great Barrier Reef there are approximately 40 species of labrid and
20 species of scarid. Scarids are herbivorous, grazing the low algal turf
that grows on most exposed surfaces of coral reefs. Labrids are basically
carnivorous but exhibit a great diversity of life styles within this general

category. For example, some labrids of the genus *Labroides* are "cleaner fishes."

Many labrids and scarids have evolved an interesting protective device operative during their sleeping periods at night. Discrete opercular glands secrete a "mucus" cocoon (Casimir, 1967) inside which the fishes sleep (Winn, 1955). It has been shown that the mucus cocoons in which some parrot fishes sleep probably protect them from predation by eels (Winn and Bardach, 1959). From the data provided by Casimir (1971) on the nature of the opercular glands that produce the sleeping cocoons of 13 labrids and 23 scarids it appears that the mucus probably contains toxic components in the form of tyrosine-containing glycoproteins secreted by granular cells distinct from those which elaborate the mucus. It is suggested here that the protection from predation observed by Winn and Bardach (1959) is more likely to be afforded by crinotoxins associated with the sleeping cocoons of these fishes, than by any mechanical properties of the cocoons.

F. Families Aluteridae, Canthigasteridae, and Diodontidae

Little is known of the crinotoxins of these fishes so far located in *Alutera scripta, Canthigaster jactator, Canthigaster rivulatus,* and *Diodon hystrix* (Halstead, 1970). However, it is well known that many plectognaths possess toxic musculature and/or viscera and discussion of the toxicity of these fishes, which are coral reef forms, has been related principally to the visceral toxins. Nonetheless, the argument that these toxins are predator deterrents is augmented by the discovery of skin toxins in the same fishes. Data pertaining to a fascinating mimic situation between *Canthigaster valentini* (the toxic model) and *Paraluteres prionurus* (the mimic) were presented by Tyler (1966). The degree of visual similarity between these two fishes of different families is such that specimens of them have been wrongly catalogued in a prestigious museum. As far as human observers are concerned, it appears that the fishes are difficult to differentiate in the field, so closely does the mimic's behavior resemble that of the model. It is not unreasonable to assume therefore that potential predators have similarly been confused.

G. Family Soleidae

Clark and Chao (1973) discovered a crinotoxin in the flatfish *Pardachirus marmoratus*. It is produced by approximately 240 glands discharging via pores (from which the milky secretion can be expressed) at the bases of the dorsal and anal fin rays. The authors did not describe the histological organization of the glands except to comment that each is lined with folds "in which the toxin is produced" (p. 53). This observation suggests that their structure may be similar to that of catfish axillary glands (Cameron and Endean, 1971) and it is in agreement with Ochiai's (1963) depiction of fin ray glands in *P. pavonius*. However, although Clark and Chao (1973) noted that the genus *Pardachirus* Günther, 1862, is characterized by pores at the dorsal and anal fin ray bases (Günther, 1862, p. 478), Ochiai's (1963) diagnosis of the genus extended the distribution of such pores to the bases of the pelvic fin rays. From Clark and Chao's figure 3 (1973, p. 55), it would seem that the pores and their associated glands are absent from the ocular side pelvic fin. This point warrants clarification. Clark and Chao noted (1973, p. 53) that the crinotoxic glands of *P. marmoratus* "appear to be enlarged dermal mucous glands or modifications of the muscles controlling movements of the dorsal and anal fins." In view of the previously cited references to the epidermal nature of the venom and poison glands of fishes (Cameron and Endean, 1972a, 1973; Quay, 1972) the second suggestion as to the derivation of the crinotoxic glands of this flatfish by Clark and Chao (1973) appears improbable.

The fin gland secretion of *P. marmoratus* has not been analyzed, but was thought to be proteinaceous by Clark and Chao. They collected freshly expressed toxin from the skin of the flatfish by pipette and diluted it with seawater to concentrations of 1:200–1:1500. When placed in such dilutions of the secretion, three species of fishes (*Mugil* sp., *Dascyllus marginatus,* and *Bathygobius fuscus*) exhibited "almost immediate distress and died within 20 minutes" (Clark and Chao, 1973, p. 53).

In view of the presence of a confirmed crinotoxin in *P. marmoratus,* the existence of gland pores at the fin ray bases in all members of the genus *Pardachirus* and the bottom-dwelling mode of life of flatfishes in general, it is highly likely that a search for crinotoxins in such fishes, especially those inhabiting coral reef environments, will be rewarding.

IV. Discussion and Conclusions

In attempting to account for the prevalence of toxic organisms in coral reef waters and of venomous and poisonous teleost fishes in particular, it appears necessary, in the absence of many relevant data, to speculate on the biological roles of such toxins. No role other than that of defense has been postulated for fish toxins and most authors have cited predator pressure as the factor evoking selection for venomousness. There can be few organisms other than fishes (including elasmobranchs) that prey on adult fishes to a significant extent in coral reef waters although of course, many organisms other than fishes prey on larval and juvenile fishes. Coral reef waters typically support an average of 69% carnivorous fishes (Bakus, 1969). For example, data collected by Hiatt and Strasburg (1960) suggest that 67% of the 233 fish species they studied from the Marshall Islands were carnivorous. Of the species examined, 114 (49%) possessed fish remains in the gut or were observed to be piscivorous. Although Hiatt and Strasburg (1960) sampled only approximately one-third of the species present, their use of several collecting techniques including poisoning, explosives, spearing, and line fishing suggests that their sample is a representative one. Comparably, Randall (1967) found that of 212 West Indian reef species, 112 (53%) contained fish remains. This figure is slightly biased because the study concentrated deliberately on fishes of sporting value, but it is of the same order as that of Hiatt and Strasburg (1960). These data, and those presented by Bakus (1969) from other authors, indicate that predation on fishes in coral reef waters is extremely high. Consequently, the fishes can be expected to have evolved means of countering potential predation and toxicity appears to be an important strategy in this regard.

A remarkable aspect of coral reef fish toxicity is the difference in prevalence of the two toxicity strategies, venomousness and poisonousness. Although there are many species of venomous coral reef teleosts their numbers, relatively, are remarkably few in comparison with the total piscine fauna of coral reefs. For example, when it is considered that estimates of Great Barrier Reef fish species approximate 1500 (Marshall, 1964) and that it is only the large scorpaenoid group (about 20 Great Barrier Reef species) and the teuthidids (siganids with approximately 10–15 Great Barrier Reef species) that contribute significantly to the venomous aspect of toxicity occurrence in coral reef fishes, it is appreciated that coral reefs are not notable for the prevalence of venomous fishes. Presumably, the development of a venom apparatus involving toxin-secreting epidermal cells and fin spines has been so expensive energetically as to be a pathway available to only a few families of teleost fishes. As mentioned earlier, it is interesting that the venom apparatus of these two, major, disparate groups of fishes is startlingly uniform in gross anatomy and histological organization. Of the coral reef fish venoms so far studied, those of the scorpaenoids and teuthidids are noteworthy for the usually intense pain they induce in human victims of envenomation. It can be assumed that this effect is an important element in successful deterrence of potential predation.

Because of the relative paucity in numbers of venomous coral reef fishes it is probable that other antipredator devices have had greater selective advantage than venomousness has had among the many families of coral reef teleosts. One of these devices could be crinotoxicity. In comparison with venomous coral reef fishes, crinotoxic species are numerous and represent many families. Furthermore, the phenomenon has only recently begun to be investigated and it can be expected to be demonstrated in many more coral reef fishes closely related to those in which it is known to occur. As an antipredator device, especially for a small-sized fish that might be engulfed whole by a predator, a crinotoxin must be distasteful and fast acting. It appears that deterrent effectiveness would be maximized if the crinotoxins were located in single cells throughout the epidermis of the body surface so that capture of the toxic fish resulted in release of toxin from the damaged cells into the mouth of the predator immediately following its initial grasping bite. Such a disposition of the toxin-elaborating cells would obviate the need for a muscular sheath encapsulating a compound gland and an accompanying nervous mechanism for control of toxin release.

One explanation for the paucity of data on crinotoxins is that small-sized fishes, which constitute a large proportion of coral reef species, are not often viewed as potential food by people from whom many authentic toxicity reports about larger fishes have been collected, larger fishes being potentially more attractive as food both aesthetically and on the return-for-effort criterion. Hence, recorded distastefulness to man is a guide for estimation of the prevalence of toxicity for only those fishes of size and anatomy appropriate for human consumption. Historically experienced distastefulness and/or lethality resulting from consumption of toxic species can be remembered by prohibitions incorporated in traditional observances. For example, that crinotoxicity has been recognized since ancient times is illustrated by the biblical admonition against eating scaleless (and finless) fishes (Deut. 14:9 and 10). This is a reflection of the apparent positive correlation between crinotoxicity and reduction of squammation in fishes reported by Cameron and Endean (1973).

It is now being realized that many small-sized and peculiarly shaped "trash" fish provide a potentially valuable nutritional source for exploitation by man. They appear ideal for production of protein concentrates for human consumption and for manufacture of "fish meal" as stock food. The prevalence of crinotoxicity should be kept in mind in designing procedures for the utilization of trash fish as a source of human food or as a source of food for domestic animals. The fish must be detoxified of any materials potentially dangerous to man and/or his domestic animals. This caution would appear to be especially applicable to coral reef fishes.

The possibility that fish crinotoxins are antibiotic against organisms other then predators has been discussed. Antibiotic activity against a wide range of threatening organisms appears to be located in the superficial integument or outer covering of animals of many taxa (see Burkholder, 1973). This is indeed a logical place in which to expect it to be manifested, especially for sessile (fixed, benthic), sedentary (resting on the bottom), and site attached species. Its incidence in sedentary coral reef fishes might be expected to be more frequent than in other coral reef fishes less intimately associated with the microbiota and invertebrate larval population on the bottom. That crinotoxins are more common than venoms in coral reef fishes appears to be related to two things; crinotoxins cannot only be defenses against predators but also they are capable, because of their location on the integument of virtually the whole body surface, of adaptation to the function of antibiosis.

From what is known of the biology of the toxic species in the 16 families of coral reef fishes mentioned in this paper it can be said that only four families (Teuthididae, Acanthuridae, Labridae, and Scaridae) contain species in which individuals are known to be numerous enough to be called "common." (For reasons discussed earlier, one of these families, the Acanthuridae, could be omitted from the list of toxic fishes.) Further, species in these four families are typically more wide-ranging in their movements, that is, less stationary, than are species in the other families. Finally, the most toxic of the toxic species (stonefishes of the family Synanceiidae) are the most stationary, being actually sedentary for much of their time. Stationariness in general and its extreme form of sedentariness appear to be more common in coral reef fishes than in temperate fishes characterized as they are by a free swimming, pelagic mode of life. Thus it is suggested that toxicity is a strategy that has allowed many coral reef fishes to be relatively stationary (site attached) compared with species inhabiting more temperate waters. Available information suggests that toxic coral reef fishes are also relatively rare (uncommon) compared with fishes of more temperate waters but data that suggest that stonefishes, for example, are rare or uncommon are meager. Such data are, of course, more difficult to gather than are those indicating a species to be common. A collateral augmentation of the effects of toxicity on the biology of coral reef fishes is the occurrence of nontoxic mimics complicating predator–prey relationships. This aspect of fish toxicity should be further investigated.

Although fishes have provided many insights into pheromones, their chemical ecology is otherwise little understood. Nothing is known of the antibiotic relationships of coral reef fishes with the multitude of diverse organisms with which they are surrounded. Possibly an important facet of the relationships of rare and stationary fishes to their biotic environment is their possession of toxic epidermal secretions. Chemical and behavioral investigations of the venoms and skin toxins of coral reef fishes could elucidate some of these relationships. With the exception of fishes exhibiting ciguateratoxin and allied phenomena (see Chapter 6 by Banner), it seems that, in general, toxicity in the form of venousness and poisonousness is a strategy allowing some coral reef fishes to exploit a stationary mode of life. The possibility that rarity is linked in some way with stationariness seems worthy of investigation in toxic coral reef fishes. If a significant percentage of toxic coral reef fishes proves to be rare and stationary, we may gain insight into two things— the high incidence of toxicity in coral reef fishes, on the one hand, and the high species diversity of coral reef fishes, on the other. Grassle (1972, 1973) has indicated the advantages of rarity as a strategy in pre- dictable heterogeneous environments such as coral reefs and has postu- lated that the high species diversity of coral reefs is a reflection of the advantages of rarity. A rare species can specialize on smaller and smaller sections of the environmental patchwork mosaic that is characteristic of coral reefs, thereby avoiding interspecific competition. Where rarity is a common strategy, species diversity will be high. But what mechanisms operate to allow a species to be rare? I suggest that the adoption of sta- tionariness as a life style may allow species to be rare by facilitating specialization on small, narrowly prescribed sections of the environment that are themselves rare but predictable in occurrence. In as much as toxicity is a specialization against particular biotic elements of the environ- mental mosaic and is correlated with stationariness, so toxicity in many coral reef fishes may be a reflection of the advantages (for these species) of a "rare and stationary" life style in a predictable coral reef environ- ment. Within this context, however, it is not yet clear what role toxicity plays in the strategies of those teuthidids, acanthurids, and scarids that are numerically common.

A general theory of the incidence of toxicity in marine organisms cannot yet be presented but it seems that toxicity is correlated with stationariness in many coral reef organisms, sponges, corals, and holo- thurians being outstanding examples. Relative rarity or commonness of toxic coral reef species appears to depend on the scales of distribution of the resources exploited.

Acknowledgments

I thank R. Endean, K. Plowman, D. R. Robertson, and P. D. Dwyer for discussions of some of the ideas presented in this paper.

References

Bakus, G. J. (1969). *Int. Rev. Gen. Exp. Zool.* 4, 275.
Bakus, G. J. (1971). *In* "Toxins of Plant and Animal Origin" (A. De Vries and E. Kochva, eds.), pp. 57–62. Gordon & Breach, New York.
Bakus, G. J., and Green, G. (1974). *Science* 185, 951.
Bean, B. A., and Weed, A. C. (1910). *Proc. U.S. Nat. Mus.* 38, 511.
Boylan, D. B., and Scheuer, P. J. (1967). *Science* 155, 52.
Burkholder, P. R. (1973). *In* "Biology and Geology of Coral Reefs" (O. A. Jones and R. Endean, eds.), Vol. 2, pp. 117–176. Academic Press, New York.
Cameron, A. M. (1974). *In* "Proc. 2nd Int. Symp. Coral Reefs, 1972, Vol. 1" (A. M. Cameron, B. M. Campbell, A. B. Cribb, R. Endean, J. S. Jell, O. A. Jones, P. Mather, and F. II. Talbot, eds.), pp. 513–518, Great Barrier Reef Committee, Brisbane, Australia.
Cameron, A. M., and Endean, R. (1966). *Toxicon* 4, 111.
Cameron, A. M., and Endean, R. (1971). *Toxicon* 9, 345.
Cameron, A. M., and Endean, R. (1972a). *Toxicon* 10, 301.
Cameron, A. M., and Endean, R. (1972b). *Toxicon* 10, 335.
Cameron, A. M., and Endean, R. (1973). *Toxicon* 11, 401.
Casimir, M. J. (1967). *Naturwissenschaften* 54, 446.
Casimir, M. J. (1971). *Mar. Biol.* 8, 126.
Clark, E., and Chao, S. (1973). *Bull. Sea Fish. Res. Stat. Haifa, Isr.* 60, 53.
Collette, B. B. (1966). *Copeia* (4), 846.
Duhig, J. V., and Jones, G. (1928a). *Mem. Queensl. Mus.* 9, 136.
Duhig, J. V., and Jones, G. (1928b). *Aust. J. Exp. Biol. Med. Sci.* 5, 173.
Endean, R. (1961). *Aust. J. Mar. Freshwater Res.* 12, 177.
Endean, R. (1962). *Aust. Nat. Hist.* 14, 21.
Eschmeyer, W. N., and Rao, K. V. R. (1973). *Proc. Calif. Acad. Sci. 4th Ser.* 39, 337.
Fishelson, L. (1973). *Z. Zellforsch.* 140, 497.
Fishelson, L. (1974). *Copeia* (2), 386.
Grassle, J. F. (1972). *5th Eur. Symp. Mar. Biol., 1970*, pp. 19–26.
Grassle, J. F. (1973). *In* "Biology and Geology of Coral Reefs" (O. A. Jones and R. Endean, eds.), Vol. 2, pp. 247–270. Academic Press, New York.
Günther, A. (1862). "Catalogue of the Fishes in the British Museum," Vol. 4. British Museum (Natural History), London.
Halstead, B. W. (1965). "Poisonous and Venomous Marine Animals of the World," Vol. 1. U.S. Govt. Printing Office, Washington, D.C.
Halstead, B. W. (1967). "Poisonous and Venomous Marine Animals of the World," Vol. 2. U.S. Govt. Printing Office, Washington, D.C.
Halstead, B. W. (1970). "Poisonous and Venomous Marine Animals of the World," Vol. 3. U.S. Govt. Printing Office, Washington, D.C.

Halstead, B. W., and Mitchell, L. R. (1963). *In* "Venomous and Poisonous Animals and Noxious Plants of the Pacific Region" (H. L. Keegan and W. V. Macfarlane, eds.), pp. 173–202. Pergamon, Oxford.

Hiatt, R. W., and Strasburg, D. W. (1960). *Ecol. Monogr.* 30, 65.

Knipper, H. (1953). *Veröeff Ueberseemus. Bremen, Reihe A.* 3, 141.

Knipper, H. (1955). *Umschau* 55, 398.

Losey, G. S. (1972). *Pac. Sci.* 26, 129.

Magnus, D. B. E. (1967). *Verh. Deut. Zool. Ges.* p. 401.

Marshall, T. C. (1964). "Fishes of the Great Barrier Reef and Coastal Waters of Queensland." Angus & Robertson, Sydney, Australia.

Ochiai, A. (1963). "Fauna Japonica. Soleina (Pisces)." Biogeographical Society of Japan, Tokyo.

Quay, W. B. (1972). *Amer. Zool.* 12, 95.

Randall, J. E. (1961). *Pac. Sci.* 15, 215.

Randall, J. E. (1967). *Stud. Trop. Oceanogr.* 5, 665.

Randall, J. E., Aida, K., Hibiya, T., Mitsuura, N., Kamiya, H., and Hashimoto, Y. (1971). *Publ. Seto Mar. Biol. Lab.* 19, 157.

Roche, E. W., and Halstead, B. W. (1972). *Calif. Fish. Bull.* 156, 1.

Springer, V. G., and Smith-Vaniz, W. F. (1972). *Smithson. Contrib. Zool.* 112, 1.

Tange, Y. (1955). *Yokohama Med. Bull.* 6, 171.

Thomson, D. A. (1964). *Science* 146, 244.

Thomson, D. A. (1968). *In* "Drugs from the Sea" (H. D. Freudenthal, ed.), pp. 203–211. Mar. Technol. Soc., Washington, D.C.

Tyler, J. C. (1966). *Notulae Natur. Acad. Natur. Sci. Philadelphia* 386, 1.

Whitley, G. P. (1935). *Rec. S. Aust. Mus.* 5, 345.

Winn, H. E. (1955). *Zoologica (New York)* 40, 145.

Winn, H. E., and Bardach, J. E. (1959). *Ecology* 40, 296.

6

CIGUATERA: A DISEASE FROM CORAL REEF FISH

Albert H. Banner

I. Introduction

In association with coral reefs throughout the tropical world are fish which, if eaten, may cause illness or even death. The fish range from small herbivores to large reef carnivores and belong to many orders; even some invertebrates have been implicated. The disease, or diseases, for there may be more than one, is known as "ciguatera." One of the outstanding characteristics of the disease is its ecology, for the same group of species of fish varies in toxicity in both space and time. A fish that is favored from the waters of one island may be highly toxic in an adjacent island, or an island that has not harbored any toxic fish for as long as tradition remembers may within a year have "all of the fish" become toxic.

The toxicity of the fish must have been known to the island people long before the advent of western exploration, for soon after the explorers

177

ventured into the region of coral reefs they began to report serious, and even lethal, cases of ciguatera. In 1601 the Dutch at Mauritius reported the disease; in 1606 the men of the Spanish explorer de Quiros were afflicted in the New Hebrides. Probably the most accurate early account, related by several observers, was illness of the crew of Captain Cook's *Resolution* after eating some *pajaros* (probably the red snapper *Lutjanus*) in the New Hebrides in 1774; the entrails also killed one of the captive pigs aboard (Cook, 1777).

The name ciguatera reaches back at least to the nineteenth century, for Poey in 1866 defined the disease as one contracted from eating fish. The name had been applied earlier to an illness found in Cuba that resulted from eating the "cigua" or "sigua," a turban shell, *Livona* (*Turbo*) *pica* L., and then was extended to the disease produced by fish (see Halstead, 1965).

The historical records of the disease and, to a lesser extent, the modern records are confused by use of the single term ciguatera to apply to a series of diseases resulting from a multiplicity of toxins of varying action. Many earlier workers lumped under the term all intoxications that resulted from eating any marine fish or invertebrates; modern workers have differentiated clearly among many of these toxins (see Section II). Even more confusing is the fact that the fish that bear the principal toxin causing typical ciguatera may concurrently bear other toxins, as reported by Banner (1967), Hashimoto *et al.* (1969b), Hashimoto (1970), Li (1970), and Yasumoto *et al.* (1971). In the main discussion that follows reference will be largely confined to the principal toxin, named "ciguatoxin" by Scheuer *et al.* in 1967. A brief discussion of the other toxins associated with ciguatera will be presented in a separate section.

The symptoms of the disease are primarily neurological, although gastrointestinal symptoms, including nausea and diarrhea, may be the first to appear. The characteristic early symptoms include the tingling of the lips, mouth, and tongue, which may be extended to an intense itching of the skin. This last symptom is so pronounced in New Caledonia that the disease is known as "La Gratte." Exhaustion and muscular weakness, particularly of the legs, become progressively worse, and in more intense cases, partial to complete paralysis may result. Generalized aches and pains, visual disturbance, and an "inversion of the senses," in which cool objects are reported to feel hot, and hot objects cold, are common. Profuse sweating, a rapid but weak pulse, and a loss of reflexes are often noted. In acute cases, the loss of reflexes becomes more widespread, clonic and tonic convulsions occur, and muscular fasciculation may be pronounced. In these cases the patient often becomes comatose. Death, when it occurs, is the result of respiratory failure. The initial symptoms usually occur within six hours after ingesting the fish. Recovery may take months, and permanent damage has been recorded (see Halstead, 1967).

The severity of the attack naturally depends upon the amount of toxin ingested relative to body size; as shown below, the viscera contain relatively more toxin than does the flesh, and severe attacks usually result from eating liver and gonads.

The symptoms are not consistent (Banner and Helfrich, 1964, from Wake; Bagnis, 1968, from Tahiti). Bagnis reported that the gastrointestinal symptoms are more common in cases caused by herbivorous fishes and cardiovascular disorders and other symptoms in cases caused by carnivores. He suggested that this variability may be due to the presence of two or more toxins in the fish.

A person, once having suffered an attack of ciguatera, becomes sensitized in some fashion, so that he may have a recurrence of symptoms if he eats fish that do not cause symptoms in others. (How much of this is psychosomatic is problematical; the author has interviewed a physician in the New Hebrides who stated a patient had a recurrence of symptoms after eating canned sardines from the Mediterranean, and Australians who insist their symptoms recur after drinking beer.)

II. Differentiation among Marine Toxins

A large number of species of both fish and invertebrates, especially in the tropics, can cause intoxication when eaten. Only a few of these toxic forms have been studied in any detail; many of the reports are based on local knowledge and have never been actually observed by professionally trained personnel.

Most of the invertebrates found to be toxic have toxins that do not resemble ciguatoxin. These include such animals as the toxic sea anemone *Rhodactis howesi* Kent from Samoa (Martin, 1960), the crabs *Zozimus aeneus* (L.), *Platypodia granulosa* (Ruppell), and *Atergatis floridus* (L.) (Hashimoto, 1970, and other publications), and various mollusks.

However, ciguatera has been attributed to at least three pelecypods and one gastropod. The giant clam, *Tridacna maxima* Roding, was originally associated with ciguatera at Bora Bora, but Bagnis (1967) decided on the basis of the symptoms in two lethal cases that the causative toxin was not similar to ciguatoxin. Banner (1967) reported at least two toxins in this clam, but his preliminary chemical tests were not definitive. McFarren *et al.* (1965) reported that an oyster, *Crassostrea virginica* (Gmelin), and a clam, *Venus mercenaria campechiensis* [= *Mercenaria campechiensis* (Gmelin)], from coastal waters of Florida contained a toxin they described as "ciguatera-like" as it was lipoidal and caused similar symptoms in test animals; neither the chemistry nor the pharmacology was investigated further. They also reported a similar toxin from a concurrent bloom of the planktonic dinoflagellate *Gymnodinium breve* Davis. The third pelecypod reported to cause symptoms similar to ciguatera was a clam of the family Arcidae from Wake Island; it has never been studied and the report of its toxicity was merely from hospital records (Banner and Helfrich, 1964).

The gastropod that was thought possibly to harbor ciguatoxin or a related compound was one of the Pacific turban shells, *Turbo angyrostoma* L. This has been reported to be toxic, particularly from the Tuamotus and from Marcus as well as several other places in the Pacific by Hashimoto *et al.* (1970). They made initial studies on the nature of the toxins and found two, one water soluble and one lipoidal; the lipoidal toxin, although similar to ciguatoxin in its chemical solubilities, caused different reactions in the test animals. The authors concluded that it was not ciguatoxin.

The only other invertebrate suspected of bearing ciguatoxin is the short-spined sea urchin, *Tripneustes gratilla* (L.). Randall, working in the Societies in 1956, heard a report from the Tahitians that this urchin, esteemed for food, was toxic in areas of the reef where the fish were toxic. He returned several specimens in the frozen state to the University of Hawaii for testing; one of these caused death in a test mongoose (Randall, 1958). No further studies have been made.

Among the fish in the tropics, there are at least four major types of toxicity in addition to ciguatera. The best known group is that labeled by Halstead (1967) as "Tetrodotoxic" and includes many species of puffers of the family Tetraodontidae as well as species in related families. The toxin appears to be endogenous in the fishes, and Tsuda *et al.* (1964) have elucidated the full chemical structure of the toxic molecule. The basic pharmacological action of the toxin appears to be an antagonism of the increased Na^+ ion permeability associated with electrical excitability in cellular membranes (Kao, 1966).

The second type of intoxication arises from a histaminelike response from eating tuna and related fish. Halstead (1967) called these fishes "Scombrotoxic." The causative toxin is produced in the early spoilage of the dark-fleshed tunalike fish by the action of the bacterium *Proteus morganii* that reduces histidine to toxic histamine and possibly related products. Patients have remarked that the toxic fish have a "sharp or peppery taste." The symptoms are typical of histaminic drugs. The disease was reviewed by Kimata (1961) and Halstead (1967).

The two other types of intoxication are less well known. The type of toxicity labeled by Halstead (1967) as "clupeotoxic" and confined to the suborder Clupeoidae, may be found in sardines, herring, shad, anchovies, and tarpon both in the Caribbean and the tropical Indo-Pacific. Because the disease may lead to death within 15 minutes to a few hours, and because the fish are plankton feeders, the toxin does not appear to be related to ciguatoxin, which has a slow onset of symptoms and is confined to fish associated by their food chain with the benthos. Nothing is known of the biological origin nor the chemical nature of the toxin; little has even been reported on the symptoms. The disease is discussed by Halstead (1967). Finally, a few species of mullet, surmullet, rudderfish, and possibly others from restricted localities are reported to cause short-lived hallucinations when eaten. Although hallucinations have been documented in a few cases (Helfrich and Banner, 1960), the disease has never been studied in the laboratory. For a review, see Halstead (1967) under "Ichthyoallyeinotoxic Fishes." (It is noteworthy that Halstead preferred his name, "ichthyoallyeinotoxism," to the term coined—and rejected—by Helfrich and Banner for the same syndrome, "ichthyosarcephialtilepsis," yet the earlier name has four more letters!)

In addition, Halstead (1967) listed other rare and unstudied types of toxicity in fish: sharks (some of which appear to carry toxins other than ciguatoxin); oil fish or escolars [whose oil, composed largely of wax esters according to Nevenzel *et al.* (1965) and Mori *et al.* (1966), is strongly purgative]; fish in several orders with toxic eggs; eels (some of which may have toxic blood); and a few perchlike fish that seem to have a toxin in their livers. On each category Halstead bestowed a characteristic name, some of which are shorter than those cited above.

III. Assays for Toxicity

In the South Pacific there are a number of popular "tests" for toxicity of fish; these include the discoloration of silver coins or copper wire and the repulsion of flies and ants. Banner *et al.* (1963) reported on controlled experiments on these popular tests and discarded them all as being completely invalid.

The basic test for any toxin or toxins that cause disease through ingestion must be a feeding test on a sensitive animal and be based on measured test meals given at a percentage of body weight. Many investigators from Hiyama (1943) on have used cats or kittens, feeding at 5–15% body weight. Although the cats are sensitive to the toxin, their absorption of the toxin cannot be quantified for they usually regurgitate part of the test meal. In a search for a better test animal, Banner *et al.* (1960) reported on attempts to use 37 species of animals, from protozoans to mammals, as test animals. Only five appeared to respond in a noticeable fashion to the oral administration of the toxic fish flesh. Two of these were mammals, the cat and the mongoose [*Herpestes auropunctatus* (Hodgson), an Indian mongoose introduced to Hawaii and elsewhere in the tropics]; the mongoose had the advantage that it seldom regurgitated the test meal. A third mammal, the mouse, did not respond reliably (it was afterward found that the laboratory mouse had such a high tolerance of the toxin that it could not eat enough of a highly toxic fish at one time to induce symptoms). The fourth animal, the painted turtle [*Pseudemys scripta* (Schoepff)] when sick or otherwise unhappy would merely withdraw into its shell, so there could be no quantification of degrees of reaction. The last animal, the stream crayfish introduced to Hawaii, *Procambarus clarki,* (Girard), could not be fed measured meals. The mongoose was chosen as the animal for standardized screening tests of raw flesh in Hawaii.

The standard technique evolved in Hawaii was to hold a trapped wild mongoose several days for observation. The animals to be tested were starved for 24 hours and then fed flesh at 10% body weight of the mongoose. The test animal was observed for 48 hours with its response rated from 0 (no response) to 5 (death within 48 hours). As the mongooses come from a wild population and are usually infected with a series of diseases (G. N. Stemmermann, personal communication), the response is only roughly quantitative, and critical tests must be run in duplicate or triplicate to avoid false positives.

Although feeding tests are necessary for screening fish for toxicity, they are not satisfactory for further studies of the toxin. The first injection tests of potentially ciguatoxic fish were initiated by Hiyama (1943), who used ethanol as a solvent. Hashimoto (1956) used acidulated methanol in his study on a toxic barracuda. Halstead, with numerous coauthors (see principally Halstead and Bunker, 1954), based a series of reports of faunal surveys upon aqueous extracts of flesh and visceral organs injected into mice by various routes. In a subsequent paper (Goe and Halstead, 1955) he cast some doubts on the reliability of his test when he reported the intoxication of a student by a fish pronounced nontoxic as a result of injection of an aqueous extract. The technique was subsequently questioned by Banner and Boroughs (1958) and most recently by Dammann (1969) and Brody (1970). A new type of aqueous injectant was reported by Keene *et al.* (1968) who used an emulsified fish tissue homogenate that subsequently was heat precipitated and centrifuged. This they injected intramuscularly into various crustaceans. The test was subsequently abandoned at the University of Hawaii because of false positives, especially with herbivorous fishes (A. H. Banner, unpublished observations). Dammann (1969) experimented with Halstead's aqueous extract on "fairy shrimp, cricket, hermit crab, fiddler crab, isopod, octopus, chicken, sand flea and fish louse" without finding a reliable test. Brody (1970) extended Dammann's list to two more species of crab and a mixed protozoan culture. Spandorf (1970) tried two species of bacteria, also with negative results.

In two papers Banner *et al.* (1960, 1961) reported on a more reliable mouse injection test. They found that the initial extraction by hot ethanol carried enough concentration of normally nontoxic compounds to prevent firm differentiation between nontoxic and moderately toxic fish. These normal components of nontoxic fish could be removed from the test extract by concentration of the ethanol solution, solvent–solvent partition of the residue between water and highly nonpolar solvents, such as petroleum ether, and the reextraction of the aqueous phase with a polar solvent such as diethyl ether. The concentrate of the diethyl ether solution was either suspended in a plant oil vehicle or emulsified with Tween 60 (polyoxyethylene sorbitan monostearate) or dried human serum (Kosaki *et al.*, 1968); it could be administered via the intravenous (IV) or intraperitoneal (IP) route. It gave a quantitatively reliable result, especially if an LD_{50} figure was obtained. Subsequent studies have indicated that any modification of the chemical extraction and purification that would give a comparable level of purification would give equally satisfactory results, and that the same syndrome in the test animals obtained from the initial ether extract was maintained through progressively higher levels of purity of the toxin. The symptoms of the test mice included diarrhea, inactivity, excessive salivation and lachrymation, pupillary miosis, and death after convulsive spasms. Aqueous extracts of other fish were found to cause death in animals, but with different symptoms (Banner, 1967; Yasumoto *et al.*, 1971). Kosaki *et al.* (1968) have indicated that the chick is as satisfactory as the mouse for this bioassay, and in an earlier paper (Kosaki and Anderson, 1968) reported that pupillary miosis in the rabbit could be used to judge the toxicity of extracts of the eel *Gymnothorax javanicus* (Bleeker).

IV. Species of Fishes Known to Be Ciguatoxic

Halstead (1967) listed well over 400 species of bony fish, exclusive of sharks, that have been reported in the literature to have produced ciguatera. However, Halstead pointed out in his footnotes that many of the older references did not differentiate between the now accepted types of toxicity such as that of the sardines and the histaminelike reaction to the pelagic tunas. Correspondingly, when the Pacific islanders report that all the fish on certain reef sections have become toxic, they are obviously referring to many or most of the fish that they commonly eat. In contrast, only a few species of fish have been tested by differential tests with appropriate solvents for lipoidal toxins; even fewer have been tested by exact pharmacological tests (see Banner, 1967; Baslow, 1969). The true figure must lie below that reported by Halstead and considerably above those that have been accurately tested.

In general, ciguatoxic species are limited to those fish that feed on algae or detritus of coral reefs, especially the surgeonfish (Acanthuridae), parrotfish (Scaridae), and the larger reef carnivores that prey largely upon these herbivores (some of the often indicted species are shown in Figs. 1–12). It is the larger carnivores that become the most

Fig. 1. Gymnothorax javanicus (Bleeker). Moray eel. Part of a day's catch at Johnston Island. These eels are the basis of the study at the University of Hawaii on the chemistry and pharmacology of ciguatoxin. (Photo by J. E. Randall.)

Fig. 2. *Ctenochaetus striatus* (Quoy and Gaimard). Surgeonfish. (Photo by J. E. Randall from Eniwetok, Marshall Islands.)

Fig. 3. *Naso unicornis* (Forsskål). Unicorn fish. (Photo by J. E. Randall from Hawaii.)

Fig. 4. *Caranx* sp. [probably *ignobilis* (Forsskål)]. Pompano, jack, or ulua. (Photo by J. E. Randall from Fanning Island, Line Islands.)

Fig. 5. Seriola dumerili (Risso). Amberjack. (Photo by J. E. Randall from St. John, Virgin Islands.)

Fig. 6. Lethrinus miniatus (Forster). Scavenger fish. (Photo by J. E. Randall from Eniwetok, Marshall Islands.)

Fig. 7. Lutjanus bohar (Forsskål). Red snapper. (Photo by J. E. Randall from Ulithi, Caroline Islands.)

Fig. 8. *Scarus jonesi* (Streets). Parrotfish. (Photo by J. E. Randall from Tahiti, Society Islands.)

Fig. 9. *Epinephelus fuscoguttatus* (Forsskål). Grouper. (Photo by J. E. Randall from Eniwetok, Marshall Islands.)

Fig. 10. *Cephalopholis argus* Block and Schneider. Spotted Seabass or Spotted Grouper. (Photo by J. E. Randall from Tahiti, Society Islands.)

Fig. 11. Plectropomus truncatus Fowler and Bean. Grouper. (Photo by J. E. Randall from Eniwetok Atoll, Marshall Islands.)

Fig. 12. Sphyraena barracuda (Walbaum). Great Barracuda. (Photo by J. E. Randall from St. John, Virgin Islands.)

dangerously toxic: reef sharks (especially of the family Carcharhinidae), moray eels (Muraenidae), jacks or pompanos (Carangidae), wrasses (Labridae), snappers (Lutjanidae), scavengers (Lethrinidae), certain inshore tunas (Scombridae), groupers (Serranidae), and barracuda (Sphyraenidae). Many other reef fish not fitting exactly into these two groups may carry the toxin, as possibly do some of the triggerfish (Ballistidae). Likewise, in general, none of the pelagic fish and few of the reef plankton feeders, or those that feed over sand, mud, or turtle grass, have been blamed for ciguatera, and in those cases the identity of the disease in the strict sense may be questioned. It is difficult to state which species is the most highly toxic throughout the Pacific, but certainly the fish of the family Lutjanidae, especially the red snapper *Lutjanus bohar* Forsskål would be high, if not highest, on the list.

V. Distribution of Ciguatoxin in a Population

All of the fish in a single population are not equally toxic; Fig. 13 gives the cumulative data on moray eels (*G. javanicus*) weighing over 2.2 kg from Johnston Island, based on the mongoose test (Banner,

1974). It should be noted that even when the flesh of eels is rated as 0 in the mongoose test, the liver may have an appreciable amount of the toxin (Yasumoto and Scheuer, 1969).

With the selection from a fish population of only the large fish, the correlation of toxicity with size is not too apparent. In the 585 eels given in Fig. 13, those of 0 toxicity averaged 8.4 kg, whereas those rated as 5 averaged 9.5 kg (original data). In the samples of *L. bohar* from Palmyra Atoll where the size range was greater, the correlation is readily apparent (Fig. 14; the significance of the contrasting data from 1962 and 1968 will be discussed in the next section). As Helfrich *et al.* (1968) pointed out, not only are the larger fish more likely to be toxic, but they also are more likely to be highly toxic; the small fish, when toxic, usually rate 1–3 on the mongoose test, whereas the largest more often rate 4 and 5. This relationship between size and toxicity has been remarked upon before by many workers, but not objectively quantified with such large samples (see Halstead, 1967). Bagnis *et al.* (1970) have shown that fish from a toxic area that appear to be nontoxic or slightly toxic by a feeding test may contain enough extractable toxin to cause symptoms when injected in mice.

Previous writers have also discussed the distribution of the toxin within various parts of the fish. Studies (A. H. Banner, unpublished observa-

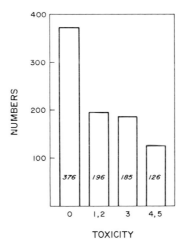

Fig. 13. Toxicity of *Gymnothorax javanicus* from Johnston Island, 883 eels all over 2.2 kg in weight (average 9.2 kg) caught from 1963 through 1969; toxicity ratings by the mongoose test. As toxicity ratings 1 and 4 appear to be transient, they have been combined with 2 and 5 in this graph. (From Banner, 1974 by the courtesy of Marcel Dekker, Inc.)

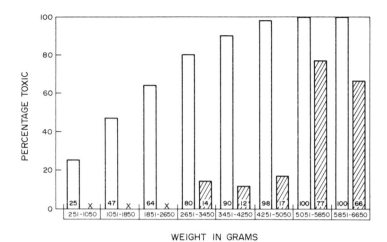

Fig. 14. Percentage of toxic *Lutjanus bohar* by weight categories, Palmyra, 1959 (solid) and 1968 (hatched) by the mongoose test; 1959 data based on 437 specimens; 1968 data based on 168 specimens. (Note: In 1968 only one specimen less than 2.6 kg was tested and only 25 in the two highest weight groups.) (From Banner, 1974 by courtesy of Marcel Dekker, Inc.)

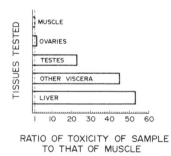

Fig. 15. Ratio of toxicity of pooled visceral samples to muscle in *Lutjanus bohar* from Palmyra; toxicity measured by the intraperitoneal injection of semipurified extract in mice and ratio based upon time to death. (Adapted from Helfrich *et al.*, 1968).

tions) at the University of Hawaii could show no statistically detectable difference between the flesh of the anterior and posterior halves of either *L. bohar* or *G. javanicus*. However, the viscera are definitely more toxic than the flesh. Helfrich *et al.* (1968) were able to show that the liver of *L. bohar* from Palmyra was about 50 times as toxic per unit weight as the flesh (Fig. 15). Yasumoto and Scheuer (1969) stated that the liver of *G. javanicus* is measurably toxic when no toxicity can be detected in the flesh by feeding tests, but did not offer any comparative quantitative data (in personal communication Yasumoto estimated that the liver was about 100 times as toxic as the flesh per unit weight, which is roughly the ratio of the weight of the musculature to the liver—in other words, the small liver contained about the same total weight of toxin as did the body muscles).

VI. Distribution of Ciguateric Fishes in Space and Time

Halstead (1967) set the limits of ciguatera between 35°N and 34°S, but pointed out that the disease is largely confined to islands in the true tropics. Several authors besides Halstead have compiled lists of areas of known toxicity, either by broad areas (e.g., Whitley, 1943; Bonder *et al.*, 1962; Banner and Helfrich, 1964) or in particular archipelagoes (e.g., Jordan, 1929; Bartsch *et al.*, 1959; Cooper, 1964; Hashimoto *et al.*, 1969a). However, these compilations should not be relied upon as more than indications as to where ciguatera may occur for three reasons. First, almost all reports were compilations of second- or third-hand information, and almost none was based on laboratory testing. Second, often the informants did not distinguish between true ciguatera and other types of intoxications, even those as unrelated as puffer and sardine poisonings. Third, as the incidence of ciguatera varies in most areas from year to year, older surveys do not give the current picture (see below).

In both the Pacific and Caribbean, ciguatera seems largely confined to islands and is not found along continental margins. It is also apparently lacking in the waters of the great islands of the Western Pacific. When the author spent a year in Thailand and Malaya he found red snappers (*Lutjanus* spp.) to be a prized food fish and ciguatera was completely unknown; in the early 1960's he imported *L. bohar* from the Manila fish market to serve as nontoxic controls in contrast with the same species from Palmyra. Li, studying ciguatoxic eels in Hong Kong, stated that the fish were not caught in the vicinity of Hong Kong, but on offshore coral islands (K. M. Li, personal communication). Yip recently (1971) reported three toxic species of *Gymnothorax* from the Hong Kong fish market, but did not specify where they were caught; moreover, as he used an aqueous extraction for his tests, it is doubtful that he was reporting upon ciguatoxin. The rarity of ciguatera along the coasts of continents and large islands causes the odd reports of ciguatera from these waters to be viewed with suspicion. However, it has been reliably reported from the Ryukyu archipelago between Japan and Taiwan (Hashimoto *et al.*, 1969a) and may occur in *Seriola aureovittata* Schlegel (= S. *dumerili* Risso ?) from off central Honshu in Japan [Hashimoto and Fusetani (1968) had some doubts as to whether the toxin they extracted was identical with that reported by Scheuer *et al.* (1967) from the central Pacific].

Only two exceptions to the general rule have been reported, for de Sylva (1963) and Morton and Burklew (1970) have reported toxicity of barracuda from the coasts of Florida and Whitley (1943) for fishes along the Great Barrier Reef of Australia; these last may be lethally toxic (Tonge *et al.*, 1967). However, close examination shows that in Australia the toxic fish are not along the continental margin itself, but are found around the offshore reefs of the broad complex. In New Guinea there were a few rather vague reports on intoxications, but these again were from offshore islands (Banner and Helfrich, 1964); the last report on intoxications from the whole Indonesian archipelago was that of Stevenson (1914).

The situation in the Philippines seems to be somewhat controversial, for Banner and Helfrich (1964) reported "both medical and fisheries officers indicated that ciguatera is unknown to responsible authorities." Yet Halstead (1967) stated that "unofficial but reliable sources [report] that during 1957–1958 in fish poisoning outbreaks more than several thousand persons were involved." He stated the only known cause was the oceanic bonito—a fish that is more associated with scombroid intoxication than ciguatera. When the author revisited the Philippines in the spring of 1968 he inquired about ciguatera, and again all interviewed professed no knowledge of the disease. Even in the Sulu Archipelago, where coral reefs flourish and the water conditions are similar to those of isolated islands of the Central Pacific, not only the officials but also the fishermen knew nothing of the disease. This is not to say that some of the offshore islands, like the Cagayan Islands west of Negros, might not have unreported ciguatera.

In general, almost any of the islands of the Central Pacific and, to a lesser extent, those of the Indian Ocean and Caribbean Sea may have a few species of fish that may be sporadically toxic. An excellent example of this low level of toxicity is Hawaii where ciguatera-type of poisonings have been known intermittently since at least 1900 (Helfrich, 1963). The poisonings were of minor nature until 1964, when a sudden outbreak resulted in two deaths and one near death (Okihiro *et al.*, 1965); since then the cases have again been mild and sporadic. Yet in any of the tropical islands many of the safe fish may suddenly become highly toxic.

In the Central Pacific and in the Caribbean, peculiar discontinuous distributional patterns are found for toxic fish. One of the best documented areas is the sparsely inhabited Line Islands lying near the equator directly south of the Hawaiian Islands (for a review of the earlier work in this archipelago, see Helfrich *et al.*, 1968). Of the four major islands, Christmas Island, the southernmost, was only moderately toxic in the 1950's and 1960's; Fanning Island, next to the north, had an outbreak in 1946 but by 1960 even *L. bohar* was being eaten; on Washington Island, the following island, toxic fish were unknown except about a year after the breakup of a wrecked freighter in 1965; and Palmyra, about 250 miles northwest of Christmas, was perhaps the most toxic area in the Pacific in the late 1950's (see Fig. 14). In the Gilbert Islands, Cooper (1964) reported that of the 16 atolls, 10 harbored toxic fish in 1962–1963, all with decreasing toxicity since a peak in the decade around 1950. On the other six atolls, toxic fish were unknown in the postwar years. She also reported that the toxic areas around the atolls were limited to small patches, with the fish in the other waters considered safe; usually these toxic zones were associated with reef passages (Fig. 16).

The seasonal variability of the toxicity of fish has been reported by numerous authors; however, other authors reportedly could not detect any seasonality in their data (for summation, see Halstead, 1967). If other fish accumulate and store toxins as does *L. bohar* (Banner *et al.*, 1966), seasonal variation in the production of toxin would not be reflected in the toxicity of the fish. It may be, however, that the toxicity of some fish, such as acanthurids, does reflect the seasonally changing toxicity of the food making up their diets. A preliminary hint of this was given by Yasumoto *et al.* (1971), who found some specimens of *Ctenochaetus striatus* (Quoy and Gaimard) collected at a different season from their main collection, carrying what appeared to be different toxins. Two other factors may account for the reported seasonality. First, the nonseasonal nature of the fish bearing ciguatoxin may be confused with fish bearing other toxins of seasonal nature, as with sardines in Fiji. Second, the seasonal change in incidence of the disease may be a reflection of the intensity of the fishing effort. L. de Vambez, then the Fishery Officer for the South Pacific Commission, suggested that decrease in ciguatera in the winter in New Caledonia might be explained by the decrease in fishing effort during the period of rough seas (personal communication).

Ciguateric fish in any particular area may change in toxicity markedly over one to several years. Helfrich and Banner (1968) have pointed

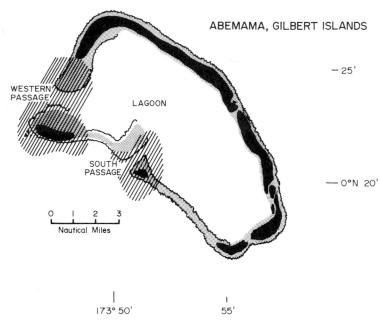

Fig. 16. Abemama Atoll, Gilbert Islands, showing areas (hatched) reported to be toxic by the inhabitants; they stated that in the stretch of reef between West and South Passages the fish were nontoxic. (Adapted from Cooper, 1964.)

out three general patterns of toxicity in the tropical Pacific: (1) where there was a sudden appearance, a rapid rise, and a slow decline in toxicity in areas where no previous toxicity was known—Palmyra is an example; (2) a similar rise and decline in toxicity in an area where ciguatera was previously known but of minor importance—the Marquesas are an example; and (3) where toxicity has apparently been continuous at the same level, high or low, over a long period of time—the New Hebrides and Jaluit Atoll in the Marshalls are excellent examples. The authors stated that when toxicity is rising, it is first noted in the reef herbivores, followed rapidly by the reef carnivores; in decline, the longer-lived carnivores such as snappers, sharks, and eels may remain toxic for years after the herbivores are reported to be nontoxic.

Several authors have recorded the rise of toxicity in areas where previously toxicity was unknown or very low (Bartsch and McFarren, 1962; Cooper, 1964). None has so fully documented the rise as did Bagnis (1969) for the atoll of Hao in the Tuamotus. His report has been reviewed by Banner (1974). Ciguatera had been unknown to the atoll previous to its conversion by the French Atomic Energy Commission (CEA) to a staging base in January, 1965. The ciguatoxic fishes appeared in each area of the lagoon within 1.5–2.0 years after the changes in the marine environment. The geographic spread of ciguatoxic fishes is shown in Fig. 17; the rise in incidence of ciguatera is shown in Fig. 18. In 1971 the fishes of the western side of the atoll were still considered to be safe. As expected, the first fishes to cause ciguatera were herbivores, the acanthurids and scarids; much later did the carnivores, such as carangids and serranids, cause the disease. In all, Bagnis found 32 species in 15 families to have caused ciguatera.

The decline of toxicity is slow and less spectacular. The documentation of a decline on the basis of medical records is doubtful, for unless the drive for protein food impels the inhabitants to again and again sample potentially toxic fish as Cooper reported for the Gilbertese (1964), the falling off of case histories merely reflects that a person once or twice poisoned stops eating local fish. It is likely that the drop

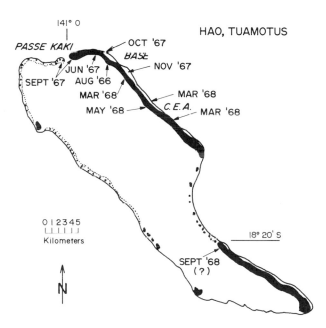

Fig. 17. Hao, Tuamotu Archipelago, showing spread of ciguatera from center of beaching area in August, 1966; data based on house-to-house survey in 1968. Even by 1971 no toxic fish were known from the southern and western portions of the atoll. (Adapted from Bagnis, 1969, in Banner, 1974 by courtesy of Marcel Dekker, Inc.)

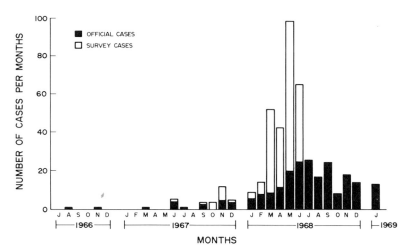

Fig. 18. Monthly incidence of ciguatera on Hao, Tuamotu Archipelago. Ciguatera was unknown to Hao previous to 1966. Solid bar represents the number of official cases reported to medical authorities; the open bar represents the number of additional cases that were not reported to medical authorities but that were discovered by a house-to-house survey. The epidemiological survey stopped in June, 1968; the official records were available through January, 1969. (Adapted from Bagnis, 1969, in Banner, 1974 by courtesy of Marcel Dekker, Inc.)

in cases shown by Bagnis from Hao thus does not represent a decrease in toxicity of the fish. However, the laboratory assays of toxicity of *L. bohar* from Palmyra for 1959 and 1968 given in Fig. 14 show a true loss of toxicity in the fish population; it is noteworthy that in 1968 it was the largest, therefore the oldest, fish that remained highly toxic.

VII. Origin and Transmission of the Toxin*

Many of the earlier suggestions as to the cause of ciguatoxicity in fishes have not survived modern scrutiny. The idea that the toxin is endogenous, similar to tetrodotoxin in puffers, has been rejected as the toxin is erratic in appearance in species of such broad phylogenetic span which are yet of such close ecological affinity. It cannot be a product

* This section is a summation of my review, "The Biological Origin and Transmission of Ciguatoxin," presented at the *Symposium on Physiologically Active Compounds from the Sea* at St. Petersburg, Florida in November, 1971 (Banner, 1974). This summation is included here as necessary for the development of this review; for fuller discussion and additional references, the reader should examine the parent article.

of bacterial decomposition of fish flesh, similar to scombrotoxicity, as the toxin is found in freshly frozen fish (Banner *et al.*, 1963). It cannot be from contamination with heavy metals, such as copper as previously suggested, or mercury as is found in the Minamata disease of Japan, for there are no heavy metals in the purified toxic extracts (see Section VIII). Instead, ciguatera is caused by a toxin that arises in the environment and is of biological origin.

Most workers in the field of marine toxins now accept the food-chain theory of transmission of ciguatoxin within the food web of coral reefs. The theory was best advanced by Randall (1958) who reviewed what was then known about the biology of ciguatoxic fishes. He rejected the idea that any of the larger reef forms, such as jellyfish, corals, balolo worms, pufferfish, and even the coarser attached algae, could be the elaborator of the toxin. He based this rejection on the knowledge of the food habits of toxic herbivores. He concluded (p. 257) that the original elaborator of the toxin was likely to be "an alga, a fungus, a protozoan or a bacterium," and he pointed out that if it were an alga, it would have to be filamentous and soft. This toxigenic form would then be eaten by the reef herbivores that in turn would be eaten by the larger reef piscivorous carnivores. He postulated that the toxin would accumulate in the carnivores; Helfrich and Banner (1968) suggested that the accumulation in the higher trophic levels could be comparable ecologically, but not physiologically, with the accumulation of modern insecticides in the trophic pyramid.

Since the publication of Randall's paper his theory has been confirmed both by field and experimental evidence. At Iao (see Section VI) the first fish to become toxic were the herbivores and detrital feeders, with the first carnivores causing the disease ten months later; presumably the lapse represents the time necessary for sufficient concentrations of the toxin to be passed through the food chain. In periods of declining toxicity, Cooper (1964) in the Gilberts, Banner (1974) at Palmyra (see Fig. 14), and Brock *et al.* (1965) at Johnston have recorded that only the larger carnivores remain toxic.

The experimental evidence also supports the food-chain hypothesis. Helfrich and Banner (1963) and Banner *et al.* (1966) reported on two experiments with captive fishes. In the first they fed a nontoxic omnivorous acanthurid, *Acanthurus xanthropterus* Cuvier and Valenciennes, with small portions of toxic fish flesh daily until the fish became lethally toxic to mongooses. In the second experiment they held a population of toxic *L. bohar* from Christmas Island in holding ponds on a nontoxic diet; at the end of 30 months of captivity, the fish showed no detectable loss of toxicity. From these two experiments they concluded that the toxicity could be induced in fishes through diet, that the toxin in the diet caused no apparent harm to the fish, and that the toxin could be accumulated in the flesh and stored there for long periods of time.

The last and most conclusive support of the food-chain theory is the work of Yasumoto *et al.* (1971) on *C. striatus* from a toxic zone in Tahiti. The fish, a detrital feeder that cannot bite off pieces of attached algae, contained either ciguatoxin or a compound indistinguishable from it by present chemical and pharmacological tests. This toxin was found in the flesh, viscera, and gut contents. The presence of the toxin in the gut contents shows that the toxin originates at the base of the food chain in recognizable form and detectable quantities, and that there is no observed biochemical alteration of the toxic moiety by the metabolism of the fishes as it is passed through the food chain.

Although this evidence supports the theory of ecological transmission of the toxin, it leaves to conjecture both the identification of the elaborator and the ecological conditions that would cause the rapid rise and slow decline of ciguatoxin in a reef community. It may be possible that ciguatoxin originates in many species or even groups of the biota and that the appearance of ciguatoxin in a reef community may be caused by a variety of ecological conditions. However, in view of what is presently known about the toxin and its appearance, it would appear to be more logical to seek a single species or genus as the elaborator and to postulate that this form is stimulated into proliferation on separated reefs by similar ecological events.

If the reasoning of Randall and the evidence of Yasumoto *et al.* are accepted, the elaborator must be fine, but could be either a fine autotroph or heterotroph. The latter authors studied the food habits of *C. striatus* and reported that in the imperfect fractionation of the gut contents, the most toxic fraction was composed not of algae but of "unidentifiable particles"; they concluded that the elaborator(s) would be "both small in size and low in specific gravity."

The concurrent paper on the biology of ciguatoxin (Banner, 1974) reviews the unsuccessful search for the elaborator among the fine algae, mostly blue-green, and an inconclusive initial study by Gundersen of microbial heterotrophs and suggests that the originator may not be an alga but rather, as Randall had suggested, a bacterium, yeast, or mold. This microbial heterotroph could live in the bottom detritus—mostly broken fronds of seaweeds—where it would be picked up in quantity by the bottom-feeding *C. striatus*. However, the bacterium, yeast, or mold might not occur in abundance in the coral reef environment but live as part of the nonpathogenic flora of the intestinal tract of the fish. There it would produce the toxin, harmless to the fish as has been shown, to be absorbed by the host and thus stored and transmitted to the rest of the ecosystem.

A number of hypotheses on the ecological causes of outbreaks must be discarded. Any postulated phenomenon that does not reach back into time would be improbable, for it could not account for the poisonings reported in the last several centuries. These postulations would include ecological disruption by the atomic testing program, modern insecticides, recent pollution, and similar changes. Similarly, ecological changes resulting from additional metal ions in the sea cannot be considered, as the atoll environments are notably deficient in metals.

Randall, in addition to supporting the food-chain hypothesis, also suggested that "new surfaces" on the coral reef might be the cause of the outbreaks. The new surfaces would be sections of the reef laid bare of its biota either by natural disasters such as hurricanes or by acts of man, such as anchoring of ships, shipwrecks, or the dumping of war surplus material. On these new surfaces would appear in early ecological succession the toxigenic form, which Randall suggests is most likely to be a blue-green alga. This influx of toxin would then spread through the ecosystem.

In the review, the author (Banner, 1974) carefully considers this hypothesis and cites more recent reef disruptions such as that on Hao, as supporting Randall's thesis. However, he also cites many cases— blasting of channels in the Gilberts, typhoon flooding in Fiji, reef disruption by the atomic testing program at Eniwetok, wholesale dredging at Johnston, even the denuding of reef surfaces by the starfish *Acanthaster*— that were followed by no reported increase in fish toxicity. He cites Randall's own report (1968) of failure to produce the toxigenic strain on artificial new surfaces (of plywood, asbestos board, etc.) in a toxic area in Tahiti.

Thus, no conclusions can be drawn about either the elaborator or the conditions that cause an outbreak. It is likely that the toxin itself is widespread and most ancient on the reefs, for all marine animals tested, in contrast with most freshwater and terrestrial animals, have developed immunity to the toxin (see Banner *et al.*, 1960). Some evidence pointed toward yeasts or molds, either in the reef environment or in the gut flora of fishes; these could be newly introduced into an ecosystem, as they could have on Hao by ship bottoms arriving from the then rampantly toxic waters of Tahiti, or they could exist on the reef to be stimulated in growth by yet unknown factors. Any ecological speculation will be without foundation until the elaborator of the toxin is isolated and studied.

VIII. Chemistry of Ciguatoxin

The original work on the chemistry of the toxin was a mere excursion into its solubilities and other characteristics. Hiyama (1943) noted that the toxin could be removed from fish flesh with ethanol and that the toxin was heat stable so that cooking did not destroy the toxicity. Hashimoto (1956), working with only a 55 gm sample of barracuda, reported that the toxin was extracted from the fish by methanol and that it was soluble in organic solvents such as acetone and ether. Banner and Boroughs (1958) and later Banner et al. (1960) confirmed Hashimoto's results and found the toxin to be soluble in a series of polar organic solvents; they also noted that the toxin could not be extracted with water. They stated that there was no apparent loss of toxicity when the fish was stored below freezing for up to six months, when it was dried, or when the initial extraction was carried on with hot solvents. In the earlier paper they found that if secondary extractions were made under a normal atmosphere, toxicity was lost, but under a nitrogen atmosphere it was retained. To the contrary, Halstead and a series of associates (in papers from 1954 to 1958) presumed they were extracting the principal toxin with water, in some cases acidulated and in others in normal saline, for use in their bioassay. Similarly, Bartsch and Mc-Farren (1962) and the group under Dammann (1969) also used aqueous extractions for their bioassay.

The use of column chromatography to purify the toxin was first hinted at, but not fully reported, by Banner et al. (1960). Hessel et al. in the same year reported on an unsuccessful technique of chromatography. In subsequent papers both Hessel and the group at the University of Hawaii reported successful chromatography (Hessel, 1961, 1963; Banner et al., 1963; Banner, 1967; Scheuer et al., 1967; Yasumoto and Scheuer, 1969).

The technique of extraction and purification at the University of Hawaii has gone through 14 modifications since 1962; the present standard technique, not previously reported in the literature, is given in Fig. 19. The yield is about 10 ppm of highly toxic raw fish. The only published reports on the structure of the molecule, named ciguatoxin, are by Scheuer et al. (1967). They reported (p. 1267) that they obtained a viscous oil, possibly pure (". . . the fact we have not obtained a stable crystalline derivative keeps open the question whether ciguatoxin is a single substance with a tendency to decompose or whether it consists of several related compounds"). They obtained 0.75 mg of toxin per kg of highly toxic fish, and the final preparation had the toxicity of 0.5 mg/kg when injected intraperitoneally into mice. Combustion data gave the empirical formula of $(C_{35}H_{65}NO_8)_n$. Other experiments indicated that the molecule contains a quarternary nitrogen atom, one or more hydroxyl groups, and a carbonyl function. It should be noted that the statement that Halstead (1967, p. 304) attributed to "Yoshida *et al.* (1965)" that the toxin "in pure form is a phospholipid" was based on a manuscript reporting earlier studies of impure extracts and the statement was never actually published. The new procedure outlined in Fig. 19 gives a yield of 5–10 mg/kg and a toxicity of 0.025 mg/kg when injected intraperitoneally into mice (P. J. Scheuer and D. B. Boglan, personal commmunication), an increase over the 1967 report.

Baslow (1969) questioned the assumption made by the University of Hawaii group that the same toxin was found in the snapper *L. bohar,* the eel *G. javanicus,* and the shark *Carcharhinus menisorrah* (Müller and Henle) (= *C. amblyrhynchos* Bleeker). Scheuer *et al.* (1967) did not suggest that the whole lipoidal molecule was identical, but that the toxic moieties in the diverse fishes were of sufficient chemical similarity to give similar physiological activity. Rayner (see Section IX) has reported pharmacological characteristics for the toxin that appear to be unique, and has found these reactions caused by the toxin from the eel, the snapper, and the acanthurid *C. striatus* (Banner, 1974).

IX. Pharmacology of Ciguatoxin

Aside from the search for a suitable bioassay and the superficial observation of symptoms, the earliest work on pharmacology was that of Hessel *et al.* (1960), who reported that when the sciatic nerve of the frog was bathed in an emulsified acetone–ether extract of a toxic *L. bohar,* its action potential would drop by 25% or more in 70 minutes. Banner *et al.* (1963) reported that an extract made from a barracuda, originally extracted with ethanol and reextracted with diethyl ether, rapidly impaired the transmission of the nervous impulse to the muscle in a frog nerve–muscle preparation. As direct stimulation of the muscle caused contraction they concluded (p. 14) that "while the action potential of a nerve may be lost from long immersion in a solution of semi-purified toxin, the immediate effect is on the nerve–muscle junction."

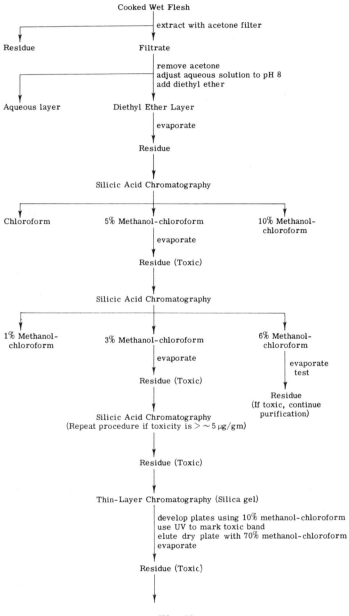

Fig. 19

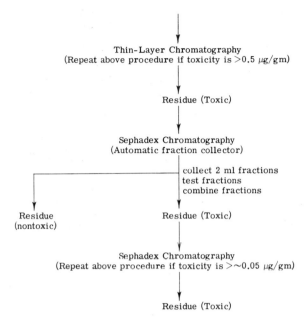

Fig. 19. Revised procedure for extraction and purification of ciguatoxin from flesh of *Gymnothorax javanicus* as developed at the University of Hawaii. (Note: All chromatography carried on in a cold room, near 4°C. Samples stored under inert atmospheres at about –20°C.)

Li (1965a,b, 1970) reported that the toxins from the red snapper, the moray eel, a grouper [*Epinephelus fuscogullatus* (Forsskål)], and a shark (*C. menisorrah*) all behaved as anticholinesterases. These conclusions were based upon the following: (1) the similarity of symptoms in animals when injected with either crude extracts of ciguatoxin or known inhibitors of cholinesterase; (2) *in vitro* tests of cholinesterase activity in human red blood cells when bathed in a solution containing ciguatoxin; and (3) the recovery of intoxicated test animals when treated with Protopam Chloride (2-formyl-1-methylpyridinium chloride oxime), a drug known for its activity against anticholinesterases. Li (in Banner, 1967; Li, 1970) pointed out that all toxic fish do not have the same anticholinesterase activity.

The first doubt of the supposed anticholinesterase activity was cast when Okihiro *et al.* (1965) reported (p. 355) on attempting to treat a near fatal hospital case of ciguatera with 2-PAM, a cholinesterase regenerator: "The results were startling, unexpected and almost disastrous." Only heroic measures, including a bedside tracheotomy and massive dosages of atropine and magnesium sulfate saved the patient. Rayner and associates in two papers (1968, 1969) reexamined the contended inhibition of cholinesterase activity. In the first paper they studied the effects of other cholinesterase inhibitors and of ciguatoxin upon the reaction of the respiratory system; in the second they used a similar series of drugs and measured the reduction of the cholinesterase activity in the blood cells in living animals. From these two studies they concluded that while there may be some inhibition of cholinesterase in in vitro preparations, the action of the toxin is definitely not that of an anticholinesterase in living systems.

Reviewing the recent work carried out in the laboratory at the University of Hawaii, Rayner (1970b) concluded that ciguatoxin has a rather widespread action on excitable membranes involving an initial increase in excitability followed later by conduction block; the hypothesis was put forward that increased Na^+ permeability might be the causative mechanism for these changes. Subsequent studies (Rayner, 1970a; Rayner and Kosaki, 1970; Setliff et al., 1971) have confirmed that ciguatoxin increases the passive permeability of frog skin preparations and frog muscle membranes to ^{22}Na, and that ciguatoxin extracted from both Gymnothorax and Ctenochaetus produces a depolarization in frog muscle cells that is specifically antagonized by the action of tetrodotoxin. This action appears to be associated with the competitive inhibition by ciguatoxin of the membrane stabilizing action of Ca^{2+} ions. The more common acute symptoms associated with ciguatera poisoning appear to be consistent with the proposed mechanism of action and a rational therapy would be to treat the membrane effects of ciguatoxin with magnesium sulfate and calcium gluconate (M. D. Rayner, personal communication). Those symptoms associated with the disfunction of the autonomic nervous system have been shown to be relieved by atropine (Okihiro et al., 1965). On the other hand, it cannot yet be suggested that this is the only mechanism responsible for all of the symptoms which characterize the ciguatera syndrome.

Intoxications by ciguatoxic fish may cause pathological damage. Banner et al. (1960) quoted a neuropathologist who stated he could find no changes in the central nervous system of two mongooses maintained intoxicated on ciguateric fish for over a month. However, Li (1970) reported demyelination in both spinal cord and sciatic nerve in adult hens that had been given a large sublethal dose of a toxic extract intramuscularly two weeks before; he did not state the purity or the source of the extract.

X. Other Toxins

Ciguatoxin, or a compound of similar solubilities and similar pharmacology, appears to be the principal toxin in the carnivorous fish of the Pacific, being found in fish as diverse as sharks, moray eels, snappers, etc., from almost all parts of the Pacific (Banner *et al.*, 1960, 1963; Banner, 1967). However, the positive results obtained by Halstead in the 1950's with his bioassay utilizing aqueous extracts gave an indication that other toxins might be found in "ciguateric" fishes. This was also indicated by reports of seasonality in toxicity, as in Fiji where the fish are reported to be highly toxic during the spawning period of the balolo worm (Banner and Helfrich, 1964), for ciguatoxin appears to be stored in at least some species of fish (see Section VII). Differences in human symptoms were also remarked upon. Dr. E. Massal was quoted as stating that the symptoms of ciguatera in Tahiti were different from those in New Caledonia (Banner *et al.*, 1963). More recently, Bagnis (1968) reported (p. 28) from 350 cases in French Polynesia that he had attended (see also Section XII): "Gastrointestinal and neurologic symptoms are more common in cases caused by eating herbivorous surgeonfishes; cardiovascular disorders and more varied symptoms are common when piscivorous groupers or snappers have caused the poisoning."

The first actual laboratory report of a different toxin was by Banner *et al.* (1963) in which they reported that *C. striatus* had a toxin that was removed by alcohol, but not soluble in diethyl ether. Banner (1967) reported three different types of intoxications from fish based primarily upon pharmacology and supplemented by tests of *in vitro* anticholinesterase activity. The fishes of the first group, which included the carnivores *Gymnothorax, Lutjanus,* and *Epinephelus*, caused death by respiratory failure and gave high anticholinesterase activity. The fishes of the second group, with *Cheilinus* and *Acanthurus* being mentioned, caused death by cardiac failure and had lower *in vitro* anticholinesterase activity. The third group, which included *Caranx* and *Sphyraena*, was intermediary between the first two. He concluded (p. 161) that these differing reactions may "indicate the presence of other toxins." This differentiation was also discussed by Li (1970).

Hashimoto and Yasumoto (1965) and Hashimoto *et al.* (1969b) reported a water-soluble toxin that they named "ciguaterin" in the liver, and in some cases in the flesh, of five species of snappers, groupers, and eels from the Ryukyu and Amami Islands. In some cases they also found an oil-soluble ciguatoxin-like compound. Ciguaterin was found to be unstable in frozen raw fish, but stable when frozen after being cooked; it caused vomiting in kittens when administered either by feeding or sub-cutaneous injection, but in all cases the test animal would recover in 24–48 hours.

The most definitive work on toxins other than ciguatoxin was that of Yasumoto *et al.* (1971) who worked with the acanthurids *C. striatus* and *Acanthurus lineatus* (L.) from Tahiti. Both fish contained an oil-soluble toxin either identical or very similar to ciguatoxin from Johnston Island eels, both in chemistry and pharmacology. In addition both carried a second toxin which was water-soluble, nondialyzable, and precipitated from concentrated solution by the addition of acetone; the last stage of purification reported upon was on a Sephadex G-100 column. When the toxin was injected intraperitoneally into mice, the mice displayed a "remarkable loss of activity, weakness in limbs, and convulsions before death that took place rather slowly: after several hours to three days, depending upon the dose" (Yasumoto *et al.* 1971, p. 730). The extract was also hemolytic and caused death in guppies when they were im-mersed in a 0.00044% solution. Like the ciguatoxin in the same fish, the toxin was found in the gut contents and in the liver; none, however, was found in the flesh.

The same authors said they had indications of possibly different toxins from the same species of fish in samples at the same locality but at a different season, but their sample was too small for further investigation.

From this evidence the authors concluded that a fish labeled as "cigua-teric" may harbor a variety of toxins of different chemistry and pharma-cology, and the variable symptoms reported probably reflect the variabil-ity in toxins. They suggested (p. 733) "As our knowledge of the differing toxins and the symptoms they produce increases, it would be well to apply more specific designations to the various illnesses."

XI. Dealing with Potentially Toxic Fish

As indicated in Section III, there is no simple test for toxicity in fish. If a fish is suspected of carrying toxin, the only way to ascertain its toxicity away from the laboratory is to feed its viscera to a cat or other animal and to watch it for symptoms for 24–48 hours. An early sign of intoxication in the cat is the loss of the ear-flick reflex when the inner ear hairs are touched.

Correspondingly, there is no way of preparing a fish carrying cigua-toxin that would render it safe for consumption. Washing does not remove the oil-soluble toxin, nor does freezing or cooking detoxify it. No studies have been made on the other toxins except that of Hashimoto *et al.* (1969b), who reported that ciguaterin is detoxified with freezing.

XII. Remedies for Intoxication

A number of remedies has been suggested for the treatment of ciguatera, including (1) native plants (Loison, 1955; also in Banner *et al.*, 1963); (2) vitamins of the B complex (Bouder and Cavallo, 1962); (3) Protopam chloride or the related PAM (2-pyridine aldoxime methochloride)[*] (Li, 1965b); and (4) neostigmine methylsulfate (trimethylammonium methylsulfate dimethylcarbamate) with other drugs (Banner *et al.*, 1963). In some cases the drugs appear to have contributed to recovery but laboratory studies with pure or semi-pure ciguatoxin do not confirm the efficacy of the drugs. Thus Shaw reported (in Banner *et al.*, 1963) what appeared to be a spectacular cure with the use of the anticholinesterase neostigmine in a case of barracuda poisoning, but Li (1965a, p. 1581) reported that physostigmine (a related compound) injected before the administration of a ciguatoxic extract in rats had "little protective action." Similarly Rayner *et al.* (1968) have reported that no aid was derived from PAM (similar to Protopam chloride) or from vitamin B_1 (M. D. Rayner, personal communication).

One of the best documented cases of an almost fatal case of ciguatera and its cure was that of Okihiro *et al.* (1965). They recorded a symptomatology in part parallel with that of a calcium deficiency. After an almost fatal attempt to use 2-PAM, they changed to massive doses of atropine for the muscarinic functions and magnesium sulfate, which they titrated against the muscular fasciculations. Later, calcium gluconate was given with methylphenidate for the coma. The use of magnesium and calcium ions thus preceded the recommendations of Rayner (see Section IX). Atropine, used in this and other cases (Shaw, in Banner *et al.*, 1963), also appears to be helpful but as yet is without a basic pharmacological rationale derived from a knowledge of specific actions of ciguatoxin.

Complicating any treatment is the possible presence of other toxins in the fish body which may demand drugs different from those used to treat ciguatoxin alone. Thus Bagnis (1968) reported that in 350 cases

[*] Li (1965b) and Okihiro *et al.* (1965) used a different chemical name for this drug than did Li (1965a, cf. p. 25).

he had treated in Tahiti the following types of symptoms as tabulated below were found to predominate.

Predominate symptoms	Number of cases
Neurologic	112
Digestive	58
Itching	29
Erythema	14
Cardiovascular	7
Neuromuscular	7
Sensory disturbances	4

From what is now known about the presence of other toxins in at least some fishes, this variety of symptoms could have been caused by a mixture of various toxins. Bagnis reported that he treated most cases symptomatically.

XIII. Public Health Significance

To one who has visited the Pacific Islands, the public health significance lies beyond the cold statistics of incidence. Statistics do, however, reflect the impact upon island cultures. Bartsch and McFarren (1962) reported that on the island of Majuro, Marshall Islands, during the year 1957, 9.3% of the island population was treated in the hospital, but that interviews of families living on various islets gave the figure of 14–15% incidence during the year. Malardé et al. (1967) carried out a house-to-house survey in rural Tahiti and interviewed 33,085 individuals. They reported that a total of 8.45% of those interviewed had fish poisoning during the year 1966, but that in some districts the incidence was as high as 22.84%. The highest incidence yet reported was on Hao, Tuamotus, where Bagnis (1969) found 224 of the 514 interviewed reported to have been intoxicated at least once, giving an incidence of 43%, and counting multiple attacks, there were actually 271 cases. The last six months of Bagnis' study saw a decrease in medically treated cases, either because of a decrease in toxicity in the fish or a decrease in use of local fishes.

It is rare for death to result from the intoxication (Bagnis, 1968), but the illness imposes an economic strain upon island economies, for those affected cannot be productive during their days or weeks of illness. Malardé et al. (1967) reported that 80% of the cases they investigated were of people of the "active age," in the 15–64 age group. In more subsistence economies, such as in the Gilbert Islands, the father and husband is unable to gather coconuts and fish for his family; in more advanced economies, the poisoned individual is unable to work for wages. Malardé *et al.* estimated that during their study year, 6580 mandays of labor were lost. In addition to the loss of labor, the economies may be displaced by the loss of market to fishermen.

An indirect effect of the toxicity of the reef fishes is the loss to the island diet of the principal source of protein. Especially on the atolls where domestic animals cannot be raised easily as food—pigs and chickens, for example, are a "feast food"—the routine protein comes from the sea. Where all of the fish become toxic, this source is denied to the people and malnutrition results unless the individuals have sufficient cash income to buy imported tinned fish and meat. There have been no studies on the results of the dietary imbalance or economic loss.

Ciguatera has been found to interfere with the development of domestic and export fisheries in some tropical "underdeveloped" areas. A noteworthy example was the attempt of the United States and the Virgin Islands governments to increase income in the Virgin Islands by increasing the local fisheries. In 1967–1968 the local fisherman landed a catch worth $781,896, yet during the same period $1,416,726 worth of seafood was imported (Dammann, 1969). The project to improve the fisheries started in 1965; in 1970, Dammann (p. 3) concluded: "This problem [of ciguatera] was viewed as being so severe, in fact, that there was little possibility of improving the inshore fishery until the total problem could be solved." Similarly, Halstead (1970b, p. 1) reported that the FAO Caribbean Fisheries Development Project vessel landed a catch of *Caranx* in Kingston, Jamaica that "severely poisoned . . . about 60 persons at the Police Officer's Mess"; Halstead cited several other outbreaks resulting from the exploratory fishing effort. For the development of tropical reef fisheries there is the vital need of either an infallible predictability as to which fish will be toxic (as individuals, as species, or from certain areas), or a simple and reliable method of testing individual fish for toxicity.

XIV. Conclusions

The disease ciguatera results from the ingestion of fishes associated with coral reefs and is widespread in the tropical Pacific and Caribbean. Although research on the principal causative toxin, ciguatoxin, has been quite productive in spite of the complexity of the problem, all areas of research must advance before any definitive answers are achieved. Biological research has shown that the toxin originates environmentally on the coral reef and is transmitted through the food web, but both the elaborator of the toxin and the ecological factors causing the increase of the toxin in the environment are unknown. Ciguatoxin has been isolated, but is not structurally identified; other toxins in fishes labeled as "ciguateric" lack more than initial exploration of their chemical characteristics. One of the pharmacological activities of ciguatoxin, that of disruption of the ionic balance of excitable cell membranes, has been established but it is not known whether this is the sole action of ciguatoxin; the actions of other toxins have not been investigated. No treatment other than symptomatic for the disease has been developed that considers the action of other possible toxins in the fishes.

The disease is of considerable importance to the public health and to the present economy of oceanic islands. The development of new fisheries in much of the tropics, as is now being tried, demands extensive research on all aspects of the problem. This research will require laboratory work to confirm field observations, and will also require consideration of all other toxins that may be found in "ciguateric fishes."

References

Bagnis, R. (1967). *Bull. Soc. Pathol. Exot.* **60**, 580.

Bagnis, R. (1968). *Hawaii Med. J.* **28**, 25.

Bagnis, R. (1969). *Rev. Corps Sante Armees* **10**, 783.

Bagnis, R., Fevai, G., also Lefevre, N., and Thevenin, S. (1970). *Rev. Int. Oceanogr. Med.* **18–19**, 5.

Banner, A. H. (1967). *In* "Animal Toxins" (F. E. Russell and P. R. Saunders, eds.), pp. 157–165. Pergamon, Oxford.

Banner, A. H. (1974) *In* "Bioactive Compounds from the Sea" (H. J. Humm and C. E. Lane, eds.), pp. 15–36. Dekker, New York.

Banner, A. H., and Boroughs, H. (1958). *Proc. Soc. Exp. Biol. Med.* **98**, 776.

Banner, A. H., and Helfrich, P. (1964). *Hawaii Inst. Mar. Biol. Tech. Rep.* No. 3, pp. 1–48.

Banner, A. H., Scheuer, P. J., Sasaki, S., Helfrich, P., and Alender, C. B. (1960). *Ann. N.Y. Acad. Sci.* **90**, 770.

Banner, A. H., Sasaki, S., Helfrich, P., Alender, C. B., and Scheuer, P. J. (1961). *Nature (London)* **189**, 229.

Banner, A. H., Shaw, S. W., Alender, C. B., and Helfrich, P. (1963). *S. Pac. Comm. Tech. Pap.* No. 141, pp. 1–17.

Banner, A. H., Helfrich, P., and Piyakarnchana, T. (1966). *Copeia* (2), 297–301.

Bartsch, A. F., and McFarren, E. F. (1962). *Pac. Sci.* **16**, 42.

Bartsch, A. F., Drachman, R. H., and McFarren, E. F. (1959). "Report of a Survey of the Fish Poisoning Problem in the Marshall Islands." Report of U.S. Pub. Health Serv. to Trust Terr. of Pacific Islands (special mimeographed report).

Baslow, M. H. (1969). "Marine Pharmacology—A Study of Toxins and Other Biologically Active Substances of Marine Origin." Williams & Wilkins Co., Baltimore, Maryland.

Bouder, H., and Cavallo, A. (1962). *Ass. Med. Nouv.-Caledonie* pp. 1–11.

Bouder, H., Cavallo, A., and Bouder, M. J. (1962). *Bull. Inst. Oceanog.* **59**, 1–66.

Brock, V. E., Jones, R. S., and Helfrich, P. (1965). *Hawaii Inst. Mar. Biol., Tech. Rep. No. 5*, pp. 1–90.

Brody, R. W. (1970). *Virgin Isl. Ecol. Res. Sta., Contrib.* No. 2, pp. 30–38.

Cook, J. (1777). "A Voyage Towards the South Pole and Round the World," Vol. II.

Cooper, M. J. (1964). *Pac. Sci.* **18**, 411.

Dammann, A. E. (1969). *Virgin Isl. Ecol. Res. Sta., Contrib.* No. 1, pp. 1–197.

Dammann, A. E. (1970). *Virgin Isl. Ecol. Res. Sta., Contrib.* No. 2, pp. 3–5.

de Sylva, D. P. (1963). *Stud. Trop. Oceanogr.* **1**, 1–179.

Goe, D. R., and Halstead, B. W. (1955). *Copeia* (3), 238.

Halstead, B. W. (1965). "Poisonous and Venomous Marine Animals," Vol. 1. US Govt. Printing Office, Washington, D.C.

Halstead, B. W. (1967). "Poisonous and Venomous Marine Animals," Vol. 2, US Govt. Printing Office, Washington, D.C.

Halstead, B. W. (1970a). "Poisonous and Venomous Marine Animals," Vol. 3, US Govt. Printing Office, Washington, D.C.

Halstead, B. W. (1970b). "Result of a Field Survey on Fish Poisoning in the Virgin and Leeward Islands During 7–18 January 1970." Dept. Fish., Food and Agricultural Organization of the United Nations (copy of typed report).

Halstead, B. W., and Bunker, N. C. (1954). *Copeia* (1), 1.

Hashimoto, Y. (1956). *Bull. Jap. Soc. Sci. Fish.* **21**, 1153.

Hashimoto, Y. (1970). *In* "Poisonous and Venomous Marine Animals" (B. W. Halstead, ed.), Vol. 3, pp. 904–910. US Govt. Printing Office, Washington, D.C.

Hashimoto, Y., and Fusetani, N. (1968). *Bull. Jap. Soc. Sci. Fish.* **34**, 618.

Hashimoto, Y., and Yasumoto, T. (1965). *Bull. Jap. Soc. Sci. Fish.* **31**, 452.

Hashimoto, Y., Konosu, S., Yasumoto, T., and Kamiya, H. (1969a). *Bull. Jap. Soc. Sci. Fish.* **35**, 316.

Hashimoto, Y., Yasumoto, T., Kamiya, H., and Yoshida, T. (1969b). *Bull. Jap. Soc. Sci. Fish.* **35**, 327.

Hashimoto, Y., Konosu, S., Shibota, M., and Watanabe, K. (1970). *Bull. Jap. Soc. Sci. Fish.* **36**, 1163.

Helfrich, P. (1963). *Hawaii Med. J.* **22**, 361.

Helfrich, P., and Banner, A. H. (1960). *J. Trop. Med. Hyg.* **63**, 83.

Helfrich, P., and Banner, A. H. (1963). *Nature* (*London*) **197**, 1025.

Helfrich, P., and Banner, A. H. (1968). *Occas. Pap. Bishop Mus.* **23**, 371.

Helfrich, P., Piyakarnchana, T., and Miles, P. S. (1968). *Occas. Pap. Bishop Mus.* **23**, 305.

Hessel, D. W. (1961). *Toxicol. Appl. Pharmacol.* **3**, 574.

Hessel, D. W. (1963). *In* "Venomous and Poisonous Animals and Noxious Plants of the Pacific Region" (H. L. Keegan and W. V. MacFarlane, eds.), p. 203. Pergamon, Oxford.

Hessel, D. W., Halstead, B. W., and Peckham, N. H. (1960). *Ann. N. Y. Acad. Sci.* **90**, 788.

Hiyama, Y. (1943). Report on an investigation of poisonous fishes of the South
    Seas (transl. by Van Campen). *U.S., Fish Wildl. Serv., Spec. Sci. Rept.–Fish.*
    25, 1950.
Jordan, D. S. (1929). *Amer. Natur.* **63**, 382.
Kao, C. Y. (1966). *Pharmacol. Rev.* **18**, 997.
Keene, E., Randall, J. E., and Banner, A. H. (1968). S. *Pac. Semin. Ichthyosarcotox-
    ism, 1968 SPC/ICHT/WP-18.*
Kimata, M. (1961). *In* "Fish as Food" (G. Borgstrom, ed.), Vol. 1, pp. 329–352.
    Academic Press, New York.
Kosaki, T. I., and Anderson, H. H. (1968). *Toxicon* **6**, 55.
Kosaki, T. I., Stephens, B. J., and Anderson, H. H. (1968). *Proc. West. Pharmacol.
    Soc.* **11**, 126.
Li, K. M. (1965a). *Science* **147**, 1580.
Li, K. M. (1965b). *Hawaii Med. J.* **24**, 353.
Li, K. M. (1970). *In* "Poisonous and Venomous Marine Animals of the World"
    (B. W. Halstead, ed.), Vol. 3, pp. 857–882. US Govt. Printing Office, Washing-
    ton, D.C.
McFarren, E. F., Tanabe, H., Silva, F. J., Wilson, W. B., Campbell, J. E., and
Loison, G. (1955). S. *Pac. Comm., Quart. Bull.,* **5**, (4), 28.
    Lewis, K. H. (1965). *Toxicon* **3**, 111.
Malardé, L., Bagnis, R., Tapu, J., Bennett, J., and Nanai, F. (1957). *Inst. Rech.
    Med. Polynesie Fr., Tech. Rep., 1967 No. 1,* pp. 1–23.
Martin, E. J. (1960). *Pac. Sci.*14, 403.
Mori, M., Saito, T., Nakanishi, Y., Miyazawa, K., and Hashimoto, Y. (1966). *Bull.
    Jap. Soc. Sci. Fish.* **32**, 137.
Morton, R. A., and Burklew, M. A. (1970). *Toxicon* **8**, 317.
Nevenzel, J., Waldtraut, R., and Mead, J. (1965). *Biochem. J.* **4**, 1589.
Okihiro, M. M., Keenan, J. P., and Ivy, A. C. (1965). *Hawaii Med. J.* **24**, 354.
Randall, J. E. (1958). *Bull. Mar. Sci. Gulf Carib.* **8**, 236.
Randall, J. E. (1968). S. *Pac. Comm. Semin. Ichthyosarcotoxism, 1968
    SPC/ICHT/WP–20.*
Rayner, M. D. (1970a). *Pharmacologist* **12**, Abstr. No. 546.
Rayner, M. D. (1970b). *In* "Proceedings of Food/Drugs from the Sea Conference,
    1969" (H. W. Youngken, ed.), pp. 345–350. Mar. Technol. Soc., Washington,
    D.C.
Rayner, M. D., and Kosaki, T. I. (1970). *Fed. Proc., Fed. Amer. Soc. Exp. Biol.*
    29, Abstr. No. 1689.
Rayner, M. D., Kosaki, T. I., and Fellmeth, E. L. (1968). *Science* **160**, 70.
Rayner, M. D., Baslow, M. H., and Kosaki, T. I. (1969). *J. Fish. Res. Bd. Can.*
    26, 2208.
Scheuer, P. J., Takahashi, W., Tsutsumi, J., and Yoshida, T. (1967). *Science* **155**,
    1267.
Setliff, J. A., Rayner, M. D., and Hong, S. K. (1971). *Toxicol. Appl. Pharmacol.*
    18, 676.
Spandorf, A. A. (1970). *Virgin Isl. Ecol. Res. Sta. Contrib. No. 2,* pp. 39–41.
Stevenson, R. L. (1914). "The Cruise of the *Janet Nichol* Among the South Sea
    Islands: A Diary by Mrs. Robert Louis Stevenson." Scribner's, New York.
Tonge, J. I., Battey, Y., and Forbes, J. J. (1967). *Med. J. Aust.* **2**, 1088.

Tsuda, K., Tachikawa, R., Sakai, K., Tamura, C., Amakasu, O., Kawamura, M., and
      Ikuma, S. (1964). *Chem. Pharm. Bull.* **12,** 642.
Whitley, G. P. (1943). *CSIR (Counc. Sci. Ind. Res.) Bull.* **159,** 1–28.
Yasumoto, T., and Scheuer, P. J. (1969). *Toxicon* **7,** 273.
Yasumoto, T., Hashimoto, Y., Bagnis, R., Randall, J. E., and Banner, A. H. (1971).
      Bull. Jap. Soc. Sci. Fish. **37,** 724.
Yip, L. (1971). *Copeia* (1), 175.

7

DESTRUCTION AND RECOVERY OF CORAL REEF COMMUNITIES

Robert Endean

I. Introduction

Until recent times, most of the principal coral reef ecosystems were remote from major centers of human population and difficult of access. This situation has now changed and the biota of coral reefs is being

215

exposed increasingly to a variety of human activities that are potentially harmful. There is a strong possibility that these activities will result in severe stresses being imposed on at least some elements of these ecosystems and that, in some areas, massive destruction of the fauna and flora will occur. Certainly such effects have stemmed from human activities in other ecosystems and concern has already been expressed about the possible adverse effects of these activities in coral reef areas. In Australia, for example, there has been major controversy about the possible harmful effects on the fauna and flora of mining limestone on reefs of the Great Barrier Reef (Clare, 1971). In addition, public disquiet about the possible deleterious effects on coral reef communities of drilling for oil in waters of the Great Barrier Reef led to the setting up in 1970 of a Royal Commission to inquire into the matter.

It would be instructive to examine the types of natural destructive agency to which the biota of coral reefs has been exposed for millenia and to compare these with the types of destruction currently being wrought by human activities on coral reefs. It would also be instructive to assess the extent, rate, and manner of recovery of a number of coral reef communities that have been subjected to destruction of different degrees of magnitude and destruction stemming from different causes. From such analyses, insight might be gained into the types of stress, both natural and induced by humans, that have adverse effects on coral reef communities and the extent to which these communities can cope with such stresses. Possibly the information obtained could be used to predict the likely effects of current and projected human activities on the biota of coral reefs. Possibly too, the information could be used to provide guidelines for developing and implementing rational policies for the conservation of the biota of coral reefs in the face of increasing pressures for the exploitation of the resources of coral reef ecosystems.

II. Factors Responsible for the Destruction of the Biota of Coral Reefs

A. General Considerations

Throughout this section attention will be focused on corals because of the basic roles they play in the construction and maintenance of coral reefs. They are responsible for creating conditions favorable for the development of complex coral reef communities. It is a feature of coral physiology that most coral species have rather narrow ambient salinity and temperature ranges, the extremes of which are near their lethal limits. In addition, any marked alteration in a variety of other parameters of their physical environment leading, for example, to low light intensities, excessive sedimentation rates, low O_2 content of the ambient seawater, etc., would be inimical to their development and, perhaps survival. However, the physical environment of the well-developed coral reef communities of the Indo-West Pacific and Caribbean regions is benign. Those fluctuations in physical parameters that occur are predictable and relatively minor compared with the fluctuations that occur in the environments of most other types of community. Even so, the fluctuations that do occur can lead to localized destruction of corals and their associates, which undoubtedly is responsible, in part, for the spatial heterogeneity found on coral reefs.

Although the roles played by corals are basic, cognizance should be taken of the important roles played by other elements of the coral reef community. For example, coralline algae have essential constructional roles (Cribb, 1973) and microorganisms make major contributions to the high productivity of coral reef communities (Di Salvo, 1973; Sorokin, 1973). Because of their great species diversity and concomitant trophic complexity that have been acquired during their evolutionary history and that manifest themselves during ecological succession, mature coral reef communities possess a multiplicity of homeostatic mechanisms that enable them to resist normal perturbations, particularly those relating to biological factors. Indeed, they are regarded as biologically accommodated communities (Sanders, 1968) with biological interactions such as competition and predation playing a major role in determining community structure and conferring stability on the community. Fluctuations in population densities of most coral reef species appear to be well buffered. It is here that animals of high trophic status might be expected to play key roles. Some of these so-called key species (Paine, 1969) might be more susceptible than corals to the adverse effects of human activities. Attention should therefore be given to the possibility that selective destruction of elements of the fauna other than corals might have profound effects on the community as a whole.

Destruction of coral reef communities, along with the reefs themselves in some cases, has occurred repeatedly throughout the geological record. However, there is no reason to believe that before this century large-scale catastrophic destruction of coral reef communities normally occurred on a time scale which could be conveniently expressed in terms of the average human life span. On the contrary, it would appear that these communities, in some areas at least, have had a long history of continuous development, although the communities have moved laterally from time

to time because of eustatic changes in sea level. Thus, coral reef communities were established at Bikini and Eniwetok as long ago as the Eocene
(Ladd, 1973). Limestone deposition on the northeastern Australian shelf
occurred during the middle Miocene (Lloyd, 1973). These limestones
belonged to a reefal facies and apparently conditions similar to those
existing today on the Great Barrier Reef came into existence along the
inner parts at that time whereas conditions similar to the area of the
outer Great Barrier Reef came into existence during the lower Pliocene.
Modern reef growth related to present sea level must have begun about
5000 years ago according to Stoddart (1973).

Although catastrophic destruction involving the bulk of a coral reef
community would appear to be a rare event if based on a time scale
expressed in terms of the average human life span, localized destruction
of part of a reef community owing to the operation of natural agencies
occurs frequently on modern coral reefs. Factors responsible for the
destruction of corals and other elements of coral reef communities are
discussed below.

B. Water Movements Associated with Tropical Storms

Severe tropical storms are a major cause of localized and occasionally
large-scale mortality of hermatypic corals. Some coral reef systems such
as the Great Barrier Reef are especially subject to hurricanes (or cyclones, as such disturbances are termed in Australia). For example, a
succession of cyclones since 1966 has caused considerable erosion at one
section of Heron Island, a coral cay in the Capricorn Group (Flood,
1974). Moorhouse (1936) has described the destruction caused to corals
at Low Isles, Great Barrier Reef, by a cyclone in 1934. The reef at Low
Isles was again affected by a cyclone in 1950. Damage caused by the
1950 cyclone was described by Stephenson et al. (1958). In 1967 a cyclone almost completely devastated the reef at Lady Elliot Island at the
southern end of the Great Barrier Reef. According to the head lighthouse keeper (Mr. J. Pope) most colonies of branching corals growing
in shallow water were smashed and coral rubble filled in pools in the
reef flat so that the reef flat assumed the appearance of a flat pavement.

In the Caribbean region hurricanes are common. Goreau (1959) has
described the havoc caused by a hurricane in 1951 to reefs in Jamaica.
Glynn et al. (1964) have described the coral destruction caused by a
hurricane in the Puerto Rico region in 1965. Stoddart (1963) gave an
account of the massive coral destruction caused by a hurricane in 1961 to
reefs in the British Honduras region of Central America. Large areas of

reefs were denuded of reef corals and branching corals were selectively destroyed over a wide area.

Damage to coral reef communities occurs principally as a result of the mechanical force exerted by the pounding surf associated with these storms. Branching corals are smashed and coral rubble rolling about in the breakers causes damage to other corals and to other organisms. Frequently, the cyclone-driven seas strike what is normally the lee side of a reef (as far as prevailing winds are concerned) where there is usually marked development of branching coral colonies. Such colonies are particularly susceptible to mechanical damage. Sometimes massive corals are torn loose from their attachment to the substratum and hurled up on reef crests to form boulders (so-called "negro heads"). The presence of such boulders on the perimeters of many reefs of the Great Barrier Reef bears testimony to the power of cyclone-driven seas.

However, damage caused by cyclones is usually localized, the region of destruction being restricted to shallow water areas in the sector of the reef directly exposed to the full force of the pounding surf. Corals in other sectors largely escape damage. Indeed, coral growth in other areas may be enhanced. For example, coral boulders that lodge in coral sand on reef flats frequently become sites of attachment for new coral colonies. Moreover, some reefs lie outside the hurricane (or cyclone) belts and are rarely exposed to damage of the type just discussed.

C. SEDIMENTATION

As noted by Wood-Jones (1910), coral colonies may be killed as a result of material in the form of silt or sand falling upon them from above or by an encroachment of accumulated sediment from below. Most colonies appear capable of removing the sediment that normally falls upon them. Colonies belonging to species possessing large polyps are generally more successful at ridding themselves of sediments than colonies belonging to species (e.g., species of *Porites*) that have small polyps (Marshall and Orr, 1931). The rate of sedimentation that exceeds the ability of corals to rid themselves of sediment no doubt varies not only from species to species but also with the type of sediment involved. However, excessive sedimentation can certainly cause the deaths of coral colonies, most species of coral being unable to withstand burial under sediment for periods longer than one or two days (Mayer, 1918a; Edmondson, 1928).

Severe tropical storms sometimes move about vast quantities of coral sand and rubble, resulting in some coral colonies being buried. Movements of sand caused by a cyclone in March 1972 were responsible for blanketing sectors of the reef crest and adjacent areas on the northern region of Heron Island reef. In some sectors corals were completely or partially buried. When examined approximately two weeks after the cyclone, coral colonies and portions of coral colonies that had been buried were dead (R. Endean and P. Alderslade, unpublished).

Sedimentation can kill corals growing in all depths of water on reefs. However, as might be expected, corals growing on the upper regions of steep slopes are less likely to be buried by sediment than corals growing elsewhere.

D. SALINITY CHANGES

Although Mayer (1918a) found that all of eight species of corals tested at Mer Island, Great Barrier Reef, withstood immersion for 4–5 hours in 50% seawater without detectable injury, most species of coral that have been studied have shown little tolerance to exposure to 50% seawater for longer periods (Mayer, 1918a; Vaughan, 1919; Edmondson, 1928). Exposure to freshwater for 30 minutes was sufficient to kill most of the species studied by Edmondson (1928).

Both branching and massive corals in shallow water habitats can be killed by a local influx of large volumes of freshwater. Heavy rain associated with a cyclone in 1918 caused the destruction of coral on certain fringing reefs in the Whitsunday area of the central Queensland coast (Hedley, 1925; Rainford, 1925). Mayor (1924), Crossland (1928), Slack-Smith (1960), Cooper (1966), and Goodbody (1961) decribed coral destruction attributed to a similar cause at Samoa, Tahiti, Moreton Bay (Queensland), Fiji, and Jamaica, respectively. Banner (1968) described the destruction of corals in Kaneohe Bay, Hawaii, caused by an influx of freshwater.

Corals are also sensitive to salinities higher than those normally encountered. Salinities 150% of normal were fatal to most corals tested within 24 hours and the majority of species tested could not survive salinities of 110% of normal for more than two weeks (Edmondson, 1928). In most regions, corals would not be subjected to salinities appreciably higher than normal and increased salinity is not usually a factor causing significant coral destruction.

E. TEMPERATURE CHANGES

Corals normally live within a narrow range of temperature. It has been known since the work of Dana (1843) that minimum ambient temperatures limit the distribution of corals. Thus, Vaughan (1919) has shown that reef corals in Florida do not grow in waters with an annual minimum temperature below 18°C. This is only a few degrees above temperatures that proved lethal to corals both from Florida and from the Great Barrier Reef (Mayer, 1918a). Likewise, maximum ambient temperatures normally encountered by corals are only a few degrees below their lethal temperatures (Mayer, 1918a,b; Mayor, 1924; Edmondson, 1928). Under normal conditions, shallow water heating by solar radiation is sufficient to inhibit coral growth. Such heating was believed responsible for the paucity of corals within 150 m of the shore at Mer Island, Torres Strait (Mayer, 1918a), for the lack of corals in shallow water at Arno Atoll (Wells, 1951), and for the lack of corals on the beach rock at Heron Island, Great Barrier Reef (Endean *et al.*, 1956).

Even at sublethal temperatures, normal behavioral and metabolic processes are affected, as noted by Mayer (1914) and Johannes (1970). Even so, it is unlikely that temperature fluctuations, apart from fluctuations occurring on a geological time scale, are normally responsible for large-scale coral mortality. There are indications that corals in some regions have adapted to a much wider range of temperatures than that normally encountered elsewhere by corals. For example, Kinsman (1964) has reported flourishing coral reefs on the Oman coast in waters having a seasonal range of 16°–40°C.

F. EMERSION AT LOW TIDE

Emersion at low tide can result in the deaths of those polyps exposed to the atmosphere. Deaths of portions of a large number of colonies of *Acropora* that appeared to stem from emersion at low tide were observed on the reef flat at Heron Island in 1970 and again in 1972 (R. Endean, unpublished). On both occasions, exceptionally cold weather coincided with spring tides. For some days after the event the upper portions of colonies that had been exposed to the atmosphere were covered with a greyish fuzz that consisted primarily of decomposing coral tissue. Extremely low tides occur sporadically at Eilat, Gulf of Aqaba, Red Sea, and one such low tide that occurred in 1970 caused considerable damage to shallow water corals (Fishelson, 1973).

Exposure of emersed corals to freshwater may lead to their death. Taylor (1968) has reported that emersed specimens of *Acropora digitifera* at Mahé in the Seychelles were killed by exposure to rain.

Water movements associated with tropical storms may cause lowering of drainage gaps in shingle ramparts which dam back water on some reef flats at low tide. Moorhouse (1936) noted that the heights of drainage gaps in the shingle ramparts at Low Isles were lowered by the 1934 cyclone and that this resulted in lowering of water level in the so-called "moat" at low tide. The tops of moat corals were exposed at low tide leading to the deaths of the exposed portions.

G. Changes in Light Intensity

Gardiner (1930) showed that the critical factor controlling the depth at which corals grow was illumination and Kawaguti (1937) has shown that the number of species of corals represented decreased markedly at depths where illumination fell to values of 15–20% of surface illumination. As noted by Stoddart (1969a), illumination decreases rapidly below 10 m.

It could be expected that the degree of turbidity of the ambient seawater would affect the depth to which light penetrates (Verwey, 1930). Information is required on the extent to which different types of suspended material reduce the amount of light received by corals growing at different depths. It is known that the normal growth rates of corals can be cut by half on a cloudy day (Goreau, 1961) and it is conceivable that a marked increase in the amount of suspended material could reduce growth rates of corals considerably and possibly to an extent which would be inimical to the survival of corals growing in deeper water. Such an increase in the amount of suspended material could occur in coastal waters after prolonged periods of rain on nearby land masses.

H. Volcanic Activity, Tectonic Uplift or Subsidence, and Earthquakes

"Foul water" released during a volcanic eruption in 1876 was reported to have killed all the corals in the southeast region of the lagoon at Cocos-Keeling Atoll (Wood-Jones, 1907, 1910). It is possible that destruction of coral due to a similar cause had occurred earlier in the region since Darwin noted a large stand of dead coral in the lagoon at Keeling Atoll in 1836 (Darwin, 1967).

Dead corals in the position of growth and unfragmented have been found emersed at low tide levels at several localities in the Solomon Islands (Stoddart, 1969a,b). Tectonic uplift was suggested as a possible cause of the coral deaths. On the other hand, sudden subsidence could result in corals being displaced below the euphotic zone.

Stoddart (1972) has studied the damage to local coral reef communities near Madang, New Guinea, caused by an earthquake in 1972. He found that damage was irregular over the area studied and much less than that associated with major hurricanes. The damage to corals was primarily structural, direct damage to polyps being caused chiefly by abrasion and crushing. Some colonies of massive corals were found to have disintegrated *in situ*. Others had been uprooted and, in some cases, overturned. Some had slid or rolled downslope. Colonies of vasiform foliacious corals belonging to such genera as *Turbinaria, Echinopora, Echinophyllia, Pectinia,* and *Mycedium* had been markedly affected and many were found to have collapsed *in situ*. Stoddart (1972) observed that in Melanesia the frequency of large earthquakes is much greater than the frequency of major hurricanes in other areas.

I. Phytoplankton Blooms

Baas-Becking (1951) has described coral deaths stemming from contact with masses of a planktonic alga *Trichodesmium* that had been washed onto reefs. *Trichodesmium erythraeum* periodically covers vast areas of sea in Barrier Reef waters. This species is reported to make antibacterial substances (Ramamurphy and Krishramurphy, 1967) and its toxicity to members of the coral reef community warrants investigation.

J. Changes in Current Flow Patterns

Changes in current flow stemming from interference to drainage patterns at Low Isles caused by a cyclone in 1934 was mentioned as a factor contributing to the deaths of corals on the reef flat at that locality (Moorhouse, 1936). It might be expected that local tidal currents, particularly on those reefs where the tidal range is considerable, would cause coral rubble to be deposited in some areas while removing it from other areas. Any change in the pattern of current flow could result in the burial of some coral colonies under coral rubble, thereby causing their destruction.

K. Predation by Animals

It has become apparent that earlier estimates (Wells, 1957; Yonge, 1963) of the number of animals specialized to feed on corals are wide of the mark. Recent work (Robertson, 1970; Glynn, 1973; Randall, 1974) has revealed that numerous species of animals, including fish belonging to at least twelve families, polychaetes, a cyclopoid copepod, a barnacle, species belonging to three genera of crabs, several species of gastropods (eolid nudibranchs and species belonging to the families Epitoniidae, Architectonidae, Ovulidae, Caralliophilidae, and Muricidae), and the asteroids *Acanthaster planci* and *Culcita novaeguineae* prey on coral polyps.

In the waters of the Great Barrier Reef only one species of gastropod and the asteroids *C. novaeguineae* and *A. planci* have been observed to kill entire colonies of hermatypic corals. The gastropod *Drupella cornus* has been observed to kill small colonies of acropores. Usually the gastropods cluster among the coralline algae on a few basal branches of such colonies during the day and ascend the branches at night. However, they have been observed feeding during the day on small acropores in shallow water near the reef crest at Mid Reef, Great Barrier Reef (R. Endean, unpublished). Although no estimates have been made of the population density of *D. cornus* on any reef or of the amounts of coral it destroys each year as a result of its feeding activities, the impression gained was that relatively few coral colonies were under attack at any one time. However, the extent and significance of the destruction of coral colonies by this predator require elucidation. The asteroid *C. novaeguineae* has been observed to kill small acropore colonies on the reef flat at Heron Island. Again the extent and significance of coral destruction by this predator require elucidation but the impression gained is that when present at normal population densities, this asteroid does not destroy significant amounts of coral.

Although most coral predators do negligible damage, this certainly is not so in the case of *A. planci* as noted by Yonge (1968). Since 1957, population explosions of *A. planci* associated with massive destruction of hermatypic corals have been recorded from many parts of the tropical Indo-West Pacific region (Chesher, 1969a,b; Endean, 1969, 1973, 1974; Randall, 1972; Endean and Chesher, 1973). These authors expressed the view that the population explosions are abnormal events, probably triggered by human activities. Other authors (Newman, 1970; Dana, 1970) have put forward the view that similar population explosions could have occurred in the recent past but have gone unnoticed. Mean population densities of *A. planci* on uninfested reefs of the Great Barrier Reef are of the order of 6/km^2 (Endean, 1974), and when in such densities, *A. planci* causes negligible damage to corals on these reefs. It has been postulated that the population density of *A. planci* is normally held at low levels by relative specific predators, particularly

Charonia tritonis, the giant triton (Endean, 1973), and possibly by certain species of fish. Collecting of these predators by humans could have triggered the *A. planci* infestations.

It should be noted that although the population density of *A. planci* is held at levels of the order of 6 individuals per km² of reef in the species-rich, biologically accommodated coral reef communities of the Indo-West Pacific region, the situation may well be different in the depauperate East Pacific coral reef communities. There, *Acanthaster* is relatively common (Dana and Wolfson, 1970) and appears to play a major role in regulating coral species diversity (Porter, 1972a). In this regard it is perhaps significant that *Charonia* is absent from the East Pacific (Beu, 1970). *Acanthaster* does not occur in the Atlantic Ocean.

Although there is dispute about the causes of the *A. planci* outbreaks, there is general agreement about the severity of the destruction of corals in some areas such as the Great Barrier Reef, where at least 150 platform reefs have been affected in the last decade (Endean, 1973, 1974; Endean and Stablum, 1973a,b), the Marianas where extensive destruction of hard corals has occurred (Chesher, 1969a,b; Randall 1973), and the Ryukyus where extensive damage to corals has been observed (Nishihira and Yamazato, 1974). It is likely that severe damage has also been inflicted by *A. planci* in recent years on the corals of reefs in other areas (e.g., reefs at Sri Lanka, the Cook Islands, the Philippines, Tahiti, Fiji) but an assessment of the damage at these other localities is not yet available. Whether normal or abnormal events, the *A. planci* infestations are undoubtedly the most important factor currently responsible for coral destruction in many areas. Destruction of the hard coral cover of affected reefs in the Great Barrier Reef region has been particularly high and, in many cases, almost total. After invasion by large numbers of *A. planci* a reef community changes rapidly from a coral-dominated community to an algae-dominated community. Corals growing at all depths on a reef and massive as well as branching species may be affected by the feeding activities of *A. planci.*

L. Penetration of the Skeletons of Corals by Organisms

A number of organisms bore into coral skeletons. Among the borers are filamentous algae, sponges, mollusks, polychaetes, sipunculids, and barnacles. In some cases living colonies are invaded by the borers. For example, poriferans belonging to the genus *Siphonodictyon* can penetrate into living colonies of several species of coral (Rützler, 1971). Cribb

(1973) has reviewed the literature relating to algae that bore into corals. Bacteria are apparently capable of weakening the attachment to the substratum of coral colonies (Di Salvo, 1969, 1972) and they could play a major role in bringing about the detachment of coral skeletons from the substratum. However, the extent to which the boring activities of various organisms weaken the attachment to the substratum of coral skeletons requires elucidation.

M. Competitive Interactions for Space

In the coral reef environment space on which benthic organisms can settle and grow is at a premium. A number of strategies have been developed by such organisms to acquire and retain space. One is the aggressive extracoelenteric feeding activity exhibited by many species of scleractinian corals (Lang, 1970; Glynn, 1973). Species that employ this strategy can be arranged in a hierarchy with the more aggressive species near the apex. Accessible portions of colonies belonging to species low in the hierarchy may be attacked by those above them in the hierarchy. In the Caribbean massive species belonging to the families Mussidae, Meandrinidae, and Faviidae are high in the hierarchy and effectively prevent faster growing acroporids from encroaching on their living space. The extent to which organisms other than corals are eliminated from the living space of corals as a result of the extracoelenteric feeding behavior of corals has yet to be studied. Obviously, this feeding behavior is of importance in ecological succession and in the distribution of organisms on reefs. However, the extent to which it results in destruction of coral colonies or other organisms requires elucidation.

Evidence is accumulating to suggest that many sedentary coral reef species produce antibiotics that inhibit the growth of other organisms in their immediate vicinity (Burkholder and Burkholder, 1958; Nigrelli, 1958; Ciereszko, 1962; Endean, 1966; Burkholder, 1973; Ciereszko and Karns, 1973). Antibiotic activity exhibited by benthic coral reef organisms is of obvious importance in preventing invasion of their tissue by pathogenic microorganisms and perhaps some parasites and in preventing the larvae of fouling forms from settling upon them. However, the extent to which antibiotic activity is involved in preventing a benthic organism from encroaching upon the living space of another, in permitting organisms to live together, and in permitting one organism to overgrow another warrants detailed examination. Certainly, some organisms appear to overgrow others. Glynn (1973), for example, has referred to the tendency of some of the larger algae, sponges, octocorals, and zoanthidians to displace coral growths.

The activities of animals such as certain fishes that abrade the surfaces of living corals and cause localized destruction of polyps may be responsible for providing a foothold for species, such as some species of alcyonarians and algae, that may compete with corals for space and a foothold for penetrating forms, such as clionid sponges.

N. HUMAN ACTIVITIES

1. Dredging, Filling, and Mining

Dredging, filling, and mining activities may be expected to result directly in localized mechanical damage to corals and other elements of the coral reef biota. In some regions damage could also stem from interference with water movements across and around reefs and possibly from lowering of water levels on reef flats at low tide. Then too, large volumes of sediment released into the ambient seawater as a result of these activities could be inimical to the establishment, development, and perhaps survival of many benthic species, particularly corals.

Johannes (1970) has reported that when an airfield was built at Castle Harbour, Bermuda, dredging and filling were responsible for the destruction by siltation of numerous coral colonies including large colonies of brain corals belonging to the genus *Diploria*. Likewise, the total destruction of reef communities occupying over 440 ha as a result of siltation associated with dredging at Johnston Island has been described by Brock *et al.* (1966) and siltation associated with dredging has been responsible for the destruction of corals in Water Bay, St. Thomas, Virgin Islands (Brody *et al.*, 1970). Reclamation work on reef flats at Okinawa has caused destruction of coral at that locality (Nishihira and Yamazato, 1974).

Release into waters near Magnetic Island, Queensland, over a number of years of spoil from harbor dredging activities has been responsible for destruction of the bulk of coral colonies that formerly flourished on the island's fringing reefs (Fig. 1). The probable consequences of the dredging activities were discussed by Bennett (1971) and Brown (1972) has given a detailed account of the coral destruction that has occurred on the fringing reefs since 1961. Acropores, particularly the tabular acropores *Acropora hyacinthus* and *Acropora corymbosa*, were especially susceptible to the accumulation of fine sediment (Fig. 2). Other species of *Acropora* and species of *Pocillopora* and *Seriatopora*

Fig. 1. (A) Flourishing coral colonies (mostly acropores) photographed at low tide at Geoffrey Bay, Magnetic Island, Queensland during the winter of 1952. (B) The same region photographed at low tide during the winter of 1971. Total loss of living corals has occurred. (Courtesy of T. W. Brown.)

were also markedly affected. Species of *Montipora* and *Porites* were slower to exhibit visible effects of the excessive siltation but many specimens eventually succumbed to the constant rain of sediment. Species

Fig. 2. Accumulated silt is visible on these corals photographed in 1971 at Nelly Bay, Magnetic Island, Queensland. The white areas are the exposed skeletons of freshly killed polyps. (Courtesy of T. W. Brown.)

belonging to the genera *Favia, Favites, Leptoria, Platygyra, Goniastrea, Symphyllia, Goniopora,* and *Fungia* appeared to be most resistant to the effects of siltation. However, a high percentage of colonies of these corals present was eventually killed in some areas. Algae invaded many areas after destruction of part of the coral cover and precipitated further destruction by trapping sediment.

During World War II (1939–1945) causeways were built around the perimeter of Palmyra Atoll in the Line Islands. These causeways prevented renewal of water in the lagoon thereby causing the deaths of the corals that had flourished there. Subsequently, algal communities dominated by *Lyngbya* replaced the corals (Dawson, 1959).

Although the guano deposits and phosphate rock on many islands associated with coral reefs have been mined extensively, there has, up to the present, been little mining activity on coral reefs themselves. However, removal of surface material from reefs for industrial purposes has been significant on reefs in India and Mauritius. Mahadevan and Nayar (1972) have estimated that 60,000 m³ of coral stones are removed annually from coral reefs in the Gulf of Mannar and Palk Bay, India. The coral is used in the carbide industry, in lime manufacture, and as building blocks. These authors advocated that coral gathering should be prohibited in some areas and that exploitation should be commensurate with coral growth rates in the region. Walker (1962) has noted that in Mauritius there is evidence of local overexploitation of reef corals that are used for lime production. Much of the lime produced is used in the sugar industry.

The skeletons of corals killed in subrecent times are dredged from a section of Moreton Bay, Queensland and used in the manufacture of cement. It can be expected that pressures for the exploitation of reef corals for cement and lime manufacture will increase markedly with the continued industrialization of countries in coralliferous areas.

2. Land Clearance

It was suggested by Fairbridge and Teichert (1948, p. 86) that sedimentation appeared to be having an adverse effect on coral growth in the vicinity of Low Isles (Great Barrier Reef) because of "colossal soil erosion during the last decade or so engendered by unplanned agriculture." These words were somewhat prophetic because it would appear that Low Isles itself is now being adversely affected by the runoff of fresh silt-laden water from the nearby mainland. In 1954, when Low Isles was resurveyed (Stephenson et al., 1958), the composition of the fauna there did not appear to have changed appreciably since 1928–1929, when it was investigated by members of the Great Barrier Reef Expedition (Stephenson et al., 1931; Manton and Stephenson, 1935). However, in 1973 (R. Endean, unpublished) it was apparent that a heavy mortality of corals in many habitats on the reef flat had occurred. This was particularly evident in the case of massive corals that formerly flourished in shallow water habitats. The cause of the mortality was not immediately apparent but freshwater runoff from the adjacent mainland is suspected as shallow water habitats were primarily affected and most areas on the reef flat were covered by silt. There was also a marked lack of echinoderms on the reef flat compared with the position in 1954 (Endean, 1956). Miss I. Bennett (personal communication, 1973) stated that changes in the fauna on the reef flat at Low Isles were apparent in 1969.

3. Blasting and Nuclear Weapons Testing

Explosives are often used to kill reef fish. Thus, Fuchs (in Johannes, 1970) has described how fishermen use dynamite to obtain fish from Truk lagoon for commercial purposes and Ramas (1969) has described the technique of fishing using dynamite employed by fishermen on coral reefs in the Philippines. In Fiji, fishing with dynamite was commonly employed prior to 1965 (Owens, 1971). Chesher (1969b) has discussed the dynamiting of fish in the Marianas and Carolines.

Blasting of channels through coral reefs and blasting of coral pinnacles that pose navigational hazards have occurred in several coral reef areas (Chesher, 1969b). Blasting associated with dredging was used in excavation of a harbor and swing basin in 1967 at Heron Island, Great Barrier Reef. All corals were killed within 150 m of the blasting and dredging sites at the time but it is not known precisely how they were killed (R. Endean, unpublished).

The reefs around many islands in the Pacific Ocean were blasted with high explosives during World War II but effects of the blasting do not appear to have been studied. However, Stoddart (1968) noted that it had been suggested (Emery *et al.*, 1954) that the so-called "decadence" (Stearns, 1945) of reefs in the Marshall Islands has stemmed from intense military bombardment, rather than from biological or geological causes.

When nuclear explosions are involved, damage to reef communities could stem from mechanical, heat, or radiation effects. A layer of radioactive mud estimated to have a mean thickness of 5 ft and a volume of 0.5 million tons was formed on the floor of the lagoon at Bikini Atoll as a result of the 1946 underwater nuclear explosion at that locality (Hines, 1962). Stoddart (1968) stated that the 1952 thermonuclear explosion at Eniwetok Atoll excavated a hole in the peripheral reef a mile wide and up to 200 ft deep. As noted by Johannes (1970) there is little information on the ecological effects of radioactive contamination of the environment on coral reef communities. This aspect warrants urgent attention in view of the continued use of islands in coralliferous areas for the testing of nuclear weapons.

4. Sewage Pollution

Deaths of corals in the southern and middle regions of Kaneohe Bay, Hawaii in recent years have been attributed, in part, to an increased volume of sewage entering the bay (Banner and Bailey, 1970; Banner, 1974). Other factors involved were increased freshwater runoff and increased siltation resulting from urbanization of the Kaneohe Bay watershed. During the first half of this century, Kaneohe Bay supported a diverse coral fauna and coral reefs were well developed. After 1950, great changes occurred, and in 1970 it was found that the southern part of the bay, which has an area of about 880 ha and a restricted water circulation, was virtually devoid of living coral. Corals transferred to the area died within a few weeks.

Two sewage systems discharge into the southern part of the bay and the volumes of sewage carried by these systems have increased markedly in recent years. In 1970, the outfall was calculated to be about 3 million gallons per day. It has been suggested that chlorine associated with the sewage may have been responsible for the observed coral mortality. Young and Chan (1970) found approximately 1.1 mg/liter of residual chlorine in effluent from the major sewage plant.

The increased sewage outflow appears to be linked with increased phosphate levels in the southern part of the bay. Caperon and Cattell (in Banner and Bailey, 1970) found that phosphate levels near the major sewer outfall increased between 1966 and 1970 at an average annual rate of 0.75 μg atoms/liter. Eutrophication stemming from increased levels of phosphate and other nutrients appears to have caused changes in the plankton community. It may also be responsible for changes in the benthic community. It was found in the summer of 1970 (Banner and Bailey, 1970) that corals in the central region of Kaneohe Bay were being invaded by, and in some cases obliterated by, an alga, *Dictyosphaeria cavernosa*. Johannes (in Banner and Bailey, 1970) showed that *D. cavernosa* in Kaneohe Bay water to which nitrates and phosphates were added grew much more rapidly than it did in the bay water alone.

The partially degraded organic matter present in sewage could settle and produce anaerobic conditions. Significantly, decreased redox potentials and high amounts of sulfate reducing bacteria were found in sediments in and near the southern sections of the bay by Sorokin (1973). He also found similar conditions downstream from a sewage outfall at Majuro Atoll.

Doty (1969) considered that increased dissolved nutrient levels associated with sewage may have led to an increase in algal growth in the vicinity of Waikiki Beach, Hawaii, and a reduction in the coral cover of these reefs. Barnes (1973) has drawn attention to the dangers presented by sewage pollution to the coral reefs of Jamaica as a result of the rapid development of the tourist industry.

5. *Thermal Pollution*

Johannes (1970) has drawn attention to the fact that the threat of destruction or modification of marine communities by heated effluents is greatest in tropical regions because, unlike the biota of other regions, corals, and hence coral reef communities, live near their upper thermal limit.

Thermal effluent from a power plant at Turkey Point in Biscayne

Bay, Florida has been responsible for a mass mortality of plants and animals extending 1.5 km from the outfall (Roessler and Zieman, 1969). Significantly, corals were killed by the effluent at greater distances from the outfall than most other species (Anonymous, 1970).

Jokiel and Coles (1974) studied the effect of thermal enrichment on hermatypic corals growing off Kahe Point, Oahu, Hawaii, where an electricity generating plant is located. It was noted that abundances of dead and damaged corals in the region correlated well with proximity to thermal effluent from the plant. An increase in thermal discharge accompanying expansion of the plant in 1972 resulted in an increase in the area of dead and damaged corals from 0.38 to 0.71 ha.

6. Desalination Effluents

The dangers to coral reef communities posed by effluents from desalination plants have been discussed by Johannes (1970). He noted that such effluents are characterized by elevated salinity and temperature and by the presence of toxic metals such as copper and zinc. The effects of elevated temperature and salinity on corals are certainly deleterious but the effects of toxic metals on the biota of coral reefs have received little study. It might be expected that corals and their associates will be just as susceptible to heavy metal pollution as other marine animals have proved to be (Halstead, 1970).

Van Eepoel and Grigg (1970) noted that corals and other invertebrates were killed to a distance of 200 m from a power desalination plant near St. Thomas, Virgin Islands.

7. Oil Pollution

The lack of reports in the literature of damage to reefs stemming from oil spills (Johannes, 1970) and the fact that corals flourish in several regions subjected to potential oil pollution would indicate that corals and other organisms present on coral reefs are resistant to this form of pollution.

However, the effects of oil on corals appear to depend a great deal on the way in which the corals are exposed to the oil. Grant (1970) placed specimens of *Favia speciosa* in seawater in a vessel and floated crude oil on the surface of the seawater. During the subsequent six days of observation, the corals showed no visible injury. Likewise, no visible signs of injury were exhibited by *Porites compressa*, *Montipora verrucosa*, and *Fungia scutaria* exposed for 2.5 hours to five different types of oil and observed for 25 days subsequently (Johannes *et al.*, 1972). On the other hand, Lewis (1971) found that four species of coral that he exposed to crude oil or an oil spill detergent in sealed vessels exhibited ruptured tissues and other signs of distress. These experiments were designed to prevent the escape of volatile oil fractions and possibly the harmful effects observed were caused by these fractions.

Experiments carried out by Johannes *et al.* (1972) have revealed that floating oil can kill coral tissue if it adheres when shallow water corals are exposed to air, as could occur during spring tides. (This could happen to many colonies growing in shallow water in many areas of the Great Barrier Reef.) Oil adhered strongly to the surfaces of branching corals of the genera *Acropora* and *Pocillopora* and was retained for weeks. With species of *Fungia* and *Symphyllia*, which possess large fleshy polyps and abundant mucus, most of the oil disappeared when the corals were submerged for a day. Species belonging to other genera tested showed degrees of adsorption and retention of oil that fell between these extremes. Destruction of coral tissue was observed in the areas where oil adhered in patches of a few mm diameter. It was not established whether heating as a result of absorption by the black surfaces created by the adhering crude oil was the prime cause of tissue death, a contributing factor, or unrelated to tissue death.

No doubt the type of crude oil involved is a factor that must be taken into account when assessing the likelihood of damage to corals from oil pollution. The effects of oil on elements of the biota other than corals remain to be investigated. If so-called key species are involved, the effects may be of great significance. The long-term chronic effects of oil pollution on the various elements of the biota of coral reefs have not been studied. In this respect, it might be noted that some oil compounds that are both soluble and toxic to marine organisms can pass unaltered through the food chain (Blumer, 1970).

Increased tanker traffic and increased offshore drilling activities in several coralliferous areas are projected. The holing of the *Oceanic Grandeur* in Torres Strait in 1970 highlighted the necessity for research into the effects of oil pollution on the biota of coral reefs generally.

8. Chemical Pollution

As noted by Halstead (1970), the bulk of problems caused by pollution are toxicological ones. Unfortunately, little work has been carried out on the toxicological effects on any element of the biota of coral reefs of compounds likely to be present as pollutants in the coral reef environment. Indeed, the exact nature of these pollutants has not been investigated. It might be expected that heavy metals and other inorganic substances and a variety of naturally occurring and man-made organic compounds regarded as pollutants in marine evironments elsewhere would be present. In this connection, Halstead (1970) has pointed out that shallow-water tropical insular regions are particularly susceptible to pollution. These are the regions where coral reefs flourish.

Pollution of the world's oceans by man-made chemicals is widespread and coral reefs have not escaped this form of pollution. Some of these chemicals, particularly pesticides that have been produced in enormous quantities, have entered marine food chains and have been widely transported. Thus, it is common knowledge that DDT residues have been found in Antarctic penguins and seals (Sladen *et al.*, 1966). Johannes (1970) reported that barracuda taken from reefs of the northern part of the Gulf of Mexico contained high levels of DDT. DDT has been used extensively in coral reef areas where agriculture is carried out on a significant scale or where there are large human populations (Chesher, 1969b; Randall, 1972).

In recent years other chlorinated hydrocarbons such as dieldrin and endrin, which have a greater toxicity for fishes and other marine organisms than DDT (Johnson, 1968), have been widely used in some coral reef areas. Randall (1972) mentioned that localized fish kills have occurred in the lagoon at Tahiti as a result of uncontrolled spraying with insecticides, particularly dieldrin. Bourns (1970) has reported that the flesh of large numbers of fish that died suddenly in the lagoon at Truk in 1970 contained the highest concentration of the pesticide endrin ever recorded in fishes to that date. Hambeuchen (in Randall, 1972) has reported how the inhabitants of Rarotonga use lindane and dieldrin to kill fishes in pools and lagoons.

Apart from fishes, it is not known what effects (acute or chronic) persistent pesticides have on corals or other elements of the coral reef biota. However, it is possible that some species may be particularly susceptible to these compounds, whereas others may be resistant. Selective elimination of some species (such as predators of the coral predator *A. planci*) could have far-reaching effects on coral reef communities. Pearson and Endean (1969), Fisher (1969), and Randall (1972) have discussed the possible involvement of persistent pesticides in triggering recent *A. planci* outbreaks.

As pointed out by Randall (1972), it is only in recent years that it has become apparent that polychlorinated biphenyl compounds (PCB's) used in the manufacture of plastics, paints, hydraulic fluids, etc., well before DDT was discovered are almost as widespread as DDT in the global environment. The effect of PCB's on the coral reef community has still to be evaluated.

Other forms of pollution in coral reef areas warrant attention. The effluent from sugar mills on the Queensland coast is a source of potential pollutants as are some of the agricultural chemicals used in tropical agriculture. Some of the detergents currently in use might be expected to have deleterious effects on corals. Barnes (1973) has shown that a mild detergent (Palmolive) at concentrations as low as 0.05% was capable of killing healthy specimens of the coral *Montastrea cavernosa* in Jamaica. Some of the dispersents currently used to disperse oil slicks should be examined for toxicity to coral reef organisms. Some biologists consider that the mass mortality of pearl shell oysters that resulted in the recent closure of most of the pearl culture establishments in the Torres Strait region may have been directly related to the use of dispersents to disperse oil slicks released from the holed *Oceanic Grandeur* in 1970.

9. Collection of Elements of Reef Biota

The indigenous populations of islands in coralliferous seas have utilized elements of the coral reef biota for millenia. Some animals, particularly fish, mollusks, crabs, turtles, and worms (such as the Palolo worm), have been used for food. Others, particularly mollusks, have been used for ornamentation (cowries, pearl shells, etc.), as receptacles for holding water (baler shells, giant clams), as trumpets (*C. tritonis*) for calling people together, and as a primitive form of currency (cowries) in some regions. However, until recently, the collection of coral reef organisms appears to have been on a limited scale that was not beyond the replacement capabilities of the coral reef community. In recent years, the picture has changed markedly. The resources of coral reef areas have come under increasing pressure for their economic exploitation, human populations on many island regions in coral reef areas have increased markedly, and modern methods of transport enable increasing numbers of people to visit coral reef areas each year.

Coral reefs do not lend themselves to conventional methods of fishing involving nets and trawls. In recent years the development of self-contained underwater breathing apparatus, spear guns, and the advent of high-powered outboard motors for dinghies have enabled the systematic exploitation of coal reef fishes on an unprecedented scale in some areas such as the Great Barrier Reef. On some reefs in this region most species of sizable fish are speared and sold as fillets of coral reef fish. Unfortunately, information is not available on the number of each fish species taken each year in Barrier Reef waters. Poisoning of reef fishes with derris and other poisons and the use of explosives in collecting reef fish has obviously increased in recent years, but again, figures are not available. In recent years too, a flourishing trade has arisen in aquarium fish from coral reefs. Most species of brightly hued fish are collected for this trade.

Polunin and Frazier (1974) referred to the frequent absence of large predatory fishes, particularly sharks (Carcharhinidae) and groupers (Serranidae), from reefs in the Western Indian Ocean that they visited in 1973. In historic times these reefs were known to possess vast numbers of such fishes. Also, larger fishes on the reefs were timid and ready to flee from divers, a behavior pattern that, according to Randall (1969), indicates that the fishes have been subjected to spear fishing. Only two of the 27 coral reefs investigated by Polunin and Frazier were noteworthy for their apparent lack of disturbance by man.

Endean and Stablum (unpublished) have found that the groper (*Promicrops lanceolatus*) will eat juvenile specimens of *A. planci*. In 1974 these authors searched 14 reefs (most of them infested with *A. planci*) in the central region of the Great Barrier Reef for specimens of *P. lanceolatus*. Only 5 specimens of *P. lanceolatus*, the largest estimated to weigh about 150 kg, were seen. Large serranids generally were rare on the 14 reefs visited.

Since World War II there has been a great upsurge of interest in the collection of mollusks. Shells have been sold in increasing quantities, not only to individuals for private collections, but also to the manufacturers of shell jewelry, ornaments, lamp shades, souvenirs, and bric-a-brac. The collecting of mollusks has had a marked affect on the molluscan fauna at some localities. Thus, Stoddart (1969b) noted that the decrease in mollusk populations at Addu Atoll between 1936 and 1964 amounted to local extinction of many species. The systematic collection of mollusks on the reef at Northwest Island, Capricorn Group, by a commercial collector in the early 1960's resulted in most species of mollusks becoming extremely scarce on the reef flat at that locality (R. Endean, unpublished). Moreover, there has been a selective collecting of some species. Large coral reef gastropods such as balers (*Melo* species), giant helmets (*Cassis cornuta*), and giant tritons (*C. tritonis*) command high prices and have been prime targets of shell collectors. The giant triton, *C. tritonis*, is a formidable predator of the crown-of-thorns starfish, *A. planci*, and it has been suggested by Endean (1969) that intensive collecting of *C. tritonis* by humans, particularly in the 1950's, may have initiated recent population explosions of *A. planci*. However, other authors (Vine, 1970; Ormond and Campbell, 1970; Weber and Woodhead, 1970) have stated that the giant triton is not sufficiently common to exert any major

form of control over *A. planci* populations. Although this is certainly
true on reefs recently and currently infested with *A. planci,* it is possible
that *C. tritonis* was formerly present in adequate numbers to exert control
over normal *A. planci* populations (Endean, 1973). Unfortunately, it
is very difficult to obtain information on the extent of collection of *C.
tritonis.* Records of collections made by commerical shell collectors in
Australia do not appear to have been kept and there is no way of estimating the numbers collected by amateur collectors and tourists. Then
too, vendors of shells are reluctant to divulge their sources of supply.

It is known that specimens of *C. tritonis* were collected, incidentally,
by the crews of luggers engaged in the trochus trade. Prior to World
War II (1939–1945), there appears to have been little demand for giant
tritons and their collecting appears to have been discouraged by the
masters of trochus luggers since uncleaned shells hanging from the luggers attracted sharks. After World War II the situation changed. Shell
collecting was taken up as a hobby by people throughout the world.
Large shells, such as the shells of the giant triton, came into great demand. From about 1947 onward, the crews of many trochus luggers
collected all giant tritons seen during their search for trochus shells
in Great Barrier Reef waters. As noted by Endean (1973), available
information indicates that thousands of specimens of *C. tritonis* were
collected during the 1950's. Some indication of the extent of the trade
can be gauged from the following statements. On August 17, 1969, Mr.
L. Ellis (personal communication), formerly a lighthouse keeper in North
Queensland, stated that the trochus lugger crews took all giant tritons
encountered, big ones as well as small ones. In October 1952, he saw
120 giant tritons laid out on a wharf at Cooktown following the arrival
of two trochus luggers. On January 8, 1969, Mr. B. Davidson (personal
communication) formerly of Palm Island, Queensland wrote: "During
the last year that the Thursday Island luggers operated along the reef,
1958, the price of trochus shell was dropping and the lugger boys used
to bring into the Palm Island Welfare Association, for sale, bags of
the tritons and at one stage 20 tea chests of the shells were on hand.
I would estimate there were about 40 shells per chest which is 800
shells at Palm Island alone. I would say that the giant tritons which
we received at Palm Island were mostly from local reefs, i.e., Bramble,
Britomart, Keeper, the Slashers and possibly Otter." On February 20,
1972, Mr. R. Grenier (personal communication) formerly of Thursday
Island, Queensland, stated that when the price of trochus shell fell following the advent of plastic buttons, the Island Industries Board at
Thursday Island encouraged the collection of the shells of giant tritons

and other large mollusks and bought part of the catch of shells from each lugger.

It is possible that intensive collection of *C. tritonis* would lead to a marked reduction in the numbers of specimens found on at least some reefs of the Great Barrier Reef. During the period 1966–1973, only 57 adult and two juvenile giant tritons were observed by the author and co-workers during visits to approximately 150 reefs, some reefs being visited on more than one occasion. During these trips specific searches for giant tritons were made. *Charonia tritonis* has been collected intensively in other areas such as the Marianas and Carolines (Chesher, 1969b). Owens (1971) noted that in February, 1970, when a ban was placed on the collection of *C. tritonis* in Fijian waters, there were 1000 specimens of the species in the Suva market.

III. Recovery of Coral Reef Communities Devastated by Catastrophic Events

A. THEORETICAL ASPECTS

Theoretical aspects relating to the recovery of coral reefs devastated by catastrophic events have been discussed by Endean (1971). It is apparent that recovery depends basically on colonization of devastated areas by coral planulae settling from the plankton and on the continued growth and reproduction of surviving coral colonies. However, complete recovery would involve the return of those species typically associated with corals and coral reefs in the particular geographical region concerned and the reestablishment of the complex relationships, trophic and otherwise, normally existing among these species.

A number of factors could affect the rate at which recolonization by corals occurs. If substantial numbers of coral colonies (representative of a large number of species) survive the catastrophic event in localized areas of a devastated reef, then recolonization should be relatively rapid compared with the situation that would arise if destruction of coral colonies had been uniformly extensive over the reef. In the latter case, an extended period of time would be required for adequate numbers of recolonizing planulae to be produced by the sparsely scattered survivors. This would be particularly so if species (probably the majority) that do not exhibit self-fertilization are involved. Another factor of importance is the ages of the surviving coral colonies. Connell (1973) found that about one-third, or fewer, of coral colonies in a shallow-water assem-

blage at Heron Island that he studied appeared to be large enough
to be mature. If the destruction of coral colonies caused by the catastrophic event were total, or near total, then the planulae responsible
for recolonization would have to originate from eggs and sperm produced
by corals on other reefs. In such cases, the presence or absence of
favorable currents for transporting the planulae would have a major
effect on the rate of recolonization. It might be expected that opportunistic species that have a high fecundity and breed throughout the year
would be well represented among the early colonizers.

As well as the availability of coral planulae, the degree of success
attending the settlement of planulae would affect the rate of recolonization. The availability of substrate suitable for settlement of coral planulae
would obviously regulate recruitment rate. If coral colonies and other
benthic organisms had been stripped from a reef area at the time of
a catastrophic event, then suitable substratum should be immediately
available for recolonization. However, if dead coral colonies remained
in situ, or if rapidly growing benthic organisms other than corals
spread over the area, then recolonization could well be hampered. Recolonizing planulae could certainly settle on the dead skeletons of coral
colonies remaining *in situ* but such recolonizers might subsequently
be lost as the dead coral colonies to which they attached would be
susceptible to biogenic erosion. As noted earlier, many organisms bore
into and abrade coral skeletons.

If organisms other than corals settle on and cover an area before
coral planulae arrive, then it might be expected that recolonization by
corals would be hampered. Algae, in particular, appear to compete with
corals for substrate (Cribb, 1973). If hard corals are selectively killed
during a catastrophic event, then the balance could well be tipped in
favor of fast-growing algae. In such cases, other benthic organisms, such
as alcyonarians, might also spread and restrict the amount of substratum
available for coral planulae. On the other hand, it is possible that the
presence of certain types of algae might facilitate settlement by corals.
Yamaguchi (1973) has reported that planulae of *Pocillopora damicornis*
settle predominantly on coralline algae encrustations and rarely on clean
surfaces.

After settlement of the planulae of hard corals, the survival and rate
of growth of the coral colonies initiated must be considered. A variety
of factors, such as the presence of loose rubble, marked sedimentation,
the activities of microphagous animals, etc., would have a bearing on
the survival of recently settled planulae. However, few data are available
for the survival of recently established coral colonies. Those that are

available indicate that mortality of recently established colonies is high. Connell (1973) found that, under normal conditions, recruitment rates of coral colonies in the areas he studied at Heron Island averaged 5 colonies/m²/year and that about half of these young colonies died within a year. Growth rates are variable among the species, and even within the one species are affected by a number of environmental factors. It is well established that branching corals (e.g., species of *Acropora* and *Pocillopora*) increase in linear dimensions more quickly than colonies of massive forms, such as *Porites* and *Favia*, but the total weight attained is much less than in the massive forms. The rate of growth in branching forms is greatest at the tips of the branches (Goreau, 1959, 1961) whereas it is fairly uniform over the surface of a colony belonging to a massive species. Using figures quoted by Stoddart (1969a)—annual increments of 5–10 cm in diameter and 2–5 cm in height for branching colonies and 0.5–2 cm in diameter for the hemispherical colonies of massive species—Endean (1971) has estimated that colonies of branching corals might attain a substantial size (50–100 cm in diameter) in ten years, and colonies of massive species might obtain a substantial size (10–40 cm in diameter) in 20 years from the time when the colonies were initiated. However, it is unlikely that growth would be uniform from year to year. Indeed, it has been found that the initial rapid growth rate of a coral colony is followed by a slowing down leading to an almost complete cessation of growth (Manton, 1932; Matoda, 1940; Abe, 1940; Goreau and Goreau, 1960). It is not known whether this slowing down is caused primarily by instrinsic factors or is a result of the effects of environmental factors. It should be noted that the prereproductive period of coral colonies may be of long duration. In the two species for which data are available, a period of 8–10 years is indicated (Connell, 1973).

Numerous environmental factors could be involved in retarding coral growth rates considerably and hence in increasing markedly the time required for colonies to obtain substantial sizes. Any of the physiochemical factors mentioned in Section II could operate to slow growth rates. Also, more subtle ecological factors, such as competition for space on which to grow, could play major roles. Indeed, it is possible that some recently established colonies will decrease in size with time. Thus, Connell (1973) found that during studies made of shallow-water aggregations of corals at Heron Island, almost as many corals occupying an area between 25 and 100 cm² lost ground as gained it each year.

It is to be expected that during the reestablishment of the hard coral cover of a devastated reef there will be a distinct succession of species, pioneer species paving the way for later colonists. Estimates are not available for the time required for the climax situation to be attained.

It should be appreciated that in some cases, particularly if human activity has been responsible for destruction of the biota of a coral reef, conditions in the area in question may no longer be conducive to coral growth and recovery may not occur.

B. RECORDED INSTANCES OF PARTIAL OR COMPLETE RECOVERY

Endean (1971) noted that within $3\frac{1}{2}$ years after a cyclone at Heron Island in 1967, recolonization of the relatively small areas of reef that had been denuded of living coral by the cyclone was well under way. The same cyclone destroyed almost all corals in quadrats in one area of the reef at Heron Island being studied by Connell (1973), who reported that $3\frac{1}{2}$ years after the cyclone about 10% of the surface enclosed by the quadrats had been recolonized and after $4\frac{1}{2}$ years, about 20%. Prior to the cyclone, 57% of the surface had been covered by corals.

Eleven years after the cyclone that struck Low Isles in 1934, coral damage was largely repaired (Fairbridge and Teichert, 1947, 1948; Fairbridge, 1950). Low Isles was again affected by a cyclone in 1950. It was estimated by Stephenson et al. (1958), who visited the island in 1954, that 10–20 years would elapse before recovery from the 1950 cyclone was complete.

In 1961, a severe hurricane affected reefs in the British Honduras region causing catastrophic damage in a zone 50–65 km wide (Stoddart, 1963, 1969c). Stoddart (1969a, p. 451) stated that three years afterward "the only corals living in any quantity were those which survived the storm itself and wide areas were blanketed by the algae *Padina* and *Halimeda*." In 1972, more than ten years after the hurricane, its effects were again studied (Stoddart, 1974). It was found that little or no recovery had taken place on reefs subjected to massive damage, whereas complete recovery had occurred on moderately or little damaged reefs. Stoddart (1974, p. 4) stated, "This suggests that there is a threshold of damage beyond which storm effects are likely to be prolonged." It was noted that in areas of maximum devastation recovery may require much longer periods than the 20–25 year period originally estimated.

Johannes (1970) reported on regrowth of coral that had apparently been destroyed by a nuclear blast at Eniwetok Atoll. The precise date of destruction was unknown but the last nuclear tests carried out in the area had occurred 13 years previously. It was found that regrowth of tabular *Acropora corymbosa* was extensive. However, coral diversity was low, only four species of coral being common whereas about 15 species are commonly represented in typical *Acropora* dominated communities at Eniwetok. It was concluded that although growth of *A. corymbosa* was impressive, the community studied had by no means recovered 13 years after the last nuclear test in the vicinity.

Grigg and Maragos (1974) studied times required for recolonization by coral communities of lava flows in Hawaii. They found that in exposed areas recovery time for communities decimated by lava flows appears to be about 20 years. However, they estimated that about 50 years may be required for complete recovery of coral communities in sheltered areas.

C. RECORDED INSTANCES OF LACK OF RECOVERY

As pointed out by Stoddart (1973), many modern Indian Ocean reef communities only patchily veneer much older and much more extensive reef structures. The reasons for the destruction and failure to recover of these earlier reefs are obscure. However, the existence of such fossil reefs serves to emphasize that the biota of a reef does not always recover from the effects of castastrophic destruction. Recovery might not occur if the devastation was caused by a natural event of exceptional severity that rendered the area unsuitable for coral growth or hastened a natural trend in that direction. Also, recovery might not occur if the destruction was caused by an abnormal event stemming from some form of human activity.

In 1918 flood rains accompanying a cyclone caused widespread destruction of fringing reefs in the Whitsunday group of islands on the central Queensland coast (Rainford, 1925). Only slight recovery was observed in some areas six years after the flood (Hedley, 1925). Unfortunately, further studies of the extent of recovery of reefs in the area have not been made. However, it was reported that in 1953, 35 years after the corals on the fringing reef at Stone Island near Bowen were killed by the flood, negligible recolonization by hard corals was in evidence (Stephenson *et al.*, 1958).

Wood-Jones (1910) reported that in 1876 all the living coral of the southeastern region of the lagoon at Cocos-Keeling Atoll was destroyed by foul water ejected from a supposed volcanic vent at the southern side of the atoll and that in 1906, the same tract of dead coral was still visible.

Johannes (1970) noted that 30 years after corals were destroyed by siltation caused by dredging and filling at Castle Harbour, Bermuda, only scattered small colonies of corals occurred and the substratum was dominated by benthic algae. The flourishing coral reefs in the lagoon at Palmyra Island that were killed because of interference with water circulation in the lagoon by the erection of causeways, were subsequently replaced by algal communities dominated by *Lyngbya* (Dawson, 1959). Corals have been virtually eliminated from areas affected by outfall of heated water from the Turkey Point powerhouse at Biscayne Bay, Florida (Johannes, 1970). Sedimentation associated with constructional activity has been responsible for destruction of corals and other benthic animals in large areas of Lindberg Bay, St. Thomas, Virgin Islands, and conditions remain unsuitable for their recovery (Van Eepoel and Grigg, 1970).

D. STUDIES OF RECOVERY AFTER DEVASTATION BY *Acanthaster*

Studies of the sequence of events that occurred on some reefs of the Great Barrier Reef devastated by *A. planci* have been made by the author and co-workers. It was found that within 2–3 weeks, the exposed skeletons of corals killed by the starfish began to acquire an algal coating that subsequently thickened and darkened (Endean and Stablum, 1973b). During this period there was an obvious breakdown of typical reef community structure, coral-associated animals being particularly affected by the change from a coral-dominated to an algae-dominated community. Coralline algae did not become apparent among the algae on the skeletons until several months after the skeletons had been exposed.

Within a few months after a reef had been devastated by *A. planci,* an obvious increase in the alcyonarian cover, particularly in lagoons and back reef areas, occurred. Frequently, these soft corals grew over the skeletons of corals killed by *Acanthaster*. In some regions, stalked algae (e.g., *Turbinaria* sp.) proliferated and covered coral skeletons. In other cases, the skeletons of branching corals fragmented and formed piles of rubble. This rubble accumulated in lagoons and back reef areas, especially around the bases of coral pinnacles.

Within 3–4 years after the starfish had devastated a reef, the first coral recolonizers were noted. However, few species were represented. *Pocillopora damicornis, Seriatopora hystrix, Stylophora pistillata,* and species of *Turbinaria, Porites,* and *Acropora* (especially *A. hyacinthus* and *A. humilis*) were among the first corals to settle. Endean and Stablum (1973b) noted an apparent relationship between the rate of recovery of an area of reef and the extent of coral destruction in the area caused by the starfish initially. There are strong indications (Endean, 1974) that recolonization by hard corals will be fastest in shallow water, on seaward slopes in the vicinity of patches of hard corals that had survived the *A. planci* infestations. On the devastated reefs studied, these patches were found mainly near reef crests and upper seaward slopes in situations exposed to considerable wave action. Wave action was usually most marked at the southeastern tips of the reefs studied and usually shallow water corals had survived in this region.

Figures for the coral cover of numerous devastated reefs several years after the devastation occurred have been presented by Endean and Stablum (1973a,b), Endean (1974), and Pearson (1974). It is apparent from their figures that a massive destruction of the hard coral cover of the reefs has taken place. In a few regions, usually near patches of corals that had survived the *A. planci* attacks, coral regrowth had been impressive, particularly where fast-growing tabular colonies of *A. hyacinthus* are well represented among the recolonizers. Thus, Endean (1974) has estimated that in October, 1971, recolonizing corals occupied 6% of the surface on the southeastern end of Gibson Reef and Pearson (1974) found that considerable recolonization had occurred on the seaward slopes of Feather Reef. However, recolonization by corals on most reefs had been surprisingly slow and, in many cases, particularly in back reef areas, was negligible 6–10 years after the destruction of corals by *A. planci* occurred. Even where recolonization was in progress, many of the recolonizers had settled on dead coral skeletons and will ultimately be lost. The presence of an extensive cover of alcyonarians on some reefs and of mats of filamentous and stalked algae on others must hamper recolonization by hard corals as must the presence of huge amounts of loose rubble formed from the fragmented skeletons of corals killed by *A. planci*.

It has been estimated that a period in excess of 20 years and possibly periods ranging from 20 to 40 years will be required for recovery of reefs of the Great Barrier Reef devastated by *A. planci* (Endean, 1971, 1973). However, the factors that triggered the *A. planci* infestations may still be operative and the possibility must be entertained that affected reefs will be reinvaded by *A. planci* during the course of recolonization by hard corals. Should this happen, then affected reefs might be impoverished indefinitely.

In some regions, which are marginal for coral growth, devastation of the hard coral cover by *A. planci* may tip the balance in favor of

algae for long periods of time. Nishihira and Yamazato (1974) have
raised the possibility that coral reef communities devastated by A. *planci*
in some areas at Okinawa will change to *Sargassum* communities.

IV. Conclusions

Because of their primary roles in reef construction and maintenance
and in the provision of shelter for other organisms, corals are of basic
importance in the coral reef community. Indeed, when corals are selectively killed *en masse* (as during A. *planci* infestations) there is an
obvious breakdown of normal coral reef community structure and coral
dominated communities are frequently replaced by communities dominated by algae. It is a feature of their physiology that corals are adversely
affected by relatively small-scale fluctuations in various physical parameters of their environment, such as temperature, salinity, etc. However,
physical conditions in environments where coral reefs flourish are relatively benign as far as corals are concerned and usually such conditions
are of importance with respect to catastrophic destruction of corals
only in situations that are marginal for coral growth or on a geological
time scale. Nonetheless, fluctuations sufficiently large to cause some coral
destruction occur sporadically. Of the destructive agencies to which
corals are subject, tropical storms assume major importance in some
areas. Water movements associated with such storms can smash the
skeletons of branching corals, move massive corals into unfavorable positions, and produce and move reef debris. Movement of reef debris,
particularly coral sand, may result in coral colonies being buried and
killed. Dilution of the ambient seawater caused by excessive rainfall
produced during such storms can result in the deaths of corals growing
in shallow water.

Emersion at low tide, blooms of at least one species of alga found
in surface waters, dilution of surface waters, and temperature fluctuations
affect principally corals in very shallow water, such as the reef flats
of fringing or platform reefs. It is here, too, that water movements associated with tropical storms cause the greatest destruction of coral. Thus,
corals in shallow water on reef crests and tops of coral pinnacles are
exposed to a greater variety of physical destructive agencies than corals
growing elsewhere. On the other hand, corals in deeper water around
the seaward slopes of reefs and in lagoons and back reef areas are
particularly prone to burial by coral rubble and coral sand. Periodic
destruction of corals in the habitats mentioned above no doubt results

in corals showing their best development on seaward slopes a few meters below reef crests where the effects of the destructive agents mentioned might be expected to be minimal. Such destruction is responsible, at least in part, for the spatial heterogeneity found on coral reefs.

Occasionally, large-scale catastrophic mortality of corals is caused by natural destructive agencies. Thus, tropical storms of unusual severity may result in large-scale mortality of corals on reefs exposed directly to the wind-driven waves accompanying the storms. However, such damage is intermittent and confined to the hurricane belts. Volcanic activity and earthquakes are capable of causing catastrophic destruction of corals but such activity is restricted to zones that are fairly well defined and the activity is intermittent on a geological time scale. Sedimentation and freshwater runoff from adjacent land masses are of importance in restricting coral growth in certain regions and, when excessive, may cause catastrophic mortality among corals.

Biotic agencies of destruction affect hermatypic corals at all depths, in all habitats and at all latitudes. These agencies include predation by animals, biogenic erosion of skeletons and bases of attachment, and competitive interactions for space. However, coral reef communities are generally regarded as very stable or predictable biotic associations because of the presence of a variety of buffering systems that protect the community against large-scale destruction. Under normal conditions, the damage caused by the biotic agencies mentioned, as well as that caused by the physical agencies mentioned, are compensated for by the relatively rapid growth rates of coral colonies. Available information indicates that some coral reefs represent thousands of years of continuous development and there is no evidence that large-scale catastrophic destruction of coral reef communities occurs regularly if a time scale based on a human lifetime is used.

A number of human activities affect corals directly or indirectly. Dredging, filling, and mining can cause mechanical damage to corals, can markedly increase the amount of sediment falling on corals, and can affect local water currents in the vicinity of corals with catastrophic results. Land clearance near shorelines frequently results in increased freshwater runoff that may result in lowered salinity and increased siltation in adjacent coastal marine waters to an extent that is inimical to coral growth. Blasting with conventional explosives and nuclear weapons testing cause localized destruction of corals and nuclear weapons testing could result in long-term radiation damage. Sewage pollution may result in eutrophication leading to invasion of reefs by algae. Thermal pollution and pollution by desalination effluents are responsible for localized destruction. Pollution from certain toxic chemicals may have acute effects on corals but long-term chronic effects are ill-understood. Likewise, the effects of oil pollution and pollution from synthetic chemicals such as the persistent pesticides may not have immediate effects on corals but may have serious chronic effects. Alternatively, they may affect corals indirectly via an adverse effect on other elements of the coral reef community. In this connection, it is possible that corals may not be the most sensitive indicators of environmental pollution.

Obviously, some aspects of the possible adverse effects of current human activities on coral reefs warrant further study. This is particularly so in the case of potential pollutants, such as oil, persistent pesticides, etc. The effects of these pollutants should be studied under a variety of experimental conditions, in a variety of coral reef habitats, and with a variety of coral reef organisms apart from corals themselves. Long-term effects, as well as short-term effects, should be carefully monitored. The danger inherent in schemes to raise fish or whales in coral lagoons when such schemes involve the nutrient enrichment of the lagoons has already been pointed out by Johannes (1970) and a great deal of pertinent research is required before any such schemes are implemented.

The selective elimination or reduction in numbers of elements of the reef biota as a result of the collecting activities of humans may have far-reaching effects on the coral reef community. This would be particularly so if key species were involved. Extensive collection of the giant triton, *C. tritonis*, and large predatory fish such as the groper, *P. lanceolatus*, are believed to be responsible for triggering population explosions of the coral predator, *A. planci*. It is important to note that the population explosions having been triggered on only a few reefs could spread through a whole ecosystem resulting in catastrophic damage. This could be happening on the Great Barrier Reef at present. It should also be appreciated that the introduction by humans of a particular species to a region from which the species has been previously excluded may have profound effects on the biota of coral reefs. There has already been speculation about the fate of Caribbean corals if *A. planci* were introduced into the Caribbean as a result of joining Pacific and Atlantic Oceans with a sea-level canal across Panama (Porter, 1972b). It has been demonstrated that *A. planci* will eat Caribbean corals.

In some cases, human activities are known to be definitely harmful. Dredging, fiilling, and mining activities that cause mechanical damage to the fauna, excessive sedimentation on reefs and/or interference with established patterns of current flow in lagoons or reef flats should be undertaken with great caution after a careful assessment of the likely effects, under local conditions, of such activities on the coral reef community. Land clearance on the shorelines or in the vicinity of streams that drain into areas where there are fringing reefs or near shore patch or platform reefs should likewise be undertaken with caution and with a full appreciation of the possible effects of such activities on the adjacent coral reefs. Attention should be given to siting outlet pipes carrying sewage and heated or highly saline effluents so that negligible damage can be caused to the biota of reefs. The use of explosives and chemicals for the capture of reef fish should obviously be banned and blasting of underwater obstacles in coral reef areas should be kept to a minimum. The collecting of mollusks, aquarium fish, and other elements of the reef biota for commercial purposes should be carefully regulated.

Recovery of devastated reefs depends on recolonization by coral planulae and on the continued growth and reproduction of survivors. The rate at which recolonization occurs appears to be inversely related to the initial extent of the devastation of hard corals and is affected by such factors as the availability of planulae, the presence of favorable water currents for carrying planulae to devastated areas, the availability of suitable substrate on which to settle, the rate of survival of settling planulae, the rate of growth and maturation of colonies initiated, interactions with other species, species succession, and the return of all species normally part of the climax community in the region. It is possible that the transplanting of corals from flourishing reefs to devastated reefs might expedite the recovery of the affected reefs. Research to assess the feasibility of transplanting corals in this way is required.

Recovery of coral reef communities from small-scale localized destruction usually requires less than ten years, providing that major sectors of the community are left intact and the area involved is not marginal for coral growth. Studies of recovery after episodes of heavy destruction that cannot be attributed to human activities have revealed that periods of time ranging from 10 to 20 years are required for full recovery of affected reef areas. However, in cases where destruction has been particularly severe, several decades might be required for complete recovery. It is possible that, as suggested by Stoddart (1974) for storm damage, there is a threshold of damage beyond which the effects of the damage may be prolonged. Apparent lack of recovery has been noted on a few occasions when destruction of corals has occurred in situations that are marginal for coral growth. However, there are indications that when human activities are responsible for coral destruction, lack of recovery may prove to be common. The new conditions created may no longer be favorable for coral growth. At the same time, it might be noted that most reported cases of destruction of the coral reef biota stemming from human activities are recent and insufficient time has elapsed for recovery to proceed very far.

Recovery of the biota of certain reefs devastated by A. *planci* is occurring but is slow and it is postulated that periods of the order of 20–40 years may be required for full recovery of reefs that have lost the bulk of their hard coral cover. However, it is possible that recovery may be long delayed because the extent of the damage may have exceeded a critical threshold value and/or because the initial causes of the outbreaks may still be operative. Indeed, if the A. *planci* outbreaks are induced by human activity, as postulated, then affected reefs may remain improverished until measures to counter the A. *planci* infestations are implemented successfully. In areas that are marginal for coral growth, coral communities may be replaced by other types of community.

Although the view of Voss (1973, p. 47), prompted by the unfortunate current condition of Florida's coral reefs, that "an unprejudiced observer might well be fearful that in the not too distant future our children may be able to learn about the coral reefs only from books and documentary films, for one of nature's unique habitats will have vanished from the face of the earth" may seem unduly pessimistic, it is apparent that human activities are affecting coral reef ecosystems on an unprecedented scale. Moreover, these ecosystems appear to be particularly susceptible to damage caused by a wide variety of human activities. The results of these activities could be catastrophic and may already be irreversible in some areas. Measures should be taken immediately by the appropriate authorities to ensure that exploitation of the renewable resources of coral reefs is compatible with the conservation of these reefs. International action is required to ensure that coral reefs do not suffer the fate that has befallen their terrestrial counterparts, the tropical rain forests which, according to Richards (1973), will probably be destroyed within the next 20–30 years, except for a few small conserved relics.

References

Abe, N. (1940). *Palao Trop. Biol. Stud.* 2, 105.

Anonymous (1970). "Thermal Pollution of Intrastate Waters—Biscayne Bay, Florida," Report. Southeast Water Lab., Fort Lauderdale, Florida.

Baas-Becking, L. C. M. (1951). *Proc., Kon. Ned. Akad. Wetensch., Ser. C* 54, 213.

Banner, A. H. (1968). *Hawaii Inst. Mar. Biol. Tech. Rep.* 15.

Banner, A. H. (1974). *In* "Proceedings of the Second International Symposium on Coral Reefs" (A. M. Cameron, B. M. Campbell, A. B. Cribb, R. Endean, J. S. Jell, O. A. Jones, P. Mather, and F. H. Talbot, eds.), Vol. 2, pp. 685–702. Great Barrier Reef Committee, Brisbane, Australia.

Banner, A. H., and Bailey, J. H. (1970). *Hawaii Inst. Mar. Biol., Tech. Rep.* **25.**

Barnes, E. S. (1973). *Mar. Pollut. Bull.* [N. S.] **4,** 102.

Bennett, I. (1971). "The Great Barrier Reef." Lansdowne, Melbourne, Australia.

Beu A. G. (1970). *Trans. Roy. Soc. N.Z. Biol. Sciences,* **11,** 205.

Blumer, M. (1970). *Proc. FAO Tech. Conf. Mar. Pollut.* FIR/MP/70/R-1.

Bourns, C. T. (1970). "Truk Island Fish Kill, April 17, 1970," Water Quality Contingency Rep. U.S. Dept. Interior Fed. Water Qual. Admin. Pacific Southwest Region.

Brock, V. E., Van Heukelem, W., and Helfrich, P. (1966). *Hawaii Inst. Mar. Biol. Tech. Rep.* **11.**

Brody, R. W., Raup, D. M., Grigg, D. I., and Van Eepoel, R. P. (1970). "A Study of the Waters, Sediments and Biota of Chocolate Hole, St. John, with Comparison to Cruz Bay, St. John," Report. Carib. Res. Inst. to Govt. of Virgin Islands Dept. Health, Div. Environ. Health.

Brown, T. W. (1972). "Silt Pollution—the Destruction of Magnetic Island's Coral Fringing Reefs" (mimeogr.) Magnetic Island, Queensland, Australia.

Burkholder, P. R. (1973). *In* "Biology and Geology of Coral Reefs" (O. A. Jones and R. Endean, eds.), Vol. 2, Biol. 1, pp. 117–182, Academic Press, New York.

Burkholder, P. R., and Burkholder, L. M. (1958). *Science* **127,** 1174.

Chesher, R. H. (1969a). *Science* **165,** 280.

Chesher, R. H. (1969b). "*Acanthaster planci*: Impact on Pacific Coral Reefs," Doc. No. PB187631. Westinghouse Electric Corporation Report to U.S. Dept. Interior, Washington, D.C.

Ciereszko, L. S. (1962). *Trans. N.Y. Acad. Sci.* [2] **24,** 502.

Ciereszko, L. S., and Karns, T. K. B. (1973). *In* "Biology and Geology of Coral Reefs" (O. A. Jones and R. Endean, eds.), Vol. 2, Biol. 1, pp. 183–203. Academic Press, New York.

Clare, P. (1971). "The Struggle for the Great Barrier Reef." Collins, London.

Connell, J. H. (1973). *In* "Biology and Geology of Coral Reefs" (O. A. Jones and R. Endean, eds.), Vol. 2, Biol. 1, pp. 205–245. Academic Press, New York.

Cooper, M. J. (1966). *Pac. Sci.* **20,** 137.

Cribb, A. B. (1973). *In* "Biology and Geology of Coral Reefs" (O. A. Jones and R. Endean, eds.), Vol. 2, Biol. 1, pp. 47–75. Academic Press, New York.

Crossland, C. (1928). *Proc. Zool. Soc. London* **27,** 717.

Dana, J. D. (1843). *Amer. J. Sci.* **45,** 130.

Dana, T. F. (1970). *Science* **169,** 894.

Dana, T., and Wolfson, A. (1970). *Trans. San Diego Soc. Nat. Hist.* **16,** 83.

Darwin, C. (1967). "The Voyage of the *Beagle.*" Aldine Press, Letchworth, Herts.

Dawson, E. H. (1959). *Pac. Natur.* **1,** 32.

Di Salvo, L. H. (1969). *Amer. Zool.* **9,** 735.

Di Salvo, L. H. (1972). *In* "Proceedings of the Symposium on Corals and Coral Reefs" (G. Mukundan and C. S. G. Pillai, eds.), pp. 67–69. Marine Biological Association of India, Cochin, India.

Di Salvo, L. H. (1973). *In* "Biology and Geology of Coral Reefs" (O. A. Jones and R. Endean, eds.), Vol. 2, Biol. 1, pp. 1–15. Academic Press, New York.

Doty, M. S. (1969). *Hawaii Bot. Sci. Pap.* **14,** 211.

Edmondson, C. H. (1928). *Bull. Bishop Mus. Honolulu* **45,** 1.

Emery, K. O., Tracey, J. I., and Ladd, H. S. (1954). *U.S., Geol. Surv., Prof. Pap.* **260-A,** 1.

Endean, R. (1956). *Univ. Queensl. Pap., Dep. Zool.* **1**, 229.

Endean, R. (1966). *Sci. J.* **2**, 57.

Endean, R. (1969). "Report on Investigations Made into Aspects of the Current *Acanthaster planci* (Crown of thorns) Infestations of Certain Reefs of the Great Barrier Reef." Fisheries Branch, Queensland Dept. of Primary Industries, Brisbane, Australia.

Endean, R. (1971). *J. Mar. Biol. Ass. India* **13**, 1.

Endean, R. (1973). *In* "Biology and Geology of Coral Reefs" (O. A. Jones and R. Endean, eds.), Vol. 2, Biol. 1, pp. 389–438. Academic Press, New York.

Endean, R. (1974). *In* "Proceedings of the Second International Symposium on Coral Reefs" (A. M. Cameron, B. M. Campbell, A. B. Cribb, R. Endean, J. S. Jell, O. A. Jones, P. Mather, and F. H. Talbot, eds.), Vol. 1, pp. 563–576. Great Barrier Reef Committee, Brisbane, Australia.

Endean, R., and Chesher, R. H. (1973). *Biol. Conserv.* **5**, 87.

Endean, R., and Stablum, W. (1973a). *Atoll Res. Bull.* **167**, 1.

Endean, R., and Stablum, W. (1973b). *Atoll Res. Bull.* **168**, 1.

Endean, R., Stephenson, W., and Kenney, R. (1956). *Aust. J. Mar. Freshwater Res.* **7**, 317.

Fairbridge, R. W. (1950). *J. Geol.* **58**, 330.

Fairbridge, R. W., and Teichert, C. (1947). *Sci. Rep. Gt. Barrier Reef Comm.* **6**, 1.

Fairbridge, R. W., and Teichert, C. (1948). *Geogr. J.* **111**, 67.

Fisher, J. L. (1969). *Science* **165**, 645

Fishelson, L. (1973). *Mar. Biol.* **19**, 183.

Flood, P. G. (1974). *In* "Proceedings of the Second International Symposium on Coral Reefs" (A. M. Cameron, B. M. Campbell, A. B. Cribb, R. Endean, J. S. Jell, O. A. Jones, P. Mather, and F. H. Talbot, eds.), Vol. 2, pp. 387–399. Great Barrier Reef Committee, Brisbane, Australia.

Gardiner, J. S. (1930). *Proc. Linn. Soc. London*, 1930–1, 65.

Glynn, P. W. (1973). *In* "Biology and Geology of Coral Reefs" (O. A. Jones and R. Endean, eds.), Vol. 2, Biol. 1, pp. 271–324. Academic Press, New York.

Glynn, P. W., Almodovar, L. R., and Gonzalez, J. G. (1964). *Carib. J. Sci.* **4**, 335.

Goodbody, I. (1961). *Ecology* **42**, 150.

Goreau, T. F. (1959). *Ecology* **40**, 67.

Goreau, T. F. (1961). *Endeavour* **20**, 32.

Goreau, T. F., and Goreau, N. (1960). *Biol. Bull.* **118**, 419.

Grant, E. M. (1970). *Queensl. Fish Notes, Dep. Primary Ind., Brisbane* [N.S.] **1**, 1.

Grigg, R. W., and Maragos. J. (1974). *Ecology* **55**, 387.

Halstead, B. W. (1970). *Proc. FAO Tech. Conf. Mar. Poll.* FIR/MP/70/R-6.

Hedley, C. (1925). *Sci. Rep. Gt. Barrier Reef. Comm.* **1**, 36.

Hines, N. O. (1962). "Proving Ground: An Account of the Radiobiological Studies in the Pacific, 1946–1961." Univ. of Washington Press, Seattle.

Johannes, R. E. (1970). *Proc. FAO Tech. Conf. Mar. Pollut.* FIR/MP/70/R-14.

Johannes, R. E., Maragos, J., and Coles, S. L. (1972). *Mar. Pollut. Bull.* [N. S.] **3**, 29.

Johnson, D. W. (1968). *Trans. Amer. Fish. Soc.* **97**, 398.

Jokiel, P. J., and Coles, S. L. (1974). *Pac. Sci.* **28**, 1.

Kawaguti, S. (1937). *Palao Trop. Biol. Stud.* **2**, 309.

Kinsman, D. J. J. (1964). *Nature (London)* **202**, 1280.

Ladd, H. S. (1973). *In* "Biology and Geology of Coral Reefs" (O. A. Jones and R. Endean, eds.), Vol. 1, Geol. 1, pp. 93–112. Academic Press, New York.

Lang, J. C. (1970). Ph.D. Thesis, Yale University, New Haven, Connecticut.

Lewis, J. B. (1971). *Mar. Pollut. Bull.* [N.S.] **2**, 59.

Lloyd, A. R. (1973). *In* "Biology and Geology of Coral Reefs" (O. A. Jones and R. Endean, eds.), Vol. 1, Geol. 1, pp. 347–366. Academic Press, New York.

Mahadevan, S., and Nayar, K. N. (1972). *In* "Proceedings of the Symposium on Corals and Coral Reefs" (G. Mukundan and C. S. G. Pillai, eds.), pp. 181–190. Marine Biological Association of India, Cochin, India.

Manton, S. M. (1932). *Sci. Rep. Gt. Barrier Reef Exped.* **3**, 157.

Manton, S. M., and Stephenson, T. A. (1935). *Sci. Rep. Gt. Barrier Reef Exped.* **3**, 273.

Marshall, S. M., and Orr, A. P. (1931). *Sci. Rep. Gt. Barrier Reef. Exped.* **1**, 94.

Matoda, S. (1940). *Palao Trop. Biol. Stud.* **36**, 61.

Mayer, A. G. (1914). *Carnegie Inst. Wash. Publ.* **183**, 1.

Mayer, A. G. (1918a). *Carnegie Inst. Wash. Publ.* **213**,1.

Mayer, A. G. (1918b). *Carnegie Inst. Wash. Publ.* **252**, 175.

Mayor, A. G. (1924). *Carnegie Inst. Wash. Publ.* **340**, 1.

Moorhouse, F. W. (1936). *Sci. Rep. Gt. Barrier Reef Comm.* **4**, 37.

Newman, W. A. (1970). *Science* **167**, 1274.

Nigrelli, R. F. (1958). *Trans. N.Y. Acad. Sci.* [2] **20**, 248.

Nishihira, M., and Yamazato, K. (1974). *In* "Proceedings of the Second International Symposium on Coral Reefs" (A. M. Cameron, B. M. Campbell, A. B. Cribb, R. Endean, J. S. Jell, O. A. Jones, P. Mather, and F. H. Talbot, eds.), Vol. 1, pp. 577–590. Great Barrier Reef Committee, Brisbane, Australia.

Ormond, R F. G., and Campbell, A. C. (1970). *Symp. Zool. Soc. London* **28**, 433.

Owens, D. (1971). *Fiji Agr. J.* **33**, 15.

Paine, R. T. (1969). *Amer. Natur.* **103**, 91.

Pearson, R. G., and Endean, R. (1969). *Queensl. Fish. Notes, Dep. Harbours Mar.* **3**, 27.

Pearson, R. G. (1974). *In* "Proceedings of the Second International Symposium on Coral Reefs" (A. M. Cameron, B. M. Campbell, A. B. Cribb, R. Endean, J. S. Jell, O. A. Jones, P. Mather, and F. H. Talbot, eds.), Vol. 2, pp. 207–215. Great Barrier Reef Committee, Brisbane, Australia.

Polunin, N. V. C., and Frazier, J. G. (1974). *Environ. Conserv.* **1**, 71.

Porter, J. W. (1972a). *Amer. Natur.* **106**, 487.

Porter, J. W. (1972b). *Bull. Biol. Soc. Wash.* **2**, 89.

Rainford, E. H. (1925). *Aust. Mus. Mag.* **2**, 175.

Ramamurphy, V. D., and Krishramurphy, S. (1967). *Ann. Sci.* **36**, 524.

Ramas, C. C. (1969). *Underwater Natur.* **6**, 31.

Randall, J. E. (1969). *Oryx* **10**, 31.

Randall, J. E. (1972). *Biotropica* **4**, 132.

Randall, J. E. (1974). *In* "Proceedings of the Second International Symposium on Coral Reefs" (A. M. Cameron, B. M. Campbell, A. B. Cribb, R. Endean, J. S. Jell, O. A. Jones, P. Mather, and F. H. Talbot, eds.), Vol. 1, pp. 159–166. Great Barrier Reef Committee, Brisbane, Australia.

Randall, R. H. (1973). *Micronesica* **9**, 213.

Richards, P. C. (1973). *Sci. Amer.* **229**, 58.

Robertson, R. (1970). *Pac. Sci.* **24**, 43.

Roessler, M. S., and Zieman, J. E. (1969). *Proc. Gulf Caribb. Fish. Inst.*, *22nd Annu. Sess.* p. 136.

Rützler, K. (1971). *Smithson. Contrib. Zool.* **77**, 1.

Sanders, H. L. (1968). *Amer. Natur.* **102**, 243.

Slack-Smith, R. J. (1960). *Univ. Queensl. Pap., Dep. Zool.* **1**, 211.

Sladen, W. J. L., Menzie, D. M., and Reichel, W. L. (1966). *Nature (London)* **210**, 670.

Sorokin, Y. I. (1973). *In* "Biology and Geology of Coral Reefs" (O. A. Jones and R. Endean, eds.) Vol. 2, Biology 1, pp. 17–45. Academic Press, New York.

Stearns, H. T. (1945). *Geol. Soc. Amer., Bull.* **36**, 783.

Stephenson, T. A., Stephenson, A., Tandy, G., and Spender, M. (1931). *Sci. Rep. Gt. Barrier Reef Exped.* **3**, 17.

Stephenson, W., Endean, R., and Bennett, I. (1958). *Aust. J. Mar. Freshwater Res.* **9**, 261.

Stoddart, D. R. (1963). *Atoll Res. Bull.* **95**, 1.

Stoddart, D. R. (1968). *Geography* **53**, 25.

Stoddart, D. R. (1969a). *Biol. Rev. Cambridge Phil. Soc.* **44**, 433.

Stoddart, D. R. (1969b). *Phil. Trans. Roy. Soc. London, Ser. B* **255**, 355.

Stoddart, D. R. (1969c). *Atoll Res. Bull.* **131**, 1.

Stoddart, D. R. (1972). *Nature (London)* **239**, 51.

Stoddart, D. R. (1973). *In* "Biology and Geology of Coral Reefs" (O. A. Jones and R. Endean, eds.), Vol. 1, Geol. 1, pp. 51–92. Academic Press, New York.

Stoddart, D. R. (1974). *In* "Proceedings of the Second International Symposium on Coral Reefs" (A. M. Cameron, B. M. Campbell, A. B. Cribb, R. Endean, J. S. Jell, O. A. Jones, P. Mather, and F. H. Talbot, eds.), Vol. 2, pp. 473–483. Great Barrier Reef Committee, Brisbane, Australia.

Taylor, J. D. (1968). *Phil. Trans. Roy. Soc. London, Ser. B* **254**, 129.

Van Eepoel, R. P., and Grigg, D. I. (1970). "Survey of the Ecology and Water Quality of Lindberg Bay, St. Thomas," Water Pollution Rep. Caribbean Res. Inst., St. Thomas, Virgin Islands.

Vaughan, T. W. (1919). *Rep. Smithson. Inst.* **17**, 189.

Verwey, J. (1930). *Proc. Pac. Sci. Congr., 4th, 1929* Vol. 2A, p. 277.

Vine, P. J. (1970). *Nature (London)* **228**, 341.

Voss, G. L. (1973). *Natur. Hist., N.Y.* **82**, 40.

Walker, H. J. (1962). *Geogr. Rev.* **52**, 325.

Weber, J. N., and Woodhead, P. M. J. (1970). *Mar. Biol.* **6**, 12.

Wells, J. W. (1951). *Atoll Res. Bull.* **9**, 1.

Wells, J. W. (1957). *In* "Treatise on Marine Ecology and Paleoecology" (J. W. Hedgpeth, ed.), Vol. 1, pp. 609–631. Waverly Press, Baltimore, Maryland.

Wood-Jones, F. (1907). *Proc. Zool. Soc. London* **518**.

Wood-Jones, F. (1910). "Corals and Atolls." Reeve, London.

Yamaguchi, M. (1973). *In* "Biology and Geology of Coral Reefs" (O. A. Jones and R. Endean, eds.), Vol. 2, Biol. 1, pp. 369–387. Academic Press, New York.

Yonge, C. M. (1963). *Advan. Mar. Biol.* **1**, 209.

Yonge, C. M. (1968). *Proc. Roy. Soc., Ser. B* **169**, 329.

Young, R. H. F., and Chan, P. L. (1970). *J. Water Pollut. Contr. Fed.* **42**, 2052.

8

CORAL ISLAND VEGETATION

F. R. Fosberg

I. Introduction

"Coral limestone," the material of coral reefs and reef debris, is a substratum covering substantial areas along seacoasts in the tropical and subtropical zones. It may be either submerged or emerged and, if the latter, it may line continental coasts, form shores and terraces around high islands, or occur as generally flat islands either on continental shelves or in the deep sea. These flat islands may lie on barrier reefs separated by varying widths of lagoon from higher land, they may be on irregularly ring-shaped reefs or atolls surrounding lagoons, or they may lie on table reefs or on linear fragments of reefs without lagoons. The islands may be associated with continental land masses or be truly oceanic, that is, never having been connected to a continent. Both islands and terraces may also be variously elevated and, if elevated, variously dissected into karstic land forms and rough or pinnacled surfaces. These different situations have a considerable influence on the vegetation that covers the limestone surface.

The limestone material is principally calcium carbonate, with usually a small percentage of magnesium carbonate, and may, in places, be substantially altered to calcium phosphate (see Section I,B). Locally, small amounts of drifted pumice enter into the loose lime sand and gravel. The limestone is an accumulation of skeletons of very diverse lime-secreting organisms, especially corals, foraminiferans, algae, and mollusks, together with some precipitated chalk as well as aragonite and calcite cement deposited on surfaces and in interstices. Small amounts of silica may be present, originating from diatoms, radiolarian shells, and volcanic ash. Where the reefs have formed around high islands or along continental shores, the limestone may be variously contaminated by weathering products of volcanic and other rocks including magnetite, ilmenite, olivine, pyroxene, and quartz sand, as well as clays. Certain common elements, some of them required by plants, are frequently in very short supply in coral rock and soils, especially on oceanic coral atolls where contamination from noncoralline rock is scarce or lacking. Such deficient elements are, for example, potassium, iron, copper, zinc, molybdenum, boron, cobalt, nickel, and manganese.

The physical nature and texture of the limestone varies enormously. Fundamentally the reef is a latticelike framework of corals and coralline algae in growth position, usually filled in with and often buried by clastic calcareous materials of various textures, from fine silt to boulder size. Such clastic material may be loose or cemented together into reef rock or beach rock. There is not complete agreement on the cause and nature of this cementation, but it is certain that several distinct phenomena are involved. Recrystallization and case hardening may have taken place in older coral rock, giving a material much more resistant to erosion and degradation.

Elevation, surface features, area, distance from sea, and soil development also have an important influence on vegetation patterns. The simplest form of coral island is the sand or gravel cay—a sand or gravel deposit or bar, lying on the surface of an intertidal or slightly subtidal reef flat. These islands are frequently surrounded by beach ridges of sand, gravel, or even boulders. Boulder ridges are considered to be the results of severe storms or hurricanes and, on atolls, are usually found on the seaward sides of islets, especially on the windward or else the direction from which most storms come. Some islets are made up of a series of parallel, somewhat overlapping, gravel ridges, probably representing successive storms. Mangrove cays are accumulations of silt and sand that do not, or scarcely, reach high tide level on reefs that are in some way protected from high-energy waves and are covered by mangrove vegetation. One of the commonest types of islet is that formed of one or more patches of reef platform lying at 2 m or less above low tide (reef flat) level, and partially or wholly covered by sand or gravel that usually extends to the leeward or lagoonward of the platform. Occasional atolls are notable for patches of slightly higher reef limestone, usually very pitted and dissected, called in Polynesia "feo." On any of these types of islets or islands, there are likely to be depressions, either muddy, or rarely hard-bottomed, extending to below high tide level and filled with water, at least at high tide. Surface texture ranges from fine sand, especially on the lagoon side, to boulder flats and ridges, commonest on the ocean side. The whole atoll or island may, in rather few examples, be elevated, relatively, from several to hundreds of meters above sea level (mean low tide). Slightly elevated atolls may still have a lagoon or, in some cases, only a central depression, especially if the elevation is greater than usual. In one or two such cases, e.g., Rennell Island, this depression may contain a freshwater lake. Older, strongly elevated coral islands are likely to be deeply dissected into a karst topography with steep sides, strongly undercut shores, and with sharp peaks and sinkholes that often form sea level lakes, ponds, or wells. Any of these types of island except the karstlike ones, can have dunes of coral sand up to 15 m or more in elevation. Any of the elevated types may, and usually do, have areas of sharp, pitted, and pinnacled surface on exposed areas of consolidated rock, termed "champignon" in the Indian Ocean, feo in Polynesia, and "dogtooth" or "iron shore" in the Caribbean. More rare are a moderately rough surface called "pavé" in the western Indian Ocean and a flat or slabby surface called "platin" in the same area.

A. SIZE

Vegetated islands occupy from a few square meters to many square kilometers in area, and occur in all shapes and proportions. The distance from shore of any locality has a strong influence on its vegetation, both because of greater or less exposure to salt spray and wind and because of increasing freshness of groundwater inland.

B. SOILS

Coral island soils are all formed of coral fragments, mollusk shells, foraminiferan tests, calcareous alga skeletons, echinoderm parts, and other coral limestone detritus, with varied amounts of humus, guano, volcanic ash, and drifted pumice incorporated (Stone, 1953; Fosberg and Carroll, 1965). In stands of *Pisonia grandis, Casuarina equisetifolia,* and possibly other trees, surface horizons of acid peatlike raw humus may accumulate and, at least under *Pisonia,* the addition of guano from fish-eating birds produces a horizon of phosphatic hardpan underlying the humus (Fosberg, 1954). These phosphatic soils are called Jemo soils and are known from the Pacific and Indian Oceans. Something similar has been found in the Caribbean but is not well known. On coarse textured material and on rough consolidated rock, highly humic soil accumulates in interstices, crevices, and pockets. In dense mixed forests black, usually fine-grained, highly humic A horizons occur in soils called Arno Atoll soils (Stone, 1951). However, the vast majority of coral atoll soils are light brown, slightly altered coral sands called Shioya soils, not very different from the material originally accumulated (Stone, 1951, 1953). The pH of unaltered or only slightly altered lime sand is about 8.3. With incorporation of humus this may be lowered to pH 7.5 or 7.0 and the raw humus under *Pisonia* is usually between pH 6.0 and 5.0 or even 4.0 where the layer is very thick. I have pointed out elsewhere that Shioya soils are deficient in almost every element essential for plant growth except calcium (Fosberg and Carroll, 1965, p. 65). Salinity varies with exposure and distance from shore (Fosberg, 1949).

C. Climate

The vegetation of any region is profoundly influenced by the climate and that of coral islands is no exception. Temperature does not vary enough to make much difference in the coral seas. Wind and especially rainfall display a great range in amount and effect. Seasonality and regularity or reliability of rainfall are also of much importance in determining or limiting vegetation.

Unfortunately, weather stations are not very plentiful on coral islands. There are, or have been, a few, notably on Kwajalein, Eniwetok, and Ujelang in the Marshall Islands, Malden in the Central Pacific, Midway Island in the Leeward Hawaiian Islands, Wake Island in the North Pacific, Alacran Reef in the Gulf of Mexico, and Mopelia in the Society Islands. Stations on high islands in the neighborhood of coral islands provide important additional data, as do shipboard observations. Shorter records are available for Assumption, Aldabra, and Diego Garcia in the Indian Ocean, Clipperton Island in the Eastern Pacific, Rangiroa in the Tuamotus, and some other islands.

Climatic summaries have been made for a few atolls and atoll areas, such as the Gilbert Islands (Sachet, 1957), Clipperton (Sachet, 1962a,b), Diego Garcia (Stoddart, 1971b), Aldabra (Farrow, 1971), and Northern Marshalls (Fosberg *et al.*, 1956), and a rainfall summary has been published for the Indian Ocean coral islands (Stoddart, 1971a). Based on scanty data, these summaries scarcely give a reliable picture of the climate of these widely distributed islands. The general climatic pattern of the earth, insofar as it is understood, gives a picture reasonably in accord with what is known of the vegetation of most of the islands, but more detailed information would give more confidence to interpretations of climatic control of vegetation on these areas that are relatively uniform in many other respects. A north–south transect from Wake Island through the Marshalls and Gilberts, from dry to wet to dry again, gives an opportunity to assess the effect of the rainfall factor on vegetation, both natural and anthropogenous.

II. Vegetation

With this background, we may consider the vegetation of the islands that are entirely or preponderantly made up of coral limestone. Unfortunately, serious study of this aspect of island geography and biology has mostly taken place after profound alteration has been made in the vegetation by human activities. The most important of these are the planting of coconuts and the mining of phosphate. These have been so wide-spread that any description of the natural vegetation of all but the driest of low coral islands, or the steepest and most dissected, or else the most waterless of elevated coral islands must now be a patchwork of reconstructions from old accounts (none of them intended as vegeta-tion descriptions), interpolations and extrapolations from study of the few remaining relatively unaltered fragments, and interpretations based on herbarium specimens, fossil soils, relict occurrence of species, geo-graphical position, and what we know of climate. No such attempt has been made for coral islands generally, though several areas have been, or are being, examined with this aim. The areas that are known best are the Micronesian atolls and the Aldabra group of slightly elevated atolls. Several individual islands outside these areas have been studied fairly thoroughly but with little time depth. Our understanding of vegeta-tion dynamics on coral islands is based principally on inference and the assumption that spatial patterns may represent chronological se-quences. With presently available information this cannot be proved but, with some reservations, the relatively meager interpretations offered here seem reasonable.

A factor that greatly influences our knowledge of coral atoll vegetation is the widely held, but erroneous, idea that the floras and vegetations of coral atolls are very much alike everywhere and therefore not much worth studying. Descriptions are few and highly generalized as a result and collections are neither adequate nor sufficiently documented to yield the information needed to give a definitive account of coral atoll vegeta-tion. Because of the higher endemism and richer floras of the high vol-canic islands, they have been studied much more and have detracted attention from the elevated atolls and limestone islands. Hence, we do not have adequate floristic lists and vegetation descriptions of many of these elevated atolls and limestone islands either. These limitations should be borne in mind in reading the following account.

III. Floras and Floristic Composition

A basic component of island floras is the pantropical strand flora—a relatively small number of species that are likely to be present on any island in the tropics that presents the proper habitats, especially sand and gravel beaches, beach ridges, and flats. Atolls have small floras and extensive strand habitats. Hence, the proportion of strand species and of other pantropical lowland plants in atoll floras is usually high, regardless of the size of the total floras.

Prominent among the pantropical strand species occurring on sea level coral atolls are

Paspalum distichum
Cyperus ligularis
Fimbristylis cymosa (*sensu lato*)
Ximenia americana
Boerhaavia repens
Sesuvium portulacastrum (*sensu lato*)
Portulaca oleracea
Caesalpinia bonduc
Caesalpinia major

Sophora tomentosa
Canavalia rosea
Tribulus cistoides
Suriana maritima
Ipomoea macrantha (*I. tuba*)
Ipomea pes-caprae (*sensu lato*)
Ipomoea stolonifera
Guettarda speciosa

Widely distributed Indo-Pacific strand species on coral atolls are

Pandanus tectorius
Digitaria pruriens
Lepturus repens
Stenotaphrum micranthum
Thuarea involuta
Cyperus javanicus
Pisonia grandis
Portulaca australis

Canavalia cathartica
Vigna marina
Pemphis acidula
Ludwigia octovalvis
Neiosperma oppositifolia
Cordia subcordata
Tournefortia argentea
Premna obtusifolia

Species that have achieved a pantropical strand distribution with the help of man are

Cynodon dactylon
Digitaria timorensis
Eleusine indica
Eragrostis tenella
Cyperus brevifolius
Casuarina equisetifolia
Portulaca oleracea
Euphorbia glomerifera

Euphorbia hirta
Euphorbia prostrata
Euphorbia thymifolia
Phyllanthus amarus
Carica papaya
Asclepias curassavica
Bidens pilosa
Vernonia cinerea

Caribbean strand species widespread on Caribbean atolls are

Cenchrus pauciflorus
Chloris petraea
Eragrostis domingensis
Cyperus planifolius
Batis maritima
Atriplex pentandra
Philoxerus vermicularis
Cakile lanceolata
Euphorbia blodgettii
Euphorbia mesambrianthemifolia
Conocarpus erecta
Opuntia dillenii

Cordia sebestena
Heliotropium curassavicum
Tournefortia gnaphalodes
Lantana involucrata
Ernodea littoralis
Scaevola plumieri
Ambrosia hispida
Borrichia arborescens
Flaveria linearis
Melanthera nivea
Wedelia trilobata

In addition to the basic strand flora, the atolls in each geographic region have a component of species peculiar to the region, though very few species are endemic to low coral atolls. Species such as *Nesogenes euphrasioides* and *Digitaria stenotaphrodes* in the Tuamotus, *Eragrostis whitneyi* and *Digitaria pacifica* in the Central Pacific, *Hedyotis roman-zofiensis* common to both of these areas, *Timonius polygama* in Southern Polynesian atolls, *Lepturus gasparricensis* on Pokak and Wake atolls, and *Nesogenes prostrata* on Agalega atoll are endemic to these regions, if not strictly to low-level atolls. Species extending from nearby high islands to low islands are *Santalum ellipticum*, *Pritchardia remota*, and *Nama sandwicensis* in the Leeward Hawaiian Islands, *Bidens hender-sonensis* var. *oenoensis* on Oeno Atoll, *Piper fragile*, *Piper ponapensis*, and *Pittosporum ferruginea* on the Caroline atolls, and *Poupartia gum-mifera*, *Lagrezia madagascariensis*, *Ficus nautarum*, *Ficus reflexa*, and *Ficus avi-avi* in Aldabra (a slightly elevated atoll), among others.

There is a common belief that the widespread strand species are monot-onously uniform and uninteresting. Logically this would not be expected and when some of the widely distributed species are closely examined, they are found to be extremely variable and the variation to show at least vague geographical patterns. Some still appear to be very uniform, such as *Suriana maritima*, *Ipomoea macrantha*, *Canavalia cathartica*, *Canavalia sericea*, *Canavalia rosea*, *Vigna marina*, *Pisonia grandis*, and *Cordia subcordata*.

Other species are moderately variable. *Ipomoea pes-caprae* has two well-marked subspecies, one centered in the Indian Ocean, the other pantropical. *Sesuvium portulacastrum* is somewhat variable generally but has a well-marked Central Pacific variety, *griseum*. *Guettarda speciosa* varies greatly in leaf shape and indument, the forma *tahitensis* being a very pubescent extreme that crops up here and there. *Scaevola taccada* has a depressed, narrow-leafed, yellowish-flowered variety *tuamotuensis* in southeastern Polynesia, a hairy, white-flowered variety *moomomiana* in Hawaii, and in the Western Pacific a generally glabrous white-flowered population and sporadic occurrences of a pubescent purple-flowered form. *Boerhaavia repens* is so variable that it has com-pletely defied attempts to work out a rational classification. *Boerhaavia tetrandra* is much more uniform, but still variable, and it may hybridize with *B. repens*. *Lepturus repens* is almost hopelessly variable, though several sets of varieties have been proposed, and even several "species" have been segregated out of it. *Tournefortia argentea*, superficially ex-tremely uniform, has been shown by unpublished studies made by St. John to show extraordinary variation in its nutlets, traditionally regarded as very significant in the taxonomy of the family Boraginaceae, to which it belongs. This list could be substantially enlarged. Many of the plants in atoll floras have not yet been adequately studied.

While sea level atolls have a limited, though interesting, flora, even a slight elevation relative to sea level is accompanied by a substantial increase in the flora, both of widely distributed species and a few local endemics. Collecting in the Tuamotu Atolls in 1934 showed that certain species were found only, in the atolls visited, on an area of slightly elevated, dissected limestone or feo. Examination of floristic lists from other atolls showed some of these same species from Niau Atoll. Information on the physiography of this closed atoll showed elevations of as much as 6 m. Among these species were *Pipturus argenteus, Capparis cordifolius, Euphorbia tahitensis, Waltheria indica, Premna obtusifolia Chomelia sambucina,* and *Morinda umbellata* var. *forsteri.*

Henderson Island, though extremely isolated from large land masses and elevated to about 30 m, has a larger flora than any of its neighboring sea level atolls, with 58 species of vascular plants. Included among eight endemics are *Santalum hendersonense* and *Bidens hendersonensis,* the latter remarkable because it is a tree 6 m or so tall. Such high island genera as *Nesoluma, Korthalsella, Pittosporum, Cassia, Canthium, Ixora,* and others contribute to the rich forest cover of this cliff-lined limestone plateau. *Thespesia populnea* and *P. tectorius* are important forest tree species.

Makatea Island, now very badly devastated by phosphate mining, had a rich flora as well, 76 native species being recorded by Wilder (1934), who probably did not locate all that were there. Phosphate mining had already been going on for some time when he visited the island in 1932. Westward in the Pacific, the floras of elevated coral islands are richer, though not well known. Niue has 166 native species. The floras of Rennell, Bellona, and the Louisiades are almost unknown. Angaur, Peliliu, and the semidrowned karstic islands south of Koror in the Palaus have rich floras now under study.

A number of elevated coral atolls are found in the Indian Ocean. Christmas Island, in the Eastern Indian Ocean, has 152 native species of vascular plants (Andrews, 1900), but is being denuded by phosphate mining. In the Western Indian Ocean lie the Aldabra Group of four atolls, all slightly elevated. They have a native flora of about 161 species compared with a total of 48 known from the Amirantes, sea level atolls in the same region.

Aldabra has strong floristic affinities with East Africa and Madagascar, but has a number of endemic species. Most of these have Malagasic affinities.

IV. Vegetation Patterns

Turning from the floristic picture, the more strictly vegetational features show a substantial diversity as well, largely related to rainfall amount and distribution. Atolls occur from just north of the Tropic of Cancer—Leeward Hawaiian Islands and Marcus Island—to just south of the Tropic of Capricorn—Ducie Island. Since, at least in the open sea, the climate is arranged in roughly parallel belts, a great range of rainfall regimes is exhibited on atolls. In the Marshall Group alone, the mean annual precipitation ranges from an estimated 600 mm in the dry north—Pokak Atoll—to possibly 6000 mm on Ebon in the south. Continuing southward through the Gilberts, Butaritari is wet but the southern Gilberts, again, become quite dry. The Central Pacific atolls contain some very dry ones such as Christmas, Jarvis, Malden, and the Phoenix Group, moderately moist ones such as Fanning, and wet islands such as Washington and Palmyra. The atolls in the Caroline Archipelago are wet and lush.

The vegetation of only a few atolls has been described in any detail. Christophersen (1927, 1931) published accounts of the Pacific Equatorial Islands, briefer ones of the Leeward Hawaiian Group, and, with E. L. Caum (1931), accounts of Johnston and Wake. Setchell (1924) described the very simple vegetation of Rose Atoll, Samoa. Taylor (1950) described Bikini and nearby atolls. Sachet (1962a,b,c) described Clipperton Island, past and present. Some of the Caribbean atolls have been described by Millspaugh (1907, 1916), Stoddart (1962), and Fosberg (1962). Hatheway (1953) described Arno Atoll in detail and subsequently Canton Island (Hatheway, 1955); Niering described Kapingamarangi in 1956. In general, however, the assumption has been made that, since coral atoll vegetation is poor and monotonous, generalized descriptions will fit any island equally well. This has even influenced observation, as well as presentation of results. Enough has been learned during the course of our own studies to identify many of the principal types of vegetation and to get some idea of their ecological relationships. The fact that the vegetation of most atolls is now replaced by coconut groves and plantations makes only an imperfect reconstruction of the original vegetation possible, even on a generalized level.

All except the driest atolls are wooded. Open scrub forest and savanna characterize the drier end of the climatic spectrum. At first sight, remarkable for the tropics, is the fact that vegetation of pure stands of single species is frequent on sea level atolls. Forests of *Pisonia grandis*, of *Neiosperma oppositifolia*, and of *Pandanus tectorius*; scrub forest of

Pemphis acidula and of *Tournefortia argentea;* scrub of *Scaevola taccada,* of *Suriana maritima,* and of *Sida fallax;* and stands of grass, *Lepturus repens,* of the sedge, *Fimbristylis cymosa,* and of the succulent *Sesurium portulacastrum,* are a few of the single species types seen on atolls. This phenomenon is unusual in the tropics, where vegetation is noted for its rich composition. It is probably due to the impoverished flora in combination with extreme conditions of dryness and salinity.

Little is known of the distribution of the several pure stand vegetation types in pre-European, let alone preaboriginal time. The only one that is documented to any extent is the *Pisonia grandis* forest. This was reported from many atolls by Agassiz (1903a,b), who observed the majority of Pacific and Indian Ocean atolls while on the cruises of the *Albatross* (1899–1902). Most of these forests have since been replaced by coconut plantations. Some former areas of this type are identifiable by beds of white-speckled, brown phosphate rock. *Pemphis* stands are commonly found on areas of elevated reef rock with little soil. Such areas are usually small and only part of them, usually in moderately dry districts, bear *Pemphis* forest.

Judging from existing remnants, the predominant forest types in most atoll regions are mixtures of a few tree species, most of which also form pure stands locally. One interpretation that can logically be made is that the mixed forest is the basic unit in any region and that in more and more extreme environments one or another of the component species assumes dominance in terms of different factors. The pure stands are, in this view, merely the extremes of several environmental gradients.

Another interpretation, in my view probably less likely, is that originally the vegetation of an atoll was mostly a mosaic of pure stands, arranged according to an environmental mosaic—in many cases possibly concentric or parallel belts depending on salinity of ground water, drainage, and exposure to salt spray. Man, by clearing and other activities, has disrupted this pattern and the habitat features that determined it, and the component species have colonized the resulting disturbed areas in various mixtures. This interpretation seems more likely for dry than wet atolls, though little enough can be reconstructed of original conditions on wet islands. Man has been there too long.

Elevated coral islands have less tendency to pure stands than low atolls, though Aldabra, which is only slightly elevated, has a number of such types. Wetter and more elevated islands seem generally to have mixed forests, richer in species, as either elevation or rainfall or both, increase. The karst islands of southern Palau, the Lau Group of Fiji, the terraced limestone of Rota in the Marianas, and the little known limestone islands of the Louisiades are examples of the floristically rich end of the mixed forest spectrum. Christmas Island, in the Eastern Indian Ocean is 355 m high and has, according to Andrews *et al.* (1900), 152 species of vascular plants. The Bahamas, which are composed entirely of limestone, have, according to Britton and Millspaugh (1920), about 1025 species and a maximum elevation of 53 m. Henderson Island, which is 33 m high but extremely distant from large land masses, has, as noted above, 62 species compared with the nearby sea level atolls of the Taumotus with 10–30 indigenous species each.

Available information, organized in any sort of usable fashion, is too scanty to enable one, at this time, to classify and describe anything like all the vegetation types found on coral islands. There are 63 definable types found on Aldabra Atoll alone, briefly described after only a two-month visit (Fosberg, 1971). Some of them are of very limited extent and some are peculiar to Aldabra. Brief characterizations of some of the more important or widespread coral island vegetation types, both natural and anthropogenous, will be attempted, starting with forest types. The diagnostic terminology used is based on the classification for general purposes formulated by Fosberg (1961) and refined by Fosberg, in Peterken (1967), with appropriate floristic terms and qualifying adjectives added.

A. *Pisonia* FOREST

Pisonia forest is a closed, broadleaf, orthophyll, evergreen to semi-deciduous, unistratal forest. This is a forest of one species, *P. grandis* (with rarely a scattering of others), with enormous smooth pale trunks of soft pulpy wood and a dense canopy that shades out most other plants. It reaches a stature of at least 30 m, and some of the trunks reach 3–4 m diameter at 1.5 m. An acidic raw humus accumulates on the ground. In most areas this species of *Pisonia* is evergreen, but it may lose its leaves during an exceptionally dry period, and then it usually flowers.

The species has a wide distribution almost entirely on islands. This has given rise to speculations that it is found only where guano accumulates. This is unlikely, as its sterile planted variety *alba* clearly has no such requirement. It is more likely that *P. grandis* cannot stand competition from aggressive species, but has adapted to most species that it normally shares islands with. The only species seen to do well in *Pisonia* forest shade is *Neiosperma oppositifolia* (*Ochrosia oppositifolia*), which has been seen competing so successfully that it seems likely that it can replace *Pisonia*, given a seed washed up and germinated in a *Pisonia* forest and sufficient time.

This is one of the commonest atoll forest types throughout the Indo-Pacific region. The species occurs on higher islands but as scattered individuals mixed with other trees.

B. *Neiosperma* Forest

Neiosperma forest is a closed, broadleaf, evergreen, subsclerophyllous unistratal forest. Commonly pure stands of *N. oppositifolia* exhibit straight, slender, clear trunks up to 15–20 m tall and umbrella-shaped crowns forming a very dense canopy of dark green foliage. Apparently no other species can gain a foothold in a dense stand of this species but a veritable lawn of very small seedlings of *Neiosperma* covers the ground in most stands. They never reach more than a dm or two in height unless there is a windfall or other break in the canopy, when a few shoot up rapidly. Well-grown seedlings of *Neiosperma* have been observed under closed stands of *Pisonia*, so it is capable of tolerating even the dense shade and root competition of a *Pisonia* forest.

This species occurs from Palmyra Atoll to the Seychelles, but has been observed forming pure stands only in the Marshall Islands. There it seems capable of crowding out other species (even *Pisonia grandis*) and forming pure stands. Vertical air photos of this vegetation type have a characteristic tessellate appearance. Curious light spots are sometimes found on such photos. When visited on the ground these are found to be of chlorotic trees, sometimes dying, with other species gaining a foothold in such spots. The cause and course of development of these areas are completely unknown. This forest type was probably more widespread in prehuman or even pre-European times but we have little information other than the wide distribution of the species itself. *Neiosperma oppositifolia* is an important component, even locally a dominant, in the forests on elevated reef limestone but appears to be confined or almost confined to islands.

C. Coconut Forest

A coconut plantation is a closed to, less often, open evergreen, megaphyllous sclerophyll forest, usually with grass, scrub, or scrub forest undergrowth. In most climatic regions if left for a long time untended it gradually becomes a mixed mesophyllous and megaphyllous evergreen forest. The trunks of the dominant species, *Cocos nucifera*, are columnar, erect or leaning, the crowns great rosettes of enormous pinnately compound palm leaves. The spacing is normally 5–10 m, often in lines or geometrically arranged, but if nuts are allowed to germinate and young trees to grow, irregularly spaced and closer, or, in dry areas, more widely spaced. The grass ground cover and the shrubby undergrowth that follow neglect by the cultivator vary greatly in floristic composition with the geographic and climatic region. Strand and substrand elements are usually well represented or even predominant. There is also variation from windward to leeward sides of an atoll islet.

This planted forest is, at the present time, areally the most important vegetation type on low coral islands and that usually thought of popularly as island vegetation. It has replaced most of the natural vegetation except where the climate is too dry, the soil too saline, or where there is no soil at all. The nuts produced by the trees are the principal source of economic income, as well as one of the best sources of drinking water and food for the indigenous inhabitants. The trees also furnish building materials, thatch, matting, fiber, and a fermented beverage.

It is doubtful if any natural stands of coconut exist, though floated nuts are seen germinating on beaches. Possibly Palmyra Atoll in the Central Pacific may be an exception, but no one knows its prehistory and it has long been altered by man. Sauer (1967) suggested that the coconut may be native in the islands of the Indian Ocean, but even there it has been domesticated for ages and is not known truly wild.

D. Breadfruit Forest

Breadfruit forest is a tall, closed, macrophyllous, evergreen, orthophyll to sclerophyll forest, with one tree stratum and, usually, a very open shrub layer, often a ground cover of vines (*Piper* spp.), ferns, or grass. The dominant tree is the breadfruit, *Artocarpus altilis*, or, locally, a hybrid complex of *A. altilis* × *A. mariannensis*. Some of the trees reach a very large size, both in height (30 m) and trunk diameter (1–2 m) on favorable islands. The canopy is very dense.

This type is usually, on low islands at least, strictly planted and tended. It is found in the interiors of moderately wet to quite wet islands, especially in the Carolines, the Maldives, and other heavily populated atoll groups. The fruit is an important source of food and the timber is used locally.

E. Coconut–Breadfruit Forest

Coconut–breadfruit forest is a tall, closed, evergreen, megaphyllous–macrophyllous sclerophyll forest, a planted mixture of the last two types, combining their characteristics.

It is more common than breadfruit forest, occurring in the interiors of many low coral islands and atolls. The extent of breadfruit seems to be limited by the distance to which heavy salt spray or wave wash penetrates, as the breadfruit is rather salt sensitive. It is not prominent on even moderately dry atolls, though individual breadfruit trees may be seen as far north as Utirik, in the Marshalls, in apparently healthy condition.

This strictly anthropogenous forest type is one of the more productive in terms of food and supports some of the densest human populations on islands, as in the Maldives.

F. *Casuarina* Forest

Casuarina forest is a tall evergreen, nonresinous, narrow sclerophyll unistratal forest, with only sparse ground cover and shrub layer. *Casuarina equisetifolia* is completely dominant, at least in drier areas. It lays down a thick layer of shed needles (photosynthetic branchlets) that, except in wet areas, inhibits seedlings of most species, including its own, from establishing themselves. Hence, the sparseness of herb and shrub layers.

Casuarina colonizes most readily bare mineral substrata such as coral and volcanic rock or sand, but it can also invade grassland or open scrub. Dominant stands of it are more frequent on at least slightly elevated coral islands than on atolls. Just what the natural range of *C. equisetifolia* was before the advent of man on the islands is not at all certain. It is now pantropical but on many low or slightly elevated islands there is no evidence that it is indigenous. On Midway Island, where it forms the principal forest cover, it was brought within the present century. All indications are that on Aldabra it was brought and planted in a number of localities by man but from each original site it is slowly spreading, invading open areas in the indigenous scrub vegetation. On the calcareous sand coastal plain of Saipan, in the Marianas, it forms open to closed forests locally. The evidence as to how long it has been there is ambiguous. Very large trees occur on Peliliu, Palau Group, but usually form only a fringe at the top of the beach, as they do on coral sand in the Seychelles. Old trees often form conspicuous buttresses. The wood is very hard and heavy, sinking in seawater. In the Western Pacific and Indian Oceans, it is often planted on beaches to stabilize them, locally forming groves or forests. It is also established to a limited extent on Caribbean atolls.

G. Mixed Forest

A mixed forest is a closed, evergreen, orthophyll forest, multistratal or unistratal, in places very rich in floristic composition compared with the types hitherto described, with no dominant species except very locally. Both stature and composition vary with habitat. This formation is found from the top of the beach on atolls and elevated limestone islands to the steep sides and tops of karstic peaks and "mogotes," giving rise to the fantastic "Chinese landscape" hills, or "cockpit country" of the larger Caribbean islands and similar topography in Palau, Fiji, and the Louisiades, though here surrounded by water rather than inland.

On the sand flats and wet, low areas of low islands and in valleys and ravines of elevated ones, a tall, species-rich forest with more than one tree stratum is usual, where such has not been replaced by coconut groves. On the steep, almost soilless slopes of wet karst areas is a dense, tangled, unistratal forest, differing in few respects, except being less rich in epiphytes, from a montane forest. On somewhat drier islands, even though somewhat elevated and essentially flat, the forest is again of low stature and unistratal, though here usually with little in the way of shrub or herb layers. On wetter elevated flat limestone plateaus, such as the northern half of Guam, this forest is tall and dense.

The composition of these facies varies with the parts of the world in which they occur. As the climate approaches the dry end of the spectrum, the tendency is toward fewer species, locally approaching dominance by one or another of them. Hence the physiognomy, though conforming to a general type, differs in detail from place to place. In some areas the predominant leaf texture is sclerophyll, rather than orthophyll. Locally, also, the foliage may be facultatively deciduous, leaves falling in dry periods or after severe storms. Flowering may occur after such occurrences. One of the simplest aspects of this type is a mixture of *Pisonia grandis* and *Cordia subcordata* found in the dry areas of the northern Marshall Islands and, formerly, on Wake Island. Locally, it approaches a pure stand of one or another component. Important species are *Thespesia populnea, Guettarda speciosa, Pisonia grandis, Intsia bijuga, Hernandia sonora, Mammea odorata, Cordia subcordata, Morinda citrifolia, Merrilliodendron megacarpum*, and *Ficus* spp. with various local species. *Artocarpus mariannensis* shares dominance with *Ficus prolixa* in certain plateau areas on Guam.

On steep karst slopes in wet areas, such as Palau, little soil exists, except in crevices and pockets. Roots spread over the wet slopes and in wet weather a film of water moves down over them. The plants lead almost the same sort of existence as epiphytes, obliged to endure occasional severe water shortages of short duration. Ferns and other epiphytes are, indeed, common here on both rocks and trees. This sort of vegetation has aptly been described as a "hydroponic forest."

H. *Pandanus* FOREST

Pandanus forest is an open to closed, megaphyllous, evergreen, sclerophyll forest or scrub forest, dominated by *P. tectorius* (*sensu lato*) with prickly short trunks, contorted thick branches, and long, hard, prickly, strap-shaped leaves which is found occasionally on coral atolls and on elevated coral limestone plateaus such as on northern Guam. There the *Pandanus* may be accompanied by *Cycas circinalis* (*sensu lato*). This forest is likely to have a well-developed shrub layer, where the fallen dry leaves are not so deep as to inhibit seedlings from getting started. The crowns are ordinarily conspicuously conical or pyramidal.

I. *Tournefortia* SCRUB AND FOREST

Tournefortia scrub and forest is a closed to open, or sparse, broadleaf, evergreen succulent scrub or scrub forest, rarely taller, trunks tending to be bent and distorted, leaves thick and with a frosty silvery pubescence. This typically forms a narrow or interrupted belt back of the seaward beach on drier atoll islets, open to sparse on extremely dry islands, where it may be called savanna (see below under *Lepturus* savanna). More often the *Tournefortia* is a component of a mixed scrub forest. *Tournefortia* is a pioneer component of atoll vegetation resulting from colonization of bars, sand flats, and dunes, often directly exposed to salt spray. It can live out its life span in closed forest, but when it dies, it is not replaced. Seedlings are ordinarily seen only in full sun on bare coral sand or gravel. Open to sparse stands of rather stunted trees or large shrubs of this species are found on dry atolls such as Pokak, in the Northern Marshalls Islands, Wake Island, and Christmas Island (Central Pacific). On the latter island, this species was scattered over savannas of *Lepturus* on coral sand, but on Pokak there is little or no grass with it when it grows on almost bare rock with soil in pits and crevices.

J. *Pemphis* SCRUB AND SCRUB FOREST

Pemphis acidula is a dense, microphyllous, evergreen, sclerophyll shrub with extremely hard wood and rigid branchlets, usually growing with very few or no other plants, is commonly found throughout the Indo-Pacific region on bare, often rough coral limestone. From a distance, this type of vegetation appears almost coniferous, though rather gray-green. It is usually very difficult to penetrate, as the stiff branches are hard to cut and when broken or cut they are painfully scratchy. Not only is *Pemphis* capable of growing on rock, but it seems to grow perfectly well drenched with salt spray or with its roots covered with sea-water at very high tides. Its tough leaves are astringent when chewed.

K. Mangrove Swamp and Mangrove Depressions

A mangrove swamp is a closed to rarely open, broad sclerophyll swamp forest or scrub, up to 15 or more meters tall, usually without undergrowth, but frequently the lower 1–2 m is a tangle of arching forked aerial or prop roots. Depending on the geographic area and climatic belt the composition may vary, but mangrove vegetation is normally of very few species, frequently an almost pure stand of *Rhizophora*, *Avicennia*, or *Bruguiera*, more rarely *Ceriops*, *Sonneratia*, or *Lumnitzera*. The mangrove fern, *Acrostichum*, is found on a few atolls, but is not common on those oceanic islands that are far from continents or larger islands.

Mangroves are found in several situations on coral islands. They may form a special kind of islet, the mangrove cay, which is just a sand or mud accumulation on a reef. These are well developed on the British Honduras atolls and some other Carribbean coral reef islands. Mangroves may live on shallow lagoon shores in the Western Pacific and Western Indian Oceans. These mangrove-lined shores and the mangrove cay type do not differ essentially from ordinary mangrove swamps. Mangrove depressions are low spots on atoll islets, often hard bottomed, extending to below the fluctuating water table, or at least below midtide level. Frequently, the seawater enters and leaves through underground connections with the sea. In other cases, there is only a slow fluctuation of groundwater, brackish or fresh. *Rhizophora* and *Sonneratia* occur in depressions that have a connection, above or below ground, with the sea. In those without such connections the brackish water genera, *Bruguiera* and *Lumnitzera*, are more prevalent. In the Marshall Islands, and probably elsewhere, are small mud-bottomed depressions carrying *Bruguiera* that have been planted by the Marshallese, who are said to have used the swollen radicles and other parts of the plants.

L. *Cordia* Scrub and Scrub Forest

On many atolls, small areas, often on lagoon beaches and beach ridges, are dominated by *C. subcordata* alone or with *Pisonia* or *Guettarda* or both. These are closed, broadleaf evergreen or semideciduous ortho-phyll scrub or scrub forest. They normally grow on sand at or near sea level but, on the north end of Guam on steep coral limestone slopes, are areas dominated by *C. subcordata*. Vegetation of this species is hard to penetrate because the lower branches spread widely close to the ground and become very tangled.

M. *Scaevola* Scrub or Scrub Forest

Scaevola taccada is one of the commonest and most widespread shrubs of Indo-Pacific shore and near shore vegetation. It forms a closed, broadleaf evergreen orthophyll scrub or rarely a scrub forest, often a pure stand but sometimes mixed with *Tournefortia* and other broadleafed shrubs. The most characteristic manifestation of this scrub is as a fringe or hedge at the top of the beach and, if on windward shores, it is strikingly wind sheared, if on lee shores, it is tall and hedgelike. On many atolls, notably Diego Garcia, in the Chagos Archipelago, there may be large areas of *Scaevola* on sand ridges and dunes. Smaller such areas are occasional on many low coral islands on rock or gravel, as well as sand substrata.

N. *Suriana* Scrub

Suriana maritima forms closed, to open, microphyllous, evergreen scrub, occurring here and there in all coral seas as a fringe at the top of the beach and, on at least one atoll, Arrecife Alacranes, in the Gulf of Mexico, an open stand of it dominates whole islets. This species can tolerate great quantities of salt spray. In the Northern Marshall Islands, it appears to be the most sensitive to low levels of radioactive fallout of all the plants present. This scrub superficially resembles *Pemphis* scrub but is a brighter green and the branches and branchlets are much less brittle.

O. *Guettarda* Scrub Forest

Guettarda speciosa is present on most atolls except the driest and the most remote. On a few it forms an open stand, as on the east end of Aldabra, on others, including other parts of Aldabra, as well as Rongerik, in the Marshalls, it may form a closed evergreen broadleaf orthophyll scrub forest. It is a shrub or small tree with large leaves, very fragrant white flowers, and globose fruits well adapted for floating. Usually it forms a component of mixed evergreen forest, rather than dominating the vegetation.

P. Mixed Subsclerophyll Scrub

On Aldabra, Astove, and probably other slightly elevated coral islands are areas of closed to open, evergreen, broadleaf, subsclerophyll scrub on rough to smooth limestone surfaces. A considerable number of species make up this vegetation, their proportions and stature varying from place to place. Vegetation physiognomically similar to this but tending to be spiny is very common on coral limestone in the Caribbean where it is also rich in species composition.

Q. *Lepturus* MEADOW AND SAVANNA

The commonest and most widespread Indo-Pacific coral atoll grass is *L. repens*. It is wiry, hard-tufted grass, the tufts usually sending out long stolons that form a tangled loose mat. On atolls in the drier zones, such as the Central Pacific atolls, the Northern Marshalls, and others, are limited meadows made up almost exclusively of *Lepturus*. It varies in stature from 1.5 to 4 or 5 dm. On Christmas Island, this grassland becomes a savanna by addition of *Tournefortia argentea,* or a dwarf shrub savanna by addition of *Heliotropium anomalum* (a silvery leafed succulent dwarf shrub), and *Sida fallax* (a tomentose small shrub) separately or in various mixtures. Similar savannas occur to a limited extent in the Northern Marshalls and Wake Island. On the latter they have been all but eliminated by airport development.

R. *Ipomoea–Wedelia* MAT

In the Marshall Islands, and probably elsewhere, after intense distur-bance and clearing of other vegetation, the pioneer vegetation is often a deep, tangled mat of creepers, principally *I. pes-caprae* and *Wedelia biflora.* This reaches a meter or more, even 2 m, in depth. Little is known of the subsequent succession from this early vegetation. Most areas where it occurs are subject to continued disturbances and no continued study of it has been made. Invasion of such a dense mat by woody species would seem to be difficult and slow.

S. TARO MARSHES

A taro marsh is a closed to open, megaphyllous, orthophyll marsh that occupies mud-bottomed depressions on many wet atolls and on some elevated coral islands, such as Angaur and Peliliu in the Palaus. Acaulescent or short thick-stemmed aroids are dominant in this planted type. *Cyrtosperma, Colocasia, Xanthosoma,* and *Alocasia* are the genera most common in these artifically dug habitats. All are planted for food, either in pure or mixed stands. All of them, except *Colocasia,* may reach very large size, up to 3 or even 4 m tall (*Cyrtosperma chamissonis*). Bananas and a number of ornamentals are occasionally planted in these pits, but on a minor scale. A large flora of marsh-dwelling weeds or "camp follower" plants share the pits and are undoubtedly carried around with planting material and in other ways by man. The local name for these gardens in the Gilbert Islands is "babai pits." The dominant species there is the babai, *C. chamissonis*, which furnishes enormous edible corms.

The distribution of these pits was formerly much greater, judging by the winding pits and ridges found on many islands where there is no taro culture today, as in the Northern Marshall Islands. Taro culture is hard work and tends to lose ground to a cash economy based on copra. In Likiep an attempt to reactivate taro culture failed after a year or two, supposedly because of the introduction of a weedy grass, *Paspalum distichum*, which is exceedingly tenacious and difficult to eliminate and capable of crowding out the taros.

T. Sea-Grass Meadows

A final type of vascular plant vegetation that should be mentioned is the widespread "turtle grass" of shallow waters in most tropical seas. Several genera of marine flowering plants are involved, depending on the region and habitat. *Thalassia* (of several species), *Halodule* (several species), *Cymodocea, Syringodium, Halophila, Enhalus*, and especially *Thalassodendron* may form pure or mixed stands, usually in rather quiet or sheltered water on mud or sand flats, or lagoon shores below usual low tide levels. Their tangled rhizomes form a dense sod that is an important binder of loose sediments and contributes to building substrata for mangroves and, eventually, dry land. On Aldabra, even on exposed high-energy shores, the reef flats are covered by a tough sod of *Thalassodendron ciliatum*, with wiry stems rising from the rhizomes and diminutive fanlike distichous crowns of purplish-green linear leaves. These so-called sea-grasses are important food for sea turtles and cover large areas in water of appropriate depths.

U. Algal Reefs

It is beyond the scope of this chapter to describe coral reefs, except to point out that many of them are composed of large proportions, even up to 90%, of calcareous algae, both Chlorophyceae (*Halimeda*) and lithothamnioid Rhodophyceae (*Porolithon, Goniolithon, Lithothamnium*, and related genera). *Halimeda* contributes large quantities of sediments, especially in lagoon bottoms. The encrusting red algae are very important in binding the components of coral reefs together. On exposed, high-energy coasts, massive species of *Porolithon* and other genera form a characteristic pink "algal ridge" and great buttresses that are the actively growing and wave resistant front of the reef. It has even been said that without the calcareous red algae to cement the corals together there would be no coral reefs, only banks and bars of clastic calcareous sediments of organic origin. Setchell (1928) was the first to point out in a substantial way the importance of algae on coral reefs.

V. Conclusions

The vegetation of coral islands, when studied seriously, gives a very useful insight into the nature and complexity of vegetation generally. Compared with that of continents and even of other islands, it is made up of relatively very few species, mostly with wide distributions. The above summary gives some idea of what a wide range of types of vegetation, and of variations within these types, even these few species can form. The responses to different climates, topographic situations, textural classes of even a single soil parent material, and kinds and intensities of animal and human exploitation and disturbance are extremely diverse, even though relatively infinitesimal compared with those of situations of greater complexity and larger floras.

When understood, the nature of the vegetation will give an indication of other, less easily observed environmental parameters. Its condition may give clues to the kinds and degree of stresses to which particular ecosystems are being subjected. It may even serve as a guide to proper land use and management on these bits of land which must often support very large population densities.

Perhaps even more important, the vegetation is the basis of most of the comfort and of the beauty for which coral islands are so justly famed.

References

Agassiz, A. (1903a). *Mem. Mus. Comp. Zool. Harvard* 23, 1–410.
Agassiz, A. (1903b). *Mem. Mus. Comp. Zool. Harvard* 29, 1–168.
Andrews, C. W. *et al.* (1900). "A Monograph of Christmas Island." British Museum (Natur. Hist.), London.
Britton, N. L., and Millspaugh, C. F. (1920). "The Bahama Flora." Published by authors. New York.
Christophersen, E. (1927). *Bishop Mus. Bull.* 44, 1–79.
Christophersen, E. (1931). *Occas. Pap. Bishop Mus.* 9(13), 1–20.
Christophersen, E., and Caum, E. L. (1931). *Bishop Mus. Bull.* 81, 1–41.

Farrow, G. E. (1971). *Phil. Trans. Roy. Soc. London, Ser. B* **260**, 67–91.

Fosberg, F. R. (1949). *Pac. Sci.* 3, 89–92.

Fosberg, F. R. (1954). *Soil Sci.* **78**, 99–107.

Fosberg, F. R. (1961). *Trop. Ecol.* **2**, 1–28.

Fosberg, F. R. (1962). *Atoll Res. Bull.* **93**, 1–25.

Fosberg, F. R. (1971). *Phil. Trans. Roy. Soc. London, Ser. B* **360**, 215–225.

Fosberg, F. R., and Carroll, D. (1965). *Atoll Res. Bull.* **113**, 1–156.

Fosberg, F. R., Arnow, T., and MacNeil, F. S. (1956). "Military Geography of the Northern Marshalls." U.S. Army Corps of Engineers, Far East, Tokyo.

Hatheway, W. H. (1953). *Atoll Res. Bull.* **16**, 1–68.

Hatheway, W. H. (1955). *Atoll Res. Bull.* **43**, 1–9.

Millspaugh, C. F. (1907). *Field Mus. Publ. Bot.* **2**, 191–245.

Millspaugh, C. F. (1916). *Field Mus. Publ. Bot.* **2**, 421–431.

Niering, W. A. (1956). *Atoll Res. Bull.* **49**, 1–32.

Peterken, G. F. (1967). *IBP Handb.* **4**, 73–120.

Sachet, M.-H. (1957). *Atoll Res. Bull.* **60**, 1–4.

Sachet, M.-H. (1962a). *Atoll Iles. Bull.* **86**, 1–115.

Sachet, M.-H. (1962b). *Proc. Calif. Acad. Sci. [Ser. 4]* **31**, 249–307.

Sachet, M.-H. (1962c). *Ann. Inst. Oceanogr. (Paris)* **40**, 1–107.

Sauer, J. (1967). "Plants and Man on the Seychelles Coast." Univ. Wisconsin Pr., Madison.

Setchell, W. A. (1924). *Carnegie Inst. Wash. Publ.* **341**, 225–261.

Setchell, W. A. (1928). *Science Ser. 2* **68**, 119–131.

Stoddart, D. R. (1962). *Atoll Res. Bull.* **87**, 1–151.

Stoddart, D. R. (1971a). *Atoll Res. Bull.* **147**, 1–21.

Stoddart, D. R. (1971b). *Atoll Res. Bull.* **149**, 27–30.

Stone, E. L. (1951). *Atoll Res. Bull.* **5**, 1–56.

Stone, E. L. (1953). *Atoll Res. Bull.* **22**, 1–6.

Taylor, W. R. (1950). "Plants of Bikini." Univ. of Michigan Press, Ann Arbor.

Wilder, G. P. (1934). *Bishop Mus. Bull.* **120**, 1–49.

9

THE BIRDS OF THE GREAT BARRIER REEF

Jiro Kikkawa

I. Introduction

Since the voyage of Lt. James Cook in 1770, ornithological collections and observations have been made in the Great Barrier Reef region by naturalists on board H.M.S. *Mermaid* and *Bathurst* (1819–1821), *Beagle* (1839–1841), *Fly* (1843–1845; see MacGillivray, 1846; Jukes, 1847), *Rattlesnake* (1847–1850; see MacGillivray, 1852), *Herald* (1869; see Rayer, cited by Sharpe, 1906), *Challenger* (1874; see Forbes, 1878; Saunders, 1878; Sclater and Salvin, 1878; Moseley, 1892), and *Alert* (1881). At the turn of the century, a few Australian ornithologists began to visit the region (Austin, 1908; Cornwall, 1903, 1909; Le Souef, 1894, 1897) culminating in an expedition to the Capricorn Group during October 1910 by the Royal Australasian Ornithologists' Union (Barrett, 1910). One of the results of this expedition was the description by Campbell and White (1910) of a new species of bird, *Zosterops chlorocephalus* (now recognized as a subspecies of *Zosterops lateralis*), the only form endemic to the Great Barrier Reef region. A most extensive survey of birds in the Great Barrier Reef region was made by MacGillivray, who visited Raine Island and many inner reef areas between 1910 and 1930. Hindwood *et al.* (1963) aboard H.M.A.S. *Gascoyne* surveyed the birds of outer reef areas and the cays of the Coral Sea in 1960 and

1961. Since 1960 some 2000 sea birds (12 species) have been banded in the area by CSIRO workers and the recoveries of *Puffinus pacificus* and *Sula leucogaster* have provided some useful information on these species (Purchase, 1969a,b, 1973). Recently, Serventy *et al.* (1971) published an excellent handbook of the Australian sea birds that contains detailed biological information on sea birds, including those breeding on the Great Barrier Reef. The sea birds of the Pacific Ocean have been studied intensively under the Smithsonian Institution Pacific Ocean Biological Survey Program 1963–1970 (Humphrey, 1965; Smithsonian Institution, 1971) and the publication of this work is still in progress (Amerson, 1969; King, 1967, 1970).

This chapter brings together scattered information on the birds of the Great Barrier Reef in order to obtain some general patterns of distribution and to point out gaps in our knowledge of the biology of coral reef birds.

II. Birds of Coral Cays and Coral Cay Islands

Sea birds of the tropical ocean are largely associated with coral cays and islands (Alexander, 1954). Birds are generally absent from a vast expanse of tropical water masses that is characterized by high temperatures (18°–28°C), high salinities (35–37‰), and poor nutrients, yet their concentration around coral reefs, lagoons, and cays often supersedes the abundance of sea birds widely distributed in the polar and temperate regions. Because of the proximity of islands or shallow reef waters of high productivity, birds are abundant generally throughout the Great Barrier Reef region and a variety of habitats provided by islands of different ages supports breeding colonies of many species.

Tropical sea birds generally have little affinity with the temperate species. Alcidae (auks) of northern waters and Spheniscidae (penguins) and Pelecanoididae (diving-petrels) of southern waters are conspicuously absent from tropical waters except for the occurrence of two species of auk on the lower California coast and one species of penguin in the Galápagos. Very few albatrosses, gulls, skuas, and fulmars stray into tropical waters. Of the latter group, only one species of gull breeds in the Great Barrier Reef region. Cold water upwellings that attract many temperate birds to parts of the tropical coast of America are not known in the Coral Sea. Birds associated with the upwellings, such as guano-forming cormorants (Murphy, 1925, 1936), are absent from the Great Barrier Reef. The characteristic sea birds of the tropical ocean are frigate-birds, pelicans, tropic-birds, and noddies. There are, in addi-

TABLE I

NUMBERS OF SEA BIRD SPECIES RECORDED FROM VARIOUS ISLAND
GROUPS OF THE TROPICAL AND SUBTROPICAL PACIFIC[a]

| Latitude range | Island groups | Number of sea bird species | |
		Breeding	Nonbreeding
30°–20°N	Bonin and Volcano	12	24
	Marcus	4	20
	Hawaii	22	50
20°–10°N	Wake	8	10
	Marianas	11	12
	Marshall	14	17
10°N–0°	Palau	12	4
	Caroline	12	6
	Gilbert	9	13
	Line	19	19
0°–10°S	Bismarck	9	17
	Solomon	8	15
	Ellice	7	9
	Phoenix	19	20
	Tokelau	5	7
	Marquesas	18	15
10°–20°S	New Hebrides	11	9
	Fiji	19	7
	Samoa	14	11
	Society	14	8
	Tuamotu	21	4
	Cook	4	7
	Great Barrier Reef	21	17
20°–30°S	New Caledonia	19	8
	Austral	13	4
	Pitcairn	14	3
	Easter	6	5
	Kermadec	13	20

[a] The data other than those from the Great Barrier Reef region are based on King (1967).

tion, large numbers of species of tern, gannet, shearwater, petrel, and storm-petrel breeding on tropical islands. In the Great Barrier Reef region one species of shearwater, one species of petrel, three species of gannet, and eight species of tern are known to breed. As can be seen from Table I, the islands of the Great Barrier Reef are among those that possess the greatest numbers of breeding species of sea birds in the tropical and subtropical Pacific.

Considered from an ecological point of view, the birds occupy a unique position in the coral sea ecosystem; they exploit all trophic levels of sea and land. The sea birds range from plankton feeders to fish eaters (Ashmole, 1971). The waders feed on tidal zone animals and the diet of land birds varies from fruits to insects at all heights of vegetation and on the ground. Sea birds make a significant contribution in the cycle of nutrients by transporting organic matter from the nutrient-rich marine environment to islands where the growth of vegetation depends on imported material (Heatwole, 1971). Migratory species disseminate many species of plants from island to island and cause development of plant communities on cays.

III. Distributional Patterns of Birds in the Great Barrier Reef Region

The region considered here covers the latitudinal range from 9°10'S (Bramble Cay) to 24°10'S (Lady Elliot Island), and Fig. 1 shows the locations of 91 islands and island groups from which three or more species of breeding birds have been recorded. Where information is available, continental and offshore islands are included as well as coral reef islands. Reference sources from which information relating to the distribution and status of the 254 species recorded from this region was obtained, are given in the Appendix. The distributional data published before 1970 were used to construct two sets of data matrices; one with 43 grid squares (areas marked by latitude and longitude degrees) by 239 species and the other with 91 islands and island groups by 133 breeding species. Exotic species and species erroneously recorded were excluded from the analyses. The classifications of both the grid squares and the island groups were made by information analysis (Williams et al., 1966) using the Canberra program CENTCLAS. This analysis was previously applied to distributional data of land birds and produced an ecologically meaningful classification of areas (Kikkawa, 1968).

The results of the analysis for the grid squares based on the presence and absence of all bird species are shown in Fig. 2, with hierarchical and geographical relations of the classified squares. The squares representing open waters of the southwest Coral Sea and coral cays of the outer Barrier Reef were grouped together generally and contained relatively few species. The squares containing species-rich continental islands of central and southern areas were grouped separately from those of Cape York Peninsula, reflecting the faunal change of the land birds north of Cooktown. In spite of the presence of several oceanic birds, Willis Island area (E) and Raine Island area (F) showed greater similarity to coastal areas than to oceanic areas. This is because many drifted land birds have been recorded from these islands, increasing the similarity with continental islands. The inner reef areas showed a greater affinity with northern areas than with outer reef areas.

The results of the analysis for the 91 islands and island groups based on the presence and absence of the breeding bird species are shown in Fig. 3. Since the majority of the breeding species are land birds, the continental islands tend to have more species than reef islands. The six that were grouped together at low levels (A–E) represent 94 species compared with the 82 species represented by 85 other islands (F–M). The two large groups (F and G) of noncontinental islands (totaling 29), which showed little affinity with other island groups, contained only 23 breeding species. Both Raine and Willis Islands were grouped here. The Capricorn Group of islands (H) also formed a distinct group, separated from other island groups of the inner reef and the continent.

Among the land birds of inner reef islands, resident populations of the Sacred Kingfisher (*Halcyon australasiae*) and the Pied Currawong (*Strepera graculina*) are restricted to the central and southern parts, whereas the migratory Torres Strait Pigeon (*Ducula spilorrhoa*) is confined to the northern part of the region. Silvereyes breed on many of the wooded islands throughout the region, but apart from the Pale Silvereye (*Zosterops citrinella albiventris*) of the far north and the Capricorn race of the Grey-breasted Silvereye (*Z. lateralis chlorocephala*) no specimens have been collected from central and northern parts of the region. Here the species and races of silvereyes are not clear (Mees, 1969; Kikkawa, 1973). The Yellow Silvereye (*Zosterops lutea*) reported by Le Souëf (1891) from Kent Island requires further investigation.

The above analyses reveal some interesting patterns of distribution in the region. First, the influence of Australian land birds is largely limited to the continental islands and islands of the inner reef. Coral cay islands are small and the habitat for land birds is much impoverished compared with continental islands. Colonization by land birds is much limited here in spite of the short distance from the mainland, and coral cay islands have the characteristics of oceanic islands. Second, near the continent the faunal composition is distinct around Cape York Peninsula. Third, the sea birds of the outer reef and Coral Sea in general show no geographical patterns of distribution, particularly among the breeding species.

For an understanding of the distribution of breeding colonies on coral cays, the habitat types of islands and the traditional aspect of colony establishment by birds need to be considered. Hindwood *et al.* (1963)

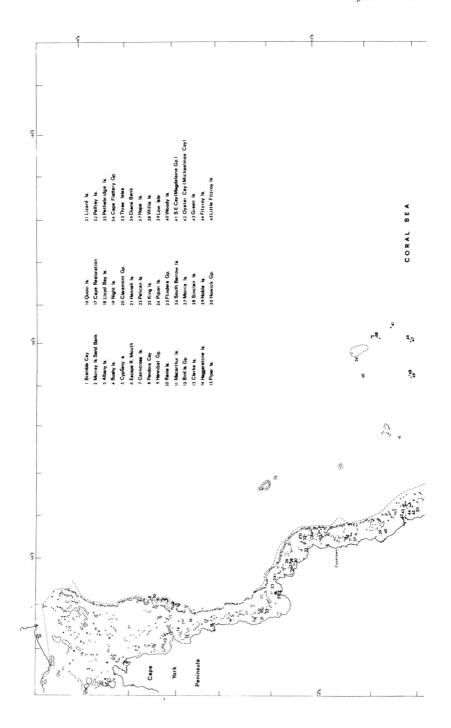

1 Bramble Cay
2 Murray Is. Sand Bank
3 Albany Is.
4 Bushy Is.
5 Cypffeny a.
6 Escape R. Mouth
7 Cairncross Is.
8 Pandora Cay
9 Hannibal Gp.
10 Raine Is.
11 Macarthur Is.
12 Bird Is. Gp.
13 Clerke Is.
14 Haggerstone Is.
15 Pipon Is.

16 Quoin Is.
17 Cape Restoration
18 Lloyd Bay Is.
19 Night Is.
20 Claremont Gp.
21 Hannah Is.
22 Pelican Is.
23 King Is.
24 Pipon Is.
25 Flinders Gp.
26 South Barrow Is.
27 Morris Is.
28 Sinclair Is.
29 Noble Is.
30 Howick Gp.

31 Lizard Is.
32 Palfrey Is.
33 Pethebridge Is.
34 Cape Flattery Gp.
35 Three Isles
36 Diana Bank
37 Hope Is.
38 Willis Is.
39 Low Isle
40 Woody Is.
41 S.E Cay (Magdelaine Gp.)
42 Oyster Cay (Michaelmas Cay)
43 Green Is.
44 Fitzroy Is.
45 Little Fitzroy Is.

CORAL SEA

Cape York Peninsula

QUEENSLAND

46 N.E. Islet (Chilcott, Coringa Gp.)	61 Flinders Reef
47 S.W Islet (Coringa Gp.)	62 Dunk Is.
48 N.E. Cay (Herald Gp.)	63 South Brook Is.
49 S.W. Cay (Herald Gp.)	64 White Rock
50 Russell Is.	65 Carola and Paget Cays (Marion Reef)
51 Turtle Islet (Lihou Reef)	66 Magnetic Is.
52 No.1 Cay (Lihou Reef)	67 Whitsunday Islands
53 No.8 Cay (Lihou Reef)	68 Cumberland Gp.
54 No.9 Cay (Lihou Reef)	69 Victor Is.
55 Herald's Beacon Islet (Mellish Reef)	70 Taffy Is.
56 West Islet (Diamond Islets)	71 Observatory Cay (Kenn Reef)
57 Mid Islet (Diamond Islets)	72 S.W. Projection Cay (Kenn Reef)
58 East Islet (Diamond Islets)	73 Cape Palmerston Is.
59 S.W (Diamond Islets)	74 Pine Islet
60 Kent (North Barnard) Is.	75 Temple Islet

76 Percy Is.
77 S.W Cay (Saumarez Reef)
78 Swain Reefs
79 Porpoise Cay and Bird Islet (Wreck Reef)
80 Keppel Gp.
81 North West Is.
82 Tryon Is.
83 Wilson Is.
84 Cato Is.
85 Wreck Is.
86 Heron Is.
87 One Tree Is.
88 Masthead Is.
89 Hoskyn Is.
90 Fairfax Is.
91 Lady Musgrave Is.

Fig. 1. Map of the Great Barrier Reef region showing the islands used in the analysis of bird distribution. The islands are numbered from north to south.

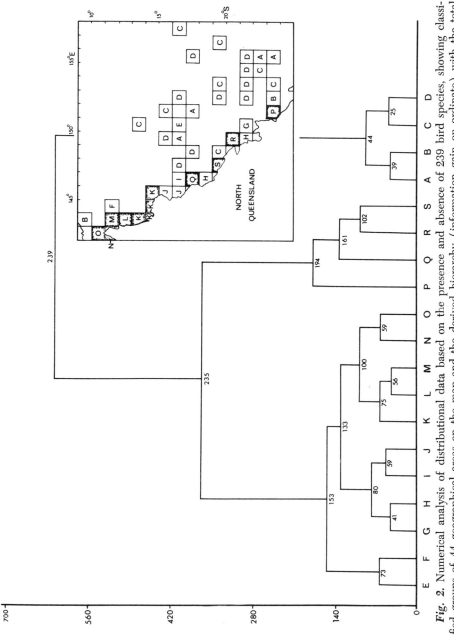

Fig. 2. Numerical analysis of distributional data based on the presence and absence of 239 bird species, showing classified groups of 44 geographical areas on the map and the derived hierarchy (information gain on ordinate) with the total number of bird species recorded from the group of areas at each fusion.

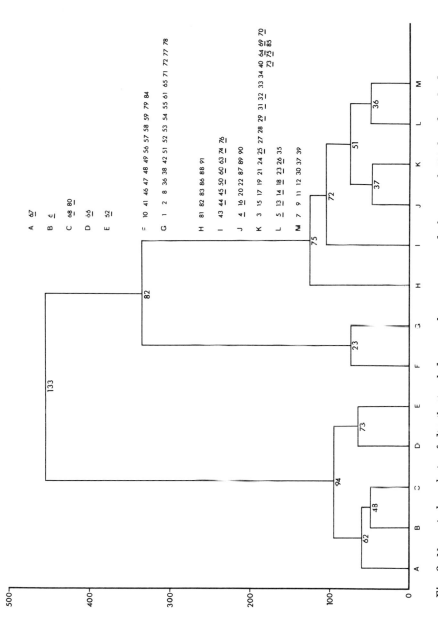

Fig. 3. Numerical analysis of distributional data on the presence and absence of 133 breeding bird species on 91 islands (see Fig. 1), (information gain on ordinate) with total number of breeding bird species recorded from the group of islands at each fusion. The numbers representing continental islands are underlined.

distinguished three types of cay or islet in the outer reef that supported different species of breeding sea birds. The unvegetated cays formed of sand and shingle generally support two or three breeding species including generally Brown Gannet (*Sula leucogaster*), Masked Gannet (*S. dactylatra*), Black-naped Tern (*Sterna sumatrana*), or Noddy (*Anous stolidus*) and, occasionally, Crested Tern (*Sterna bergii*) or Sooty Tern (*Sterna fuscata*) in addition.

The cays covered, or partly covered, with grass, creepers, and succulents, but with no trees, generally support more species than those without any vegetation. Up to seven species from the following selection may breed on such cays: Wedge-tailed Shearwater (*Puffinus pacificus*), Lesser Frigate-Bird (*Fregata ariel*), Brown Gannet, Red-footed Gannet (*Sula sula*), Masked Gannet, Red-tailed Tropic-Bird (*Phaëthon rubricauda*), Little Tern (*Sterna albifrons*), Sooty Tern, and Noddy. Cays with herbage and trees support the greatest number of breeding species. In addition to the species breeding on grass-covered cays, Greater Frigate-Bird (*Fregata minor*) and White-capped Noddy (*Anous minutus*) commonly breed on such cays. Wooded cays naturally have more land birds than other cays, but the number of breeding species is still small compared with the number on continental islands.

The type of vegetation and species of trees present may govern the distribution of nesting birds on the island. In the Capricorn and Bunker Groups, wooded islands typically have a row of tall *Casuarina* on one side of the island and dense shrubs on the other. In between, *Pisonia* may grow up to 40 ft (13 m) interspersed with patches of *Pandanus*, *Ficus*, and *Celtis* forming a lower canopy. *Pandanus* occurs on low-lying areas, sometimes forming a dense cover. The White-breasted Sea-Eagle (*Haliaeëtus leucogaster*) and Reef Heron (*Egretta sacra*) breed on all wooded islands here but, as can be seen in Table II, other species are not equally represented. The distribution of the Grey-breasted Silvereye is associated with figs (*Ficus opposita*), while the Pied Currawong, when it used to breed, occurred only on densely wooded islands (MacGillivray, 1926, 1928).

However, similar islands do not necessarily have similar breeding species. Some species seem to have traditional sites for breeding; the Australian Pelican (*Pelecanus conspicillatus*), for example, is known to breed on Pelican Island (so named by Capt. James Cook), Sinclair Island, Howick Island Group, and Hope Island in northern parts of the region, but is absent from many similar islands in the vicinity. The conditions that govern the distribution of the Australian Pelican in the Great Barrier Reef region are not known. The breeding sites of Torres Strait Pigeons

TABLE II

DISTRIBUTION OF BREEDING BIRDS (X) ON ISLANDS OF THE CAPRICORN AND BUNKER GROUPS[a]

Bird	Islands in Capricorn Group							Islands in Bunker Group		
	North West	Tryon	Wilson	Wreck	Heron	Ore Tree	Mast-head	Hoskyn	Fairfax	Lady Mus-grave
Wedge-tailed Shearwater	X	X	X	X	X		X	X	sX	X
Brown Gannet								X	X	X
Little Pied Cormorant				X						
Reef Heron	X	X	X	X	X	X	X		X	X
White-breasted Sea-eagle	X	X	X	pX	pX	pX	X	X	pX	X
Feral Domestic Fowl (introduced)	X				X					
Banded Land Rail	X	X			X	sX	X			
Pied Oyster-catcher	?	sX			pX		sX	?	sX	sX
Sooty Oyster-catcher	?	pX	sX	sX	X	sX	sX	X	sX	sX
White-capped Noddy	X	X	X		pX	X	X		X	X
Silver Gull	X	X	X	X	pX	sX	X		X	X
Little Tern									X	
Bridled Tern	X	X		X		X	X	X	X	X
Lesser Crested Tern	X					X	X	X	X	
Crested Tern		X	X			X	X		X	X
Roseate Tern		X	X	X		X			X	X
Black-naped Tern	X	X	X	X	sX	X			X	
Bar-shouldered Dove	sX	sX	sX	sX	sX		X			X
Sacred Kingfisher	?				sX		sX		sX	
Black-faced Cuckoo-shrike					sX	sX				
Golden-headed Fantail-Warbler										
Capricorn Silvereye	X	X	sX	sX	X	sX	X			X
Pied Currawong	X	pX			rX		pX			

[a] Species known to have bred only in the past and species represented by a relatively small breeding colony are prefixed by "p" and "s," respectively.

also appear to be traditional. The pigeons breed and roost in large numbers on islands off the coast of Cape York Peninsula. Each day they fly across the sea to rain forest areas of the mainland for feeding; they fly in small flocks low above the water (the destination often not visible). Once the pigeons returning to Hope Island from widely scattered sites of the mainland were counted for 15 minutes (17.30–17.45, October 26, 1968) from a ship. A total of 199 flocks consisting of 1103 birds (flock size, 5.5 ± 0.291) was sighted in this period. What proportion of the population on this island was represented in this count is not known. The Torres Strait Pigeon is a summer visitor to the region.

In some highly social species there is a very strong tendency for all breeding birds to try to nest in an established colony rather than in new areas that are apparently equally suitable for nesting. Ashmole (1962) found that many Black Noddies (*Anous tenuirostris*) on Ascension Island in the Atlantic attempted to breed in the overcrowded colony without success. He suggested that, in spite of such failure to breed, it is normally advantageous for them to nest among other individuals of the species as they suffer less predation in a dense colony than at a new site and that the presence of a colony is the best indication of a suitable nesting site for the young birds attempting to breed for the first time.

Among breeding land birds, the Capricorn race of the Grey-breasted Silvereye showed very little interchange of individuals (up to 1%) among breeding populations of different islands (evidence based on 1500 birds banded in the Capricorn Group, mostly on Heron Island). As yet, behavioral aspects of birds associated with dispersal or site attachment have not been studied in the Great Barrier Reef region. Oceanic birds do not remain on the island after breeding and their distribution during the nonbreeding season is little known. The Wedge-tailed Shearwater returns to the same island each year [evidence based on banding by Booth (1970) at Heron Island]. Other available evidence based on banding shows that the Brown Gannet breeding on Fairfax Island migrates to coastal areas of North Queensland after breeding (Purchase, 1969a,b). Recoveries of banded juvenile Sooty Terns from the Philippines (Lane, 1967) suggest somewhat directional movements of young birds away from the breeding grounds of the South Pacific, but no large scale banding has been carried out in the Great Barrier Reef region to discover the range of dispersal of this species in the nonbreeding period. Robertson (1969) reported that Sooty Terns banded as young on Dry Tortugas in the Gulf of Mexico migrated across the Atlantic in their first autumn to the Gulf of Guinea on the West African coast. These young apparently stay away from the breeding ground for at least two years. Most of the young reared in the colony ultimately returned there to breed and they may tend to seek nesting space near the natal nesting site. Since there are about as many nonbreeding birds as are breeding birds in the colony, Robertson (1969) considered the long absence and delayed maturity of juveniles and subadults as an important factor reducing competition and causing selection for young with migratory habits.

Shearwaters, skuas, and many waders migrate across the tropical sea to spend the southern winter in the northern Pacific or the northern winter in southern waters, but of these, only some species of waders are found regularly on the Great Barrier Reef. Of the three species of shearwater [Fleshy-footed Shearwater (*Puffinus carneipes*), Short-tailed Shearwater (*Puffinus tenuirostris*), and Sooty Shearwater (*Puffinus griseus*)] that breed in southern waters of Australia and migrate to the northern hemisphere, only the Fleshy-footed Shearwater has been re-corded from the Coral Sea (Hindwood *et al.*, 1963; Norris, 1967). The Southern Skua (*Stercorarius skua*), which ranges the southern seas, sel-dom enters the tropics, whereas the Pomarine Skua (*Stercorarius po-marinus*) and the Arctic Skua (*Stercorarius parasiticus*) visit southern waters of Australia from the northern hemisphere. Apart from isolated sightings of Southern Skuas (Cooper, 1948), they are not known from the Great Barrier Reef region. Wintering populations of waders are com-mon in summer in the region and during migration some large flocks may appear. Their competitive and social relations with local oyster-catchers (two breeding species) require investigation. Some waders, such as the Turnstone (*Arenaria interpres*), Grey-tailed Tattler (*Tringa brevipes*), and Bar-tailed Godwit (*Limosa lapponica*), remain through the winter months in small numbers. At present there is no banding program to study the migration of waders in the area.

Many species of Australian land birds appear in the Great Barrier Reef region during migration. For example, 26 species of land birds, not known to breed on the coral cay islands, have been recorded from Heron Island (Kikkawa, 1970). Some species, such as the Rufous Whis-tler (*Pachycephala rufiventris*) and Leaden Flycatcher (*Myiagra rube-cula*), visit the island regularly, though never in large numbers, whereas others have obviously drifted to the island. The mainland form of *Zosterops lateralis* migrating in eastern Australia is known to drift to Heron Island in winter, sometimes in numbers sufficient to cause severe competition for food (Kikkawa, 1970). The records kept at the weather station on Willis Island of Australian land birds reaching the island show that the following species have drifted at least 290 miles east of the continental shore in the past: Nankeen Kestrel (*Falco cenchroides*), Brolga (*Grus rubicundus*), Banded Land Rail (*Rallus philippensis*), Eastern Swamphen (*Porphyrio porphyrio*), Spur-winged Plover, (*Vanellus novaehollandiae*), Purple-crowned Pigeon (*Ptilinopus superbus*), Torres Strait Pigeon, Diamond Dove (*Geopelia cuneata*), Oriental Cuckoo (*Cuculus saturatus*), Golden Bronze-Cuckoo (*Chrysococcyx lucidus*), Grey Swiftlet (*Collocalia francica*), Azure Kingfisher (*Alcyone azurea*), Little Kingfisher (*Alcyone pusilla*), Forest Kingfisher (*Halcyon macleayii*), Mangrove Kingfisher (*Halcyon chloris*), Eastern Broad-billed Roller (*Eurystomus orientalis*), Welcome Swallow (*Hirundo tahitica*), Tree Martin (*Petrochelidon nigricans*), Black-faced Cuckoo-Shrike (*Coracina novaehollandiae*), Australian Ground Thrush (*Zoothera dauma*), Leaden Flycatcher, Satin Flycatcher (*Myiagra cyanoleuca*), Pictorella Finch (*Lonchura pectoralis*)(?), and Magpie Lark (*Grallina cyanoleuca*). Studies of these incidences would reveal the time and the route of migration on the mainland and the pattern of dispersal of inland nomadic and resident species.

IV. Breeding of Birds on Coral Cays and Oceanic Islands

The laying seasons and clutch sizes of breeding birds in the Great Barrier Reef region are summarized in Table III. Comparable information is absent in the case of the Little Pied Cormorant (*Phalacrocorax melanoleucos*) and Red-backed Sea-Eagle (*Haliastur indus*), which are also known to breed on some coral cay islands.

The evolution of a small clutch size (many tropical sea birds lay only one egg and the clutch of one must have evolved from a larger clutch size) in many different taxa suggests that the distribution and abundance of food resources in the tropics and the evolved mechanisms of food collecting by parent birds are not suitable for raising more than one young at a time. Lack (1954) pointed out that if one type of individual lays more eggs than another and the difference is genetic, then the more fecund type must come to predominate over the other. If, however, the individuals laying more eggs leave fewer, not more, descendants by failing to care for more young or living a shorter life span on the average, then a small clutch size will be favored. Wynne-Edwards (1962) contended that the consistent laying of a clutch of one has evolved as an adaptation to limit the population size (restrictive adaptation) below the level at which the population may overexploit its food supply. The possibility of such evolution involving group selection is negated by the arguments of Ashmole (1963b) and the view that the reduced clutch size in tropical sea birds is the direct result of selection through food supply is favored (Lack, 1968). Stonehouse (1963) weighed eggs of sea birds on Ascension Island and found that the boobies (*Sula* spp.) having a clutch size of two produced the smallest eggs in proportion to body weight (4%), whereas other species with a clutch size of one produced eggs weighing up to 22% of the body weight. In birds that lay a single large egg and rear a slow-growing young, energy for breeding may be required for a long period. During the production of the egg and the long period of incubation that follows, the demand on concentrated food may be just as great as after the egg hatches. If the egg is lost, laying of a replacement occurs only after a long time. Thus the small clutch size may be an adaptation to the tropical environment in which the supply of food is stable for a longer period but less seasonal than in temperate waters. *Sula* spp. on Ascension Island lay two eggs but normally only one young is reared (Dorward, 1962). Both the Masked Gannet and Brown Gannet in the Great Barrier Reef region show the same trend. Among other sea birds that lay more than one egg in the Great Barrier Reef region (Table III), the Silver Gull and the Little Tern breed more commonly outside the tropics.

In recent years breeding cycles of tropical sea birds have been studied in detail on Ascension Island at 8°S, 14°W, (see *Ibis* **103b**, 1962–1963), the Galápagos Islands at 0°, 90°W (Harris, 1969b), and Christmas Island at 2°N, 157°W (see Schreiber and Ashmole, 1970), and comparison of the breeding seasons of sea birds among these islands has been made by Schreiber and Ashmole (1970) and Ashmole (1971). Serventy *et al.* (1971) made a generalization that along the Queensland coast and on the inner reef islands of the Great Barrier Reef most sea birds breed in spring and summer but on the outer reef islands and the northern Coral Sea atolls there is a double season regime with autumn nesting apparently predominant. They list the following species as having a double nesting season over the range of their distribution: Masked Gannet, Brown Gannet, Red-footed Gannet, Lesser Frigate-bird, Red-tailed Tropic-Bird, Australian Pelican, Pied Cormorant, Noddy, Caspian Tern, Silver Gull, Bridled Tern, Lesser-crested Tern, Crested Tern, Sooty Tern, and Roseate Tern. It will be useful to comment on the laying seasons of sea birds in the Great Barrier Reef region in the light of work elsewhere.

Following the order of listing of species in Table III, the Wedge-tailed Shearwater in the region has a regular laying period in the southern season (November–December) corresponding with the laying at Christ-

TABLE III

BREEDING SEASONS AND CLUTCH SIZES OF SOME ISLAND BIRDS IN THE GREAT BARRIER REEF REGION[a]

| Species | Breeding | | Clutch size | | Remarks |
	Laying seasons	Variation	Mode	Range	
Wedge-tailed Shearwater (*Puffinus pacificus*)	Nov.–Dec.	Season regular	1		Summer breeder, arriving in the region during Oct.
Red-tailed Tropic-Bird (*Phaëthon rubricauda*)	June–Nov. (Raine Is. and Coringa Gp.)	Fresh eggs found almost all months of year	1		Breeding colonies small
Australian Pelican (*Pelecanus conspicillatus*)	April–Aug.	Winter breeding	2	1–4	Spring breeding elsewhere
Masked Gannet (*Sula dactylatra*)	April–Jan., peak Aug. (Raine Is.) Nov. and April (Willis Is.)	Season irregular or extended	2	1–2	Breeding cycle annual, brood size 1
Brown Gannet (*Sula leucogaster*)	April–Dec., peak Aug. (Raine Is.), Oct. and Apr. (Willis Is.), Oct. (Bunker Gp)	Season irregular or extended in north, regular in Wreck Rfs. and Bunker Gp. (Oct. or August)	2	1–2	Breeding cycle annual, brood size 1
Red-footed Gannet (*Sula sula*)	June–Dec.	Season extended	1		
Lesser Frigate-Bird (*Fregata ariel*)	May–Aug.		1		
Greater Frigate-Bird (*Fregata minor*)	June–Nov.	Season irregular from island to island	1		
Reef Heron (*Egretta sacra*)	Aug.–Dec.	Season extended	3	1–3	Brood size 2 (mode)
Osprey (*Pandion haliaëtus*)	June	Season regular	3	1–3	
White-breasted Sea-Eagle (*Haliaëtus leucogaster*)	June–Sept.		2		
Banded Land Rail (*Rallus philippensis*)	Nov.–May		5, 6	2–6	Populations fluctuate greatly

Species					Remarks
Pied Oyster-Catcher (*Haëmatopus ostralegus*)	July–Oct.	Season regular	2		
Sooty Oyster-Catcher (*Haëmatopus unicolor*)	July–Nov.	Season regular	2		
White-capped Noddy (*Anous minutus*)	Oct.–April, peak Nov.	Season extended	1		Breeding cycle annual
Noddy (*Anous stolidus*)	Peak Nov. and April	Season irregular, fresh eggs found in almost all months of year, double peaks	1		Great mortality of eggs and young in nesting colonies known
Caspian Tern (*Hydroprogne caspia*)	May–Sept.	Mainly winter laying	1	1–2	Breeding colonies small and scattered
Silver Gull (*Larus novaehollandiae*)	June–Feb. peak Oct.	Season extended, double peak	2	1–3	Latitudinal variations of clutch size not clear
Little Tern (*Sterna albifrons*)	Sept.–Oct.	Season regular	2, 3		Very few breeding colonies known
Bridled Tern (*Sterna anaethetus*)	Oct.–Dec.	Season regular	1		
Lesser Crested Tern (*Sterna bengalensis*)	Sept.–Dec.	Season regular	1		A record of nesting in non-breeding plumage (Mast-head Is.)
Crested Tern (*Sterna bergii*)	Oct.–Jan., peak Dec. (Capricorn Gp.), July and Nov. (Raine Is.), April–May (Willis Is.)	Season irregular, fresh eggs found in almost all months of year, double peaks	1		
Roseate Tern (*Sterna dougalli*)	Oct.–Dec., April–June	Season regular in south, double peaks in north	2	1–3	A record of mortality of young in July (Mac-arthur Is.), suspected to have been caused by cyclone

TABLE III (*Continued*)

Species	Breeding Laying seasons	Breeding Variation	Clutch size Mode	Clutch size Range	Remarks
Sooty Tern (*Sterna fuscata*)	May–Aug. (Raine Is.), April–Sept. (Willis Is.), April–Oct. (Oyster Cay)	Season irregular from island to island, from year to year, double peaks	1	1–2	Great mortality of eggs and young in nesting colonies known, suspected to have been caused by exposure due to dying out of vegetation
Black-naped Tern (*Sterna sumatrana*)	Oct.–Dec.	Season regular	1, 2	1–4	Breeding cycle annual
Bar-shouldered Dove (*Geopelia humeralis*)	Oct.–Dec.	Season regular	2	1–2	Species sedentary
Torres Strait Pigeon (*Ducula spilorrhoa*)	Sept.–Dec.	Season regular	1	1–2	Migrant to breeding grounds
Sacred Kingfisher (*Halcyon australasiae*)	Sept.–Dec.	Season regular	4	4–6	Species sedentary
Mangrove Kingfisher (*Halcyon chloris*)	Sept.–Dec.	Season regular	3	3–4	Migrant to breeding grounds
Yellow-breasted Sunbird (*Nectarinia jugularis*)	April–May, July–Jan., peak Sept.–Oct.	Season extended	2	2–3	
Capricorn Silvereye (*Zosterops lateralis chlorocephala*)	Aug.–April, peak Oct.	Commencement varying from year to year	3	1–4	Up to three clutches raised successfully per season, brood size 2 (mode)
Varied Honeyeater (*Meliphaga versicolor*)	May–Oct.	Mostly winter nesting	2	2–3	

TABLE III *(Continued)*

Species	Breeding		Clutch size		Remarks
	Laying seasons	Variation	Mode	Range	
White-breasted Wood-Swallow (*Artamus leucorhynchus*)	Sept.–Dec.	Regular	3	3–4	Partial migrant
Pied Currawong (*Strepera graculina*)	Sept.–Nov.	Season regular	3	2–5	Sedentary on southern wooded cays, partial migrant on central continental islands

a Compiled from authorities listed in references for the Appendix.

mas Island (Schreiber and Ashmole, 1970) in the northern season (May–June). This is in contrast with the resident species of shearwater *Puffinus lherminieri* at the Galápagos, which shows no seasonality although pairs lay about every nine months (Snow, 1965a; Harris, 1969a). The tendency to breed synchronously was brought about by food shortages, which were frequent and unpredictable, and the availability of food for egg formation was considered to be the controlling factor of breeding in this species (Harris, 1969a).

The Red-tailed Tropic-Bird occurs in only a few small colonies in the Great Barrier Reef region and the laying season is not well defined though eggs have been recorded mostly in southern winter. On Christmas Island this species nests throughout the year, but the peak laying is found in northern summer (Schreiber and Ashmole, 1970) in the same months as the peak laying in the Great Barrier Reef region. Related species, *Phaëthon aethereus* on Daphne at the Galápagos (Snow, 1965b) and *P. aethereus* and *P. lepturus* on Ascension Island (Stonehouse, 1962) lay in all months. Competition for nesting sites has been put forward as a possible cause for the breakdown of a fixed annual cycle on these islands. A small colony on Plaza at the Galápagos has a defined annual cycle (laying August–February) (Harris, 1969b).

In all three gannets that breed in the Great Barrier Reef region (*Sula dactylatra, S. leucogaster,* and *S. sula*) the season is irregular or extended from winter to summer in northern parts of the reef. The peak laying appears to differ from island to island, and from year to year on the same islands. All three species breed on Christmas Island and show a tendency to have two laying peaks (northern spring and late summer) each year, but their individual cycles are not known (Schreiber and Ashmole, 1970). *Sula dactylatra* at the Galápagos shows an annual cycle of breeding coinciding with southern spring to summer, though different colonies on different islands are out of phase by two to four months (Harris, 1969b). The availability of food may directly control the laying of at least *S. sula* at the Galápagos, where the breeding cycle is a little more than a year (Nelson, 1969). On Ascension Island *S. leucogaster* shows synchronized laying at eight-month intervals (Dorward, 1962).

There is little information available on the Lesser Frigate-Bird (*Fregata ariel*) and Greater Frigate-Bird (*F. minor*) of the Great Barrier Reef region, but they generally lay in the southern summer. The season differs from island to island in the latter species and this agrees with observations made by Harris (1969b) at the Galápagos. Nelson (1967) suggested that the young in this species are so slow growing that successful breeding can occur only in every other year. However, Harris (1969b) contended that the lack of a permanent nest site and pair bond in this species may enable birds to move from one colony to another and breed every 18 months. On Christmas Island both species seem to have a relatively short laying season in northern spring and individual cycles last two years with successful breeding (Schreiber and Ashmole, 1970). Other species of frigate-birds, *Fregata aquila* on Ascension Island (Stonehouse and Stonehouse, 1963) and *F. magnificens* at the Galápagos (Harris, 1969b), seem to have an extended laying season over nine or ten months (little or no laying occurs in January and February).

Among noddies, the White-capped Noddy (*Anous minutus*), which nests on trees, has a defined laying season in the southern part of the Reef, but the Noddy (*A. stolidus*) nesting on the ground may lay at any time while having two peaks of laying on some islands. The breeding regime of *A. stolidus* is consistent with the findings of Dorward and Ashmole (1963) on Ascension Island and of Schreiber and Ashmole (1970) on Christmas Island. At the Galápagos the colony sizes of this species are small and there is no marked synchronization of laying (Harris, 1969b). *Anous tenuirostris*, which is considered to be conspecific with *A. minutus* (Moynihan, 1959), nests on cliffs on Ascension Island and has a laying season from April to August (Ashmole, 1962). On Christmas Island this species has a definite spring (northern) laying season with individual cycles of 12 months (Schreiber and Ashmole, 1970).

Among terns, the Crested Tern (*Sterna bergii*) and the Sooty Tern (*S. fuscata*) appear to have laying seasons that vary from island to island and from year to year, though within each colony the breeding seems to be synchronous. The latter species may have two peaks in the long breeding season at Michaelmas Cay. Serventy (1952) showed that this species has two distinct laying seasons in the Sahul Shelf region off Western Australia. Other species of tern have a well-defined laying season in southern spring. Detailed studies of *S. fuscata* on Ascension Island (Ashmole, 1963a) revealed that the cyle of breeding in this species is ten lunar months and nonannual. Ashmole suggested that the length of the cycle was determined primarily by the time required for breeding activities, subsequent molt, and the preliminaries for the next breeding period, and that the absence of strong seasonal changes in the marine environment made it possible to breed at different times of the year. Synchronous breeding was considered advantageous because of the predation of eggs and young, though colonial breeding habits were most likely to have evolved and be maintained by social responsiveness. On Christmas Island this species shows semiannual laying in December–January and June–July, with individual cycles lasting

12 months in case of successful breeding or six months in case of failure (Schreiber and Ashmole, 1970). Records of S. *fuscata* at the Galápagos are too scattered to be readily interpreted (Harris, 1969b).

Although information on the breeding regimes of sea birds in the Great Barrier Reef region is still scanty, the above comparison with available information elsewhere reveals some interesting features. Many species have characteristic strategies of breeding in tropical parts of the world, indicating that the modes of life adopted by them and the selective forces acting on them do not vary very much throughout the tropics. The laying season in southern parts of the Reef (Capricorn and Bunker Groups) is limited to southern spring and summer. Here the subtropical winter may inhibit breeding, at least in the Brown Gannet. The spring–summer laying season is retained in the tropical parts of the reef by the Wedge-tailed Shearwater, White-capped Noddy, Little Tern, Bridled Tern, Lesser-Crested Tern, Crested Tern, Roseate Tern, and Black-naped Tern. At Christmas Island, north of the Equator, the first two species mentioned lay in northern spring. Although greatly variable, the peaks of laying in the Red-tailed Tropic-Bird, Masked Gannet, Brown Gannet, Red-footed Gannet, and Noddy seem to occur at the same time of year across the Equator, whereas those in the Lesser Frigate-Bird and Sooty Tern occur at different times (same seasons) of the year. These species show a complex pattern of breeding wherever they occur.

The evolution of breeding seasons in temperate regions is considered to be a result of selective forces favoring individuals that breed at a time when they can produce and rear the greatest number of young and, of the factors that produce such selective forces (ultimate factors), the availability of food for the young is considered the most important (Lack, 1954). Since breeding activities of sea birds start long before such factors operate, there must be other factors that trigger the activities (proximate factors). In the tropics, where seasons are not well marked, food as an ultimate factor may not have a polarizing effect on the breeding season; thus proximate factors may not operate selectively. There are obviously internal rhythms controlling the breeding cycle which may be shorter than a year depending on the minimum time required for the completion of breeding and subsequent molt, as in the case of the Sooty Tern discussed above. In such circumstances birds may try to breed as frequently as they can and occasionally suffer great mortality in the breeding colony when they are hit by local food shortages, tropical cyclones, or prolonged droughts on the island reducing the cover. If food shortages occur irregularly and inhibit or suspend breeding, the food supply may directly control breeding and the distinction between ultimate and proximate factors may disappear. Because many sea birds require energy for breeding for a long time before the feeding of young starts and the demand for food by young is limited by the small brood size of one, the use of energy is spread evenly over a very long time. If, in fact, this is how adaptation of sea birds in the tropics has occurred, then interspecific competition for food will not be reduced by having different breeding seasons on the same islands. Competitive exclusion, on the other hand, may emphasize ecological segregation among closely related species occurring sympatrically but, as pointed out by Ashmole (1968) in his study of five sympatric species of tern, coexistence of a number of divergent forms is not necessarily an indication of competitive exclusion.

Food shortages and other environmental factors with prolonged effects may bring out of phase breeders in phase with the majority, but synchronization of breeding is also brought about by social facilitation in colonial breeders. Predation was considered to act as a selective force for synchronous breeding (Ashmole, 1962), but Harris (1969b) argued that since predation no longer existed in the case of *Anous tenuirostris* on Ascension Island, synchrony would not be retained if the advantages were only to reduce the chance of predation. Synchronous breeding probably has social significance that relates to the utilization of resources (both food and nesting sites). This aspect requires much more work. Competition within the species for nesting sites and food in the breeding season may also have produced a tendency for many sea birds to have prolonged juvenile periods (see Ashmole, 1963b).

In the Great Barrier Reef region the breeding biology of sea birds has not been studied in detail. Since many islands supporting breeding colonies are readily accessible from the mainland or established island resorts, they would provide suitable opportunities for making comparative studies.

V. Behavior and Evolution of Land Birds

Island populations of land birds provide unique opportunities for the study of the mechanisms of evolution. On the coral cay islands of the Great Barrier Reef very few species of land birds breed and there is, as yet, little evidence that speciation has occurred in them. Nevertheless, the fact that species occur where there are very few competitors and predators suggests possibilities of behavioral and ecological changes in isolated populations. In the following some interesting topics of study are listed for common species.

The Banded Land Rail (*Rallus philippensis*) is known to fluctuate greatly in number but its population dynamics have not been investigated. On Heron Island the recent increase in number coincided with a drastic decrease in the number of rats and feral domestic fowl as a result of killing on the island (Kikkawa, 1970). The Bar-shouldered Dove (*Geopelia humeralis*) is another common ground feeding species but with a low reproductive rate (Table III). It appears to have a stable population and its life cycle is worth investigating on islands. It is also a suitable subject of study for feeding and courtship behavior that can be observed more readily on islands than elsewhere.

A long-term study of solitary sea-eagles by banding would be able to establish their traditional use of nests, longevity, home range, and the pattern of dispersal among islands. In contrast, the Torres Strait Pigeon, with its highly social roosting and nesting habits, as well as its peculiar habit of commuting to the mainland feeding areas, will be an interesting species to study.

Recher and Recher (1969) gave a general account of Reef Herons with a large number of nonbreeders in a resident population. Their study of foraging and territorial behavior revealed that breeding birds defend foraging territories (Recher, 1972; Recher and Recher, 1972). The Reef Heron has two color phases: the ratio of the white to the gray phase is 2:1 or greater in the Capricorn Group. The white phase is generally more abundant than the gray phase in tropical areas, but the change of the exact ratio along the Great Barrier Reef is yet to be documented. Because the two phases interbreed commonly, it would be interesting to find out if the young birds were imprinted on the color of the parents and if such color imprinting affected their mate selection in adult life. The effect of mate selection must inevitably appear in the ratio of the phases in the population.

McBride *et al.* (1969) studied the social organization of the feral Domestic Fowl (*Gallus gallus*) on North West Island and found that although mating occurred throughout the year, actual breeding was restricted to the spring (September–December) when six classes of male could be identified, ranging from the dominant and territorial, to the subordinate and nonterritorial. Hens became solitary after laying a clutch of eggs, and reared the brood. In the nonbreeding season the social phase changed to a pattern of overlapping home ranges. Because dispersal is prevented on the island, a study of this kind is valuable in understanding the changes of social organization in relation to population density or food supply.

The only species of land bird known to have been morphologically differentiated is the race of silvereye *Zosterops lateralis chlorocephala*. As shown in Table IV, this race has greater body size and bill size than the mainland race, which is often drifted to islands during its autumn migration. The density of the island race may reach as high as 500 pairs per 100 acres (40 ha), which is greater than the highest density estimated for all land birds in a complex rain forest of the mainland. Such a high density may be caused by a superabundance of food and an absence of other competing species on the island. The available food in the normal habitat, however, is so heavily taxed by fellow feeders that many silvereyes constantly explore and exploit new sources of food. On Heron Island, silvereyes search nests of white-capped Noddies for insects and fly into buildings to take food. They also feed frequently on the ground where their food overlaps with that of the Bar-shouldered Dove and the Banded Land Rail. The extent to which such expansion of niche is possible must be determined by increased degree of predation and competition with other species in relation to the abilities of silvereyes. However, since the species utilizes a wide variety of habitats and occupies a wide range of niches on the mainland, particularly if flocks concentrate during winter, it would be hard to establish the degree of niche expansion that this species could have achieved on small islands. It would be even more difficult to relate the niche expansion to the absence of other species which might normally utilize the types of resource greatly exploited by silvereyes.

The effect of high density is also apparent in the social behavior of silvereyes; winter flocks are not integrated and aggressive encounters are frequent on Heron Island. Only when a cyclone reduces the population to a low level, are winter flocks distinguishable. The population, however, recovers its high density in one breeding season. It is significant that although many other species of land birds reach the island (Kikkawa, 1970), practically none of them has colonized the island in recent years. The island silvereye is more aggressive than its mainland counterpart (Morris, 1968) and there is a trend for aggressive birds to survive better than submissive birds during the winter (J. Kikkawa, unpublished). The breeding success of dominant birds may not be as high as that of submissive birds in some years (Wilson, 1970). Selection of certain agonistic behavior patterns in this population is currently under investigation.

Increased body size, bill size, and tarsus length in the island form of silvereyes have been commented on by Mees (1969) as advantages during the cyclone season. It is also possible that these may be a result of selection common to other island species that show the same trend

TABLE IV

Measurements of Two Races of *Zosterops lateralis* Found on Heron Island in Winter[a]

| | Island form, Z. l. chlorocephala (May, 1966) | | | | | | Mainland form, Z. l. familiaris (Winter, 1966-1970) | | |
| | Adults (1 year or older) | | | Juveniles (after molting) | | | | | |
	Sample size	Range	Mean ± S.E.	Sample size	Range	Mean ± S.E.	Sample size	Range	Mean ± S.E.
Wing (mm)	21	61.5–68.0	64.8 ± 0.36	165	59.5–65.5	63.0 ± 0.10	71	55.0–61.0	58.2 ± 0.24
Tail (mm)	21	46.0–51.0	49.3 ± 0.32	143	46.0–51.0	48.0 ± 0.12	70	39.5–47.0	43.7 ± 0.17
Tarsus (mm)	20	18.7–21.0	19.7 ± 0.16	165	17.7–21.0	19.7 ± 0.05	70	16.4–18.5	17.3 ± 0.06
Exposed culmen (mm)	21	10.7–12.3	11.5 ± 0.09	163	10.4–12.3	11.5 ± 0.03	70	8.8–10.5	9.5 ± 0.05
Weight in starved condition (gm)	20	12.2–16.0	14.1 ± 0.26	164	10.2–15.9	13.6 ± 0.07	54	8.0–14.1	9.9 ± 0.20

[a] All measurements were taken from live birds and the wing was not flattened. After Kikkawa (1970).

elsewhere (Murphy, 1938; Amadon, 1953; Grant, 1965, 1966; Keast, 1968). However, the fact that large size is generally advantageous in competition for food is significant in crowded populations. It would be worth surveying those species that show similar trends elsewhere, to see if they occur normally in crowded conditions.

Acknowledgments

I wish to thank Mr. J. N. Butler for making available the list of birds recorded at the Willis Island Weather Station since 1947. I am most grateful to Mrs. Carolyn Jeffrey who made a comprehensive literature survey of the birds of the Great Barrier Reef region for this article and to Dr. W. T. Williams, C.S.I.R.O. Division of Tropical Agronomy, Townsville, who conducted the computer analysis of distributional data.

References

Alexander, W. B. (1954). "Birds of the Ocean," 2nd ed. Putnam, New York.
Amadon, D. (1953). *Bull. Amer. Mus. Natur. Hist.* **100**, 397.
Amerson, A. B., Jr. (1969). *Atoll Res. Bull.* **127.**
Ashmole, N. P. (1962). *Ibis* **103b**, 235.
Ashmole, N. P. (1963a). *Ibis* **103b**, 297.
Ashmole, N. P. (1963b). *Ibis* **103b**, 458.
Ashmole, N. P. (1968). *Syst. Zool.* **17**, 292.
Ashmole, N. P. (1971). *In* "Avian Biology" (D. S. Farner and J. R. King, eds.), Vol. 1, pp. 223–286. Academic Press, New York.
Austin, T. P. (1908). *Emu* **7**, 176.
Barrett, C. (1910). *Emu* **10**, 181.
Booth, J. (1970). *Sunbird* **1**, 85.
Campbell, A. J., and White, S. A. (1910). *Emu* **10**, 195.
Cooper, R. P. (1948). *Emu* **48**, 107.
Cornwall, E. M. (1903). *Emu* **3**, 45.
Cornwall, E. M. (1909). *Emu* **8**, 138.
Dorward, D. F. (1962). *Ibis* **103b,** 174.
Dorward, D. F., and Ashmole, N. P. (1963). *Ibis* **103b**, 447.
Forbes, W. A. (1878). *Challenger Rep., Zool.* **2**(8), 84.
Grant, P. R. (1965). *Evolution* **10**, 355.
Grant, P. R. (1966). *Postilla* **98**, 1.
Harris, M. P. (1969a). *Ibis* **111**, 139.
Harris, M. P. (1969b). *J. Zool.* **159**, 145.
Heatwole, H. (1971). *Ecology* **52**, 363.
Hindwood, K. A., Keith, K., and Serventy, D. L. (1963). *Div. Wildl. Res., Tech. Pap.* 3, 1–44.
Humphrey, P. S. (1965). "Smithsonian Year," p. 24. Smithsonian Press, Washington, D.C.
Jukes, J. B. (1847). "Narative of the Surveying Voyage of H.M.S. *Fly*," Vol. 1. Boone, London.
Keast, A. (1968). *Evolution* **22**, 762.

Kikkawa, J. (1968). *J. Anim. Ecol.* **37**, 143.
Kikkawa, J. (1970). *Sunbird* **1**, 34.
Kikkawa, J. (1973). *Sunbird* **4**, 30.
King, W. B. (1967). "Seabirds of the Tropical Pacific Ocean." U.S. Nat. Mus. Smithson. Inst., Washington, D.C.
King, W. B. (1970). *U.S., Fish Wildl. Serv., Spec. Sci. Rep.–Fish.* **586**, 1–136.
Lack, D. (1954). "The Natural Regulation of Animal Numbers." Oxford Univ. Press (Clarendon), London and New York.
Lack, D. (1968). "Ecological Adaptations for Breeding in Birds." Methuen, London.
Lane, S. G. (1967). *Aust. Bird Bander* **5**, 57.
Le Souëf, D. (1891). *Victorian Natur.* **8**, 163.
Le Souëf, D. (1894). *Victorian Natur.* **11**, 3.
Le Souëf, D. (1897). *Victorian Natur.* **14**, 19.
McBride, G., Parer, I. P., and Foenander, F. (1969). *Anim. Behav. Monogr.* **2**, 127.
MacGillivray, J. (1846). *Zoologist* **4**, 1473.
MacGillivray, J. (1852). "Narrative of the Voyage of H.M.S. *Rattlesnake*," Vol. 1, pp. 42–75 and 76–120; Vol. 2, pp. 33–84 (facsimile ed., Boone, London, 1967).
MacGillivray, W. (1926). *Emu* **25**, 229.
MacGillivray, W. (1928). *Emu* **27**, 230.
Mees, G. F. (1969). *Zool. Verh.* **102**, 85, 86, 276, and 323.
Morris, D. K. (1968). B.Sc. Hon. Thesis, Biology Library, University of Queensland.
Moseley, H. N. (1892). "An Account of Observations Made During the Voyage of H.M.S. *Challenger* Round the World in the Years 1872–1876," pp. 299–302.
Moynihan, M. (1959). *Amer. Mus. Nov.* **1928**, 1.
Murphy, R. C. (1925). "Bird Islands of Peru." Putnam, New York.
Murphy, R. C. (1936). "Oceanic Birds of South America," 2 vols. Amer. Mus. Natur. Hist., New York.
Murphy, R. C. (1938). *Science* **88**, 533.
Nelson, J. B. (1967). *Nature (London)* **214**, 318.
Nelson, J. B. (1969). *J. Anim. Ecol.* **38**, 181.
Norris, A. Y. (1967). *Emu* **67**, 33.
Purchase, D. (1969a). *CSIRO Div. Wildl. Res., Tech. Pap.* **18**, 66.
Purchase, D. (1969b). *CSIRO Div. Wildl. Res., Tech. Pap.* **19**, 49.
Purchase, D. (1973). *CSIRO Div. Wildl. Res., Tech. Pap.* **27**, 48.
Recher, H. F. (1972). *Emu* **72**, 126.
Recher, H. F., and Recher, J. A. (1969). *Aust. Natur. Hist.* **16**, 151.
Recher, H. F., and Recher, J. A. (1972). *Emu* **72**, 85.
Robertson, W. B., Jr. (1969). *Nature (London)* **223**, 632.
Saunders, H. (1878). *Challenger Rep., Zool.* **2**(8), 133.
Schreiber, R. W., and Ashmole, N. P. (1970). *Ibis* **112**, 363.
Sclater, P. L., and Salvin, O. (1878). *Challenger Rep., Zool.* **2**(8), 117.
Serventy, D. L. (1952). *Emu* **52**, 33.
Serventy, D. L., Serventy, V., and Warham, J. (1971). "The Handbook of Australian Sea Birds." A. H. and A. W. Reed, Sydney, Australia.
Sharpe, R. B. (1906). "History of the Collections." Brit. Mus. (Birds), London.
Smithsonian Institution. (1971). *Atoll Res. Bull.* **148**, 6.
Snow, D. W. (1965a). *Auk* **82**, 591.
Snow, D. W. (1965b). *Condor* **67**, 210.
Stonehouse, B. (1962). *Ibis* **103b**, 124.

Stonehouse, B. (1963). *Ibis* **103b**, 474.
Stonehouse, B., and Stonehouse, S. (1963). *Ibis* **103b,** 409.
Williams, W. T., Lambert, J. M., and Lance, G. N. (1966). *J. Ecol.* **54,** 427.
Wilson, J. M. (1970). B.Sc. Hon. Thesis, Biology Library, University of Queensland.
Wynne-Edwards, V. C. (1962). "Animal Dispersion in Relation to Social Behaviour."
    Oliver & Boyd, Edinburgh.

Appendix

Birds recorded in the Great Barrier Reef region including continental islands and surrounding waters of the region. Known breeding sites are indicated by an asterisk. For clarity, references are enclosed in square brackets.

Casuariiformes
  Casuariidae
    Casuarius casuarius (Linnaeus, 1758)
      Cassowary: Dunk Is.° [Banfield, 1913]
Procellariiformes
  Diomedeidae
    Diomedea chrysostoma Forster, 1785
      Grey-headed Albatross: Raine Is., Howick Gp. [Hull, 1925]
    Diomedea exulans Linnaeus 1758
      Wandering Albatross: Open Sea (20°S, 149°–150°E) [MacGillivray, 1927]; Whitsunday Islands [Amiet, 1958]; One Tree Is. [Domm and Recher, 1973]; Fairfax Is. [Booth, 1970]; Cato Is. [Hindwood *et al.*, 1963; Norris, 1967]
    Phoebetria fusca Hilsenberg, 1822
      Sooty Albatross: One Tree Is. [A. E. Chilvers, personal communication]
  Procellariidae
    Macronectes giganteus (Gmelin, 1789)
      Giant Petrel: Fairfax Is. [Booth, 1970]
    Pachyptila turtur (Kuhl, 1820)
      Fairy Prion: Wreck Is. [Booth, 1970]
    Pachyptila desolata Gmelin, 1789
      Dove Prion: One Tree Is. [G. F. van Tets, personal communication]
    Pterodroma arminjoniana (Giglioli and Salvadori 1868)
      Trinidad Petrel: Raine Is.° [Warham, 1961; Lavery and Grimes, 1971]; No. 8 Sandbank [Warham, 1959]
    Pterodroma nigripennis (Rothschild, 1893)
      Black-winged Petrel: Heron Is. [Slater, 1970; Serventy *et al.*, 1971; as *Pterodroma hypoleuca* (Salvin, 1888) by Reid, 1965, Lavery, 1969, and Booth, 1970]; Tryon Is. Lady Musgrave Is. [R. Elks, personal communication]
    Pterodroma rostrata (Peale, 1848)
      Tahiti Petrel: Open Sea (19°32'S, 153°05'E, 20°26'S, 153°09'E, 21°13'S 153°11'E–21°16'S 153°12'E, 22°S, 156°15'E) [Norris, 1967]
    Daption capensis (Linnaeus, 1758)
      Cape petrel: Brampton Is. [Serventy *et al.*, 1971]; Heron Is. [Booth, 1970]

Puffinus carneipes Gould, 1844
Fleshy-footed shearwater: Open Sea (16°47'S, 152°27'E–17°03'S 152°48'E, 19°32'S 153°05'E–20°26'S 153°09'E) [Norris, 1967]; Kenn Rf., Wreck Rf., Cato Is. [Hindwood *et al.*, 1963]; Masthead Is. [Hindwood, 1945]
Puffinus gavia (Forster, 1844)
Fluttering shearwater: Open Sea (24°05'S 153°24'E–24°15'S 153°25'E) [Norris, 1967]
Puffinus lherminieri Lesson, 1839
Audubon's shearwater: Townsville (offshore) [Alexander, 1928]
Puffinus pacificus (Gmelin, 1879)
Wedge-tailed shearwater: Raine Is.* [MacGillivray, 1910, 1914, 1917; Alexander, 1925a; Warham, 1959, 1961; Hindwood *et al.*, 1963; Lavery and Grimes, 1971; Serventy *et al.*, 1971; Storr, 1973]; Montague Is. [Alexander, 1920]; Willis Is.* [Davis, 1923a,b; Alexander, 1925a; Hogan, 1925; Lawry, 1926; Serventy, 1959; Hindwood *et al.*, 1963; Serventy *et al.*, 1971]; Mid Islet* (Willis Gp.), S.E. Cay* (Magdelaine Gp.), N.E.* and S.W.* Islets (Coringa Gp.), N.E.* and S.W. Cays (Herald Gp.), Turtle Islet*, No. 1 Cay*, No. 9 Cay* (Lihou Rf.), Mid*, S.W.*, and West* Islets (Diamond Islets), Bird Is.* (Wreck Rf.) [Hindwood *et al.*, 1963; Serventy *et al.*, 1971]; Whitsunday Gp. [Marshall, 1934]; Keppel Gp. [Wolstenholme, 1925]; Capricorn Gp.* [Alexander, 1925a; Gilbert, 1925; MacGillivray, 1926; Napier, 1928; Cooper, 1948; Serventy *et al.*, 1971; Storr, 1973]; North West Is.* [Gilbert, 1925; Napier, 1928; Nebe, 1928; MacGillivray, 1928,1931; McNeill, 1946; Cooper, 1948; McBride *et al.*, 1969; Lavery and Grimes, 1971]; Tryon Is.* [Gilbert, 1925; MacGillivray, 1928; Lavery and Grimes, 1971]; Wilson Is.* [Gilbert, 1925; Cooper, 1948; Lavery and Grimes, 1971]; Cato Is.* [Hindwood *et al.*, 1963; Serventy *et al.*, 1971]; Wreck Is.* [Cooper, 1948; Booth, 1970; Lavery and Grimes, 1971]; Erskin Is.* [Lavery and Grimes, 1971]; Heron Is.* [MacGillivray, 1928; Yonge, 1930; Cooper, 1948; Gillham, 1961; Miles, 1964; Keast, 1966; Shipway, 1969; Kikkawa, 1970; Booth, 1970; Lavery and Grimes, 1971]; Masthead Is.* [Campbell and White, 1910; Barrett, 1919; MacGillivray, 1928; Nebe, 1932; Cooper, 1948; Lavery and Grimes, 1971]; One Tree Is. [Domm and Recher, 1973]; Bunker Gp.* [Napier, 1928; Serventy *et al.*, 1971; Storr, 1973]; Hoskyn Is.* [MacGillivray, 1928; Lavery and Grimes, 1971]; Fairfax Is.* [MacGillivray, 1928; Booth, 1970; Lavery and Grimes, 1971]; Lady Musgrave Is. [MacGillivray, 1928; Napier, 1928; Lavery and Grimes, 1971]; Lady Elliot Is.* [Fien, 1971; Serventy *et al.*, 1971; Storr, 1973]; Open Sea [Hindwood *et al.*, 1963]; Open Sea (13°17'S 150°05'E–13°21'S 150°06'E, 15°38'S 151°39'E 15°57'S 151°50'E 19°44'S 156°38'E–19°50'S 156°33'E, 19°32'S 153°05'E–20°26'S 153°09'E, 21°13'S 153°11'E–21°16'S 153°12'E, 24°05'S 153°24'E–24°15'S 153°25'E) [Norris, 1967]
Hydrobatidae
Fregetta grallaria
White-bellied Storm-Petrel: Open Sea (13°17'S 150°05'E–13°21'S 150° 06'E, 15°10'S 151°39'E–15°20'S 151°40'E, 15°38'S 151°39'E–15°57'S 151°50'E, 16°47'S 152°27'E–17°03'S 152°48'E, 19°32'S 153°05'E–20°26'S 153°09'E, 19°41'S 153°36'E–20°02'S 153°31'E, 20°25'S 153°06'E, 22°07'S 154°20'E–22°18'S 154°13'E [Norris, 1967]; Cato Is. [Hindwood *et al.*, 1963]
Oceanites oceanicus (Kuhl, 1820)

Wilson storm-petrel: Bowen (offshore) [Alexander, 1925b; Serventy, 1952]; Capricorn Gp. [MacGillivray, 1931]; Heron Is. (offshore) [Kikkawa, 1970]; Bunker Gp. [Alexander, 1925b]

Pelagodroma marina (Latham, 1790)

White-faced storm-petrel: Willis Is. [J. N. Butler, personal communication, 1968]

Pelicaniformes

Phaëthontidae

Phaëthon lepturus Daudin, 1802

White-tailed Tropic-Bird: Willis Is. [Serventy, 1959; J. N. Butler, personal communication, 1968]; Open Sea (15°38'S 151°38'E–15°57'S 151°50'E) [Norris, 1967]; 280 miles N.E. of Brisbane [Hindwood *et al.*, 1963]

(*Phaëthon aethereus* Linnaeus, 1758 Red-billed Tropic-Bird: Raine Is. [Sclater and Salvin, 1878]?)

Phaëthon rubricauda Boddart, 1783

Red-tailed Tropic-Bird. Bramble Cay [MacGillivray, 1914]; Raine Is.* [J. MacGillivray, 1846; W. MacGillivray, 1914, 1918b; Alexander, 1925a; Warham, 1961; Hindwood *et al.*, 1963; Lavery and Grimes, 1971; Serventy *et al.*, 1971; Storr, 1973]; N.E.* and S.W. Cays (Herald Gp.) [Hindwood *et al.*, 1963; Serventy *et al.*, 1971]; Willis Is. [Davis, 1923b; Hogan, 1925; Serventy, 1959; J. N. Butler, personal communication, 1968]; S.W. Islet* (Coringa Gp.) [Hindwood *et al.*, 1963; Serventy *et al.*, 1971]; Dunk Is. [Tarr, 1948]; One Tree Is. [Domm and Recher, 1973]; Fairfax Is. [Booth, 1970]

Pelecanidae

Pelecanus conspicillatus Temminck, 1824

Australian pelican: Raine Is. [Warham, 1961]; Piper Is. [Warham, 1962]; Aye Is.* [MacGillivray, 1910; Serventy *et al.*, 1971]; Stainer Is. [Warham, 1962]; Pelican Is.* [MacGillivray, 1852; Warham, 1962; Kikkawa, 1969; Serventy *et al.*, 1971]; Wharton Rf. [Warham, 1962]; Pipon Is. [Hull, 1925; Warham, 1962]; South Barrow Is., Morris Is., Coombe Is.*, Sinclair Is.* [Warham, 1962; Serventy *et al.*, 1971]; Howick Gp.* [MacGillivray, 1910, 1918b; Warham, 1962; Storr, 1973]; Pethebridge Is. [Warham, 1962] Cape Flattery* [MacGillivray, 1910]; Three Isles [Warham, 1962]; Pickersgill Rf. [Le Souëf, 1897]; Hope Is.* [Le Souëf, 1894, 1897; Storr, 1973]; Gubbins Rf. [Warham, 1962]; Whitsunday Gp. [Marshall, 1934]; Rock near Brampton Is.* [Storr, 1973]; Cumberland Gp. [Roberts, 1957]; One Tree Is. [Domm and Recher, 1973]

Sulidae

Sula bassana (Linnaeus, 1758)

Gannet: Wreck Rock [Wodzicki and Stein, 1958]

Sula dactylatra Lesson, 1831

Masked gannet: Pandora Cay* [Warham, 1961; Lavery and Grimes, 1971; Serventy *et al.*, 1971; Storr, 1973]; Raine Is.* [MacGillivray, 1846; Sclater and Salvin, 1878; Moseley, 1892; MacGillivray, 1910, 1914, 1918b; Alexander, 1925a; Warham, 1961; Hindwood *et al.*, 1963; Lavery and Grimes, 1971; Serventy *et al.*, 1971; Storr, 1973]; Cay A* (Flinders Rf.), Diana Bk.*, N.E. and S.E.* Cays (Moore Rf.), Mid Islet* (Willis Gp. [Hindwood *et al.*, 1963; Serventy *et al.*, 1971]; Willis Is.* [Davis, 1923a,b; Alexander, 1925a; Hogan, 1925; Lawry, 1926; Reithmüller, 1931; Serventy, 1959; Cays A, B (Holmes

Rf.), N.W. and S.E.° Cays (Magdelaine Cays), N.E.° and S.W.° Cays (Herald Gp.), N.E.° and S.W.° Cays (Coringa Gp.), Turtle Islet°, No. 1°, No. 8°, No. 9°, No. 2, and No. 3 Cays (Lihou Rf.), North Cay, Herald's Beacon Islet° (Mellish Rf.), West°, Mid°, East°, and S.W.° Islets (Diamond Islets), Carola° and Paget° Cays (Marion Rf.), North Rf. Cay (Frederick Rf.), Observatory Cay° (Kenn Rf.), N.E. and S.W.° Cays (Saumarez Rf.), [Hindwood *et al.*, 1963; Serventy *et al.*, 1971]; Arlington Rf. [Alexander, 1926]; Swain Rf.° [Gillett and McNeill, 1959; Serventy *et al.*, 1971; Storr, 1973]; Porpoise Cay°, Bird Islet°, West Islet (Wreck Rf.), Cato Is.° [Hindwood *et al.*, 1963; Serventy *et al.*, 1971]; One Tree Is. [Domm and Recher, 1973]; Open Sea (15°38'S 151°39'E–15°57'S 151°50'E, 16°47'S 152°27'E–17°03'S 152°48'E) [Norris, 1967]

Sula leucogaster (Boddaert, 1783)

Brown Gannet: Bramble Cay° [MacGillivray, 1852; MacGillivray, 1914; Alexander, 1925a; Lavery and Grimes; 1971; Serventy *et al.*, 1971; Storr, 1973]; Murray Is. Sandbank [Warham, 1961]; Pandora Cay° [Warham, 1961; Lavery and Grimes, 1971; Serventy *et al.*, 1971; Storr, 1973]; Raine Is.° [J. MacGillivray, 1846; Sclater and Salvin, 1878; Moseley, 1892; W. MacGillivray, 1910,1914,1918b; Alexander, 1925a; Warham, 1961; Lavery and Grimes, 1971; Serventy *et al.*, 1971; Storr, 1973]; Ashmore Sand Banks° [MacGillivray, 1910; Alexander, 1925a; Lavery and Grimes, 1971; Serventy *et al.*, 1971; Storr, 1973]; Eel Rf., Waterwitch Rf., Pipon Is., Rocky Isle, Decapolis Rf., Gubbins Rf. [Warham, 1962]; Howick Is. Gp. [MacGillivray, 1910]; Diana Bk.° [Hindwood *et al.*, 1963; Serventy *et al.*, 1971]; Willis Is.° (Davis, 1923a,b; Alexander, 1925a; Hogan, 1925; Lawry, 1926; Reithmüller, 1931; Serventy, 1959; J. N. Butler, personal communication, 1968]; Mid Islet° and North Cay (Willis Gp.) [Hindwood *et al.*, 1963; Serventy *et al.*, 1971]; Low Is. [Young, 1929; White, 1946]; Oyster Cay (Michaelmas Cay) [Alexander, 1926; White, 1946; Kikkawa, 1969]; Cays A, B (Holmes Rf.), N.W. and S.E.° Cays (Magdelaine Cays), N.E.° and S.W.° Cays (Coringa Gp.), N.E.° and S.W.° Cays (Herald Gp.), Turtle Is.°, Observatory Cay, No. 1°, No. 8°, No. 9°, No. 2, No. 3, No. 4, and No. 5 Cays (Lihou Rf.), Herald's Beacon Islet° (Mellish Rf.), West°, Mid°, East°, and S.W.° Islets (Diamond Islets), Cays A°, B (Flinders Rf.) [Hindwood *et al.*, 1963]; Dunk Is. [Austin, 1950]; White Rock [Warham, 1962]; Paget° and Carola° Cays, (Marion Rf.) [Hindwood *et al.*, 1963; Serventy *et al.*, 1971]; Whitsunday Gp. [Marshall, 1934; Brown 1949]; Cumberland Gp. [Roberts, 1957]; North Rf.° and Observatory Cays (Frederick Rf.), Observatory and S.W. Projection° Cays (Kenn Rf.), N.E.° and S.W.° Cays (Saumarez Rf.) [Hindwood *et al.*, 1963; Serventy, *et al.*, 1971]; Swain Rf.° [Gillett and McNeill, 1959; Cameron, 1969; Lavery and Grimes, 1971; Serventy *et al.*, 1971; Storr, 1973]; Unnamed Cay, Porpoise Cay°, Bird Is.° and West Islet (Wreck Rf.) [Hindwood *et al.*, 1963; Serventy *et al.*, 1971]; Capricorn Gp. [Cooper, 1948]; North West Is. [Campbell and White, 1910; MacGillivray, 1931; Cameron, 1969]; Tryon Is. (offshore) [MacGillivray, 1931]; Cato Is.° [Hindwood *et al.*, 1963; Serventy *et al.*, 1971]; Wreck Is. [Booth, 1970]; Heron Is. [Kikkawa, 1970]; Masthead Is. [Campbell and White, 1910]; One Tree Is. [Domm and Recher, 1973]; Bunker Gp.° [Cooper, 1948; Keast, 1966; Serventy *et al.*, 1971., Storr, 1973]; Hoskyn Is.° [MacGillivray, 1928; Nebe, 1932; Lavery and Grimes, 1971]; Fairfax Is.° [MacGillivray, 1928; Nebe, 1932;

Gillett and MacNeill, 1959; Booth, 1970; Lavery and Grimes, 1971]; Lady Musgrave Is.* [MacGillivray, 1928; Gillett and McNeill, 1959; Lavery and Grimes, 1971]; Lady Elliot Is. [Fien, 1971]; Open Sea (13°17′S 150°05′E– 13°21′S 150°06′E, 15°10′S 151°39′E–15°20′S 151°40′E, 15°38′S 151°39′E– 15°57′S 151°50′E, 16°47′S 152°27′E–17°03′S 152°48′E, 20°25′S 153°06′E, 22°07′S 154°20′E–22°18′S 154°13′E, 23°21′S 153°24′E–23°36′S 153°26′E) [Norris, 1967]

Sula sula (Linnaeus, 1766)

Red-footed Gannet; Raine Is.* [Sclater and Salvin, 1878; Moseley, 1892; Mac-Gillivray, 1910, 1914, 1918b; Alexander, 1925a; Warham, 1961; Hindwood *et al.*, 1963; Lavery and Grimes, 1971; Serventy *et al.*, 1971; Storr, 1973]; N.E. and S.E. Cays (Moore Rf.) [Hindwood *et al.*, 1963]; Willis Is.* [Davis, 1923a,b; Hogan, 1925; Lawry, 1926; Reithmüller, 1931; Serventy, 1959; J. N. Butler, personal communication, 1968]; Fitzroy Is. [White, 1946]; Cays A, B (Holmes Rf.), S.E. Cay* (Magdelaine Cays), N.E.* and S.W.* Cays (Coringa Cp.), N.E.* and S.W.* Cays (Herald Gp.), No. 4 Cay (Lihou Rf.), North Cay (Mellish Rf.), West*, Mid*, East*, and S.W.* Islets (Diamond Gp.), North Rf. Cay (Frederick Rf.), Observatory Cay (Kenn Rf.), Bird Is.* (Wreck Rf.), Cato Is.* [Hindwood *et al.*, 1963; Serventy *et al.*, 1971]; Fairfax Is. [Booth, 1970]; Open Sea [Hindwood *et al.*, 1963]; Open Sea (15°10′S 151°39′E–15°20′S 151°40′E, 19°32′S 153°05′E–20°26′S 153°09′E, 20°25′S 153°06′E) [Norris, 1967]

Phalacrocoracidae

Phalacrocorax carbo (Linnaeus, 1758)

Black Cormorant: Pethebridge Is. [Warham, 1962]; North West Is. [Campbell and White, 1910]; One Tree Is. [C. Hulsman, personal communication]

Phalacrocorax melanoleucos (Vieillot, 1817)

Little Pied Cormorant: Pipon Is., Morris Is., Coquet Is., Pethebridge Is. [Warham, 1962]; North West Is. [Gilbert, 1925; MacGillivray, 1926; Cameron, 1969]; Tryon Is. [Gilbert, 1925; MacGillivray, 1926]; Wreck Is.* [Cooper, 1948; Booth, 1970]; Heron Is. [Kikkawa, unpublished]; One Tree Is. [MacGillivray, 1928; Domm and Recher, 1973]; Masthead Is. [Cooper, 1948]; Fairfax Is. [Booth, 1970]

Phalacrocorax sulcirostris (Brandt, 1837)

Little Black Cormorant: Willis Is. [Serventy, 1959]; Heron Is., One Tree Is. [MacGillivray, 1928; Domm and Recher, 1973]

Phalacrocorax varius (Gmelin, 1789)

Pied Cormorant: Gubbins Rf. [Warham, 1962]; Dunk Is. [Tarr, 1948]; Capricorn Gp. [Campbell and White, 1910]; Heron Is. [Kikkawa, 1970]; One Tree Is. [Domm and Recher, 1973]; Masthead Is. [Campbell and White, 1910]

Anhingidae

Anhinga anhinga (Linnaeus, 1766)

Australian darter: Murray Is. Sandbank [Warham, 1961]

Fregatidae

Fregata ariel (Gray, 1845)

Lesser Frigate-bird: Bramble Cay [MacGillivray, 1941]; Keats Is.* [Lavery and Grimes, 1971]; Escape River Mouth [MacGillivray, 1910]; Pandora Cay [Warham, 1961]; Raine Is.* [J. MacGillivray, 1846; W. MacGillivray, 1910, 1914, 1918b; Alexander, 1925a; Warham, 1961; Hindwood *et al.*, 1963; Lavery and

Grimes, 1971; Serventy et al., 1971; Storr, 1973]; Cape Restoration Is. [MacGillivray, 1910]; Diana Bk. [Hindwood et al., 1963]; Willis Is. [Davis, 1923a,b; Hogan, 1925; Lawry, 1926; Serventy, 1959; J. N. Butler, personal communication, 1968]; Cays A, B (Holmes Rf.), S.E. Cay* (Magdelaine Cays), N.E.* and S.W.* Cays (Coringa Gp.), N.E. Cay* (Herald Gp.), West* and S.W.* Islets (Diamond Gp.) [Hindwood et al., 1963; Serventy et al., 1971]; Whitsunday Gp. [Marshall, 1934]; North Rf. and Observatory Cays (Frederick Rf.) [Hindwood et al., 1963]; Swain Rf.* [Gillett and McNeill, 1959; Serventy et al., 1971; Storr, 1973], Bird Is.* (Wreck Rf.) [Hindwood et al., 1963; Serventy et al., 1971], North West Is. [MacGillivray, 1928, 1931; Cameron, 1969]; Tryon Is. [Campbell and White, 1910]; Cato Is.* [Hindwood et al., 1963; Serventy et al., 1971]; Heron Is. [MacGillivray, 1928; Cooper, 1948; Kikkawa, 1970]; One Tree Is. [Domm and Recher, 1973]; Masthead Is. [Barrett, 1919; MacGillivray, 1928; Cooper, 1948]; Hoskyn Is. [Nebe, 1932]; Fairfax Is. [MacGillivray, 1928; Booth, 1970]; Lady Musgrave Is. [MacGillivray, 1928]; Open Sea (16°10'S 157°14'E, 23°21'S 153°24'E–23°36'S 153°26'E) [Norris, 1967]

Fregata minor (Gmelin, 1789)

Greater Frigate-bird: Bramble Cay [Hedley, 1926]; Keats Is. Oomaga Is. [Lavery and Grimes, 1971]; Raine Is. [Sclater and Salvin, 1878; Moseley, 1892; Warham, 1961]; Willis Is. [Serventy, 1959; J. N. Butler, personal communication, 1968]; S. E. Cay (Moore Rf.), S.E. Cay* (Magdelaine Cays), N.E.* and S.W. Cays* (Coringa Gp.), N.E.* and S.W.* Cays (Herald Gp.), Observatory Cay (Lihou Rf.), West*, Mid*, and East* Islets (Diamond Gp.) [Hindwood et al., 1963; Serventy et al., 1971]; Whitsunday Gp. [Brown, 1949]; Heron Is. [Cooper, 1948]; Masthead Is. [Gilbert, 1925; MacGillivray, 1928; Cooper, 1948]; One Tree Is. [C. Hulsman, personal communication]; Fairfax Is. [Booth, 1970]; Lady Elliot Is. [Fien, 1971]; Open Sea [Hindwood et al., 1963]; Open Sea (23°21'S 153°24'E–23°36'S 153°26'E) [Norris, 1967]

Ciconiiformes

Ardeidae

Ardea novaehollandiae Latham, 1790

White-faced Heron: Escape River Mouth* [MacGillivray, 1910]; Clerke Is., Pipon Is. [Warham, 1962]; Willis Is. [Serventy, 1959; J. N. Butler, personal communication, 1968]; Dunk Is.* [Tarr, 1948; Austin, 1950]; Hayman Is.* [Brown, 1949]; North Is.* (Keppel Gp.) [Sharland, 1925; Wolstenholme, 1925]; North West Is. [Gilbert, 1925; MacGillivray, 1926]; Tryon Is. [MacGillivray, 1928]; Wilson Is. [Gilbert, 1925; MacGillivray, 1926]; Wreck Is. [Booth, 1970]; Heron Is. [Kikkawa, 1970; Booth, 1970] One Tree Is. [Domm and Recher, 1973]; Fairfax Is. [Booth, 1970]; Lady Elliot Is. [Fien, 1971]

Ardea sumatrana Raffles, 1822

Great-billed Heron: Dunk Is. [Tarr, 1948]

Butorides striatus (Linnaeus, 1766)

Mangrove Heron: Kypeny Is.* [MacGillivray, 1914]; Bird Is.* (Cape York) [MacGillivray, 1914]; Clerke Is.* [Warham, 1962]; Haggerstone Is.* [MacGillivray, 1918b]; Lloyd Bay Is.* [MacGillivray, 1918b]; King Is.*, Pipon Is. South Barrow Is.*, Sinclair Is., Coquet Is.,* Three Isles* [Warham, 1962]; Dunk Is.* [Tarr, 1948; Austin, 1950]; Hayman Is.* [Brown, 1949]; North Is.* (Keppel Gp.) [Sharland, 1925; Wolstenholme, 1925]; Heron Is. [Recher and Recher, 1969]

Egretta alba (Linnaeus, 1758)
  White Egret: Escape River Mouth [MacGillivray, 1910]; Raine Is. [Warham, 1961]; Willis Is. [Serventy, 1959; J. N. Butle, personal communication, 1968]; Fairfax Is. [Booth, 1970]
Egretta sacra (Gmelin, 1789)
  Reef Heron: Bushy Is.* [MacGillivray, 1914]; Cypheny Is.* (Albany Pass.) [MacGillivray, 1910, 1914]; Wyburn Rf. [Warham, 1962]; Cairncross Is.* [MacGillivray, 1914]; Hannibal Gp.* [MacGillivray, 1914, 1918a; Raine Is.* [J. MacGillivray, 1846; W. MacGillivray, 1914; Warham, 1961; Hindwood *et al.*, 1963]; Macarthur Is.* [MacGillivray, 1914]; Bird Is.* (Cape York) [MacGillivray, 1910]; Sir Charles Hardy Gp.* [MacGillivray, 1910, 1918a]; Clerke Is.*, Eel Rf. Piper Is.*, Chapman Is.* [Warham, 1962]; Haggerstone Is.*, Quoin Is.*, Lloyd Bay Is.* [MacGillivray, 1918a]; Cape Restoration Is.*, Claremont Gp.,* Aye Is., Pelican Is.* [MacGillivray, 1910]; Pipon Is. [Warham, 1962]; Flinders Gp.* [Hull, 1925]; South Barrow Is.*, Morris Is.*, Coquet Is.*, Three Isles* Palfrey Is., Rocky Isle [Warham, 1962]; Howick Gp., Cape Flattery* [MacGillivray, 1910]; Pickersgill Rf., Hope Is.* [Le Souëf, 1897]; Willis Is. [Serventy, 1959; Hindwood *et al.*, 1963; J. N. Butler, personal communication, 1968]; Low Is.* [Young, 1929; White, 1946; Warham, 1962]; Woody Is. [White, 1946]; Green Is.* [Alexander, 1926; White, 1946]; Fitzroy Is.* [Alexander, 1926]; N.E. Cay (Herald Gp.) [Hindwood *et al.*, 1963]; Russell Is. [Warham, 1962]; Dunk Is.* [Tarr, 1948; Austin, 1950]; Magnetic Is.* [Alexander, 1926]; Whitsunday Gp.* [Marshall, 1934; Brown, 1949]; Cumberland Gp.* [Roberts, 1957]; Red Bill Is.*, Victor Is.*, Taffy Is.* [Austin, 1908]; North Is.* (Keppel Gp.) [Sharland, 1925; Wolstenholme, 1925]; Capricorn Gp* [Gilbert, 1925; Napier, 1928]; North Rf. (Capricorn Gp.) [Barrett, 1919]; North West Is.* [Gilbert, 1925; MacGillivray, 1926, 1928, 1931; Napier, 1928; Cameron, 1969]; Tryon Is.* [Campbell and White, 1910; Barrett, 1919; Gilbert, 1925; MacGillivray, 1926, 1931]; Wilson Is.* [Gilbert, 1925; MacGillivray, 1926; Cooper, 1948]; Wreck Is.* [Cooper, 1948; Booth, 1970]; Heron Is.* [Campbell and White, 1910, Barrett, 1919; MacGillivray, 1928; Nebe, 1928, 1932; Cooper, 1948; Gillham, 1961; Recher, 1972a,b; Kikkawa, 1970; Booth, 1970; Recher and Recher, 1969, 1972]; One Tree Is.* [MacGillivray, 1928; Kikkawa, 1970; Recher, 1972a; Recher and Recher, 1972; Domm and Recher, 1973]; Masthead Is.* [Hedley, 1906; Barrett, 1919; Cooper, 1948]; Bunker Gp.* [Napier, 1928]; Fairfax Is.* [MacGillivray, 1928; Booth, 1970]; Lady Musgrave Is.* [MacGillivray, 1928]; Lady Elliot Is.* [Fien, 1971]
Ixobrychus flavicollis (Latham, 1790)
  Black Bittern: Lloyd Bay Is.* [MacGillivray, 1918a]; Dunk Is. [Tarr, 1948]; North West Is. [Gilbert, 1925; MacGillivray, 1926]
Nycticorax caledonicus (Gmelin, 1789)
  Nankeen Night Heron: Cairncross Is.* [MacGillivray, 1914]; Pandora Cay* [Warham, 1961]; Hannibal Is. [MacGillivray, 1918a]; Raine Is.* [MacGillivray, 1914, 1918a; Warham, 1961; Hindwood *et al.*, 1963]; Macarthur Is. [MacGillivray, 1914]; Clerke Is. [Warham, 1962]; Cape Restoration Is.*, Pelican Is. [MacGillivray, 1910]; Sinclair Is., Pethebridge Is.* [Warham, 1962]
Ciconiidae
Xenorhynchus asiaticus (Latham, 1790)
  Jabiru: Escape River Mouth [MacGillivray, 1910]; Magnetic Is. [Enwright, 1940; Storr, 1973]

Threskiornithidae *Platalea regia* Gould, 1838
   Royal Spoonbill: Escape River Mouth [MacGillivray, 1910]
Threskiornis molucca (Cuvier, 1829)
   Australian White Ibis: Willis Is. [J. N. Butler, personal communication, 1968];
   Dunk Is. [Austin, 1950]; Fairfax Is. [Booth, 1970]
Threskiornis spinicollis (Jameson, 1835)
   Straw-necked Ibis: Heron Is. [Kikkawa, 1970]
Anseriformes
   Anatidae
   Anas castanea (Eyton, 1838)
      Chestnut Teal: Facing Is. [MacGillivray, 1852]
   Anas superciliosa Gmelin, 1789
      Black Duck: Facing Is. [MacGillivray, 1852]
   Cygnus atratus (Latham, 1790)
      Black Swan: Heron Is. [Kikkawa, 1970]; One Tree Is. [Domm and Recher,
      1973]
Falconiformes
   Accipitridae
   Accipiter fasciatus (Vigors and Horfield, 1827)
      Australian Goshawk: Dunk Is., Goold Is., Magnetic Is. [Storr, 1973]; Hayman
      Is.* [Brown, 1949]; North Is.* (Keppel Gp.) [Sharland, 1925; Wolstenholme,
      1925]
   Accipiter novaehollandiae (Gmelin, 1788)
      Grey Goshawk: Dunk Is. [Austin, 1950]; One Tree Is. [Domm and Recher,
      1973]
   Aquila audax (Latham, 1801)
      Wedge-tailed Eagle: Dunk Is. [Banfield, 1913]; Magnetic Is. [Enwright, 1940]
   Aviceda subcristata (Gould, 1838)
      Crested Hawk: Dunk Is. [Austin, 1950]
   Circus approximans Peale, 1848
      Swamp Harrier: Three Isles [Warham, 1962]
   Elanus notatus Gould, 1838
      Black-shouldered Kite: Albany Is. [Warham, 1962]
   Haliaeëtus leucogaster (Gmelin, 1788)
      White-breasted Sea Eagle: Albany Rock [Warham, 1962]; Bushy Is.*, Cairncross
      Is.* Macarthur Is.*, Bird Is.* [MacGillivray, 1914]; Haggerstone Is.* [MacGil-
      livray, 1918b]; Palfrey Is. [Warham, 1962]; Hope Is.* [Le Souëf, 1897]; Low
      Is.* [Young, 1929]; Green Is.* [Cornwall, 1909]; Dunk Is. [Banfield, 1913;
      Tarr, 1948; Austin, 1950] South Brook Is. [Warham, 1962]; Magnetic Is.*
      [Alexander, 1926]; Hayman Is. [Brown 1949]; Hook Is.* [Booth, 1970]; Whit-
      sunday Gp. [Marshall, 1934]; Cumberland Gp.* [Roberts, 1957]; Temple
      Is.* [Austin, 1908]; North West Is.* [Campbell and White, 1910; Gilbert,
      1925; MacGillivray, 1926, 1928, 1931; Nebe, 1928; Cameron, 1969]; Tryon
      Is.* [Gilbert, 1925; MacGillivray, 1926, 1928, 1931]; Wilson Is.* [Gilbert,
      1925; MacGillivray, 1926; Cooper, 1948] Wreck Is.* [Nebe, 1932; Booth,
      1970]; Heron Is.* [MacGillivray, 1928; Cooper, 1948; Keast, 1966; Kikkawa,
      1970]; One Tree Is.* [Jukes, 1847; MacGillivray, 1928; Gillet and McNeill,
      1959; Keast, 1966; Domm and Recher, 1973]; Erskine Is.* [Campbell and

White, 1910; Barrett, 1919]; Masthead Is.° [Campbell and White, 1910; Barrett, 1919; MacGillivray, 1928]; Hoskyn Is.° [MacGillivray, 1928; Nebe, 1928]; Fairfax Is.° [Nebe, 1928; Booth, 1970]; Lady Musgrave Is.° [MacGillivray, 1928; Nebe, 1928]

Haliastur indus (Boddaert, 1783)
  Red-backed Sea Eagle: Hope Is.° [MacGillivray, 1852]; Dunk Is.° [Banfield, 1913; Tarr, 1948; Austin, 1950]: Magnetic Is.° [Enwright, 1940]; Hook Is.° [Booth, 1970]; Whitsunday Gp.° [Marshall, 1934; Brown, 1949]; Cockermouth Is. (Cumberland Gp.) [Roberts, 1957]; North Is.° (Keppel Gp.) [Sharland, 1925; Wolstenholme, 1925]; North West Is. [MacGillivray, 1931]

Haliastur sphenurus (Vieillot, 1818)
  Whistling Eagle: Albany Is. [Warham, 1962]

Pandionidae
Pandion haliaëtus (Linnaeus, 1758)
  Osprey: Albany Is.° [Warham, 1962]; Cairncross Is.° [MacGillivray, 1914]; Hannibal Gp.° [MacGillivray, 1914, 1918b]; Macarthur Is.° [MacGillivray, 1914, 1918b]; Bird Is.° [MacGillivray, 1914; Warham, 1962]; Haggerstone Is., Lloyd Bay Is. [MacGillivray, 1918b]; Chapman Is.°, Waterwitch Rf., Wharton Rf., Pipon Is.° [Warham, 1962]; Flinders Gp., South Barrow Is.°, Noble Is.° [Hull, 1925]; Howick Is. Gp.° [MacGillivray, 1910]; Coquet Is. [Hull, 1925; Warham, 1962]; Sinclair Is., Lizard Is., Palfrey Is., Pethebridge Is., Three Isles° [Warham, 1962]; Low Is.° [White, 1946; Warham, 1962]; Woody Is.° [White, 1946]; Little Fitzroy Is. [Warham, 1962]; Dunk Is.° [Jackson, 1909; Banfield, 1913; Tarr, 1948; Austin, 1950]; White Rock° [Warham, 1962]; Whitsunday Gp.° [Marshall, 1934; Brown, 1949]; Armit Is. [Hull, 1925]; Cumberland Gp.° [Roberts, 1957]; Temple Is.° [Austin, 1908]; North Is.° (Keppel Gp.) [Sharland, 1925; Wolstenholme, 1925]; Heron Is. [Kikkawa, unpublished].

Falconidae
Falco berigora Vigors and Horsfield, 1827
  Brown Hawk: Dunk Is. [Tarr, 1948]; Palm Is. [Storr, 1973]; North Is. (Keppel Gp.) [Sharland, 1925]

Falco cenchroides Vigors and Horsfield, 1827
  Nankeen Kestrel: Flinders Gp. [Hull, 1925]; Willis Is. [Serventy, 1959; J. N. Butler, personal communication, 1968]; Dunk Is., Magnetic Is. Brampton Is. [Storr, 1973]; Hayman Is. [Brown, 1949]; Cumberland Gp. [Roberts, 1957]; Fairfax Is. [Booth, 1970]

Falco hypoleucos Gould, 1841
  Grey Falcon: Dunk Is. [Banfield, 1913; Tarr, 1948]

Falco peregrinus Tunstall, 1771
  Peregrine Falcon: Lloyd Bay Is. [MacGillivray, 1918b]; Oyster Cay (Michaelmas Cay) [Alexander, 1926]; Hayman Is. [Brown, 1949]; One Tree Is. [Domm and Recher, 1973]

Falco longipennis Swainson, 1837
  Little Falcon: (Wreck Is., Fairfax Is. [Booth, 1970]?)

Galliformes
  Megapodiidae
Alectura lathami Gray, 1831
  Brush Turkey: Dunk Is.° [Austin, 1950]; Whitsunday Gp.° [MacGillivray, 1852]; Percy Is.° [Coppinger, 1883]

Megapodius freycinet Gaimard, 1823
    Scrub Fowl: Cairncross Is.° Low Is.° [MacGillivray, 1852]; Haggerstone Is.
    [Storr, 1973]; Clerke Is.° [Warham, 1962]; Fitzroy Is.° [White, 1946]; No.
    IV Is. (Frankland Gp.), Southernmost Is.° (Frankland Gp.), No. I Is. (Barnard
    Gp.) [MacGillivray, 1852; Storr, 1973]; Russell Is.° [Warham, 1962]; Kent Is.°
    (North Barnard Is.) [MacGillivray, 1852; Le Souëf, 1891; Warham, 1962];
    Dunk Is.° [Jackson, 1909; Banfield, 1913; Le Souëf, 1915; Tarr, 1948; Austin,
    1950; Storr, 1973]; Whitsunday Gp.° [MacGillivray, 1852; Marshall, 1934;
    Storr, 1973]; Armit Is. [Hull, 1925]; Brampton Is.° Carlyle Is., St. Bees Is.,
    Keswick Is. (Cumberland Gp) [Roberts, 1957; Storr, 1973]; Scawfell Is.
    (Cumberland Gp.) [Austin, 1908; Roberts, 1957; Storr, 1973]
Phasianidae
    Coturnix ypsilophorus Bosc, 1792
        Brown Quail: North Is.° (Keppel Gp.) [Sharland, 1925; Wolstenholme, 1925]
    Gallus gallus Linnaeus, 1758
        Fowl (introduced): North West Is.° [MacGillivray, 1926, 1927, 1931; Nebe,
        1928; Cooper, 1948; Tarr, 1950; Cameron, 1969; Cribb, 1969; McBride *et al.*,
        1969]; Heron Is.° [Cooper, 1948; Tarr, 1950; Kikkawa, 1970]
    Pavo cristatus Linnaeus, 1758
        Peacock (introduced): Heron Is.° [Kikkawa, 1970]
Numididae
    Numida meleagris (Linnaeus, 1758)
        Guinea Fowl (introduced): Heron Is.° [Kikkawa, 1970]
Gruiformes
    Turnicidae
    Turnix maculosa (Temminck, 1815)
        Red-backed Quail: Albany Is. [Forbes, 1878]
    Turnix velox (Gould, 1841)
        Little Quail: Heron Is. [Booth, 1970]
    Gruidae
    Grus rubicundus (Perry, 1810)
        Brolga: Escape River Mouth [MacGillivray, 1910]; Willis Is. [Hogan, 1925;
        Serventy, 1959]
    Rallidae
    Amaurornis olivacea (Meyen, 1834)
        Bush-hen: Fitzroy Is.° [White, 1946]
    Gallinula tenebrosa Gould, 1846
        Dusky Moorhen: Magnetic Is. [Enwright, 1940]
    Porphyrio porphyrio (Linnaeus, 1758)
        Swamphen: Raine Is. [Warham, 1961]; Willis Is. [Hogan, 1925; Serventy, 1959;
        J. N. Butler, personal communication, 1968]; Magnetic Is. [Lavery and Hop-
        kins, 1963]; Carlyle Is.° (Cumberland Gp.) [Roberts, 1957]; Heron Is. [Kik-
        kawa, 1970]; Fairfax Is. [Booth, 1970]
    Purzana cinerea (Vieillot, 1819)
        White-browed Crake: Dunk Is. [Tarr, 1948]
    Rallus pectoralis Temminck, 1831
        Lewin Water Rail: Raine Is. [Forbes, 1878]
    Rallus philippensis Linnaeus, 1766

Banded Land Rail: Pandora Cay* [Warham, 1961]; Raine Is.* [Moseley, 1892; J. MacGillivray, 1946; W. MacGillivray, 1910, 1917; Warham, 1959, 1961; Hindwood *et al.*, 1963]; Quoin Is.* [MacGillivray, 1971]; Claremont Gp.* [MacGillivray, 1852]; Pelican Is.* [MacGillivray, 1852; MacGillivray, 1910]; Morris Is.* [Warham, 1962]; Noble Is.* [Hull, 1925]; Eagle Is.* [MacGillivray, 1852]; Willis Is.* Davis, 1923a,b; Hogan, 1925; Lawry, 1926; Reithmüller, 1931; Serventy, 1959] S.E. Cay* (Magdelaine Cays), N.E.* and S.W.* Cays (Coringa Gp.), N.E.* and S.W.* Cays (Herald Gp.), No. 1 Cay* (Lihou Rf.), West*, Mid*, East*, and S.W.* Islets (Diamond Islets), Bird Is.* (Wreck Rf.) [Hindwood *et al.*, 1963]; North West Is.* [MacGillivray, 1928; Cooper, 1948]; Tryon Is.* [Campbell and White, 1910; Gilbert, 1925; MacGillivray, 1926, 1928]; Cato Is.* [Hindwood *et al.*, 1963]; Wreck Is. [Booth, 1970] Heron Is.* [MacGillivray, 1928; Cooper, 1948; Kikkawa, 1970]; One Tree Is.* [Kikkawa, 1969; Domm and Recher, 1973]; Masthead Is.* [Campbell and White, 1910; Cooper, 1948]; Fairfax Is. [Booth, 1970]; Lady Musgrave Is.* [MacGillivray, 1928]

Otididae

Ardeotis australis (Gray, 1829)

Australian Bustard: Facing Is. [MacGillivray, 1852]

Charadriiformes

Jacanidae

Irediparra gallinacea (Temminck, 1828)

Lotus Bird (Jacana): Fairfax Is. [Booth, 1970]

Haematopodidae

Haematopus ostralegus Linnaeus, 1758

Pied Oyster-catcher: Cairncross Is.,* Hannibal Gp.* [MacGillivray, 1914]; Macarthur Is.* [MacGillivray, 1914, 1917]; Piper Is.* [Warham, 1962]; Claremont Gp.,* Aye Is. [MacGillivray, 1910]; Flinders Gp.* [Hull, 1925]; Pipon Is.*, South Barrow Is.*, Morris Is.*, Sinclair Is.*, Coquet Is.*, Pethebridge Is.* [Warham, 1962]; Dunk Is. [Tarr, 1948]; Magnetic Is. [Lavery and Hopkins, 1963]; Whitsunday Gp.* [Marshall, 1934; Brown, 1949]; Cumberland Gp.* [Roberts, 1957]; Cape Palmerston Is.*, Temple Is.* [Austin, 1908]; North Is.* (Keppel Gp.) [Sharland, 1925; Wolstenholme, 1925]; Capricorn Gp.* [Campbell and White, 1910]; North West Is. [Gilbert, 1925; MacGillivray, 1926; Cameron, 1969]; Wilson Is. [Gilbert, 1925; MacGillivray, 1926]; Wreck Is. [Booth, 1970]; Heron Is. [Kikkawa, 1970]; One Tree Is. [Domm and Recher, 1973]; Masthead Is.* [Cooper, 1948]; Fairfax Is.* [Booth, 1970]; Lady Musgrave Is.* [MacGillivray, 1928; Storr, 1973]; Lady Elliot Is. [Fien, 1971]

Haematopus unicolor Forster, 1844

Sooty Oyster-catcher: Bushy Is.*, Cairncross Is.*, Hannibal Gp.* [MacGillivray, 1914]; Macarthur Is.* [MacGillivray, 1914, 1917]; Bird Is. [MacGillivray, 1914]; Wharton Rf., South Barrow Is.*, Sinclair Is.*, Coquet Is.*, Pethebridge Is.* [Warham, 1962]; Whitsunday Gp.* [Marshall, 1934]; Hayman Is. [Brown, 1949]; Cumberland Gp.* [Roberts, 1957]; Taffy Is.*, Cape Palmerston Is.* [Austin, 1908]; North Is. (Keppel Gp.) [Wolstenholme, 1925]; Capricorn Gp.* [Campbell and White, 1910]; North West Is. [MacGillivray, 1931; Cameron, 1969]; Tryon Is.* [Gilbert, 1925; MacGillivray, 1926, 1928]; Wilson Is.* [MacGillivray, 1928; Cooper, 1948]; Wreck Is.* [MacGillivray, 1928; Cooper, 1948; Booth, 1970]; Heron Is.* [Barrett, 1919; Kikkawa, 1970]; One Tree Is.*

[Domm and Recher, 1973]; Masthead Is.* [Barrett, 1919; Cooper, 1948]; Fair-
fax Is.* [MacGillivray, 1928; Booth, 1970]; Lady Musgrave Is.* [MacGillivray,
1928]; Lady Elliot Is. [Amiet, 1957]
Charadriidae
Charadrius asiaticus Pallas, 1773
   Oriental Dotterel: North West Is., Masthead Is. [Campbell and White, 1910]
Charadrius bicinctus Jardine and Selby, 1827
   Double-banded Dotterel: Low Is. [Young, 1929]
Charadrius cucullatus (Vieillot, 1818)
   Hooded Dotterel: Whitsunday Gp. [Marshall, 1934]
Charadrius leschenaultii Lesson, 1926
   Large Sand-Dotterel: North West Is. [MacGillivray, 1926]; Heron Is. [Kikkawa,
   unpublished]; Lady Elliot Is. [Fien, 1971]
Charadrius mongolus Pallas, 1776
   Mongolian Sand-Dotterel: Sue Islet, Claremont Gp. [McGill and Keast, 1945];
   Low Is. [White, 1946]; Heron Is. [Cooper, 1948; Kikkawa, 1970]; One Tree
   Is. [Domm and Recher, 1973]
Charadrius ruficapillus Temminck, 1821
   Red-capped Dotterel: Escape River Mouth* [MacGillivray, 1910]; Dunk Is.*
   [Tarr, 1948]; North West Is., Tryon Is., Heron Is. [MacGillivray, 1928]; One
   Tree Is. [Domm and Recher, 1973]
Pluvialis dominica (Muller, 1776)
   Eastern Golden Plover: Bramble Cay [MacGillivray, 1852]; Albany Is. [War-
   ham, 1962]; Pandora Cay [Warham, 1961]; Raine Is. [MacGillivray, 1917;
   Warham, 1961]; Hindwood et al., 1963]; Sir Charles Hardy Gp. [MacGillivray,
   1910]; Sinclair Is., Coquet Is., Lizard Is., Palfrey Is., Pethebridge Is., Three
   Isles [Warham, 1962]; Willis Is. [Hogan, 1925; Serventy, 1959; J. N. Butler,
   personal communication, 1968]; Low Is. [Young, 1929; White, 1946]; Green
   Is. [White, 1946]; N.E. Cay (Coringa Gp.), N.E. and S.W. Cays (Herald
   Gp.), Observatory Cay, No. 1 and No. 3 Cays (Lihou Rf.), Herald's Beacon
   Is. (Mellish Rf.), Mid and S.W. Islets (Diamond Islets) [Hindwood et al.,
   1963]; Dunk Is. [Tarr, 1948]; Magnetic Is. [Hopkins, 1948]; North Rf. Cay
   (Frederick Rf.), Bird Is. (Wreck Rf.) [Hindwood et al., 1963]; Capricorn
   Gp. [MacGillivray, 1928; Napier, 1928]; North West Is. [Campbell and White,
   1910; Gilbert, 1925; MacGillivray, 1926]; Tryon Is. [Gilbert, 1925; MacGil-
   livray, 1926]; Wilson Is. [Gilbert, 1925; MacGillivray, 1926]; Cato Is. [Hind-
   wood et al., 1963]; Wreck Is. [Booth, 1970]; Heron Is. [Cooper, 1948; Kik-
   kawa, 1970; Booth, 1970]; One Tree Is. [Domm and Recher, 1973]; Masthead
   Is. [Campbell and White, 1910]; Bunker Gp. (MacGillivray, 1928; Napier,
   1928]; Fairfax Is. [Booth, 1970]; Lady Elliot Is. [Fien, 1971]
Pluvialis squatarola (Linnaeus, 1758)
   Grey Plover: Raine Is. [MacGillivray, 1917]; Three Isles [Warham, 1962]; Willis
   Is. [J. N. Butler, personal communication, 1968]; Dunk Is. [Tarr, 1948]; North
   West Is. [Gilbert, 1925; MacGillivray, 1926, 1928; Cameron, 1969]; Wilson
   Is. [Gilbert, 1925]; Heron Is. [Cooper, 1948; Kikkawa, 1970]
Vanellus miles (Boddaert, 1783)
   Masked Plover: Escape River Mouth° [MacGillivray, 1910]
Vanellus novaehollandiae Stephens, 1819
   Spur-winged Plover: Willis Is. [Serventy, 1959; J. N. Butler, personal communi-
   cation, 1968]

Scolopacidae
Arenaria interpres (Linnaeus, 1758)
  Turnstone: Pandora Cay [Warham, 1961]; Raine Is. [Forbes, 1878; Moseley, 1892; MacGillivray, 1917; Warham, 1961; Hindwood *et al.*, 1963]; Aye Is. [MacGillivray, 1910]; Clerke Is., King Is., Sinclair Is., Pethebridge Is. [Warham, 1962]; Willis Is. [Hogan, 1925; Serventy, 1959]; North Cay (Willis Gp.) [Hindwood *et al.*, 1963]; Low Is. [White, 1946; Warham, 1962]; Russell Is. [Warham, 1962]; Oyster Cay (Michaelmas Cay) [Alexander, 1925a; Kikkawa, 1969]; N.W. and S.E. Cays (Magdelaine Cays), N.E. and S. W. Cays (Coringa Gp.), S.W. Cay (Herald Gp.), Observatory Cay, No. 2 and No. 4 Cays (Lihou Rf.), Mid, East, and S.W. Islets (Diamond Islets), Paget Cay (Marion Rf.), North Rf. Cay (Frederick Rf.), Porpoise Cay and West Islet (Wreck Rf.) [Hindwood *et al.*, 1963]; Bird Is. (Wreck Rf.) [Amiet, 1957; Hindwood *et al.*, 1963]; North West Is. [Campbell and White, 1910; Gilbert, 1925; MacGillivray, 1926, 1931; Cooper, 1948]; Tryon Is. [Campbell and White, 1910; Gilbert, 1925; MacGillivray, 1926; Cooper, 1948]; Wilson Is. [Gilbert, 1925; MacGillivray, 1926; Cooper, 1948]; Cato Is. [Hindwood *et al.*, 1963]; Wreck Is. [Cooper, 1948; Booth, 1970]; Heron Is. [Cooper, 1948; Kikkawa, 1970]; One Tree Is. [Domm and Recher, 1973]; Erskin Is. [Cooper, 1948]; Masthead Is. [Campbell and White, 1910; Cooper, 1948]; Bunker Gp. [MacGillivray, 1928; Napier, 1928]; Fairfax Is. [Booth, 1970]; Lady Elliot Is. [Fien, 1971]
Calidris acuminatus (Horsfield, 1821)
  Sharp-tailed Sandpiper: Raine Is. [MacGillivray, 1917; Warham, 1961]; Aye Is. [MacGillivray, 1910]; Pipon Is. [Warham, 1962]; North West Is. [Gilbert, 1925; MacGillivray, 1926, 1928]; Wilson Is. [Cooper, 1948]; Heron Is., One Tree Is. [MacGillivray, 1928; Domm and Recher, 1973]
Calidris albus (Pallas, 1764)
  Sanderling: Whitsunday Gp. [Marshall, 1934]; Fairfax Is. [Booth, 1970]
Calidris canutus (Linnaeus, 1758)
  Knot: Raine Is. [Amiet, 1957]; One Tree Is. [Domm and Recher, 1973]
Calidris ferrugineus (Pontoppidan, 1763)
  Curlew Sandpiper: Pipon Is. [Warham, 1962]; Willis Is. [J. N. Butler, personal communication, 1968]; Dunk Is. [Tarr, 1948]; Heron Is. [Cooper, 1948]
Calidris ruficollis (Pallas, 1776)
  Little Stint: Albany Is. [Warham, 1962]; Escape River Mouth [MacGillivray, 1910]; Raine Is. [Hindwood *et al.*, 1963]; Cape Restoration Is. [MacGillivray, 1910]; Pipon Is., Sinclair Is., Coquet Is., Lizard Is. [Warham, 1962], Willis Is. [J. N. Butler, personal communication, 1968]; Dunk Is. [Tarr, 1948]; Capricorn Gp. [MacGillivray, 1928]; Heron Is. [Cooper, 1948]; One Tree Is. [Domm and Recher, 1973]; Masthead Is. [Campbell and White, 1910]; Bunker Gp. [MacGillivray, 1928]; Lady Elliot Is. [Fien, 1971]
Calidris tenuirostris (Horsfield, 1821)
  Great Knot: Sue Islet (Torres St.) [Serventy, 1944]; One Tree Is. [Domm and Recher, 1973]
Gallinago megala Swinhoe, 1861
  Pin-tailed Snipe: Dunk Is. [Tarr, 1948]
Limosa lapponica (Linnaeus, 1758)
  Bar-tailed Godwit: Raine Is. [Hindwood *et al.*, 1963]; Aye Is., Bird Is. [MacGillivray, 1910]; Clerke Is., South Barrow Is., Coquet Is., Pethebridge Is. [Warham, 1962]; Willis Is. [Davis, 1923a,b], Low Is. [Young, 1929]; Green Is.

[White, 1946]; Herald's Beacon Is. (Mellish Rf.) [Hindwood *et al.*, 1963]; Dunk Is. [Tarr, 1948]; Whitsunday Gp. [Marshall, 1934]; North Rf. Cay (Frederick Rf.), Observatory Cay (Kenn Rf.), Bird Is. (Wreck Rf.) [Hindwood *et al.*, 1963], North West Is. [Gilbert, 1925; MacGillivray, 1926, 1931; Cooper, 1948]; Tryon Is. [Gilbert, 1925; MacGillivray, 1926]; Cato Is. [Hindwood *et al.*, 1963]; Heron Is. [Kikkawa, 1970]; One Tree Is. [Domm and Recher, 1973]; Masthead Is. [Barrett, 1919; Cooper, 1948]; Bunker Gp. [MacGillivray, 1928]; Lady Elliot Is. [Fien, 1971]

Limosa limosa (Linnaeus, 1758)

Black-tailed Godwit: Haggerstone Is. [MacGillivray, 1917]; North West Is. [Campbell and White, 1910]; One Tree Is. [MacGillivray, 1928]

Numenius madagascariensis (Linnaeus, 1766)

Eastern Curlew: Bushy Is. [MacGillivray, 1914]; Cape Restoration Is., Claremont Gp., Cape Flattery Is. [MacGillivray, 1910]; Sinclair Is., Pethebridge Is. [Warham, 1962]; Willis Is. [Serventy, 1959; J. N. Butler, personal communication, 1968]; Low Is. [Young, 1929]; Whitsunday Gp. [Marshall, 1934]; Cumberland Gp. [Roberts, 1957]; Bird Is. [MacGillivray, 1910], North Is. (Keppel Gp.) [Sharland, 1925; Wolstenholme, 1925]; North West Is. [Campbell and White, 1910]; Heron Is. [Cooper, 1948; Kikkawa, 1970]; One Tree Is. [Domm and Recher, 1973]; Fairfax Is. [Booth, 1970]

Numenius minutus Gould, 1841

Little Whimbrel: Willis Is. [Serventy, 1959; Hindwood *et al.*, 1963; J. N. Butler, personal communication, 1968]; Herald's Beacon Is. (Mellish Rf.) [Hindwood *et al.*, 1963]; Magnetic Is. [Lavery and Hopkins, 1963]; North West Is. [Gilbert, 1925; MacGillivray, 1926]; Heron Is. [Cooper, 1948; Kikkawa, 1970]

Numenius phaeopus (Linnaeus, 1758)

Whimbrel: Albany Is. [Warham, 1962]; Bushy Is. [MacGillivray, 1914]; Raine Is. [Warham, 1961]; Clerke Is. [Warham, 1962]; Cape Restoration Is., Claremont Gp. [MacGillivray, 1910]; Pipon Is., South Barrow Is., Sinclair Is., Coquet Is., Pethebridge Is. [Warham, 1962]; Cape Flattery Is. [MacGillivray, 1910]; Green Is. [White, 1946]; N.W. Cay (Magdelaine Cays), No. 4 Cay (Lihou Rf.), East and S.W. Islet (Diamond Islets) [Hindwood *et al.*, 1963]; Dunk Is. [Tarr, 1948]; Whitsunday Gp. [Marshall, 1934; Brown, 1949]; Cumberland Gp. [Roberts, 1957]; Bird Is. [MacGillivray, 1910]; Capricorn Gp. [MacGillivray, 1928]; North West Is. [Campbell and White, 1910; Gilbert, 1925; MacGillivray, 1926, 1931]; Heron Is. [Cooper, 1948; Kikkawa, 1970]; One Tree Is. [Domm and Recher, 1973]; Lady Elliot Is. [Fien, 1971]; Bunker Gp. [MacGillivray, 1928]

Tringa brevipes (Vieillot, 1816)

Grey-tailed Tattler: Willis Is. [Serventy, 1959]; Low Is. [Young, 1929; White, 1946]; Dunk Is. [Tarr, 1948]; North Is. (Keppel Gp.) [Wolstenholme, 1925]; Capricorn Gp. [Campbell and White, 1910; MacGillivray, 1928; Bryant, 1933]; North West Is. [Gilbert, 1925; MacGillivray, 1926, 1931; Bryant, 1933]; Wreck Is. [Booth, 1970]; Heron Is. [Cooper, 1948; Kikkawa, 1970]; One Tree Is. [Domm and Recher, 1973]; Bunker Gp. [MacGillivray, 1928]; Fairfax Is. [Booth, 1970]; Lady Elliot Is. [Fien, 1971]

Tringa cinerea (Gueldenstaedt, 1774)

Terek Sandpiper: Pipon Is. [Warham, 1962]; Dunk Is. [Tarr, 1948]; North

West Is. [MacGillivray, 1928]; Heron Is. [Kikkawa, 1970]; One Tree Is. [Domm and Recher, 1973]; Fairfax Is. [Booth, 1970]

Tringa glareola Linnaeus, 1758

Wood Sandpiper: Bird Is. [Jones, 1943]; Willis Is. [Davis, 1923a,b]

Tringa hypoleucos Linnaeus, 1758

Common Sandpiper: Albany Is., King Is., Pipon Is. [Warham, 1962]; Dunk Is. [Tarr, 1948]; Magnetic Is. [Lavery and Hopkins, 1963]; Capricorn Gp. [Campbell and White, 1910]; One Tree Is. [MacGillivray, 1928; Domm and Recher, 1973]

Tringa incana (Gmelin, 1789)

Wandering Tattler: N.W. Cay (Magdelaine Cays), Observatory Cay (Lihou Rf.), Bird and West Islets (Wreck Rf.) [Hindwood *et al.*, 1963]; North West Is. [MacGillivray, 1931; Bryant, 1933; Serventy, 1944]

Tringa nebularia (Gunnerus, 1767)

Greenshank: Dunk Is. [Tarr, 1948]; Heron Is. [Cooper, 1948]

Tringa stagnatilis (Bechstein, 1803)

Marsh Sandpiper: Capricorn Gp. [MacGillivray, 1928]

Burhinidae

Burhinus magnirostris (Latham, 1801)

Southern Stonecurlew: Escape River Mouth° [MacGillivray, 1910]; Dunk Is.° [Jackson, 1909; Tarr, 1948; Austin, 1950]; Magnetic Is.° [Enwright, 1940; Hopkins, 1948]; Whitsunday Gp.° [Marshall, 1934; Brown, 1949; Roberts, 1957]; Cape Palmerston Is., Temple Is.° [Austin, 1908]; North Is.° (Keppel Gp.) [Wolstenholme, 1925]

Esacus magnirostris (Vieillot, 1816)

Beach Stonecurlew: Escape River Mouth° [MacGillivray, 1910]; Macarthur Is.° [MacGillivray, 1914, 1918a]; Sir Charles Hardy Gp.° [MacGillivray, 1910, 1918a]; Clerke Is.° [Warham, 1962]; Haggerstone Is.° [MacGillivray, 1918a]; Claremont Gp.° [MacGillivray, 1910]; Pipon Is. [Warham, 1962]; Flinders Gp.° [Hull, 1925]; South Barrow Is., Sinclair Is.°, Coquet Is.°, Pethebridge Is., Rock Is., Three Isles° [Warham, 1962]; Dunk Is.° [Banfield, 1913; Austin, 1950]; Whitsunday Gp.° [Marshall, 1934]; Cumberland Gp.° [Roberts, 1957]; North Is.° (Keppel Gp.) [Wolstenholme, 1925; Amiet, 1957]; Fairfax Is. [Booth, 1970]

Glareolidae

Stiltia isabella (Vieillot, 1868)

Australian Pratincole: Heron Is. [Kikkawa, 1970]

Stercorariidae

Stercorarius skua (Brunnich, 1764)

Southern Skua: Capricorn Gp. [Cooper, 1948]; Masthead Is. [Gilbert, 1925]

Laridae

Anous minutus Boie, 1844

White-capped Noddy: Island near Darnley Is.° [MacGillivray, 1914; Lavery and Grimes, 1971; Serventy *et al.*, 1971]; Raine Is. [MacGillivray, 1846; Warham, 1961; Hindwood *et al.*, 1963; Lavery and Grimes, 1971]; Bird Is. [MacGillivray, 1914]; Quoin Is.° [MacGillivray, 1917; Alexander, 1925a; Lavery and Grimes, 1971; Serventy *et al.*, 1971]; Oyster Cay (Michaelmas Cay) [Alexander, 1926]; S.E. Cay° (Magdelaine Cays), N.E.° and S.W.° Cays (Coringa Gp.), N.E.° and S.W.° Cays (Herald Gp.), West°, Mid°, S.W.°, and East°

Islets (Diamond Islets) [Hindwood *et al.*, 1963; Serventy *et al.*, 1971]; Capricorn Gp.* [Gilbert, 1925; Alexander, 1925; Serventy *et al.*, 1971]; North West Is.* [Campbell and White, 1910; Gilbert, 1925; MacGillivray, 1926, 1928; Napier, 1928; Nebe, 1928; McNeill, 1946; Cooper, 1948; Cameron, 1969; McBride *et al.*, 1969; Lavery and Grimes, 1971]; Port Curtis Is. [Cooper, 1948]; Tryon Is.* [MacGillivray, 1928; Lavery and Grimes, 1971]; Wilson Is. [Gilbert, 1925]; Heron Is.* [Campbell and White, 1910; MacGillivray, 1928; Cooper, 1948; Gillham, 1961; Keast, 1966; Shipway, 1969; Kikkawa, 1970; Booth, 1970; Lavery and Grimes, 1971]; One Tree Is. [Domm and Recher, 1973]; Masthead Is.* [Hedley, 1906; Campbell and White, 1910; Barrett, 1919; MacGillivray, 1928; Nebe, 1932; Cooper, 1948; Lavery and Grimes, 1971]; Hoskyn Is.* [MacGillivray, 1928; Lavery and Grimes, 1971; Serventy *et al.*, 1971]; Fairfax Is.* [MacGillivray, 1928; Nebe, 1928; Booth, 1970; Lavery and Grimes, 1971; Serventy *et al.*, 1971]; Lady Musgrave Is.* [MacGillivray, 1928; Napier, 1928; Nebe, 1928, 1932; Lavery and Grimes, 1971; Serventy *et al.*, 1971]

Anous stolidus (Linnaeus, 1758)

Noddy: Bramble Cay* [MacGillivray, 1914; Alexander, 1925a; Lavery and Grimes, 1971; Serventy *et al.*, 1971]; Murray Is. Sandbank* [Warham, 1961]; Albany Rock [Warham, 1962]; Pandora Cay* [Warham, 1961; Serventy *et al.*, 1971]; Raine Is.* [MacGillivray, 1846; Saunders, 1878; Moseley, 1892; MacGillivray, 1910, 1914, 1917; Warham, 1961; Hindwood *et al.*, 1963; Lavery and Grimes, 1971; Serventy *et al.*, 1971]; Bird Is.* [MacGillivray, 1914]; Ashmore Sandbank, Cape Restoration Is. [MacGillivray, 1910]; Pipon Is. [Warham, 1962]; Howick Gp.* [MacGillivray, 1910; Alexander, 1925a; Lavery and Grimes, 1971; Serventy *et al.*, 1971]; Cays A and B (Flinders Rf.), Diana Bk.*, S.E. Cay* (Moore Rf.) [Hindwood *et al.*, 1963; Serventy *et al.*, 1971]; Willis Is.* [Davis, 1923a,b; Alexander, 1925a; Hogan, 1925; Lawry, 1926; Reithmüller, 1931; Serventy, 1959; Serventy *et al.*, 1971]; Mid Is.* and North Cay* (Willis Gp.) [Hindwood *et al.*, 1963]; Woody Is. [White, 1946]; N.W. and S.E.* Cays (Magdelaine Cays), Cay B (Holmes Rf.) [Hindwood *et al.*, 1963; Serventy *et al.*, 1971]; Upolu Bank* [Cornwall, 1903; MacGillivray, 1914; Alexander, 1925a; White, 1946; Lavery and Grimes, 1971; Serventy *et al.*, 1971]; Oyster Cay* (Michaelmas Cay) [Cornwall, 1903; MacGillivray, 1914; Alexander, 1925a; Yonge, 1930; White, 1946; Kikkawa, 1969; Lavery and Grimes, 1971; Serventy *et al.*, 1971]; N.E.* and S.W.* Cays (Coringa Gp.), N.E.* and S.W. Cays (Herald Gp.), Turtle Islet*, Observatory Cay, No. 1*, No. 8*, No. 9*, No. 2, No. 4, and No. 7* Cays (Lihou Rf.), Herald's Beacon Islet* (Mellish Rf.), West*, Mid*, S.W*., and East Islets (Diamond Islets) [Hindwood *et al.*, 1963; Serventy *et al.*, 1971]; Dunk Is. [Tarr, 1948]; White Rock [Warham, 1962]; North Barnard Is.* [Serventy *et al.*, 1971]; Swain Rf.* [Gillett and MacNeill, 1959]; Paget and Carola Cays (Marion Rf.), North Rf.* and Observatory Cays (Frederick Rf.) [Hindwood *et al.*, 1963; Heatwole, 1971; Serventy *et al.*, 1971]; Observatory* and S.W. Projection Cays* (Kenn Rf.), S.W.* and N.E. Cays (Saumarez Rf.), Unnamed Cay, Porpoise Cay* West Islet* Bird Islet* (Wreck Rf.) [Hindwood *et al.*, 1963; Serventy *et al.*, 1971]; North West Is. [Gilbert, 1925; MacGillivray, 1926]; Cato Is.* [Hindwood *et al.*, 1963; Serventy *et al.*, 1971]; Masthead Is. [Gilbert, 1925]; Lady Elliot Is.* [Fien, 1971]

Chlidonias leucoptera (Temminck, 1815)

White-winged Black Tern: Ayr (offshore) [Amiet, 1956]
Gelochelidon nilotica (Gmelin, 1789)
Gull-billed Tern: Piper Is., Coquet Is., Pethebridge Is. [Warham, 1962]
Hydroprogne caspia (Pallas, 1770)
Caspian Tern: Raine Is.* [MacGillivray, 1846; Serventy *et al.*, 1971]; Claremont
Gp. [MacGillivray, 1910]; Albany Is.*, King Is.*, Wharton Rf.* [Warham,
1962; Lavery and Grimes, 1971; Serventy *et al.*, 1971]; Pipon Is.* (Hull, 1925;
Warham, 1962; Lavery and Grimes, 1971]; Flinders Gp.*, Stapleton Is.* [Hull,
1925]; South Barrow Is., Morris Is.*, Sinclair Is.*, Coquet Is. [Warham, 1962];
Lizard Is.* [MacGillivray, 1846; Serventy *et al.*, 1971]; Pickersgill Rf., Hope
Is. [Le Souëf, 1897]; Willis Is. [Serventy, 1959; J. N. Butler, personal commu-
nication, 1968]; Low Is. [White, 1946]; Dunk Is. [Tarr, 1948]; Pelican Rock*
(Mackay), Creek Rock* (Yeppoon) [Serventy *et al.*, 1971]; Masthead Is. [Gil-
bert, 1925; Cooper, 1948]
Larus novaehollandiae Stephens, 1826
Silver Gull: Tuesday Rock* [MacGillivray, 1914; Lavery and Grimes, 1971;
Serventy *et al.*, 1971]; Pandora Cay* [Warham, 1961]; Raine Is. [MacGillivray,
1846; Saunders, 1878; Moseley, 1892; MacGillivray, 1910; Warham, 1961;
Hindwood *et al.*, 1963]; Macarthur Is.*, Bird Is.* (Cape York) [MacGillivray,
1914; Lavery and Grimes, 1971; Serventy *et al.*, 1971]; Cape Restoration Is.
[MacGillivray, 1910]; Claremont Gp.* [MacGillivray, 1910; Wheeler and Wat-
son, 1963; Lavery and Grimes, 1971; Serventy *et al.*, 1971]; Wharton Rf. [War-
ham, 1962]; Boulder Rock*, Flinders Gp. [Hull, 1925]; Howick Gp.* [MacGil-
livray, 1910; Wheeler and Watson, 1963; Lavery and Grimes, 1971, Serventy
et al., 1971]; Coquet Is.* [Hull, 1925; Warham, 1962]; Miles Rf., Palfrey
Is., Pethebridge Is., Gubbins Rf., Three Isles [Warham, 1962]; Hope Is. [Le
Souëf, 1897]; Low Is.* [Wheeler and Watson, 1963; Lavery and Grimes, 1971;
Serventy *et al.*, 1971]; Woody Is., Oyster Cay (Michaelmas Cay) [White,
1946]; White Rock* [Warham, 1962]; Ocean Creek Sandbank [Lavery and
Grimes, 1971], Holbourne Is.* [Wheeler and Watson, 1963; Lavery and
Grimes, 1971; Serventy *et al.*, 1971]; Whitsunday Gp.* [Marshall, 1934; Brown,
1949; Wheeler and Watson, 1963; Lavery and Grimes, 1971]; Cumberland
Gp.* [Roberts, 1957]; Cape Palmerston Is.* [Austin, 1908; Wheeler and Wat-
son, 1963; Lavery and Grimes, 1971; Serventy *et al.*, 1971]; Bird Rock*
[Wheeler and Watson, 1963; Lavery and Grimes, 1971]; Swain Rf. [Gillett
and MacNeill, 1959]; North Is. (Keppel Gp.) [Sharland, 1925]; Capricorn
Gp.* [Serventy *et al.*, 1971]; North West Is.* [Campbell and White, 1910;
Gilbert, 1925; MacGillivray, 1926, 1928, 1931; Napier, 1928; Cameron, 1969;
Lavery and Grimes, 1971]; Tryon Is.* [Campbell and White, 1910; Gilbert,
1925; MacGillivray, 1926, 1928; Lavery and Grimes, 1971]; Wilson Is.* [Gil-
bert, 1925; Wheeler and Watson, 1963; Lavery and Grimes, 1971]; Wreck
Is.* [Booth, 1970]; Heron Is.* [Cooper, 1948; Wheeler and Watson, 1963;
Kikkawa, 1970; Booth, 1970; Lavery and Grimes, 1971]; One Tree Is.*
[Wheeler and Watson, 1963; Lavery and Grimes, 1971; Domm and Recher,
1973]; Masthead Is.* [Campbell and White, 1910; Barrett, 1919; Nebe, 1928;
Cooper, 1948; Wheeler and Watson, 1963; Lavery and Grimes, 1971]; Bunker
Gp.* [Napier, 1928; Serventy *et al.*, 1971]; Port Curtis Is. [Cooper, 1948];
Fairfax Is.* [Nebe, 1928; Wheeler and Watson, 1963; Booth, 1970; Lavery and
Grimes, 1971]; Lady Musgrave Is.* [Jukes, 1847; MacGillivray, 1928; Napier,

1928; Nebe, 1932; Wheeler and Watson, 1963; Lavery and Grimes, 1971];
Lady Elliot Is. [Fien, 1971]

Sterna spp.

South Barnard Is. [Barnard, 1892]

Sterna albifrons Pallas, 1764

Little Tern: Murray Is. Sandbank [Warham, 1961]; Pipon Is.* [Warham, 1962;
Serventy *et al.*, 1971; Lavery and Grimes, 1971]; Sinclair Is.*, Pethebridge
Is. [Warham, 1962]; Willis Is.* [Serventy, 1959; Hindwood *et al.*, 1963; J. N.
Butler, personal communication, 1968]; Low Is. [White, 1946]; Observatory
Cay* (Lihou Rf.) [Hindwood *et al.*, 1963]; Michaelmas Cay [Storr, 1973];
Dunk Is. [Tarr, 1948; Lavery and Grimes, 1971]; Victor Is.* [Austin, 1908;
Lavery and Grimes, 1971; Serventy *et al.*, 1971]; Mud Is.*, Pelican Is.* (Bun-
daberg) [Serventy *et al.*, 1971]; Capricorn Gp. [Campbell and White, 1910;
Cooper, 1948; Keast, 1966]; North West Is. [Gilbert, 1925; MacGillivray, 1928,
1931]; Tryon Is. [Gilbert, 1925; MacGillivray, 1931]; Wilson Is. [Gilbert, 1925;
MacGillivray, 1926]; Wreck Is. [Booth, 1970]; Heron Is. [Kikkawa, 1970;
Lavery and Grimes, 1971]; One Tree Is. [Domm and Recher, 1973]; Fairfax
Is.* [Booth, 1970]; Lady Musgrave Is. [MacGillivray, 1928]; Lady Elliot Is.*
[Fien, 1971; Storr, 1973]

Sterna anaethetus Scopoli, 1786

Bridled Tern: East Strait Is.*, Hammond Rock* [Lavery and Grimes, 1971;
Serventy *et al.*, 1971]; Channel Rock* [MacGillivray, 1914; Lavery and Grimes,
1971; Serventy *et al.*, 1971]; Albany Rock* [Warham, 1962; Lavery and
Grimes, 1971; Serventy *et al.*, 1971]; Bushy Is.* [MacGillivray, 1910, 1914;
Lavery and Grimes, 1971; Serventy *et al.*, 1971]; Rock Is.*, Bird Is.* [Lavery
and Grimes, 1971]; Raine Is.* [MacGillivray, 1910, 1917; Warham, 1961;
Lavery and Grimes, 1971; Serventy *et al.*, 1971]; Quoin Is.*, Lloyd Bay Is.*
[MacGillivray, 1917; Lavery and Grimes, 1971; Serventy *et al.*, 1971]; Cairn-
cross Is.*, North Barnard Is.* [Serventy *et al.*, 1971]; Cape Restoration Is.*,
Claremont Gp.*, Aye Is.*, Howick Gp., Pelican Is.* [MacGillivray, 1910;
Lavery and Grimes, 1971; Serventy *et al.*, 1971]; Wharton Rf.*, Miles Rf.,
Pethebridge Is.* [Warham, 1962; Lavery and Grimes, 1971; Serventy *et al.*,
1971]; Hope Is.* [Le Souëf, 1897; Lavery and Grimes, 1971; Serventy *et al.*,
1971]; Low Is.*, Woody Is.* [White, 1946; Lavery and Grimes, 1971; Serventy
et al., 1971]; Oyster Cay (*?), Dunk Is. (*?) [Lavery and Grimes, 1971]; Little
Fitzroy Is. [Warham, 1962]; Whitsunday Gp. [Marshall, 1934]; Beverley Gp.*,
Red Bill Is.*, Reid Is.* [Austin, 1908; Larvery and Grimes, 1971]; Swain Rf.*
[Gillett and MacNeill, 1959; Serventy *et al.*, 1971]; Capricorn Gp.* [Gilbert,
1925; Keast, 1966]; North West Is.* [Campbell and White, 1910; MacGillivray,
1926; Cooper, 1948; Serventy *et al.*, 1971]; Tryon Is.* [Gilbert, 1925; Mac-
Gillivray, 1926, 1928; Lavery and Grimes, 1971; Serventy *et al.*, 1971]; Wilson
Is. [Gilbert, 1925]; Heron Is. [Kikkawa, 1970]; Wreck Is.* [Booth, 1970]; One
Tree Is.* [MacGillivray, 1928; Lavery and Grimes, 1971; Serventy *et al.*,
1971; Domm and Recher, 1973]; Masthead Is.* [Campbell and White, 1910;
Barrett, 1919; MacGillivray, 1928; Cooper, 1948; Lavery and Grimes, 1971;
Serventy *et al.*, 1971]; Fairfax Is.* [Booth, 1970]; Hoskyn Is.*, Lady Musgrave
Is.* [MacGillivray, 1928; Lavery and Grimes, 1971; Serventy *et al.*, 1971],
Lady Elliot Is.* (Fein, 1971]

Sterna bengalensis Lesson, 1831

Lesser Crested Tern: Escape River Mouth [MacGillivray, 1910]; Ashmore Sandbanks [MacGillivray, 1917]; Cape Restoration Is. [MacGillivray, 1910]; King Is.°, Pipon Is. [Warham, 1962]; Flinders Gp. [Hull, 1925]; Howick Is. Gp. [MacGillivray, 1910]; Pickersgill Rf.° [Le Souëf, 1897]; Hope Is.° [Le Souëf, 1894]; Low Is.° [White, 1946; Serventy *et al.*, 1971]; Woody Is. [White, 1946]; Oyster Cay° (Michaelmas Cay) [MacGillivray, 1914; White, 1946; Lavery and Grimes, 1971; Serventy *et al.*, 1971]; Upolu Bank° [Cornwall, 1903; MacGillivray, 1914; Lavery and Grimes, 1971; Serventy *et al.*, 1971]; Green Is., Fitzroy Is. [White, 1946]; Little Fitzroy Is. [Warham, 1962]; North and South Barnard Is.° [Serventy *et al.*, 1971; Lavery and Grimes, 1971]; Whitsunday Gp. [Marshall, 1934]; Capricorn Gp.° [Campbell and White, 1910; Keast, 1966]; North West Is. [Gilbert, 1925; MacGillivray, 1928, 1931; Cooper, 1948]; Tryon Is. [Cooper, 1948]; Wilson Is. [Gilbert, 1925; MacGillivray, 1926; Cooper, 1948]; Wreck Is. [Cooper, 1948]; Heron Is. [Cooper, 1948; Kikkawa, 1970]; Erskine Is. [Cooper, 1948]; One Tree Is.° [Domm and Recher, 1973]; Masthead Is.° [Barrett, 1919; Cooper, 1948; Serventy *et al.*, 1971; Lavery and Grimes, 1971]; Fairfax Is.° [Booth, 1970]

Sterna bergii Lichtenstein, 1823

Crested Tern: Bramble Cay° [J. MacGillivray, 1852; W. MacGillivray, 1914; Serventy *et al.*, 1971]; A Rock° [Lavery and Grimes, 1971]; Pandora Cay° [Warham, 1961; Lavery and Grimes, 1971; Serventy *et al.*, 1971]; Raine Is.° [MacGillivray, 1914, 1917; Warham, 1961; Hindwood *et al.*, 1963; Lavery and Grimes, 1971; Serventy *et al.*, 1971]; Ashmore Sandbanks° Quoin Is.° [MacGillivray, 1917; Lavery and Grimes, 1971; Serventy *et al.*, 1971]; Dhu Reef [Lavery and Grimes, 1971]; Eel Rf., Waterwitch Rf., King Is.°, Pipon Is., Morris Is.°, Coquet Is., Miles Rf., Pethebridge Is., Rocky Is., Decapolis Rf. [Warham, 1962]; Lizard Is.° [Lavery and Grimes, 1971; Serventy *et al.*, 1971]; Diana Bk.° [Hindwood *et al.*, 1963; Serventy *et al.*, 1971]; Willis Is.° [Davis, 1923a,b; Hogan, 1925; Lawry, 1926; Reithmüller, 1931; Serventy, 1959; J. N. Butler, personal communication, 1968]; Low Is., Woody Is. [White, 1946]; Cay B (Holmes Rf.), N.W. Cay (Magdelaine Cays) [Hindwood *et al.*, 1963]; Upolu Cay° [Serventy *et al.*, 1971]; Oyster Cay° (Michaelmas Cay) [Cornwall, 1903; MacGillivray, 1914; Alexander, 1926; White, 1946; Kikkawa, 1969; Lavery and Grimes, 1971]; Green Is. [White, 1946]; N. E. Cay° (Coringa Gp.), Observatory Cay, No. 4 Cay (Lihou Rf.), S. W. Islet (Diamond Islets) [Hindwood *et al.*, 1963]; North Barnard Is. [Warham, 1962; Lavery and Grimes, 1971]; White Rock° [Warham, 1962]; Dunk Is. [Tarr, 1948; Austin, 1950]; Whitsunday Gp. [Marshall, 1934; Brown, 1949]; Cumberland Gp. [Roberts, 1957]; North Rf. and Observatory Cays (Frederick Rf.), S.W.° and N.E. Cays (Saumarez Rf.), Unnamed Cay, Porpoise Cay, and West Islet (Wreck Rf.) [Hindwood *et al.*, 1963; Serventy *et al.*, 1971]; Swain Rf.° [Gillett and McNeill, 1959]; North Is. (Keppel Gp.) [Sharland, 1925; Wolstenholme, 1925]; North West Is.° [Gilbert, 1925; MacGillivray, 1926, 1931; Cooper, 1948; Lavery and Grimes, 1971]; Tryon Is. [Gilbert, 1925; MacGillivray, 1926, 1931; Cooper, 1948]; Wilson Is.° [Gilbert, 1925; MacGillivray, 1926; Cooper, 1948; Lavery and Grimes, 1971; Serventy *et al.*, 1971]; Wreck Is. [Cooper, 1948]; Heron Is. [Cooper, 1948; Kikkawa, 1970]; Erskine Is. [Cooper, 1948]; One Tree Is.° [Gillett and McNeill, 1959; Keast, 1966; Lavery and Grimes, 1971; Domm and Recher, 1973]; Masthead Is.* [Barrett, 1919; Gilbert, 1925; MacGillivray, 1926, 1928; Napier, 1928; Nebe, 1928, 1932; Cooper, 1948; Keast, 1966; Lavery and Grimes, 1971; Serventy *et al.*, 1971]; Fairfax Is.* [MacGillivray, 1928; Booth, 1970; Lavery and Grimes, 1971; Serventy *et al.*, 1971]; Lady Musgrave Is.* [MacGillivray, 1928; Lavery and Grimes, 1971; Serventy *et al.*, 1971]; Lady Elliot Is.* [Fien, 1971; Serventy *et al.*, 1971]

Sterna dougalli Montagu, 1813

Roseate Tern: Murray Is. Sandbank [Warham, 1961]; Channel Rock*, East Strait Is.* [Lavery and Grimes, 1971]; Bushy Is.* [MacGillivray, 1910, 1914; Lavery and Grimes, 1971; Serventy *et al.*, 1971]; Escape River Mouth [MacGillivray, 1910]; Cairncross Is.*, Macarthur Is.* [MacGillivray, 1914; Lavery and Grimes, 1971; Serventy *et al.*, 1971]; Bird Is.* [MacGillivray, 1852; Lavery and Grimes, 1971]; Cockburn Rf. [Lavery and Grimes, 1971]; Cape Restoration Is., Night Is.* [MacGillivray, 1910]; Willis Is. [Davis, 1923b; Hogan, 1925; Serventy, 1959]; Frankland Is.* [Lavery and Grimes, 1971]; Capricorn Gp.* [MacGillivray, 1931; Keast, 1966]; Tryon Is.* [Napier, 1928]; Wilson Is.* [Gilbert, 1925; MacGillivray, 1926, 1928; Lavery and Grimes, 1971; Serventy *et al.*, 1971]; Heron Is. [Kikkawa, 1970]; One Tree Is.* [MacGillivray, 1928; Lavery and Grimes, 1971; Serventy *et al.*, 1971; Domm and Recher, 1973]; Fairfax Is.* [Booth, 1970]; Lady Musgrave Is.* [MacGillivray, 1928; Lavery and Grimes, 1971; Serventy *et al.*, 1971]; Lady Elliot Is. [Fien, 1971]

Sterna fuscata (Linnaeus, 1766)

Sooty Tern: Bramble Cay* [MacGillivray, 1914; Alexander, 1925a; Lavery and Grimes, 1971; Serventy *et al.*, 1971]; Murray Is. Sandbank*, Pandora Cay* [Warham, 1961; Lavery and Grimes, 1971; Serventy *et al.*, 1971]; Cairncross Is.* [MacGillivray, 1852]; Raine Is.* [MacGillivray, 1846; Saunders, 1878; Moseley, 1892; MacGillivray, 1910, 1914, 1917; Alexander, 1925a; Warham, 1961; Hindwood *et al.*, 1963; Lavery and Grimes, 1971; Serventy *et al.*, 1971]; Cape Restoration Is. [MacGillivray, 1910]; Tydeman Reef Cay*, Tydeman Cay* [Lavery and Grimes, 1971]; Pethebridge Is. [Warham, 1962]; S.E. Cay (Moore Rf.), S.E. Cay (Magdelaine Cays), Flinders Rf., North Cay, and Mid Islet* (Willis Gp.) [Hindwood *et al.*, 1963]; Willis Is.* [Davis, 1923a,b; Hogan, 1925; Lawry, 1926; Reithmuller, 1931; Serventy, 1959; Serventy *et al.*, 1971]; Low Is.* [Young, 1929; Warham, 1962]; Cays A and B (Holmes Rf.) [Hindwood *et al.*, 1963]; Upolu Cay* [Alexander, 1925a, 1926; White, 1946; Cornwall, 1903; Keast, 1966; Lavery and Grimes, 1971; Serventy *et al.*, 1971]; Oyster Cay* (Michaelmas Cay) [MacGillivray, 1914; Alexander, 1925a, 1926; Yonge, 1930; White, 1946; Keast, 1966; Kikkawa, 1969; Lavery and Grimes, 1971; Serventy *et al.*, 1971]; N.E.* and S.W.* Cays (Coringa Gp.), N.E. and S.W.* Cays (Herald Gp.), Turtle Islet,* No. 1*, No. 8*, No. 4, and No. 9 Cays (Lihou Rf.), Herald's Beacon Is.* (Mellish Rf.), West*, East*, and S.W.* Islets (Diamond Islets) [Hindwood *et al.*, 1963; Serventy *et al.*, 1971]; Dunk Is. [Tarr, 1948]; Whitsunday Passage [Roberts, 1957]; Paget Cay* (Marion Rf.), North Rf. Cay (Frederick Rf.), Observatory* and S.W. Projection* Cays (Kenn Rf.), Bird* and West Islets (Wreck Rf.), Cato Is.* [Hindwood *et al.*, 1963; Serventy *et al.*, 1971]; North West Is. [Cameron, 1969]; Lady Musgrave Is. [MacGillivray, 1928]; Open Sea (15°10′S 151°39′E–15°20′S, 151°40′E, 15°38′S 151°39′E–15°57′S, 51°50′E, 16°10′S 157°14′E, 16°47′S 152°27′E–17°03′S 152°48′E, 19°44′S 156°38′E–19°50′S 156°33′E, 19°32′S 153°05′E–20°26′S 153°09′E,

19°41'S 153°36'E–20°02'S 153°31'E, 22°07'S 154°20'E–22°18'S 154°13'E, 23°21'S 153°24'E–23°36'S 153°26'E) [Norris, 1967]

Sterna hirundo Linnaeus, 1758

Eastern Common Tern: Warrior Rf. [Hindwood, 1944]; Bird Is. (Cape York) [Hitchcock, 1965]; Low Is. [White, 1946]; Green Is. [Hitchcock, 1965]

Sterna sumatrana Raffles, 1822

Black-naped Tern: East Strait Is.*, Rocky Is.* [Lavery and Grimes, 1971]; Murray Is. Sandbank [Warham, 1961]; Albany Rock* [Warham, 1962; Lavery and Grimes, 1971; Serventy *et al.*, 1971]; Bushy Is.* [MacGillivray, 1910, 1914; Lavery and Grimes, 1971; Serventy *et al.*, 1971]; Kypenny Is.* [MacGillivray, 1914; Lavery and Grimes, 1971; Serventy *et al.*, 1971]; Escape River Mouth [MacGillivray, 1910]; Pandora Cay [Warham, 1961]; Macarthur Is. [MacGillivray, 1914]; Bird Is.* (Cape York) [J. MacGillivray, 1852; W. MacGillivray, 1914; Lavery and Grimes, 1971; Serventy *et al.*, 1971]; Clerke Is.* [Warham, 1952; Lavery and Grimes, 1971; Serventy *et al.*, 1971]; Sir Charles Hardy Is.* [Lavery and Grimes, 1971]; Lloyd Bay Is.* [MacGillivray, 1917; Serventy *et al.*, 1971]; Claremont Gp. [MacGillivray, 1910]; Hannah Is., Wharton Rf., Pipon Is., Morris Is.*, Miles Rf., Palfrey Is., Pethebridge Is. [Warham, 1962]; Rocky Is.* [Lavery and Grimes, 1971]; Willis Is. [Hogan, 1925; Serventy, 1959; J. N. Butler, personal communication, 1968]; Piper Is.* [Serventy *et al.*, 1971]; Cays A* and B* (Flinders Rf.), North Cay* (Willis Gp.) [Hindwood *et al.*, 1963]; Low Is.*, Woody Is.* [White, 1946; Lavery and Grimes, 1971; Serventy *et al.*, 1971]; Cays A and B (Holmes Rf.), N.W. Cay* (Magdelaine Cays) [Hindwood *et al.*, 1963]; Oyster Cay (Michaelmas Cay), Green Is. [White, 1946]; Little Fitzroy Is. [Warham, 1962]; S.W. Islet* (Coringa Gp.), N.E. and S.W.* Cays (Herald Gp.), Observatory Cay, No. 8, No. 2*, No. 4*, and No. 7 Cays (Lihou Rf.), East and S.W. Islets (Diamond Islets) [Hindwood *et al.*, 1963; Serventy *et al.*, 1971]; Kent Is. (North Barnard Is.) [Warham, 1962]; Dunk Is.* [Austin, 1950; Lavery and Grimes, 1971; Serventy *et al.*, 1971]; Carola* and Paget Cays (Marion Rf.), Observatory Cay (Frederick Rf.), Observatory Cay* (Kenn Rf.), Unnamed Cay*, Porpoise Cay and West Islet (Wreck Rf.), S.W. Cay (Saumarez Rf.), Cato Is. [Hindwood *et al.*, 1963; Serventy *et al.*, 1971]; Swain Rf. [Gillett and McNeill, 1959]; North West Is. [MacGillivray, 1931; Cooper, 1948]; Tryon Is.* [Napier, 1928; MacGillivray, 1928, 1931; Cooper, 1948]; Wilson Is.* [Gilbert, 1925; MacGillivray, 1926, 1928; Nebe, 1932; Cooper, 1948; Lavery and Grimes, 1971; Serventy *et al.*, 1971]; Wreck Is.* [Nebe, 1932; Cooper, 1948; Booth, 1970; Lavery and Grimes, 1971]; Heron Is.* [MacGillivray, 1928; Cooper, 1948; Kikkawa, 1970; Booth, 1970; Serventy *et al.*, 1971]; Erskine Is. [Cooper, 1948]; One Tree Is.* [MacGillivray, 1928; Lavery and Grimes, 1971; Domm and Recher, 1973]; Masthead Is. [Barrett, 1919; Cooper, 1948]; Fairfax Is.* [Booth, 1970]; Lady Musgrave Is. [MacGillivray, 1928]; Lady Elliot Is. [Fien, 1971]; Open Sea (17°10'S 151°30'E) [Norris, 1967]

Columbiformes

Columbidae

Chalcophaps indica (Linnaeus, 1758)

Green-winged Pigeon: Low Is., Green Is. [White, 1946]; South Brook Is.* [Warham, 1962]; Dunk Is.* [Tarr, 1948; Austin, 1950]; Magnetic Is.* [Enwright, 1940]; Cumberland Gp. [Roberts, 1957]

Columba leucomela Temminck, 1821
  White-headed Pigeon: Dunk Is., Palm Is. [Storr, 1973]; Hayman Is. [Brown, 1949]
Ducula spilorrhoa (Gray, 1858)
  Torres Strait Pigeon: Double Is.° [White, 1946]; Warrior Is.°, Half-Way Is.° [Jardine, 1904]; Albany Is.° [Warham, 1962]; Cypheny Is.° [MacGillivray, 1910; Warham, 1962]; Escape River Mouth° [MacGillivray, 1910]; Cairncross Is.° [MacGillivray, 1852; Jardine, 1904]; Raine Is. [Warham, 1961]; Bird Is.° (Cape York) [J. MacGillivray, 1852; W. MacGillivray, 1910]; Clerk Is.° [Warham, 1962]; Piper Is.° [MacGillivray, 1852; Warham, 1962]; Lloyd Bay Is.° [MacGillivray, 1910, 1917]; Night Is.° [J. MacGillivray, 1852; W. MacGillivray, 1910]; Hannah Is.°, King Is.°, Pipon Is.°, South Barrow Is.°, Coquet Is.°, Miles Rf., Lizard Is.°, Palfrey Is.° Pethebridge Is.°, Three Isles°, Gubbins Rf. [Warham, 1962]; Cape Flattery Is.° [MacGillivray, 1910]; Hope Is.° [Le Souëf, 1894, 1897; Kikkawa, 1969]; Willis Is. [Serventy, 1959]; Low Is.° [Young, 1929; Yonge, 1930; White, 1946; Warham, 1962]; Woody Is.° [White, 1946]; Green Is.° [Cornwall, 1903, 1909; White, 1946]; Fitzroy Is. [Warham, 1962]; Little Fitzroy Is. [White, 1946; Warham, 1962]; Russell Is. [Warham, 1962]; Kent Is.° (North Barnard Is.) [Le Souëf, 1891; Warham, 1962]; Dunk Is.° [Jackson, 1909; Banfield, 1913; Le Souëf, 1915; Tarr, 1948; Austin, 1950]; South Brook Is.° [Warham, 1962]; Magnetic Is. [Hopkins, 1948; Lavery and Hopkins, 1963]; Whitsunday Gp. [Marshall, 1934; Roberts, 1957]; Cumberland Gp. [Storr, 1973]; Ridge Is.° [Cornwall, 1910]
Geopelia cuneata (Latham, 1801)
  Diamond Dove: Escape River Mouth° [MacGillivray, 1910]; Willis Is. [J. N. Butler, personal communication, 1968]; Magnetic Is.° [Enwright, 1940]
Geopelia humeralis (Temminck, 1821)
  Bar-shouldered Dove: Clerke Is.° [Warham, 1962]; Escape River Mouth°, Cape Restoration Is.° [MacGillivray, 1910]; Hannah Is.° [Warham, 1962]; Flinders Gp. [Hull, 1925]; Morris Is.°, Sinclair Is.°, Clerke Is.° Coquet Is.°, Lizard Is.°, Palfrey Is.° [Warham, 1962]; Hope Is.° [Le Souëf, 1897]; Low Is.° [MacGillivray, 1852]; Dunk Is.° [Tarr, 1948; Austin, 1950]; Magnetic Is.° [Alexander, 1926; Enwright, 1940; Hopkins, 1948]; Whitsunday Gp.° [Marshall, 1934]; Hayman Is. [Brown, 1949], Armit Is. [Hull, 1925]; Brampton Is.° [Roberts, 1957]; North Is.° (Keppel Gp.) [Sharland, 1925]; North West Is.° [Campbell and White, 1910; Gilbert, 1925; MacGillivray, 1926, 1928; Cooper, 1948]; Tryon Is.° [Campbell and White, 1910; Gilbert, 1925; MacGillivray, 1926]; Wilson Is.° [MacGillivray, 1926]; Wreck Is.° [Cooper, 1948; Booth, 1970]; Heron Is.° [Cooper, 1948; Keast, 1966; Kikkawa, 1970]; Masthead Is.° [Campbell and White, 1910; Barrett, 1919; Cooper, 1948]; Lady Musgrave Is.° [MacGillivray, 1928]
Geopelia striata (Linnaeus, 1766)
  Peaceful Dove: Dunk Is.° [Tarr, 1948; Austin, 1950]; Magnetic Is.° [Alexander, 1926; Enwright, 1940]; Hayman Is.° [Brown, 1949]; North Keppel [Storr, 1973]; Tryon Is. [MacGillivray, 1931]
Lopholaimus antarcticus (Shaw, 1794)
  Top-knot Pigeon: No. 4 Is. (Frankland Gp.) [MacGillivray, 1852]
Macropygia phasianella (Temminck, 1821)
  Brown Pigeon: Dunk Is.° [Tarr, 1948; Austin, 1950]; Magnetic Is.° [Enwright, 1940; Hopkins, 1948]

Ptilinopus magnificus (Temminck, 1821)
   Wompoo Pigeon: Green Is. [Storr, 1973]; Dunk Is.* [Austin, 1950]
Ptilinopus regina Swainson, 1825
   Red-crowned Pigeon: Escape River Mouth* [MacGillivray, 1910]; Green Is. [Alexander, 1926; White, 1946], Dunk Is.* [Tarr, 1948; Austin, 1950], South Brook Is.* [Warham, 1962]; Whitsunday Gp.* [Marshall, 1934]; Hayman Is.* [Brown, 1949]; North West Is. [Cameron, 1969]; Heron Is. [Cooper, 1948; Kikkawa, 1970]
Ptilinopus superbus (Temminck, 1810)
   Purple-crowned Pigeon: Willis Is. [J. N. Butler, personal communication, 1968]; Low Is. [Young, 1929]
Psittaciformes
   Psittacidae
      Cacatua galerita (Latham, 1790)
         Sulphur-crested Cockatoo: Fitzroy Is.* [Alexander, 1926; Warham, 1962]; Kent Is. (North Barnard Is.) [Le Souëf, 1891]; Dunk Is.* [Banfield, 1913; Le Souëf, 1915; Tarr, 1948; Austin, 1950]; Magnetic Is.* [Alexander, 1926; Enwright, 1940]; Whitsunday Gp. [Marshall, 1934; Brown, 1949]; Hook Is.* [Booth, 1970]; Hayman Is. [Storr, 1973]; Cumberland Gp. [Austin, 1908; Roberts, 1957]; Long Is. [Coppinger, 1883]; Percy Is. [Storr, 1973]
      Calyptorhynchus magnificus (Shaw, 1790)
         Red-tailed Black Cockatoo: Percy Is. [Coppinger, 1883]
      Trichoglossus haematodus (Linnaeus, 1771)
         Rainbow Lorikeet: Lloyd Bay Is.* [MacGillivray, 1910, 1918b]; Dunk Is. [Banfield, 1913]; Magnetic Is. [Alexander, 1926; Enwright, 1940]; Whitsunday Gp.* [Brown, 1949; Roberts, 1957]; Cumberland Gp.* [Roberts, 1957]; Fairfax Is. [Booth, 1970]; Facing Is. [MacGillivray, 1852]
Cuculiformes
   Cuculidae
      Cacomantis variolosus (Vigors and Horsfield, 1826)
         Brush Cuckoo: Dunk Is.* [Austin, 1950]; Pine Islet* [Makin, 1961]; Capricorn Gp. [Campbell and White, 1910]
      Centropus phasianinus (Latham, 1801)
         Pheasant Coucal: Escape River Mouth* [MacGillivray, 1910]; South Barrow Is. [Warham, 1962]; Fitzroy Is.* [White, 1946]; Dunk Is.* [Le Souëf, 1915]; Magnetic Is.* [Alexander, 1926; Enwright, 1940]; Hayman Is. [Brown, 1949; Storr, 1973]; Whitsunday Gp.* [MacGillivray, 1852; Marshall, 1934]; Cumberland Gp.* [Roberts, 1957]; Beverley Gp.* [Austin, 1908]; Percy Is.* [Coppinger, 1883]; North Is.* (Keppel Gp.) [Sharland, 1925]
      Chrysococcyx basalis (Horsfield, 1821)
         Horsfield Bronze Cuckoo: Pine Islet* [Makin, 1961]; North West Is. [Cameron, 1969]; One Tree Is. [Domm and Recher, 1973]
      Chrysococcyx lucidus (Gmelin, 1788)
         Golden Bronze Cuckoo: Willis Is. [J. N. Butler, personal communication, 1968]; Capricorn Gp. [Campbell and White, 1910]; North West Is. [MacGillivray, 1931]; Heron Is. [Kikkawa, 1970]; One Tree Is. [Domm and Recher, 1973]; Masthead Is. [Barrett, 1919]; Fairfax Is. [Booth, 1970]
      Cuculus saturatus Blyth, 1843
         Oriental Cuckoo: Willis Is. [Davis, 1923b; Hogan, 1925; Serventy, 1959; J. N. Butler, personal communication, 1968]; Lady Elliot Is. [Fien, 1971]

Cuculus pallidus (Latham, 1801)
    Pallid Cuckoo: Magnetic Is. [Storr, 1973]
Eudynamys cyanocephala (Latham, 1801)
    Koel: Dunk Is.* [Banfield, 1913; Tarr, 1948]; Magnetic Is.* [Enwright, 1940];
    Tryon Is., Heron Is. [Campbell and White, 1910]; Wreck Is. [Booth, 1970]; One
    Tree Is. [Domm and Recher, 1973], Cato Is. [Hindwood *et al.*, 1963]
Scythrops novaehollandiae Latham, 1790
    Channel-billed Cuckoo: Dunk Is. [Storr, 1973]; Cumberland Gp. [Roberts, 1957]
Strigiformes
  Tytonidae
    Tyto alba (Scopoli, 1769)
      Barn Owl: Fairfax Is. [Booth, 1970]; One Tree Is. [A. E. Chilvers, personal
      communication]
    Tyto novaehollandiae (Stephens, 1826)
      Masked Owl: Percy Is. [Storr, 1973]
    Tyto longimembris (Jerdon, 1839)
      Eastern Grass Owl: Palm Is. [Storr, 1973]
  Strigidae
    Ninox novaeseelandiae (Gmelin, 1788)
      Boobook Owl: Magnetic Is.* [Enwright, 1940]; Whitsunday Gp.* [Marshall,
      1934]; Cumberland Gp.* [Roberts, 1957]; North Is.* (Keppel Gp.) [Sharland,
      1925; Wolstenholme, 1925]; Fairfax Is. [Booth, 1970]
    Ninox rufa (Gould, 1846)
      Rufous Owl: Dunk Is. [Banfield, 1906]
Caprimulgiformes
  Caprimulgidae
    Caprimulgus macrurus Horsfield, 1821
      Large-tailed Nightjar: Dunk Is.* [Le Souëf, 1915; Tarr, 1948; Austin, 1950]
    Eurostopodus albogularis (Vigors and Horsfield, 1826)
      White-throated Nightjar: Dunk Is.* [Tarr, 1948]
Apodiformes
  Apodidae
    Chaetura caudacuta (Latham, 1901)
      Spine-tailed Swift: Albany Is. [Warham, 1962]; Wilson Is., Heron Is., One Tree
      Is. [MacGillivray, 1928; Domm and Recher, 1973]
    Collocalia francica (Gmelin, 1789)
      Grey Swiftlet: Willis Is. [J. N. Butler, personal communication, 1968]; Fitzroy
      Is. [Warham, 1962]; Timana Is.* [Hamilton-Smith, 1965]; Bedarra Is.* [Busst,
      1956]; Dunk Is.* [Banfield, 1913, Le Souëf, 1915; Tarr, 1948; Austin, 1950];
      Thorpe Is., Richards Is., Goold Is. [Storr, 1973]
Coraciiformes
  Alcedinidae
    Alcyone azurea (Latham, 1801)
      Azure Kingfisher: Hope Is.* [Le Souëf, 1897]; Willis Is. [J. N. Butler, personal
      communication, 1968]; Kent Is.* (North Barnard Is.) [Le Souëf, 1891]; Dunk
      Is. [Storr, 1973]
    Alcyone pusilla (Temminck, 1836)
      Little Kingfisher: Flinders Gp. [Hull, 1925]; Willis Is. [J. N. Butler, personal
      communication, 1968]

Dacelo leachii Vigors and Horsfield, 1827
  Blue-winged Kookaburra: Dunk Is. [Storr, 1973]; Magnetic Is.* [Alexander, 1926; Enwright, 1940]
Dacelo novaeguineae (Hermann, 1783)
  Laughing Kookaburra: Whitsunday Gp.* [Marshall, 1934; Roberts, 1957]; Hayman Is.* [Brown, 1949]
Halcyon australasiae (Vieillot, 1818)
  Sacred Kingfisher: Hannibal Gp., Macarthur Is., Bird Is. (Cape York) [MacGillivray, 1914]; Lloyd Bay Is. [MacGillivray, 1918b]; Willis Is. [Davis, 1923b; Hogan, 1925; Serventy, 1959]; Low Is. [White, 1946; Warham, 1962]; Russell Is.* [Warham, 1962]; Dunk Is. [Tarr, 1948; Austin, 1950]; South Brook Is.* [Warham, 1962]; Magnetic Is. [Enwright, 1940]; Hayman Is.* [Brown, 1949]; Cumberland Gp.* [Roberts, 1957]; Pine Islet* [Makin, 1961]; Saumarez Rf. [Heatwole, 1968]; North West Is.* [Campbell and White, 1910; Gilbert, 1925; MacGillivray, 1926, 1928, 1931; Cooper, 1948]; Tryon Is.* [Gilbert, 1925; MacGillivray, 1926, 1928, 1931]; Wilson Is.* [Gilbert, 1925; MacGillivray, 1926]; Wreck Is.* [Booth, 1970]; Heron Is.* [MacGillivray, 1928; Nebe, 1932; Kikkawa, 1970; Booth, 1970]; One Tree Is. [Domm and Recher, 1973]; Masthead Is.* [Barrett, 1919; Cooper, 1948]; Fairfax Is.* [Booth, 1970]
Halcyon chloris (Boddaert, 1783)
  Mangrove Kingfisher: Lloyd Bay Is. [MacGillivray, 1918b]; Night Is.* [MacGillivray, 1910]; Hannah Is.*, Pipon Is., Coquet Is.*, Palfrey Is., Pethebridge, Is.* [Warham, 1962], Hope Is. [MacGillivray, 1852]; Willis Is. [J. N. Butler, personal communication, 1968]; Low Is.* [Young, 1929]; Dunk Is.* [Tarr, 1948; Austin, 1950]; South Brook Is.* [Warham, 1962]; Hook Is.* [Brown, 1949]; Pine Islet*, Percy Is.* [Makin, 1961]; Cumberland Gp., Northumberland Gp. [Storr, 1973], North West. Is. [Cameron, 1969]
Halcyon macleayii Jardine and Selby, 1830
  Forest Kingfisher: Sir Charles Hardy Gp. [MacGillivray, 1910]; Clerke Is. Waterwitch Rf. [Warham, 1962]; Noble Is.* [Hull, 1925]; Willis Is. [J. N. Butler, personal communication, 1968]; Kent Is.* (North Barnard Is.) [Warham, 1962]; Dunk Is.* [Tarr, 1948; Austin, 1950]; Magnetic Is.* [Alexander, 1926]; Percy Is.* [Makin, 1961]; North Is.* (Keppel Gp.) [Sharland, 1925, Wolstenholme, 1925]; North West Is. [Cameron, 1969]; Fairfax Is. [Booth, 1970]
Tanysiptera sylvia Gould, 1850
  White-tailed Kingfisher: Torres Strait Area (Keast, 1966)
Meropidae
Merops ornatus Latham, 1801
  Rainbow Bird: Raine Is. [Warham, 1961; Hindwood *et al.*, 1963]; Dunk Is. [Le Souëf, 1915; Austin, 1950]; Magnetic Is. [Alexander, 1926; Enwright, 1940]; Whitsunday Gp. [Brown, 1949]; North Is. (Keppel Gp.) [Sharland, 1925]
Coraciidae
Eurystomus orientalis (Linnaeus, 1766)
  Eastern Broad-billed Roller: Sir Charles Hardy Gp. [MacGillivray, 1910]; Willis Is. [Hogan, 1925; Serventy, 1959; J. N. Butler, personal communication, 1968]; Magnetic Is. [Enwright, 1940]; Pine Islet*, Percy Is.* [Makin, 1961]; North West Is. [Campbell and White, 1910]; Wreck Is. [Booth, 1970]; Heron Is. [Kikkawa, 1970]; One Tree Is. [Domm and Recher, 1973]; Fairfax Is. [Booth, 1970]

332

Passeriformes
  Pittidae
    Pitta versicolor Swainson, 1825
      Noisy Pitta: Haggerstone Is. [MacGillivray, 1918b]; Dunk Is., Palm Is. [Storr, 1973]; Heron Is. [Kikkawa, 1970]
  Hirundinidae
    Hirundo tahitica Gmelin, 1789
      Welcome Swallow: Pipon Is., White Rock [Warham, 1962]; Willis Is. [Hogan, 1925]; Magnetic Is.* [Alexander, 1926; Enwright, 1940]; Whitsunday Gp.* [Marshall, 1934; Brown, 1949]; Cumberland Gp.* [Roberts, 1957]; Beverley Gp. [Austin, 1908]; North Is.* (Keppel Gp.) [Wolstenholme, 1925]; North West Is. [MacGillivray, 1931]; Heron Is. [Kikkawa, 1970]; One Tree Is. [Domm and Recher, 1973]; Fairfax Is. [Booth, 1970]
    Petrochelidon ariel (Gould, 1843)
      Fairy Martin: Magnetic Is. [Storr, 1973]; Heron Is. [Kikkawa, 1970]; Fairfax Is. [Booth, 1970]
    Petrochelidon nigricans (Vieillot, 1817)
      Tree Martin: Raine Is. [MacGillivray, 1846; Warham, 1961]; Willis Is. [Hogan, 1925; Serventy, 1959; J. N. Butler, personal communication, 1968]; Dunk Is. [Austin, 1950]
  Motacillidae
    Anthus novaeseelandiae (Gmelin, 1789)
      Australian Pipit: North Is.* (Keppel Gp.) [Sharland, 1925; Wolstenholme, 1925]
  Campephagidae
    Coracina hypoleuca (Gould, 1848)
      White-breasted Cuckoo-shrike: Low Is. [White, 1946]; Dunk Is.* [Tarr, 1948]
    Coracina lineata (Swainson, 1825)
      Barred Cuckoo-shrike: Dunk Is.* [Tarr, 1948; Austin, 1950]; Wreck Is. [Booth, 1970]; Heron Is. [Kikkawa, 1970]
    Coracina novaehollandiae (Gmelin, 1789)
      Black-faced Cuckoo-shrike: Sir Charles Hardy Gp. [MacGillivray, 1910]; Willis Is. [Hogan, 1925; Serventy, 1959]; Dunk Is. [Tarr, 1948]; Magnetic Is.* [Enwright, 1940]; Hayman Is.* [Brown, 1949]; Pine Islet*, Percy Is.* [Makin, 1961]; North West Is. [Cameron, 1969]; Heron Is.* [Kikkawa, 1970]; One Tree Is. [Domm and Recher, 1973]
    Coracina robusta (Latham, 1801)
      Little Cuckoo-shrike: Low Is., Woody Is., Dunk Is., Goold Is., Palm Is. [Storr, 1973]; Heron Is. [Kikkawa, 1970]
    Coracina tenuirostris (Jardine, 1831)
      Cicada Bird: Dunk Is. [Storr, 1973]; North West Is., Tryon Is. [Campbell and White, 1910]
    Lalage leucomela (Vigors and Horsfield, 1827)
      Varied Triller: Dunk Is.* [Tarr, 1948; Austin, 1950]; Whitsunday Gp.* [Brown, 1949; Roberts, 1957]; Cumberland Gp.* [Roberts, 1957]; Masthead Is. [Campbell and White, 1910; Cooper, 1948]; Fairfax Is. [Booth, 1970]
    Lalage sueurii (Vieillot, 1818)
      White-winged Triller: Dunk Is. [Austin, 1950]; Capricorn Gp. [Campbell and White, 1910]; Wilson Is. [Gilbert, 1925; MacGillivray, 1926]; Heron Is. [Kik-

kawa, unpublished]; One Tree Is. [Domm and Recher, 1973]; Masthead Is. [Cooper, 1948]

Muscicapidae (Turdinae)

Zoothera dauma (Latham, 1790)

Australian Ground Thrush: Willis Is. [J. N. Butler, personal communication, 1968]

(Sylviinae)

Acrocephalus stentoreus (Ehrenberg, 1833)

Reed-Warbler: Pine Islet [Makin, 1961]; North West Is. [Cameron, 1969]; Wilson Is., Heron Is. [Kikkawa, 1970]

Cisticola exilis (Vigors and Horsfield, 1827)

Golden-headed Fantail-Warbler: Pelican Is., South Molle Is. [Storr, 1973]; Whitsunday Gp.* [Roberts, 1957]; One Tree Is.* [Domm and Recher, 1973]

Gerygone olivacea (Gould, 1838)

White-throated Warbler: Magnetic Is.* [Alexander, 1926]

Gerygone palpebrosa Wallace, 1865

Black-throated Warbler: Albany Is.* [Warham, 1962]; Palm Is. [Storr, 1973]

(Malurinae)

Megalurus timoriensis Wallace, 1863

Tawny Grassbird: Dunk Is. [Storr, 1973]; North Is.* (Keppel Gp.) [Wolstenholme, 1925]; Heron Is. [Kikkawa, unpublished]

(Muscicapinae)

Peneoenanthe pulverulenta (Bonaparte, 1851)

Mangrove Robin: Clerke Is.* [Warham, 1962]

(Monarchinae)

Monarcha leucotis Gould, 1850

White-eared Flycatcher: Dunk Is.* [MacGillivray, 1852; Banfield, 1913; Alexander, 1926; Austin, 1950]; Goold Is. [Storr, 1973]; Magnetic Is.* [Alexander 1926; Lavery and Hopkins, 1963]; Hayman Is.* [Brown, 1949]; Pine Islet* [Makin, 1961]; One Tree Is. [Domm and Recher, 1973]

Monarcha melanopsis (Vieillot, 1818)

Black-faced Flycatcher: Raine Is. [MacGillivray, 1918b]; Green Is., Dunk Is., Magnetic Is. [Storr, 1973]; Pine Islet* [Makin, 1961]; Heron Is. [Kikkawa, 1970]; One Tree Is. [Domm and Recher, 1973]

Monarcha trivirgata (Temminck and Laugier, 1826)

Spectacled Flycatcher: Little Fitzroy Is.*, Kent Is.* (North Barnard Is.) [Warham, 1962]; Dunk Is.* [Austin, 1950]; Palm Is. [Storr, 1973]; Magnetic Is.* [Enwright, 1940]; Hayman Is.* [Brown, 1949]; Cumberland Gp.* [Roberts, 1957]; Pine Islet* [Makin, 1961]

Myiagra cyanoleuca (Vieillot, 1818)

Satin Flycatcher: Willis Is. [J. N. Butler, personal communication, 1968]; Fitzroy Is., Magnetic Is. [Storr, 1973]; North West Is. [Cameron, 1969]; Heron Is. [Kikkawa, 1970]; One Tree Is. [Domm and Recher, 1973]

Myiagra rubecula (Latham, 1801)

Leaden Flycatcher: Albany Is. [Warham, 1962]; Escape River Mouth* [MacGillivray, 1910]; Raine Is., Ashmore Sandbanks [MacGillivray, 1918b]; Sir Charles Hardy Gp. [MacGillivray, 1910, 1918b]; Quoin Is., Forbes Is. [MacGillivray, 1918]; Cape Restoration Is.* [MacGillivray, 1910]; Recapolis Rf. [Warham, 1962]; Willis Is. [J. N. Butler, personal communication, 1968]; Green

Is. [Kikkawa, unpublished]; Dunk Is.* [Tarr, 1948; Austin, 1950]; Magnetic
Is.* [Alexander, 1926; Enwright, 1940]; Whitsunday Gp.* [Marshall, 1934;
Brown, 1949]; Capricorn Gp. [Campbell and White, 1910]; Heron Is. [Kik-
kawa, 1970]; Fairfax Is. [Booth, 1970]

Myiagra ruficollis (Vieillot, 1818)
  Broad-billed Flycatcher: Haggerstone Is.* [MacGillivray, 1918b]; Dunk Is.*
  [Tarr, 1948]

Piezorhynchus alecto (Temminck and Laugier, 1827)
  Shining Flycatcher: Dunk Is.* [Tarr, 1948]; Magnetic Is.* [Lavery and Hopkins,
  1963]

Seisura inquieta (Latham, 1801)
  Restless Flycatcher: Fairfax Is. [Booth, 1970](?)

(Pachycephalinae)
Colluricincla harmonica (Latham, 1801)
  Grey Shrike-Thrush: Dunk Is.* [Tarr, 1948]

Colluricincla megarhyncha (Quoy and Gaimard, 1830)
  Rufous Shrike-Thrush: Escape River Mouth* [MacGillivray, 1910]; Fitzroy Is.*
  [Warham, 1962]; Dunk Is.* [Le Souëf, 1915; Tarr, 1948; Austin, 1950]; Bar-
  nard Gp., Palm Is. [Storr, 1973]; Magnetic Is.* [Lavery and Hopkins, 1963];
  Whitsunday Gp.* [Marshall, 1934; Roberts, 1957]

Pachycephala melanura Gould, 1842
  Mangrove Golden Whistler: Cairncross Is. [Storr, 1973]; Clerke Is.* [Warham,
  1962]; Haggerstone Is.* [MacGillivray, 1918b; Galbraith, 1967]; Whitsunday
  Gp. [Brown, 1949; Galbraith, 1967]

Pachycephala pectoralis (Latham, 1801)
  Golden Whistler: Goold Is. [Storr, 1973]; Whitsunday Gp. [Marshall, 1934]

Pachycephala rufiventris (Latham, 1801)
  Rufous Whistler: Dunk Is.* [Tarr, 1948; Austin, 1950]; Magnetic Is.* [Alex-
  ander, 1926; Enwright, 1940]; Hayman Is.*, Hook Is.* [Brown, 1949]; Pine
  Islet* [Makin, 1961]; North West Is. [MacGillivray, 1931]; Wreck Is. [Booth,
  1970]; Heron Is. [Campbell and White, 1910; Kikkawa, 1970]; One Tree Is.
  [Domm and Recher, 1973]; Masthead Is. [Campbell and White, 1910]; Fairfax
  Is. [Booth, 1970]

Pachycephala griseiceps Gray, 1858
  Grey Whistler: Dunk Is.* [Tarr, 1948; Austin, 1950]

(Rhipidurinae)
Rhipidura fuliginosa (Sparrman, 1787)
  Grey Fantail: Dunk Is. [Austin, 1950]; Magnetic Is. [Alexander, 1926]; Hayman
  Is.* [Brown, 1949]; Heron Is. [Kikkawa, 1970]; One Tree Is. [Domm and
  Recher, 1973]

Rhipidura leucophrys (Latham, 1801)
  Willie Wagtail: Magnetic Is. [Storr, 1973]; Hayman Is.* [Brown, 1949; Storr,
  1973]; Whitsunday Gp.* [Roberts, 1957]; Saumarez Rf. [Heatwole, 1968]; North
  West Is. [MacGillivray, 1931]; Heron Is. [Roberts, 1957]

Rhipidura rufifrons (Latham, 1801)
  Rufous Fantail: Albany Is. [Warham, 1962]; Sir Charles Hardy Gp., Cape Restoration Is.* [MacGillivray, 1910]; Barnard Gp. [Storr, 1973]; Dunk Is.* [Austin,
  1950]; Magnetic Is.* [Enwright, 1940]; Heron Is. [Kikkawa, 1970]

Rhipidura rufiventris (Vieillot, 1818)

Northern Fantail: Hope Is. [Le Souëf, 1897]; Dunk Is.* [Austin, 1950]; Fairfax Is. [Booth, 1970](?)

Dicaeidae

Dicaeum hirundinaeum (Shaw and Nodder, 1792)

Mistletoe Bird: Albany Is.* [Warham, 1962]; Escape River Mouth* [MacGillivray, 1910]; Turtle Head Is. [Storr, 1973]; Dunk Is.* [Tarr, 1948; Austin, 1950]; Magnetic Is.* [Alexander, 1926; Enwright, 1940]; Hayman Is. [Brown, 1949; Storr, 1973]; Whitsunday Gp.* [Marshall, 1934]; Cumberland Gp.* [Roberts, 1957]

Nectariniidae

Nectarinia jugularis (Linnaeus, 1766)

Yellow-breasted Sunbird: Darnley Is., Keats Is., East Strait Is. [Storr, 1973]; Albany Is.*, Cypheny Is.*, Clerke Is.* [Warham, 1962]; Eborac Is., Turtle Head Is., Forbes Is., Lloyd Bay Is. [Storr, 1973]; Escape River Mouth* [MacGillivray, 1910]; Flinders Gp.* [Hull, 1925]; Green Is.* [Storr, 1973; Kikkawa, unpublished]; Little Fitzroy Is.*, Russell Is.* [Warham, 1962]; Dunk Is.* [Le Souëf, 1915; Tarr, 1948; Austin, 1950]; South Brook Is.* [Warham, 1962]; Palm Is. [Storr, 1973]; Magnetic Is.* [Alexander, 1926; Enwright, 1940; Hopkins, 1948; Lavery, and Hopkins, 1963]; Whitsunday Gp.* [MacGillivray, 1852; Marshall, 1934; Brown, 1949]; Cumberland Gp.* [Roberts, 1957]

Zosteropidae

Zosterops citrinella Bonaparte, 1850

Pale Silvereye: Island near Darnley Is.* [MacGillivray, 1914; Campbell, 1932]; Warrior Is.* [MacGillivray, 1918b; Mack, 1932]; Sue Is.* [Campbell, 1932]; Cairncross Is.* [MacGillivray, 1914; Mack, 1932]; Eborac Is., Cape Grenville Is. [Storr, 1973]; Haggerstone Is.* [MacGillivray, 1918b; Ashby, 1925]; Forbes Is.* [MacGillivray, 1918b; Ashby, 1925]; Quoin Is. [Mees, 1969]; Murray Is.* [Campbell, 1932]; Palfrey Is. [Warham, 1962]; Eagle Islet [Mees, 1969]

Zosterops lateralis (Latham, 1801)

Grey-breasted Silvereye: Low Is.* [MacGillivray, 1852]; Green Is.* [White, 1946; Kikkawa, 1973]; Magnetic Is.* [Alexander, 1926]; Whitsunday, Gp.* [Hull, 1925; Marshall, 1934; Brown, 1949]; Cumberland Gp.* [Roberts, 1957]; Capricorn Gp.* [Campbell and White, 1910; Mees, 1969]; North West Is.* [Campbell and White, 1910; Gilbert, 1925; MacGillivray, 1926, 1928, 1931; Cooper, 1948; Cameron, 1969]; Tryon Is.* [Campbell and White, 1910; Gilbert, 1925; MacGillivray, 1926, 1928; Cooper, 1948]; Wilson Is.* [Gilbert, 1925; MacGillivray, 1926, 1928; Cooper, 1948; Kikkawa, unpublished]; Wreck Is.* [Cooper, 1948; Booth, 1970]; Heron Is.* [MacGillivray, 1928; Cooper, 1948; D'Ombrain, 1964; Keast, 1966; Kikkawa, 1970]; Erskine Is.* [Cooper, 1948]; One Tree Is.* [MacGillivray, 1928; Cooper, 1948; Domm and Recher, 1973]; Masthead Is.* [Cooper, 1948]; Lady Musgrave Is.* [MacGillivray, 1928; Booth, 1970]; Hoskyn Is. [Storr, 1973]; Fairfax Is. [Booth, 1970]

Zosterops lutea Gould, 1843

Yellow Silvereye: Kent Is. (North Barnard Is.) [Le Souëf, 1891](?)

Meliphagidae

Lichmera indistincta (Vigors and Horsfield, 1827)

Brown Honeyeater: Percy Is. [Storr, 1973]; North Is.* (Keppel Gp.) [Wolstenholme, 1925]; Heron Is. [Kikkawa, 1970]; Fairfax Is. [Booth, 1970](?)

Meliphaga fasciogularis (Gould, 1851)

Mangrove Honeyeater; Green Is.* [Cornwall, 1909]; Dunk Is.* [Le Souëf, 1915; Austin, 1950]; Whitsunday Gp.* [Brown, 1949]; Victor Is.* [Cornwall, 1909]; One Tree Is. [Domm and Recher, 1973]

Meliphaga gracilis (Gould, 1866)
Graceful Honeyeater: Whitsunday Gp.° [Marshall, 1934; Gannon, 1962]

Meliphaga notata (Gould, 1867)
Lesser Lewin Honeyeater: Albany Is., Turtle Head Is. [Storr, 1973]; Escape River Mouth*, Night Is.* [MacGillivray, 1910]; Dunk Is.* [Tarr, 1948; Austin, 1950; Gannon, 1962]; Bird Is.* (Cape York) [MacGillivray, 1910]

Meliphaga versicolor (Gould, 1842)
Varied Honeyeater: Albany Is., Cairncross Is. [Storr, 1973]; Bushy Is.*, Hannibal Gp.*, Macarthur Is.*, Bird Is.* (Cape York) [MacGillivray, 1914]; Clarke Is.* [Warham, 1962]; Lloyd Bay Is.* [MacGillivray, 1910, 1918b]; King Is.*, Pipon Is.*, Morris Is.*, Sinclair Is., Coquet Is.*, Pethebridge Is.*, Three Isles* [Warham, 1962]; Hope Is.* [Le Souëf, 1897]; Low Is.* [Young, 1929; White, 1946; Warham, 1962]; Green Is., Double Is., Frankland Is., South Barnard Is. [Storr, 1973]; Dunk Is.* [Tarr, 1948; Austin, 1950]; North Is.* (Keppel Gp.) [Sharland, 1925; Wolstenholme, 1925]; Victor Is., South Molle Is. [Storr, 1973]

Meliphaga virescens (Vieillot, 1817)
Singing Honeyeater; Flinders Gp. [Hull, 1925]; Dunk Is.* [Tarr, 1948]

Myzomela dibapha (Latham, 1801)
Scarlet Honeyeater: Clerke Is. [Warham, 1962]

Myzomela erythrocephala Gould, 1839
Red-headed Honeyeater: Haggerstone Is.° [MacGillivray, 1918b]

Myzomela obscura Gould, 1842
Dusky Honeyeater: Mai Is. [Storr, 1973]; Dunk Is.* [Le Souëf, 1915; Tarr, 1948; Austin, 1950]; Magnetic Is.* [Alexander, 1926; Enwright, 1940]; Hayman Is.*, Hook Is.*, South Molle* (Whitsunday Gp.) [Brown, 1949]; Cumberland Gp.* [Roberts, 1957]

Philemon argenticeps (Gould, 1839)
Silver-crowned Friar-Bird: Magnetic Is. [Lavery and Hopkins, 1963]

Philemon citreogularis (Gould, 1837)
Little Friar-Bird: Heron Is. [Kikkawa, 1970; Booth, 1970]

Philemon corniculatus (Latham, 1790)
Noisy Friar-Bird: Dunk Is.* [Tarr, 1948]; Magnetic Is.* [Enwright, 1940]; North Is.* (Keppel Gp.) [Wolstenholme, 1925]

Philemon novaeguineae (Muller, 1843)
Helmeted Friar-Bird: Magnetic Is.° [Alexander, 1926; Hopkins, 1948]; Whitsunday Gp.* [Marshall, 1934]

Plectorhyncha lanceolata Gould, 1838
Striped Honeyeater: Goold Is. [Gannon, 1962]

Ramsayornis modesta (Gray, 1858)
Brown-backed Honeyeater: Dunk Is.° [Tarr, 1948]; Goold Is. [Storr, 1973]
Estrildidae
Aegintha temporalis (Latham, 1801)
Red-browned Finch: Magnetic Is.° [Enwright, 1940]

Erythrura trichroa (Kittlitz, 1835)
Blue-faced Finch: Lloyd Bay Is. [MacGillivray, 1918; Marshall, 1948]; Double Is. [Storr, 1973]

Lonchura castaneothorax (Gould, 1837)
    Chestnut-breasted Finch: Albany Is., Mai Is. [Storr, 1973]; Cypheny Is.* [Warham, 1962]
Lonchura pectoralis (Gould, 1840)
    Pictorella Finch: Willis Is. [Serventy, 1959; J. N. Butler, personal communication, 1968](?)
Stizoptera bichenovii (Vigors and Horsfield, 1827)
    Banded Finch: Magnetic Is.* [Enwright, 1940]
Taeniopygia guttata (Vieillot, 1817)
    Zebra Finch: North Is. (Keppel Gp.) [Sharland, 1925; Wolstenholme, 1925]
Proceidae
Passer domesticus (Linnaeus, 1758)
    House Sparrow (introduced): One Tree Is. [Domm and Recher, 1973]; Lady Elliot Is.* [Fien, 1971]
Sturnidae
Aplonis metallica (Temminck, 1824)
    Australian Shining Starling: Raine Is., Lloyd Bay Is. [MacGillivray, 1918b]; Dunk Is.* [Banfield, 1913; Le Souëf, 1915; Tarr, 1948; Austin, 1950]; South Brook Is.* [Warham, 1962]; Whitsunday Gp. [Roberts, 1957]
Sturnus vulgaris Linnaeus, 1758
    Starling (introduced): Lloyd Bay Is., Dunk Is., South Brook Is., Whitsunday Is. [Storr, 1973]; Heron Is. [Kikkawa, 1970]; One Tree Is. [Domm and Recher, 1973]
Oriolidae
Oriolus flavocinctus (Vigors, 1826)
    Yellow Oriole: Dunk Is. [Tarr, 1948]
Oriolus sagittatus (Latham, 1801)
    Olive-backed Oriole: Claremont Is. [Storr. 1973]; Dunk Is. [Austin, 1950]; Magnetic Is.* [Enwright, 1940]; Pine Islet* [Makin, 1961]; North West Is. [Cameron, 1969]; Heron Is. [Kikkawa, 1970]; Fairfax Is. [Booth, 1970]
Sphecotheres flaviventris Gould, 1850
    Yellow Figbird: Albany Is. [Storr, 1973]; Dunk Is.* [Tarr, 1948]; Palm Is. [Storr, 1973]; Magnetic Is.* [Enwright, 1940]
Sphecotheres vieilloti Vigors and Horsfield, 1827
    Southern Figbird: Magnetic Is.* [Alexander, 1926; Enwright, 1940]; Heron Is. [Kikkawa, 1970]; Fairfax Is. [Booth, 1970](?)
Dicruridae
Dicrurus hottentottus (Linnaeus, 1766)
    Spangled Drongo: Dunk Is. [Le Souëf, 1915; Tarr, 1948; Austin 1950]; South Brook Is. [Warham, 1962]; Palm Is. [Storr, 1973]; Magnetic Is.* [Le Souëf, 1894]; Whitsunday Gp. [Marshall, 1934; Brown, 1949]; Hook Is. [Storr, 1973]; Cumberland Gp.* [Roberts, 1957]; North West Is. [Cameron, 1969]; Heron Is. [Kikkawa, 1970]; One Tree Is. [Domm and Recher, 1973]
Grallinidae
Grallina cyanoleuca (Latham, 1801)
    Magpie Lark: Willis Is. [Serventy, 1959; J. N. Butler, personal communication, 1968]; Low Is. [Young, 1929]; Dunk Is.* [Tarr, 1948]; Magnetic Is.* [Alexander, 1926; Enwright, 1940]; Hayman Is.* [Brown, 1949]; North West Is. [Cameron, 1969]; Wreck Is. [Booth, 1970]; Heron Is. [Kikkawa, 1970]; One Tree Is. [Domm and Recher, 1973]

Artamidae
Artamus leucorhynchus (Linnaeus, 1771)
  White-breasted Wood-swallow: Cypheny Is.*, Clerke Is.* [Warham, 1962];
  Haggerstone Is.*, Lloyd Bay Is.* [MacGillivray, 1918b]; Cape Restoration Is.*,
  Night Is.* [MacGillivray, 1910]; Waterwitch Rf., Hannah Is.*, King Is.*,
  Pipon Is., South Barrow Is.*, Pethebridge Is.* Three Isles* [Warham, 1962];
  Low Is. [Young, 1929; White, 1946]; Woody Is., Green Is.* [White, 1946];
  Little Fitzroy Is.*, Russell Is.*, Kent Is.* (North Barnard Is.), White Rock*
  [Warham, 1962]; Dunk Is.* [Le Souëf, 1915; Tarr, 1948; Austin, 1950];
  Whitsunday Gp.* [Marshall, 1934]; Taffy Is.* [Austin, 1908]; Fairfax Is.
  [Booth, 1970]
Artamus personatus (Gould, 1841)
  Masked Wood-Swallow: Dunk Is., Daydream Is. [Banfield, 1906; Brown, 1949]
Cracticidae
Cracticus nigrogularis (Gould, 1837)
  Pied Butcher-bird: Little Fitzroy Is.* [Warham, 1962]; Magnetic Is.* [En-
  wright, 1940]
Cracticus quoyi (Lesson, 1827)
  Black Butcher-bird: Escape River Mouth* [MacGillivray, 1910]; Kent Is.*
  (North Barnard Is.) [Le Souëf, 1891]
Gymnorhina tibcen (Latham, 1801)
  Black-backed Magpie: Dunk Is. [Banfield, 1913]
Strepera graculina (White, 1790)
  Pied Currawong: Dunk Is. [Austin, 1950]; Magnetic Is.* [Alexander, 1926; En-
  wright, 1940; Hopkins, 1948; Lavery and Hopkins, 1963]; Whitsunday Gp.*
  [Marshall, 1934; Brown, 1949; Roberts, 1957]; Cumberland Gp.* [Austin,
  1908; Roberts, 1957]; Percy Is.* [White, 1922]; Capricorn Gp.* [Campbell
  and White, 1910]; North West Is.* [Gilbert, 1925; MacGillivray, 1926, 1928,
  1931; Cooper, 1948; Cameron, 1969]; Tryon Is.*, Heron Is.* [MacGillivray,
  1928]; Masthead Is.* [Barrett, 1919]
Ptilonorhynchidae
Ailuroedus crassirostris (Paykull, 1815)
  Green Catbird: Wreck Is. [Booth, 1970]
Chlamydera nuchalis (Jardine and Selby, 1830)
  Great Bower-Bird: Whitsunday Gp.* [Thorogood, 1941]
Paradisaeidae
Phonygammus keraudrenii (Lesson and Garnot, 1826)
  Manucode: Albany Is.* [Warham, 1962]; Dunk Is. [Chisholm, 1961]
Ptiloris magnificus (Vieillot, 1819)
  Magnificent Rifle-Bird: Albany Is.* [Warham, 1962]
Ptiloris victoriae Gould, 1850
  Victoria Rifle-Bird: Kent Is.* (North Barnard Is.) [Le Souëf, 1891]; Kent Is.
  Is. (Barnard Gp.) [MacGillivray, 1852]
Corvidae
Corvus coronoides Vigors and Horsfield, 1827
  Australian Raven: Whitsunday Gp. [Marshall, 1934]
Corvus orru Bonaparte, 1851
  Australian Crow: Flinders Gp*, Armit Is.* [Hull, 1925]; Hayman Is.* [Brown,
  1949]; Cumberland Gp.* [Austin, 1908; Roberts, 1957]; Cape Palmerston Is.*

Austin, 1908]; Percy Is.* [Coppinger, 1883]; Temple Is. [Storr, 1973]; North Is.* (Keppel Gp.) [Sharland, 1925]

Appendix References

Alexander, W. B. (1920). *Emu* 20, 14–24.
Alexander, W. B. (1925a). *Rep. Gt. Barrier Reef Comm.* 1, 47–51.
Alexander, W. B. (1925b). *Emu* 25, 120–121.
Alexander, W. B. (1926). *Emu* 25, 245–260.
Alexander, W. B. (1928). *Emu* 27, 286–287.
Amiet, L. (1956). *Emu* 56, 95–99.
Amiet, L. (1957). *Emu* 57, 236–254.
Amiet, L. (1958). *Notornis* 7, 219–230.
Ashby, E. (1925). *Emu* 25, 112–119.
Austin, C. N. (1950). *Emu* 49, 226–231.
Austin, T. P. (1908). *Emu* 7, 176–178.
Banfield, E. J. (1906). *Emu* 6, 14–15.
Banfield, E. J. (1913). "My Tropic Isle," 3rd ed. Fisher Unwin, London.
Barnard, H. (1892). *Victorian Natur., Melbourne* 9, 7–8.
Barrett, C. (1919). "In Australian Wilds," Chapter X, pp. 200–222. Melbourne Publ., Melbourne, Australia.
Booth, J. (1970). *Sunbird* 1, 85–92.
Brown, A. G. (1949). *Emu* 49, 44–49.
Bryant, C. E. (1933). *Emu* 32, 294–297.
Busst, J. (1956). *Emu* 56, 437–438.
Cameron, A. C. (1969). *Queensl. Natur.* 19, 99.
Campbell, A. G. (1932). *Emu* 32, 91–94.
Campbell, A. J., and White, S. A. (1910). *Emu* 10, 195–204.
Chisholm, A. H. (1961). *Emu* 61, 195.
Cooper, R. P. (1948). *Emu* 48, 107–126.
Coppinger, R. W. (1883). "Cruise of *Alert*—Four Years in Patagonian, Polynesian and Mascarene Waters (1878–82)," Chapter IX, pp. 180–193. W. Swan Sonnenschein and Co., London.
Cornwall, E. M. (1903). *Emu* 3, 45–47.
Cornwall, E. M. (1909). *Emu* 8, 138–141.
Cornwall, E. M. (1910). *Emu* 9, 138–141.
Cribb, A. B. (1969). *Queensl. Natur.* 19, 82–85.
Davis, J. K. (1923a). *Emu* 22, 180–187.
Davis, J. K. (1923b). "Willis Island—A Storm Warning Station in the Coral Sea," pp. 105–111. Critchley Parker Hayes, Melbourne, Australia.
D'Ombrain, A. F. (1964). *Emu* 63, 334–335.
Domm, S., and Recher, H. F. (1973). *Sunbird* 4, 63–86.
Enwright, W. J. (1940). *Emu* 40, 167–169.
Fien, I. (1971). *Sunbird* 2, 63–67.
Forbes, W. A. (1878). *Challenger Rep., Zool.* 2(8), 84–93.
Galbraith, I. C. J. (1967). *Emu* 66, 289–294.
Gannon, G. R. (1962). *Emu* 62, 145–166.
Gilbert, P. A. (1925). *Aust. Zool.* 4, 210–226.

Gillett, K., and McNeill, F. (1959). "The Great Barrier Reef and Adjacent Isles." Coral Press, Sydney, Australia.

Gillham, M. E. (1961). *Proc. Roy. Soc. Queensl.* **73**, 79–92.

Hamilton-Smith, E. (1965). *Emu* **65**, 152–155.

Heatwole, H. (1968). *Emu* **68**, 132.

Heatwole, H. (1971). *Ecology* **52**, 363–366.

Hedley, C. (1906). *Proc. Linn. Soc. N.S.W.* **31**, 453–479.

Hedley, C. (1926). *Emu* **25**, 280–281.

Hindwood, K. A. (1944). *Emu* **44**, 41–43.

Hindwood, K. A. (1945). *Emu* **44**, 241–248.

Hindwood, K. A., Keith, K., and Serventy, D. L. (1963). *CSIRO Div. Wildl. Res. Tech. Pap.* **3.**

Hitchcock, W. B. (1965). *Emu* **64**, 157–171.

Hogan, J. (1925). *Emu* **24**, 266–275.

Hopkins, N. (1948). *Emu* **47**, 331–348.

Hull, A. F. B. (1925). *Aust. Zool.* **4**, 9–16.

Jackson, S. W. (1909). *Emu* **8**, 233–283.

Jardine, F. L. (1904). *Emu* **3**, 181–185.

Jones, J. (1943). *Emu* **43**, 107–112.

Jukes, J. B. (1847). "Narrative of the Surveying Voyage of H.M.S. *Fly*," Vol. 1. Boone, London.

Keast, A. (1966). "Australia and the Pacific Islands." Random House, New York.

Kikkawa, J. (1969). *Queensl. Littoral Soc. Newslett.* **30**, 1–8.

Kikkawa, J. (1970). *Sunbird* **1**, 34–47.

Kikkawa, J. (1973). *Sunbird* **4**, 30–37.

Lavery, H. J. (1969). "List of Birds in Queensland." Winston Churchill Memorial Trust, Canberra.

Lavery, H. J., and Grimes, R. J. (1971). *Queensl. Agr. J.* **97**, 106–113.

Lavery, H. J., and Hopkins, N. (1963). *Emu* **63**, 242–252.

Lawry, K. (1926). *Emu* **26**, 69–71.

Le Souëf, D. (1891). *Victorian Natur., Melbourne* **8**, 148–164.

Le Souëf, D. (1894). *Victorian Natur., Melbourne* **11**, 3–29.

Le Souëf, D. (1897). *Victorian Natur., Melbourne* **14**, 19–34.

Le Souëf, D. (1915). *Emu* **14**, 163–166.

McBride, G., Parer, I. P., and Foenander, F. (1969). *Anim. Behav. Monogr.* **2**, 127–181.

McGill, A. R., and Keast, J. A. (1945). *Emu* **44**, 202–216.

MacGillivray, J. (1846). *Zoologist* **4**, 1473–1481.

MacGillivray, J. (1852). "Narrative of the Voyage of H.M.S. *Rattlesnake*," Boone, London (facsimile ed., 1967).

MacGillivray, W. (1910). *Emu* **10**, 216–233.

MacGillivray, W. (1914). *Emu* **13**, 132–186.

MacGillivray, W. (1917). *Emu* **17**, 63–87.

MacGillivray, W. (1918a). *Emu* **17**, 145–148.

MacGillivray, W. (1918b). *Emu* **17**, 180–212.

MacGillivray, W. (1926). *Emu* **25**, 229–238.

MacGillivray, W. (1927). *Emu* **27**, 92–101.

MacGillivray, W. (1928). *Emu* **27**, 230–249.

MacGillivray, W. (1931). *Emu* **30**, 270–276.

Mack, G. (1932). *Emu* **31**, 290–301.

McNeill, F. (1946). *Aust. Mus. Mag.* **9**, 99–104.

Makin, D. (1961). *Emu* **61**, 139–141.

Marshall, A. J. (1934). *Emu* **34**, 36–44.

Marshall, A. J. (1948). *Emu* **47**, 305–310.

Mees, G. F. (1969). *Zool. Verh.* **102**, 86–88, 276–278, and 323.

Miles, J. A. R. (1964). *Emu* **63**, 420–421.

Moseley, H. N. (1892). "Notes by a Naturalist—An Account of Observations Made during the Voyage of H.M.S. *Challenger* Round the World in the Years 1872–1876 under the Command of Capt. Sir. G. S. Nares and Capt. F. T. Thomson," pp. 299–302. Murray, London.

Napier, S. E. (1928). "On the Barrier Reef—Notes from an Oologist's Pocketbook," pp. 41–67. Angus and Robertson, Sydney, Australia.

Nebe, J. (1928). *Queensl. Natur.* **6**, 102–108.

Nebe, J. (1932). *Queensl. Natur.* **8**, 54–59.

Norris, A. Y. (1967). *Emu* **67**, 33–55.

Recher, H. F. (1972a). *Emu* **72**, 126–130.

Recher, H. F. (1972b). *Ibis.* **114**, 552–555.

Recher, H. F., and Recher, J. A. (1969). *Aust. Natur. Hist.* **16**, 151–155.

Recher, H. F., and Recher, J. A. (1972). *Emu* **72**, 85–90.

Reid, A. J. (1965). *Emu* **64**, 99–100.

Reithmüller, E. (1931). *Emu* **31**, 142–146.

Roberts, P. E. (1957). *Emu* **57**, 303–310.

Saunders, H. (1878). *Challenger Rep. Zool.* **2**(8), 133–140.

Sclater, P. L., and Salvin, O. (1878). *Challenger Rep., Zool.* **2**(8), 117–132.

Serventy, D. L. (1944). *Emu* **43**, 274–280.

Serventy, D. L. (1952). *Emu* **52**, 105–116.

Serventy, D. L., Serventy, V., and Warham, J. (1971). "The Handbook of Australian Sea-Birds." A. H. and A. W. Reed, Sydney, Australia.

Serventy, V. (1959). *Emu* **59**, 167–176.

Sharland, M. S. R. (1925). *Emu* **24**, 229–230.

Shipway, A. K. (1969). *Emu* **69**, 108–109.

Slater, P. (1970). "A Field Guide to Australian Birds: Non-Passerines." Rigby, Adelaide, Australia.

Storr, G. M. (1973). "List of Queensland Birds." Western Australian Museum, Perth, Australia.

Tarr, H. E. (1948). *Emu* **48**, 8–13.

Tarr, H. E. (1950). *Emu* **49**, 189–198.

Thorogood, H. (1941). *Emu* **40**, 418–419.

Warham, J. (1959). *Emu* **59**, 154–158.

Warham, J. (1961). *Emu* **61**, 77–93.

Warham, J. (1962). *Emu* **62**, 99–111.

Wheeler, W. R., and Watson, I. (1963). *Emu* **63**, 99–173.

White, H. L., (1922). *Emu* **21**, 164–167.

White, S. R. (1946). *Emu* **46**, 81–122.

Wodzicki, K., and Stein, P. (1958). *Emu* **58**, 289–312.

Wolstenholme, H. (1925). *Emu* **24**, 230–235 and 243–251.

Yonge, C. M. (1930). "A Year on the Great Barrier Reef." Putnam, New York.

Young, J. E. (1929). *Queensl. Natur.* **7**, 6–12.

10

TURTLES OF CORAL REEFS AND CORAL ISLANDS

H. Robert Bustard

I. Introduction

The world's seven species of sea turtles are grouped into two families and five genera. Only three species commonly frequent coral reefs and their associated cays to feed and/or nest; these are the green turtle, *Chelonia mydas* (L.), the hawksbill or tortoise-shell turtle, *Eretmochelys imbricata* (L.), and the loggerhead, *Caretta caretta* (L.).

II. Food

Turtles are such an integral part of coral reef ecology that it is surprising that so little ecological work has been carried out on the group. For instance, nothing is known about their efficiency of converting energy within the reef community and no precise data are available about their role in grazing or in the reef food chains.

All hatchling turtles are carnivorous, feeding on small animals in the plankton. So far as is known, young of all species go through a planktonic

343

phase far out to sea. During early life they are extremely buoyant and poor divers. Observations on juveniles during the first year of life are virtually nonexistent once they enter the sea, minutes after emerging from the nest. Failure to recapture individuals as a result of local inshore effort in several countries is further evidence for dispersal at sea. There are only two literature records referring to substantial recaptures of young in their first year. One (Hughes, 1965) referred to the leathery turtle (*Dermochelys coriacea*) and the other to the loggerhead (Bustard, 1975b). Following storms in early winter, large numbers of loggerheads aged between $1\frac{1}{2}$ and $3\frac{1}{2}$ months are washed ashore on Perth beaches in Western Australia and on the south coast of that state between Augusta and Denmark. Presumably these are carried south from nesting grounds to the north on the slow current that passes along the coast of Western Australia in winter.

In the green turtle the carnivorous hatchling phase is said to change, at about one year of age, to the adult herbivorous diet consisting of marine algae, including representatives of the genera *Zostera, Thallassina, Enhalus, Posidonia,* and *Halodule* (Parsons, 1962; Hirth and Carr, 1970). In the Galapagos green turtles are said to feed extensively on mangrove leaves (Colnett, 1798; von Hagen, 1949). Although it is certainly true on the basis of the small amount of data available that adult green turtles are overwhelmingly vegetarian in most parts of the world, they will still accept animal food. In captivity, these turtles have usually been fed entirely on fish or meat. At the southern end of the Barrier Reef, I have often seen them attacking large jellyfish on the surface. In some years there may be vast numbers of jellyfish and on occasions many of them have pieces similar to the shape of a turtle's jaws bitten from their bells.

Loggerheads will readily attack these jellyfish too, but it is known that this species remains predominantly carnivorous throughout life. The food of the loggerhead includes crabs, shellfish, fish, sponges, jellyfish, and sometimes algae (Carr, 1952). I possess the remains of a clam (*Tridacna fossor*) that was taken by a loggerhead on the Great Barrier Reef. The turtle literally bit one valve of the shell in half, despite a shell thickness of 8 mm. In view of this it seems likely that loggerheads would readily crunch up coral to gain access to prey detected hiding beneath or among coral. Since specimens of *T. fossor* occur embedded in coral, similar behavior is usually necessary to secure them. Undoubtedly, the large populations of loggerheads that migrate to favored coral cays for nesting and spend at least three to four months in the vicinity must impose quite a substantial drain on the local food supplies.

This is assuming that they feed normally during the nesting season. Certainly there is no reason to believe that the attendant males do not feed.

The hawksbill turtle becomes omnivorous after the hatchling phase. On the basis of scant data, the hawksbill is considered to feed largely on mollusks, crustaceans, ascidians, jellyfish, and marine algae (Carr, 1952). The hooked jaws of the hawksbill are well adapted to prying mollusks or crustaceans out of crevices in or around coral.

III. Predators

Turtles themselves provide food for other animals and, because they range from very small to very large, they may at some stage be eaten by an impressive list of carnivorous land and sea creatures. At hatching, Australian green turtles weigh about 22 gm and assuming a conservative maximum adult weight of 156 kg, then the increase in biomass during life is more than 7000-fold, which is of a similar order to figures proposed for large Cretaceous dinosaurs (Colbert, 1962).

Juvenile turtles face heavy predation during their dash from the nest to the sea on many of the world's nesting beaches. Hendrickson (1958) estimated loss of 40% of hatchlings in Sarawak due to terrestrial predators. In various parts of the world these include seabirds (especially gulls), mammals (including rats), pythons and other snakes, monitor lizards (*Varanus*), and land crabs (Hendrickson, 1958; Carr, 1968). Ghost crabs of the genus *Ocypode* (Fig. 1) are a particularly important predator as they can be extremely numerous, are active at night when most hatchlings are emerging, and are alert hunters.

Egg mortality may be even more severe. Despite the attempts made by the turtles to disguise the site where the eggs are buried, they fall prey to a host of animals, many of which rely on smell to detect them. These include ants of the genus *Dorylus* (Bass *et al.*, 1965) *Ocypode* crabs, monitor lizards (*Varanus*), dingoes and other wild dogs, foxes, pigs, peccaries, and racoons (Hendrickson, 1958; Carr, 1968). On Heron Island we have estimated terrestrial predation on hatchlings as a mere 4–5% and there is no egg predation (cf. figures given above by Carr and Hendrickson).

When hatchlings enter the sea at night one commonly hears sounds of attacks made on them by inshore fish. On entering the water the hatchlings make at once for the edge of the reef and many fall victim to carnivorous coral reef fish. The black-tipped reef shark (*Carcharhinus*

Fig. 1. A ghost crab (*Ocypode ceratophthalma*) eating a hatchling green turtle on a Great Barrier Reef cay.

spallanzani) is certainly one of the important predators on the Great Barrier Reef. I have recorded more than 20 freshly consumed hatchlings in the stomach of a single shark of this species measuring about 6 ft in total length. Once again, quantitative data are lacking, but it would seem that predation is particularly severe in the first few hours of life. The hatchlings are particularly vulnerable when crossing the shallow reef platform, since during this period they are readily detected by all nearby fish on the reef. Once they reach deeper water, the fact that they spend most time at the surface provides a degree of safety because only fish a short distance below are likely to notice them. Hatchling green turtles are black above and immaculate white below and this countershading undoubtedly reduces predation during the planktonic phase of life in the genus *Chelonia*. It would disguise them from fish below and from predaceous birds above (Bustard, 1970). However, countershading does not occur in all species of sea turtles, being absent from hawksbill and loggerhead hatchlings, for instance, which are, respectively, pale yellowish brown and brown to red-brown on both dorsal and ventral surfaces. Hatchling loggerheads may be even darker ventrally.

Predation continues throughout immature life in all species, but at a much reduced rate as the turtles increase in size. Hendrickson (1958) proposed that in Malaysia shallow water predators might destroy half the hatchlings in the first hour or so after entering the water and that loss during the subsequent first week at sea might account for a further 75%. Most authorities would agree with Hendrickson that most of this predation occurs within the first months of life, particularly within a matter of hours or days of entering the water. Survivorship is considered in more detail below but, even if one assumes survival into adulthood of 2–3 per thousand of the hatchling turtles, then the production of food for other predators is seen to be enormous.

Although it is true that they rapidly outgrow most potential predators, predation continues throughout life even for adults of large species such as green turtles and loggerheads. I have seen many adults with large pieces bitten from the carapace, usually at the rear. Sometimes it was obvious that the damage was recent. These injured areas may include a back limb bitten off high up the femur. Loss of, or extensive damage to, a rear limb is a common occurrence in both green and loggerhead turtles. Individuals also have been sighted emerging to nest with one front flipper missing at the shoulder. Damage of the kind described in this paragraph is assumed to be caused by shark predation. As pointed out by Hendrickson (1958), we see only those individuals that escape! We have no data on the frequency of attack or resultant mortality. I know of one eyewitness account in Australian waters of a large loggerhead that surfaced near a Queensland fisheries patrol vessel. Two tiger sharks (*Galeocerdo* sp.) and a hammerhead shark (*Sphyrna lewini*) closed in on the turtle and within a little over a minute only a pool of blood remained. Norman and Fraser (1948) described a shark attack on a large loggerhead. The shark was presumed to be a *Carcharodon*. An early Indonesian reference cited by Hendrickson (1958) described extensive slaughter of adult turtles on the breeding beaches by tigers and wild dogs (*Cuon javanicus*). Tigers also roamed the turtle beaches in Trengganu, Malaya (Hendrickson, 1958).

IV. Epiphytes and External Parasites

The boring barnacle, *Stephanolepas muricata*, attacks turtles and in some cases it may be so numerous as to seriously debilitate or perhaps even cause the death of the host. I have seen hawksbill carapaces riddled with its holes. Turtles also provide a settling site for other species of barnacles that colonize the carapace, flippers, or even the head. Barnacles are much more common on loggerheads than green turtles. They also occur frequently on hawksbills. The common species is *Chelonibia testudinaria*. The goose barnacle (*Lepas anatifera*) also sometimes occurs on turtles, particularly on hatchlings during their planktonic phase. Turtles also act as host to isopod crustaceans (including the genus *Eurydice*), which mainly occur under peeling scutes, particularly in the loggerhead, and to marine leeches of the genus *Ozobranchus*. Various algae may also grow on the carapace, particularly in the loggerhead.

V. Temperature Relationships

Turtles, like most reptiles, seek warm conditions whenever possible in order to elevate their body temperature. Most reptiles do this by absorption of radiant heat (basking in the sun) and under such conditions body temperatures may be of the order of 10–20°C above ambient shade temperatures. Turtles have reduced scope for behavioral thermoregulation in the water. However, adults of many species often spend hours at a time floating at the surface. Not only are they able to gain heat by radiation effects, but the surface water is also much warmer than bottom water, so that heat loss is reduced. When they dive to rest, usually under coral ledges with the head facing inwards, the low water temperatures at the bottom result in a slowing of metabolic activity and a reduced oxygen requirement.

The dark dorsal coloration of many species of hatchling turtles, for instance, green turtles and loggerheads, probably plays an important role in elevating the hatchling turtles' body temperature above that of the surrounding water during the first months of life when they spend most of their time floating at the surface. The hatchlings are extremely buoyant and at rest float with a considerable portion of the carapace out of the water. Parts of the head and front flippers are usually also exposed (Fig. 2). The figure illustrates one of two typical front flipper resting positions. In the other position the flippers are folded back on top of the edges of the carapace. Certainly the dark dorsal coloration increases absorption of radiant energy (Bustard, 1970). Increased body temperature will result in faster growth owing to a stimulatory effect on metabolism. A more rapid growth rate during an extremely vulnerable stage of the life history must have survival value. Hatchling green turtles start regular diving at 2–3 months of age when their weight has increased 60-fold to about 1200 gm. The black pigmentation is gradually lost with increase in size and regular diving so that at six months of age they

Fig. 2. Hatchling green turtle floating on the surface of the sea. The pale areas are above the water (Bustard, 1970).

are much lighter in dorsal coloration (O. L. Tanis, personal communication).

VI. Migration

Certain species of sea turtles undergo lengthy migrations. The extensive tagging carried out by Carr and associates on the green turtle in Costa Rica has resulted in recoveries of individuals from as far distant as Mexico adjacent to Yucatan, from off extreme southern Florida, and from Isla de Margarita, Venezuela (Carr, 1968). Green turtles tagged on Ascension Island, Atlantic Ocean, have been recaptured on the Brazilian coast (Carr, 1968). The shortest distance to the South American coast is about 1400 miles from Ascension and the journey involves crossing the Brazilian Basin where the sea is more than 5000 m deep. Tag recoveries from my own green turtle program on the Great Barrier Reef are shown in Fig. 3. There, the trend to move north after breeding is apparent. Some individuals were recaptured at great distances, the Papuan recapture being about 900 miles in a direct line, or after crossing areas of deep sea as in the case of the three New Caledonian recaptures.

Fig. 3. Recovery sites of green and loggerhead sea turtles tagged at Heron Island and adjacent cays and at Bundaberg on the mainland. Green turtles are indicated by continuous lines and loggerheads by broken lines. The lines do not necessarily indicate the route followed.

The loggerhead is also known to undergo lengthy migrations on the basis of limited tagging operations. Caldwell *et al.* (1959) recorded a recapture about 1000 shoreline miles from the place of tagging after about 302 days. The turtle was tagged at Hutchinson's Island opposite Jensen Beach, Martin County, Florida, and trawled off the mouth of the Mississippi River. Even by the most direct route this is a distance of about 750 miles. Hughes *et al.* (1967) reported a loggerhead recaptured at a distance of 1650 miles after only 91 days in South Africa and Hughes and Mentis (1967) reported the recapture of another loggerhead 1500 miles from the location of tagging in Tongaland, Natal, South

Africa. Bustard and Limpus (1970) recorded a loggerhead tagged near Bundaberg in southeast Queensland, Australia, and recaptured at the Trobriand Islands near Boli Point, Kiriwina, which is near Losuia. The recapture took place only about 63 days after the turtle was last sighted at Mon Repos beach near Bundaberg. The distance traveled in a straight line is 1100 miles and the probable course (plotted in Fig. 3) is 1200 miles. However, if the turtle followed the coastline the distance would have been about 2000 miles. Much of the journey would be against the current, since at that time of year the prevailing current is moving southward down the east coast of Australia. Bustard and Limpus (1975) recorded another loggerhead, tagged near Bundaberg, that went around Cape York peninsula into the Gulf of Carpentaria to Duyfken Point, which is about 20 miles WNW of Weipa. This is a minimum distance of 1350 miles from Bundaberg. The distances moved in a short time by both loggerhead and green turtles, often without assistance from, or indeed against the prevailing current, are a clear indication that these are active movements.

Turtles of both sexes and of all three species are seen around the reefs of the Capricorn cays throughout the year. This indicated that all turtles do not necessarily leave, although outside the breeding season numbers appear to be very greatly reduced. If the majority of the turtles marked while breeding remained in the general vicinity or dispersed randomly, one would expect most recaptures of them to occur off south and central Queensland where man's fishing and trawling effort is greatest. It is significant that there have only been three recaptures of them on the adjacent mainland and this, together with the general distribution of the recaptures shown in Fig. 3, strongly suggests that the spent animals travel long distances, that is, migrate, from the nesting grounds.

Tagging programs have indicated that turtles may return to the same beach to nest in subsequent nesting seasons (usually a few years later). Carr (1968) has provided a stimulating discussion of the navigational problems for turtles migrating to their nesting beaches. However, the percentage return has been puzzlingly low, especially when the probable longevity of adults is taken into account. The greatest number of returns for the green turtle was obtained by Carr for Costa Rica, where he recorded 447 returns at the nesting beach in subsequent years from a tagged population of 5758 individuals (A. Carr, personal communication, 1970). It is noteworthy that 55 of these returns occurred after intervals of between five and nine years (Carr and Carr, 1975). Of 635 green turtles tagged on Ascension Island, only eight were recaptured in the next nesting cycle (three after two years, and two after a four-year interval (A. Carr, personal communication, 1970). T. Harrisson (personal communication, 1970) recorded very few recaptures of tagged green turtles in subsequent years in the Sarawak turtle islands despite comprehensive work extending over more than a decade. Moreover, there was no human predation (for religious reasons) on the adult turtles. Harrisson states that the available data very strongly imply that, in Sarawak at least, green turtles participate in only two nesting cycles (assuming the tags remain in place). In the Capricorn cays of the Great Barrier Reef my team has tagged 3825 green turtles and 665 loggerheads, but so far only very few have been recaptured back at the nesting beaches. Those individuals recaptured, together with tags returned from turtles found elsewhere, have always shown the tag to be in excellent condition, so that tag loss cannot be an explanation.

Allowing for a time lapse of four years between nesting cycles, which is so far the most common interval between nesting cycles noted at Heron Island, a marked population of 859 green turtles (tagged previously at the island) was available for recapture there during the summers of 1968–1969 and 1969–1970, yet recaptures totaled only nine. From a sample of 139 green turtles tagged on Northwest Island four years previously, two recaptures were made there in 1969–1970 (no search was carried out there the previous year). Possible implications of the low recapture rate for green turtles are considered in Section IX.

If we assume a nesting cycle of no more than three years for the loggerheads on Heron Island, as is borne out by the data, we had 153 tagged and available for recapture there, yet we recorded only ten recaptures in subsequent nesting seasons. One individual returned after an absence of only a single year and nested again. This same individual was recaptured on its third (recorded) nesting cycle two years later.

There are seven islands in the Capricorn Group that are used by turtles and these are situated 8–17 miles from Heron Island. In view of this, it is noteworthy that despite mark–recapture operations on four of the islands during the summer of 1969–1970, all recaptures but one from previous years were made on the island where they were originally tagged. The exception, a loggerhead tagged on Heron, was recaptured eight miles distant on Wreck Island.

VII. Nesting

All species of sea turtles are well adapted to an aquatic way of life, with streamlined carapaces (cf. the highly domed carapaces of land tortoises) and flipperlike limbs. Male turtles never leave the water once they enter it, minutes after emerging from the nest. Female turtles normally leave the water only for nesting.

In an area of the Pacific, female green turtles have been recorded ashore lying in the sun on the beach (Dampier, 1717; Bryan, 1915; Fryke and Schweitzer, 1929; Kenyon and Rice, 1959). No one has suggested why this trait should be shown by only certain Pacific green turtle populations. Presumably it serves to elevate their body temperatures considerably above levels that they can attain by basking at the water's surface. Aborigines on Mornington Island in the Gulf of Carpentaria, Australia, who say the trait occurs there during winter, claim it is most pronounced during the mating season and is resorted to by the females to escape the attentions of the promiscuous males. Further investigation is required. Their aquatic adaptations make turtles clumsy on land. This is the case particularly with large green turtles. The green turtle progresses on land by synchronous movements of all four limbs, a pull–push movement by the fore and rear flippers, respectively, whereas loggerheads and hawksbills achieve much more efficient locomotion by the usual alternate limb movements of terrestrial quadrupeds.

Coral cays provide very important, although not the only, nesting grounds for green, loggerhead, and hawksbill turtles. In most of their range all three species show a marked preference for nesting on small remote islands as against mainland beaches. The vital importance of coral cays or small continental or oceanic islands in the biology of sea turtles is a result of this nesting pattern. Predation is always most severe on the mainland, followed by large islands that support a well diversified fauna. On small islands, particularly cays, the terrestrial vertebrate fauna is impoverished, hence egg and hatchling predation are likely to be low. For instance, on cays on the Great Barrier Reef there are usually no terrestrial vertebrates other than birds. In eastern Australia and northern Queensland all the most frequented nesting grounds occur on islands although a few secondary rookeries occur on the mainland. The preference for islands is clearly shown in the figures of counts made in a survey I conducted along the 3250 mile Queensland coastline and also on offshore islands in November–December, 1969. Of a count of 2077 freshly made turtle tracks, 252 (12%) occurred on mainland beaches and 1825 (88%) were on islands.

During the nesting sequence female turtles have to move up the beach to a position on the high beach platform above the spring high tide mark before laying their eggs. The positional cues used are imperfectly understood but, at the southern end of the Barrier Reef, green turtles will not nest in the absence of tall vegetation and all dig their nests within the vegetation zone. This ensures that nests are above the highest fortnightly tides. Having selected a nesting site, turtles of all species clear a depression of greater or lesser extent, termed the body pit, before commencing excavation of the pear-shaped chamber that will contain the eggs. The function of the body pit is presumably to reach moister sand in which it is possible to dig a narrow-necked hole straight downward with a reduced likelihood of cave-ins. Nesting success is greatly reduced during prolonged dry weather but tree rootlets help to bind the sand together resulting in success being achieved in the drier sand in which they are present. This situation is shown diagrammatically in Fig. 4 and was discussed at length by Bustard and Greenham (1968).

The body pit also results in the eggs being placed at a greater depth in the sand, since the egg chamber, which is dug to the full reach of the rear flippers, commences at the foot and rear of the body pit well below the level of the surrounding sand. The front flippers play the major role in construction of, and in subsequently filling in, the body pit. The egg chamber is dug entirely by the rear flippers (Fig. 5) and, after egg laying is complete, these are used to carefully pack sand over the egg mass. During the filling in process an attempt is

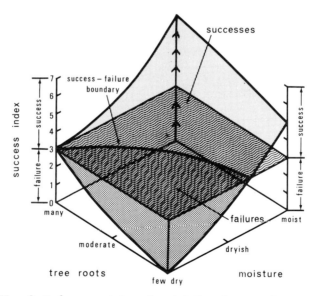

Fig. 4. Hypothetical representation of probability of success for egg chambers dug in sand with varying degrees of moisture and number of tree rootlets (Bustard and Greenham, 1968).

Fig. 5. A loggerhead turtle completing the excavation of its egg chamber on Wreck Cay, Great Barrier Reef.

made to disguise the location of the eggs by carrying the body pit forward, filling in behind, and digging out in front. This trait is particularly well developed in the green turtle, in which the body pit is frequently extended for three to four yards after egg laying, resulting in a very large area of disturbed sand (Fig. 6). There are considerable differences in the details of the nesting habits of the green turtle in various parts of the world (Deraniyagala, 1932; Moorhouse, 1933; Banks, 1937; Cozzolino, 1938; Hendrickson, 1958; Carr and Ogren, 1960; Bustard and Greenham, 1969; Hirth and Carr, 1970) and between the different genera [Caldwell *et al.* (1959) and Bustard *et al.* (1975) for *Caretta*, and Carr *et al.* (1966) and Hirth and Carr (1970) for *Eretmochelys*].

It follows that turtles play an important role in erosion of their favored nesting beaches, partly through their effect on the outer vegetation zone. Cays are dynamic entities constantly undergoing erosive and accretive processes and thereby changing shape. The vegetation of the bank region helps to consolidate the sand, thereby reducing erosion. Turtles potentiate erosive processes due to their destruction of the vegetation in this region. An examination of the outer vegetation fringing a cay that is an important turtle rookery during summer shows an absence of young bushes of *Scaevola, Messerschmidia, Pandanus,* and *Casuarina* trees.

Fig. 6. Area of disturbed sand following nesting by a single green turtle on a Great Barrier Reef cay.

Quite clearly, no regeneration is taking place in this zone of the cay. A somewhat more detailed examination will also indicate the destructive effect that green turtles have on the adult *Scaevola* and *Messerschmidia*. However, an examination of the same cay prior to the arrival of the turtles discloses an abundance of seedlings unless the season has been extremely dry. These seedlings, which will be particularly abundant on newly formed areas of high beach platform, are all destroyed after several weeks of turtle nesting activity on the cay. Further details are given by Bustard (1975d).

Turtles also directly undermine the bank and move sand seaward. The fortnightly spring high tides reach the bank and, where this is well developed, result in a pronounced cliffing effect. The first turtles to arrive thereafter are unable to climb the vertical section of the bank and are compelled to nest at the foot. In the process they dig into and undermine the bank, and also move sand seaward. These activities result in the bank being eroded back toward the interior of the island. Subsequent turtles are able to climb the inclined plane that results and either nest on the bank slope or on top of the bank, moving more sand seawards. If an erosive cycle is occurring, then this sand is removed by the next spring high tides and the process commences again. The

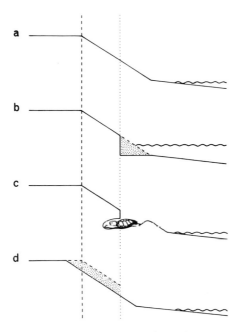

Fig. 7. A diagrammatic representation of the role of the green turtle in bank erosion on nesting cays. In each section of the figure the high beach platform, the bank (inclined slope), beach (very shallow slope), and the sea are indicated. Sand just displaced is dotted. (a) Situation at the start of an erosive cycle. (b) Cliffing of bank by fortnightly high tides. (c) Turtle, unable to climb bank, digs into base, and (d) undermines it, resulting in the top of the bank being shifted backward toward the center of the island, and the slope of the bank being restored to (a).

cycle is shown diagrammatically in Fig. 7. On small cays where nesting is particularly heavy, it may result in fairly rapid destruction of the nesting area (cay) as occurred at tiny Aves Cay in the eastern Caribbean (Carr, 1968).

VIII. Interactions with Terrestrial Animals

The adult turtles have few interactions with terrestrial animals. However, following extensive erosion of one area on Heron Island, green turtles were nesting in an area of mutton bird (*Puffinus pacificus*) nest burrows. Turtle activity had a most deleterious effect on the mutton birds (by digging into their burrows) and it appeared unlikely that any chicks were fledged in the area regularly invaded by nesting turtles.

Similarly, terns that nest on the ground on the high beach platform risk loss of their eggs from turtles moving up or down the beach. On Wreck Island the crested tern (*Sterna bergii*) rookery is, in fact, sited on a section of the high beach platform that is protected from turtle access by extensive large coral boulders on the seaward side.

IX. Population Biology

Much of the basic natural history of many species of sea turtles has been elucidated in the last 15 years, particularly as a result of the work of Carr (Carr, 1962; Carr and Giovannoli, 1957; Carr and Ogren, 1960; Carr *et al.*, 1966). Harrisson was responsible for the tag being used universally and for much research and conservation, especially of the green turtle (Harrisson, 1951, 1954, 1956) and Hendrickson (1958) has provided the most comprehensive paper on the green turtle. Working on a totally protected population in Australia, we have been able to lay the foundations of a detailed population ecology study in the last six years. The production side of the life table is now well known (Bustard, 1975a). During a nesting year, most species of sea turtles, including the green and loggerhead, lay several clutches of between 40 and 200 eggs each (there are inter- as well as extra-specific differences) at approximately fortnightly intervals (Hendrickson, 1958, for *C. mydas*; Bustard, 1975a, for *C. mydas* and *Caretta*). The nesting season varies considerably in length in different parts of the world probably as a result of latitude. Near the equator nesting may occur in all months of the year (Hendrickson, 1958). The number of clutches laid during a season also shows geographic variation.

As Heron Island is a small cay, all nesting turtles can be recorded throughout the summer; hence the data obtained there are unique in their completeness during the period of observations. In all years the turtles probably completed one nesting prior to our arrival. Making allowance for this, the mean number of lays was 3.3 in summer 1965–1966, 4.6 in 1966–1967, and 4.3 in 1967–1968.

The arrival of the first turtles is remarkably regular from year to year, generally occurring within several days of October 20. During the next four weeks the numbers build up to a maximum that is sustained throughout December and January. In February numbers start to drop off again.

Larger turtles lay more eggs in a clutch than do smaller ones. There is no correlation between turtle size and egg weight in the green turtle (presumably mean egg weight is a result of natural selection). Since egg weight is also independent of clutch size, egg biomass increases similarly to clutch size with increase in size of the nesting turtle. This relationship is shown graphically in Fig. 8 for 212 clutches of the green turtle at Heron Island in summer 1967–1968. In view of a presumed optimum egg weight on evolutionary grounds (in terms of resources within the egg to nourish the developing embryo) it is interesting to note that mean egg weight varies considerably in different parts of the green turtle's range. For instance, Hendrickson (1958) gave a mean of 36 gm (range 28.6–44.7) for Sarawak and the mean for Heron Island, Australia, based on fifty clutches of eggs was 51.6 gm (range 44.0–60.4) (Bustard and Limpus, 1969). However, calorific measurements had not been made.

The heavy utilization of cays for nesting results in intraspecific competition for a nesting site. This leads to an appreciable destruction of incubating eggs by subsequent nesting turtles as was pointed out by Moorhouse (1933) and Harrisson (1953). The phenomenon was studied for the green turtle on Heron Island and it was demonstrated, by using

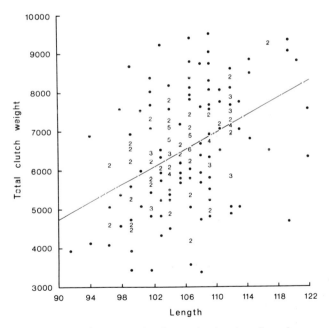

Fig. 8. The relationship between clutch weight (gm) and turtle carapace length (cm) for the green turtle population at Heron Island in summer 1967–1968. Numbers designate several points superimposed on each other.

a discrete biosimulation technique, that nest destruction was dependent on population density (Bustard and Tognetti, 1969). This could be a mechanism that plays at least a contributory role in population regulation. Further investigation is warranted.

Interspecific competition can also be important. Using biosimulation techniques, Bustard and Matters (1975) have shown how a population of nesting loggerheads may be adversely affected due to competition for nest sites by a green turtle population utilizing the same cay for nesting. As can be seen from Fig. 9, while their own population size is still small, the loggerheads undergo substantial loss of incubating eggs as a result of nesting by the green turtles. Due to their relative nesting position on the beach, greens are potentially much more destructive to loggerheads (turtle for turtle) than vice versa.

Under natural conditions at Heron Island, predators are absent and most eggs hatch. In 1966–1967 a sample of 26 undisturbed green turtle

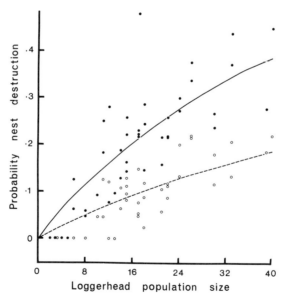

Fig. 9. The probability of nest destruction resulting from intra- and interspecific competition for nesting sites on a cay (Heron Island). Graphed are the destruction of loggerhead nests by subsequent nesting loggerheads (lower broken curve) and total nest destruction suffered by the loggerhead population (upper continuous curve). The different curves result from substantial interaction (nest destruction) by a nesting population of green turtles. As can be seen from the figure, the destruction caused by the green turtles is very substantial. From Bustard and Matters (1975).

nests gave 87.9% emergence and in 1967–1968 a sample of 40 nests of green turtles produced 84.9% emergence. Most clutches contain a percentage of infertile eggs or eggs in which the embryo dies at an extremely early stage of development (6.9 and 9.0% in the above samples). The balance of the loss is divided between embryos that die at an advanced stage and hatchlings that fail to emerge from the nest. Each category usually accounts for only a few percent. It is noteworthy that using the most careful techniques of hatchery operation, including the reburying of eggs within two hours of collection, a decrease in the number of hatchlings emerging from their nests of about 20% occurs (Bustard, 1975d).

An examination of the debit side of the population equation immediately shows that information is lacking on juvenile turtles, once they leave the shore. Research workers are still a long way from being able to construct any sort of life table for any turtle species. For instance, data on growth, survivorship, and longevity are lacking for natural populations.

Green turtles commence nesting at a shell length of 88 cm, measured over the curve. On the basis of captive growth studies of turtles kept under ideal conditions by Mr. and Mrs. O. L. Tanis of Brisbane (Bustard and Tanis, 1975), I would give a tentative age at first breeding for Australian green turtles as eight years. However, Carr (1968), basing his prediction on Caribbean populations of the same species, has suggested five years and Hendrickson (1958) thinks Asian green turtles mature at between four and six years old. In order to obtain data on more natural immature growth rate, I operated a hatchery at Heron Island for three years commencing in summer 1965–1966. All hatchlings were marked for subsequent identification into year classes before being allowed to enter the sea in the usual manner. It is hoped that some of these marked hatchlings will be recaptured and measured while nesting several years hence.

Nesting female green turtles measure from 88 to 127 cm on the Great Barrier Reef. Tag recapture data on nesting females can provide information on growth rate from first nesting size onward. (Reptiles, like other ecototherms, continue growth throughout life and typically reach sexual maturity long before "maximum" size is attained.) Our limited Australian recapture data are somewhat problematical in this regard. Of 11 green turtles recaptured after intervals of up to four years at sea, nine definitely showed no measurable growth. In only one was there a strong indication of an increase from 113 to 115 cm. The 1 cm increase in the other could have been caused by experimental error. Similarly, 8 of 11 loggerheads showed no growth after periods of up to three years at sea. In only two individuals was there clear indication of growth after three years at sea. One increased by 2.5 cm from an initial carapace length of 104 cm and the other by 4 cm from 94 cm. These data tend to indicate that either (a) growth is extremely slow in both species once sexual maturity is attained, and hence the large individuals are extremely old, or (b) that size at sexual maturity varies widely and little growth occurs subsequently. The second alternative would, however, be unusual in reptiles, as stated above. An age determination technique is required to settle this problem and we are currently critically investigating dating methods using skeletal material in a range of reptiles including sea turtles.

Data on survivorship could theoretically be obtained by massive marking programs on hatchlings, together with intensive recapturing activities at sea. The technical problems involved are immense. First, no one has designed an economic physical tag that can be inserted into or affixed to a hatchling without debilitating it and that can be detected again after several years' growth. The marginal shield clipping method that we used may suffice, as a definite year–class indicator would be adequate. Regeneration is poor, hence the mark should be readily picked up some years hence. It has the disadvantage that the animal does not carry a return address and the word "reward." However, this can be reduced to some extent by wide publicity (Bustard, 1969). Second, but equally important, is the virtual absence of sightings of small turtles at sea. Certainly the recapture of an adequate number of the various growth stages would be an enormous undertaking.

Since green and loggerhead turtles nest at intervals of several years, and since the nesting cays are visited by large numbers of turtles every year, clearly several population groups use the same cays for nesting. This phenomenon is of considerable interest in their population ecology. For instance, at the present time we do not know how discrete these population groups are or if juveniles usually recruit to the population that produced them.

An examination of a few population parameters including, where appropriate, frequency distributions of size, shell shape, postocular count, and number of marginals and inframarginals demonstrates that at Heron Island each year's population appears to be a real entity. That is to say, the population characters in any one year generally show better agreement with those of the population present at the time of the last nesting of that population than with any of the intermediate populations. That this occurs, despite the very low proportion of recaptures in green turtles, seems to be evidence that the nesting population comes from a discrete population (Bustard, 1975c).

The frequency distribution of size for both green and loggerhead populations typically shows a very small number of individuals at about first breeding size (new recruits?) and a small number of large individuals. The green turtle peaks occur at about 105 cm. It would appear that most individuals are lost from the population before they approach maximum size. These data suggest that either growth becomes extremely slow after reaching a size of about 105 cm, so that most individuals do not live long enough to reach maximum sizes, or that loss from the population is rapid above this size. Some circumstantial evidence of this exists for both species, but at present it is impossible to say which alternative applies.

An examination of the data on damage, grouped according to turtle size, demonstrates clearly that this is not cumulative throughout life as might be expected. In the green turtle incidence of damage, which is presumably usually a result of shark attack in all cases, is greatest in the smaller females and thereafter drops steeply and remains similar throughout life. In loggerheads a peak is reached slightly more than halfway through the size range shown by breeding females. The fall in percent damaged above this size class indicates that substantial loss from the population occurs among young breeding female green turtles and that either loss at a much lower level continues throughout life or that larger turtles do not sustain shark injuries. It seems likely that both factors are important. In loggerheads the continuing accumulation of damage suggests little mortality until a certain size is reached after which substantial losses from the population occur.

The very small percent recapture of green turtles, the discrete nature of the characters of each season's nesting population, together with the tendency for these characters to repeat when the turtles are next due to nest, suggest a hypothesis that cannot be either proved or disproved at present. As can be seen from Fig. 10, there are pronounced currents moving toward the Capricorn Islands from the north and northeast at the time of year the turtles are migrating to their nesting cays. Hence the Capricorn turtles could be parts of much larger populations that happen to get caught in this current and proceed with it to the nesting cays. The data presented earlier in the chapter on recaptures in subsequent nesting years indicate that once in the general area, the turtles are able to locate their own nesting island and return to it to nest. This hypothesis raises a further question that cannot be answered at present, namely, what happens to the turtles that do not reach the south-

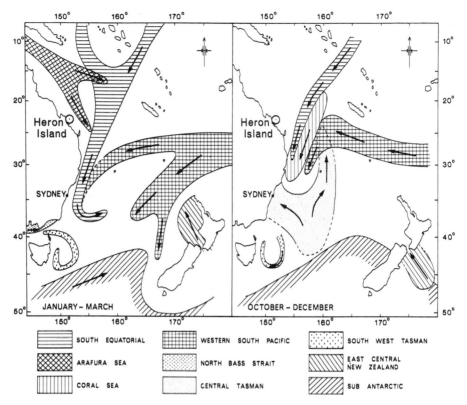

Fig. 10. The general surface water circulation off Eastern Australia when turtles are presumably migrating to or from Heron Island and other adjacent cays at the south of the Great Barrier Reef. After Rochford (1959).

ern area of the Great Barrier Reef in a nesting year? Do they breed, and if so, where?

X. Man the Predator or Competitor for Land

As with so many large animals in the world today, the green turtle, which has inhabited the warm oceans of earth since late Cretaceous times (about 90 million years ago), is seriously depleted in numbers as a result of gross overexploitation by man, extending over several centuries in some parts of the world. The hawksbill turtle may even face extinction during this century unless effective conservation measures can be implemented without delay.

Long before European exploration and colonization, turtles and their eggs were a highly esteemed article of diet among coastal-dwelling people throughout the tropics and subtropics. It seems that the turtles were able to sustain this level of predation since it was often sporadic, many of the favored rookeries were not inhabited by man, and human population density was usually low. MacGillivray (1852) cited many instances of the utilization of turtles by Australian aborigines and Torres Strait islanders. Native peoples generally catch a large percentage of their turtles at sea when they are not breeding. However, it is now certain that even without European man becoming involved in their slaughter or utilization, hunted species such as the green and hawskbill can no longer withstand the level of predation imposed by present local inhabitants in many places. This is a result of many factors, the most important being the very large increases in the size of human populations this century together with their mobility. The breakdown of old tribal rivalries and possession of motor boats has allowed numbers of people to regularly visit cays that formerly were visited only once or twice a year. Hence, even in areas of the world such as Fiji where there are many uninhabited cays and volcanic islands providing ideal conditions for nesting, turtle numbers have decreased sharply. The fact that the turtles are known to return to lay at fortnightly intervals enables the local people to note the date if they miss the turtle at its first nesting and to catch it the next time. Even when the turtle is missed, the eggs are taken, so the picture is one of little breeding success, even on many of the smaller islands, combined with a continuing drain on the remnants of the breeding populations.

European participation in a turtle fishery has usually proved disastrous owing to the large numbers of nesting females taken on the beaches (Musgrave and Whitley, 1926; Anonymous, 1969). Ingle and Walton Smith (1949) and Parsons (1956, 1962) provided particularly detailed accounts of turtle fisheries. Long (1774) and Anonymous (1957) dealt with the fishery in the Cayman Islands, the site recently selected for the world's first green turtle farming venture.

Yet another danger imposed by European man is land alienation. Beachside development for hotels and beach homes, together with coastal highways, have ruined many turtle rookeries. Bright light, so much a part of modern commercialism, tends to frighten away the adult turtles and because the newly emerged hatchlings are attracted to light, prevents them from reaching the sea.

The danger of land alienation can be adequately met only by the creation of National Parks specifically for sea turtles, sited to protect areas of important rookeries. Due to the green turtle's habit of high density nesting in isolated areas, these National Parks often need only be extremely small. In order to protect all the key turtle rookeries in Queensland and the Great Barrier Reef, the total area required would only be about 10 square miles! In addition to creation of special National Parks, it is essential to enact protective legislation. This should totally protect all species of sea turtle and their eggs at all times (as is the case in Queensland). If it is desired to commercialize turtle products or use them extensively for local people, then turtles should be specially bred for this purpose. It seems almost certain that the present decade will see turtle farms, incorporating their own breeding stock, in operation in many parts of the world. It would also seem to be feasible to take a specified number of turtles if the eggs and newly born young (both liable to heavy predation) were protected. Suggestions that this be done were made from the start of the century (see Yonge, 1930; Dresden and Goudriaan, 1948; Hendrickson, 1968), yet the first large-scale scheme has just started. Any such schemes must be under strict scientific management.

Due to their strong migratory habits sea turtles pose problems requiring concerted international action, as with whales. The International Union for the Conservation of Nature and Natural Resources (I.U.C.N.) has recently established a Sea Turtle Group within its Survival Services Commission and it is to be hoped that this will result in an awakening of interest in sea turtles (Anonymous, 1969). Properly managed turtle farms could provide substantial protein in many parts of a hungry world and also a cash crop for coastal people throughout the tropics and subtropics. They are also of very considerable scientific interest as an archaic reptile group that appears to have evolved little since the Cretaceous.

Acknowledgment

I am indebted to Dr. R. D. Hughes and Mr. J. Harris for critical reading of the manuscript. The Australian work described in this paper was mostly carried out at Heron Island and I would like to thank the Great Barrier Reef Committee, and in particular Dr. Robert Endean, for providing accommodation and research facilities for my team at their Heron Island Research Station. I would also like to thank the Fisheries Branch of the Queensland Department of Primary Industry for authorizing me to carry out research on totally protected fauna.

References

Anonymous. (1957). "Cayman Islands." Reports for 1955 and 1956. HM Stationery Office, London.

Anonymous. (1969). "Marine Turtles," New Ser. Suppl. Pap. No. 20. I.U.C.N. Publ.

Banks, E. (1937). *Sarawak Mus. J.* **4**, 523.

Bass, A. J., McAllister, H. J., and van Schoor, H. J. (1965). *Lammergeyer* **3**, 12.

Bryan, W. A. (1915). "Natural History of Hawaii." Hawaiian Gazette, Honolulu.

Bustard, H. R. (1969). *Pac. Isl. Mon.* **40**(10), 88.

Bustard, H. R. (1970). *Herpetologica* **26**, 224.

Bustard, H. R. (1975a). In preparation.

Bustard, H. R. (1975b). In preparation.

Bustard, H. R. (1975c). In preparation.

Bustard, H. R. (1975d). "Turtles on the Great Barrier Reef." Collins, London (in press).

Bustard, H. R., and Greenham, P. M. (1968). *Ecology* **49**, 269.

Bustard, H. R., and Greenham, P. (1969). *Herpetologica* **25**, 93.

Bustard, H. R., and Limpus, C. (1969). *Herpetologica* **25**, 29.

Bustard, H. R., and Limpus, C. (1970). *Herpetologica* **26**, 258.

Bustard, H. R., and Limpus, C. (1975). *Brit. J. Herpetol.* (in press).

Bustard, H. R., and Matters, D. (1975). In preparation.

Bustard, H. R., and Tanis, O. L. (1975). In preparation.

Bustard, H. R., and Tognetti, K. P. (1969). *Science* **163**, 939.

Bustard, H. R., Greenham, P., and Limpus C. (1975). *Proc., Kon. Ned. Akad. Wetensch., Ser. C* (in press).

Caldwell, D. K., Carr, A., and Ogren, L. H. (1959). *Fla. State Mus. Biol. Sci., Bull.* **4**, 295.

Carr, A. (1952). "Handbook of Turtles." Cornell Univ. Press (Comstock), Ithaca, New York.

Carr, A. (1962). *Pap., Interdisciplinary Conf. Use Telemetry Anim. Behav. Physiol., 1962* p. 179.

Carr, A. (1968). "The Turtle." Cassell, London.

Carr, A., and Carr, M. H. (1975). *Ecology* (in press).

Carr, A., and Giovannoli, L. (1957). *Amer. Mus. Nov.* **1835**.

Carr, A., and Ogren, L. (1960). *Bull. Amer. Mus. Natur. Hist.* **121**, 1.

Carr, A., Hirth, H., and Ogren, L. (1966) *Amer. Mus. Nov.* **2248**.

Colbert, E. H. (1962). "Dinosaurs: Their Discovery and Their World." Hutchinson, London.

Colnett, J. (1798). "A Voyage to the South Atlantic and 'Round Cape Horn into the Pacific Ocean." Bennett, London.

Cozzolino, A. (1938). *Riv. Biol. Colon.* **1**, 241.

Dampier, C. W. (1717). "A New Voyage 'Round the World." James Knapton, London.

Deraniyagala, P. E. P. (1932). *Ceylon J. Sci., Sect. B* **17**, 44.

Dresden, D., and Goudriaan, J. (1948). "Rapport ten Behoeve van het Velvaartsplan Nederlandsche Antillen." Stockum, The Hague.

Fryke, C., and Schweitzer, C. (1929). "Voyages to the East Indies." Cassell, London (reprint of 1700 edition).

Harrisson, T. (1951). *Sarawak Mus. J.* **5**, 593.

Harrisson, T. (1953). *Straits Times Annu.* p. 106.

Harrisson, T. (1954). *Sarawak Mus. J.* **6**, 126.

Harrisson, T. (1956). *Sarawak Mus. J.* **7**, 504.

Hendrickson, J. R. (1958). *Proc. Zool. Soc. London* **130**, 455.

Hendrickson, J. R. (1968). *Pap., S. Pac. Comm., 3rd Tech. Meet. Fish., 1968.*

Hirth, H., and Carr, A. (1970). *Verh. Kon. Akad. Wetensch. (Kon. Wetensch).* **58**, 1.

Hughes, G. R. (1969). *Afr. Wildl.* **23**, 5.

Hughes, G. R., and Mentis, M. T. (1967). *Lammergeyer* **3**, 55.

Hughes, G. R., Bass, A. J., and Mentis, M. T. (1967). *Lammergeyer* **3**, 5.

Ingle, R. M., and Walton Smith, F. G. (1949). "Sea Turtles and the Turtle Industry of the West Indies, Florida and the Gulf of Mexico, with Annotated Bibliography." Univ. of Miami Press, Miami.

Kenyon, K. W., and Rice, D. W. (1959). *Pac. Sci.* **13**, 215.

Long, E. (1774). "History of Jamaica." Lowndes, London.

MacGillivray, J. (1852). "Narrative of the Voyage of H.M.S. *Rattlesnake*," Vols. 1 and 2. T. & W. Boone, London.

Moorhouse, F. W. (1933). *Rep. Gt. Barrier Reef Comm.* **4**, 1.

Musgrave, A., and Whitley, G. P. (1926). *Aust. Mus. Mag.* **2**, 331.

Norman, J. R., and Fraser, F. C. (1948). "Giant Fishes, Whales and Dolphins." Putnam, London.

Parsons, J. J. (1956). *Univ. Calif., Berkeley, Publ. Geog.* **12**, 1.

Parsons, J. J. (1962). "The Green Turtle and Man." Univ. of Florida Press, Gainesville.

Rochford, D. J. (1959). *CSIRO Aust. Div. Fish. Oceanogr., Tech. Pap.* No. 7.

von Hagen, V. W. (1949). "Ecuador and the Galápagos Islands." Univ. of Oklahoma Press, Norman.

Yonge, C. M. (1930). "A Year on the Great Barrier Reef." Putnam, New York.

11

THE ECOLOGY AND BIOGEOGRAPHY OF CORAL CAYS*

Harold Heatwole

I. Introduction

A treatment of coral reefs would be incomplete without consideration of the cays associated with them. Cays frequently constitute a conspicu-

* Though I have imposed no regional restrictions on my treatment, it will naturally emphasize those areas with which I have had most personal experience. Most of the information summarized here is unpublished. Some arises from two projects still in progress: (1) A biotic survey of islands of the Great Barrier Reef, 73 of which have now been examined. (2) A three-year study of the community ecology of One Tree Island, Great Barrier Reef. Much of the remainder is based on a faunal survey of 140 Caribbean Islands (in collaboration with Richard Levins) and a herpetofaunal survey of the Louisiade, Lusancay, and Trobriand Islands of Papua-New Guinea. I am grateful to the National Science Foundation of the United States (Grants GB-2906 and GB-7088) and to the Fairbridge Expedition to New Guinea for support of these projects.

ous feature of reef physiognomy and their origin and development are intimately tied up with that of the rest of the reef. The parent mineral material of cays is derived from coral itself and other reef organisms such as mollusks, calcareous algae, foraminiferans, and other lesser contributors. Even much of the organic material ultimately has a marine origin, e.g., guano deposited by fish-eating sea birds. As will be discussed in more detail below, a considerable number of biotic interactions closely link the insular and marine communities in exchanges of materials and energy. Some organisms require both environments for successful maintenance and/or completion of their life cycle, e.g., terrestrial hermit crabs, some isopods, and amphipods. Thus, coral cays can be logically considered not only as a product of the reef but as an extension of the reef ecosystem. Indeed, one of the fascinating aspects of reef ecology is assessment of the extent to which marine and insular biotic communities interact, the organisms and pathways involved, and the way physical characteristics of islands influence these processes.

Cays are, however, discrete in many ways. There is a sharp discontinuity between island and sea not only in the ambient medium but also in the fauna and flora. This aids in clearly delimiting the insular biota that can then be studied as a unit. A second effect of the clearly defined boundaries of insular communities is that assessment of the relative isolation of populations is much easier than is true on mainland areas. Problems of dispersal and considerations of changes in the biota involve known boundaries and clearly defined barriers. The relative ease with which different organisms can cross such barriers, the degree of isolation of the cay from other islands or a mainland, as well as the characteristics of the island itself, all have a bearing on the composition of the insular community and hence the biotic interactions occurring there. Consequently biogeographic considerations are important to an understanding of the community ecology of coral cays.

II. Vegetation

Coral cays range from completely bare to heavily forested. The vegetation types can be conveniently categorized according to the following classification.

Strand Vegetation. The vegetation on very small cays consists of a sparse ground layer of widespread, often tropicopolitan, species. This is usually a mixture of grasses (*Thuarea, Cenchrus, Stenotaphrum, Sporobolus,* and *Lepturus*), vines (*Vigna* and *Ipomoea*), succulents (*Sesu-*

vium and *Portulaca*), and herbs (e.g., *Cakile*). On larger, more stable cays this type of cover remains on the upper beach and surrounds a central, more heavily vegetated area (Fig. 1A).

Herb Flat. Many cays are covered by low vegetation of dense cover (Fig. 1B) containing, in addition to the above mentioned strand species, a variety of herbs, grasses and small woody plants (e.g., *Boerhaavia*, *Wedelia*, and *Achyrantha*). The parasitic *Cassythea* is a common feature.

Shrubs and Shrub Ring. Many Great Barrier Reef cays have a ring of tall shrubs or trees around the periphery of the island between the strand vegetation and the herb flat or forest (Fig. 1C). Common species in Australia are *Messerschmidia argentea*, *Scaevola*, and sometimes *Casuarina*.

In the Caribbean, the ringlike configuration is not common, and there are, as well as on occasional Barrier Reef cays, open stands of shrubs or small trees covering much of the island. Common species in the Caribbean are *Coccoloba* and *Suriana*.

Forest. The most heavily vegetated cays on the Barrier Reef are those containing groves of *Pandanus* trees or *Pisonia* forests (Figs. 1D and 1E). These frequently contain accumulations of leaf litter and a thick humus layer. Shade is often so dense that a ground layer is almost completely absent. Forested Caribbean cays usually appear more xeric (Fig. 1F) and have a wide variety of tree species derived from larger, nearby rocky islands.

Mangroves. Mangroves constitute a special community sometimes associated with coral cays, in some cases being represented by only a solitary seedling or tree near the beach (Fig. 2A), in others by more extensive stands.

Succulent Mat. Many Caribbean and Australian cays have dense carpets of low, succulent plants. These are often of single species composition. Common components are *Sesuvium* and *Portulaca* (Fig. 2B).

Various islands show mixtures of these vegetation types. For example, One Tree Island, Great Barrier Reef, (5 ha in area) has strand vegetation on the beach, a shrub ring enclosing a well-developed herb flat, and both *Pandanus* groves and *Pisonia* forests inland. Around a central brackish pond is a dense mat of succulents.

In general, it seems that as one progresses from the structurally simple to the more complex vegetation types, regional differences become increasingly important. For example, strand vegetation is similar in appearance and even species composition throughout the tropics whereas the physiognomy and floristics of coral cay forests varies greatly among different areas.

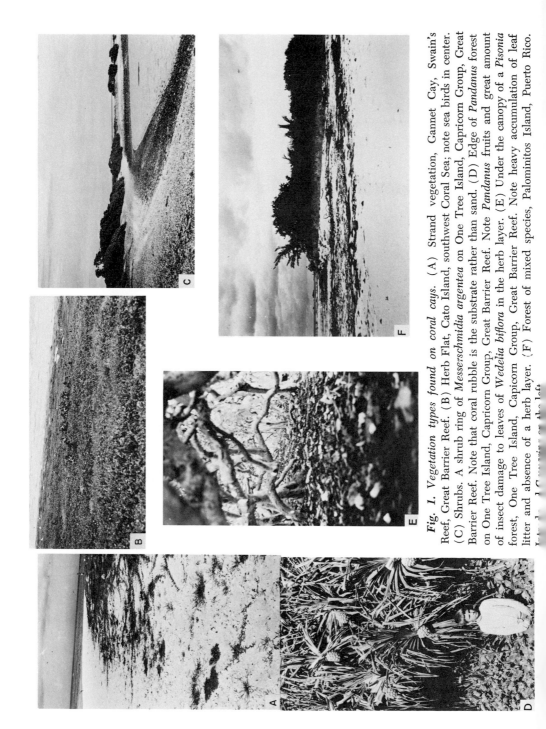

Fig. 1. Vegetation types found on coral cays. (A) Strand vegetation, Gannet Cay, Swain's Reef, Great Barrier Reef. (B) Herb Flat, Cato Island, southwest Coral Sea; note sea birds in center. (C) Shrubs. A shrub ring of *Messerschmidia argentea* on One Tree Island, Capricorn Group, Great Barrier Reef. Note that coral rubble is the substrate rather than sand. (D) Edge of *Pandanus* forest on One Tree Island, Capricorn Group, Great Barrier Reef. Note *Pandanus* fruits and great amount of insect damage to leaves of *Wedelia biflora* in the herb layer. (E) Under the canopy of a *Pisonia* forest, One Tree Island, Capricorn Group, Great Barrier Reef. Note heavy accumulation of leaf litter and absence of a herb layer. (F) Forest of mixed species, Palominitos Island, Puerto Rico.

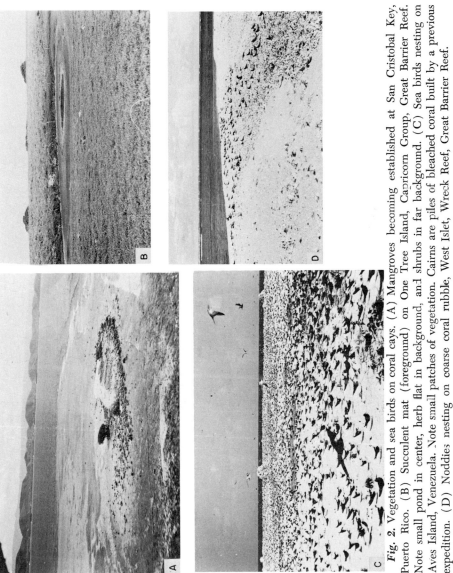

Fig. 2. Vegetation and sea birds on coral cays. (A) Mangroves becoming established at San Cristobal Key, Puerto Rico. (B) Succulent mat (foreground) on One Tree Island, Capricorn Group, Great Barrier Reef. Note small pond in center, herb flat in background, and shrubs in far background. (C) Sea birds nesting on Aves Island, Venezuela. Note small patches of vegetation. Cairns are piles of bleached coral built by a previous expedition. (D) Noddies nesting on coarse coral rubble, West Islet, Wreck Reef, Great Barrier Reef.

III. Fauna

A. SEA BIRDS

Sea birds are the most conspicuous faunal element on coral cays, sometimes nesting there in truly prodigious numbers (Fig. 2C). Gannets, terns, gulls, and Frigate birds are the most abundant. On the Great Barrier Reef, Mutton birds, and Sea Eagles are also common. The ecological significance of these birds is tremendous. Indeed, on some of the smaller cays they supersede plants as the community dominants not only in biomass and influence on community physiognomy but also in energetic importance.

Hindewood *et al.* (1963) listed 13 species of sea birds observed to nest on the cays of the southwestern Coral Sea. Although as many as 11 species sometimes nested on the same cay, there is frequently a tendency for a given island to have a large concentration of one species. Some of this may result from the social tendencies of the species involved. In other cases it may reflect rather narrow habitat preferences. For example, nests of the Common Noddy (*Anous stolidus*) usually have small coral fragments and/or pieces of brightly colored shells associated with them. I found this species nesting only on those islands that had coarse-textured substrates. Indeed, on West Islet, Wreck Reef, Great Barrier Reef, which consisted of fine sand with a central area of coarser rubble, I noticed that nesting noddies covered the coarser part but did not occur on the fine sand (Fig. 2D). By contrast, the Masked Gannet (*Sula dactylatra*) nests only on fine sand, a response that results in these two species nesting on different islands, or if together, on different parts of the same island. Vegetation is necessary for some species, e.g., the White-capped Noddy (*Anous minutus*) and the Red-footed Gannet (*Sula sula*). Gillham (1961) found that various insular birds required vegetation for nesting but that the resulting guano and trampling caused the site to become unsuitable and resulted in the birds moving to another place. When not in use, the vegetation recovered and a cycle was thereby generated. Michael Byer (personal communication) postulated a similar phenomenon on a Caribbean coral cay (Aves Island, Venezuela).

B. OTHER BIRDS

In addition to sea birds, several other avian species are ecologically important on Great Barrier Reef cays. The Reef Heron (*Demigretta sacra*) is a conspicuous element on forested cays. Resident land birds are not common. However, land rails (*Hypotaenidia phillippensis*) are found on a large number of heavily vegetated Barrier Reef cays and some of the islands of the Capricorn and Bunker Groups have dense populations of Silvereyes (*Zosterops lateralis*). Nesting doves of various species are also frequently observed on the cays of the Barrier Reef and the Caribbean. Cays near to mainlands may occasionally have mainland species nesting there.

A number of species stop briefly on coral cays during migratory flights. In addition, land birds occasionally accidentally disperse seaward (Heatwole, 1968). Eleven visits to One Tree Island over the course of two years yielded 12 "accidental" land birds of nine different species.

C. REPTILES

Reptiles are perhaps the second most important vertebrate group. Almost all vegetated cays in the Puerto Rico–Virgin Island archipelago have resident ground lizards of the genera *Ameiva* (Heatwole and Torres, 1967) and *Sphaerodactylus*. Those with trees or bushes often have, in addition, tree lizards (genus *Anolis*). Many Pacific islands have lizards. Considering their sizes and degrees of isolation, New Guinea cays contain a surprising variety of geckos and skinks. For example, Gabagabatau of the Conflict group has an area of only 3 ha yet contains four species of lizard.

On the Barrier Reef, land reptiles are not common. None of the outer reef or southwest Coral Sea cays possesses lizards. The most distant Australian coral cays known to have a native reptilian fauna are Green Island (13 km offshore) and Nymph Island lying between the mainland and a large continental island (Lizard Island) that has a reptilian fauna. It is 19 km from the mainland and 20 km from Lizard Island. Both Green and Nymph Islands have skinks and geckos. Lizards have been observed on Heron Island (70 km offshore), Wilson Island (72 km), and Lady Elliott Island (83 km). In these cases, however, the animals were probably inadvertently transported by humans. Except for Wilson Island, it is doubtful if they became permanently established.

D. OTHER VERTEBRATES

Other vertebrates are not common on coral cays. Rats have been frequently introduced by man. In the Caribbean goats were widely released on uninhabited cays and have drastically altered the original vegetation. Bats are occasionally present; the Flying Fox (*Pteropus*) was observed on almost every coral cay containing arborescent vegetation in the Louisiade Island groups east of New Guinea. Very few other native mammals occur on coral cays. Amphibians are almost never found on coral cays.

E. INVERTEBRATES

A wide variety of invertebrates is present, representing almost every terrestrial group. A few species even occur on cays that are completely devoid of vegetation (Heatwole, 1971).

IV. Number of Species

It has long been recognized that islands have fewer species than comparable areas of mainland. Insular biotas were considered "depauperate" because low species diversity was believed to result from the inability of most species to cross the seawater barrier and then only as a rare, fortuitous event. In the case of continental islands, numbers of species would be expected to be somewhat higher as a result of enrichment by species left stranded at the time of separation from the mainland. Coral cays, however, even when occurring on continental shelves, have

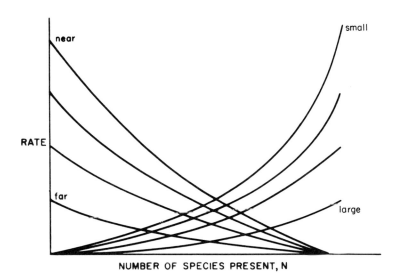

Fig. 3. Theoretical relation of extinction and immigration curves to island size and distance from mainland. Equilibrium number of species for any given combination is where the two lines cross. From MacArthur and Wilson (1963).

been formed *in situ* without previous connection with a mainland. They are thus biogeographically more analogous to oceanic islands than to continental ones. Also, the small size of many does not favor species enrichment through intrainsular adaptive radiation. MacArthur and Wilson (1963) have postulated that number of species on an island represents an equilibrium between immigration and extinction rates, these in turn being influenced by size of island and its distance from a mainland (Fig. 3).

V. Species Turnover

Few intensive studies have been carried out on cays for sufficiently long periods to enable species turnover to be evaluated. An exception is the study of Heatwole and Levins (1973). They made periodic trips to Cayo Ahogado, a small sand cay 1.1 km off the coast of Puerto Rico. The vegetated part of this cay was only about 10 m in diameter. During a period of more than two years, 36 species of plants were recorded with no more than 18 present at any one time. The ants, spiders, and other invertebrates also showed high rates of turnover. The most striking result was the appearance of eight individuals of three species of lizards at various times and their subsequent disappearance after intervals of 1–4 months.

High species turnover has also been noted on One Tree Island, Great Barrier Reef. Visits were at 2-month intervals and, over a period of 2 years, additional species of insects with high population densities were encountered on each trip; some previously abundant ones had disappeared each time. Some of the apparent turnover is almost certainly attributable to seasonal life cycles of animals, although the tropical environment would tend to minimize this effect. In the case of plants, species present only as seeds in the ground would be overlooked. However, the effect is not entirely a seasonal one as the species composition of the insect fauna differed greatly between July 1968 and July 1969. Similarly, some species that newly appeared subsequently remained at high population densities for an entire year.

Heatwole (1971) thoroughly examined a vegetation-free sand cay (North Reef Cay, Frederick Reef, Great Barrier Reef) in August, 1967 and again in the same month of 1969. On the first trip eight species of terrestrial invertebrates were detected. On the second one, three species were found with only one common to both collections. As both trips were made at the same time of year, seasonal differences are not responsible for the results. In view of the smallness of this cay (4875 m²) and the fact that it was examined in its entirety both times, it is unlikely that the observed discrepancies resulted solely from overlooking species. Consequently, high species turnover is implied.

Another method of assessing species turnover is to compare the results of several independent floral surveys made at different times. For example, the plants of Heron Island, Great Barrier Reef, were examined in 1927 by MacGillivray and Rodway (1931), in 1958 by Gillham (1963), and a third time in 1960 by Fosberg (1961b). The first survey listed 25 species, the second 35, and the third 40 (exclusive of those introduced by humans); only 17 species were common to all three surveys. Some relatively rare species overlooked one or more times may have contributed to this discrepancy but to invoke either this or seasonal changes (given the life history of the plants involved) to account for all the differences does not seem reasonable in view of the small size of the island. Morning glories were recorded in 1931 and 1955 (Gillham, 1963) but not later; I have since searched the entire island repeatedly for them but without success.

VI. Dispersal and Immigration

The above discussion may have seemed to imply that immigration to a coral cay is a lottery, every mainland form holding a ticket, each with an equal chance of winning. This is not true. Not all species are equally capable of being dispersed and hence the sea barriers will selectively filter out some species. In addition, even among species that are equally subject to being dispersed, say by flotsam, for example, there are probably differences in capacity to survive the rigors of the voyages or to become established once the destination has been reached (Levins and Heatwole, 1963).

Ridley (1930) reviewed sea transport of plants and saltwater tolerances of seeds. Some of the common strand species found on coral cays remained capable of germination after long periods in seawater (up to 10% germination after 90 days). Some germinated underwater and the seedlings floated. Many seeds or plant parts have specialized structures facilitating flotation.

Few quantitative studies have been made on the tolerances of animals to the conditions of salinity, temperature, or desiccation they are likely to encounter during either flotsam or wind dispersal. However, Brown and Alcala (1957) found that the eggs of some widely distributed Pacific geckos survived exposure to seawater for at least 11 days (and probably longer). Levins and Heatwole (in prep.) found that some Caribbean anoline lizards survived up to 9.2 days in seawater whereas frogs from the same habitats lasted only 1.75 hours or less. Much more attention to the dispersal physiology of coral cay animals is needed.

Few instances of flotsam transport have been directly observed. However, rattlesnakes, boas, crocodiles, rabbits (see King, 1962), and ants (Wheeler, 1916) have been found on floating objects at sea. Almost no attempt to assess flotsam dispersal quantitatively has been made. King (1962) observed natural rafts in the Rio Tortuguero, Costa Rica, and observed that a number succeeded in passing through the surf and drifted out to sea. He did not study frequency of occurrence of terrestrial organisms on them.

Heatwole and Levins (1972) analyzed 59 items of flotsam (coconuts, logs, sticks, etc.) collected at sea, but within 10 miles of land and found that 15 (25.4%) contained at least one live terrestrial animal. In all, 17 families of insects of four orders (Isoptera, Dermaptera, Coleoptera, and Diptera) were represented, as well as pseudoscorpions, snails, spiders, mites, millipedes, isopods, and worms. This strongly suggests that flotsam transport occurs with a surprisingly high frequency and is a significant feature of insular biogeography. Eight coconuts taken 150 miles from land lacked live terrestrial animals.

Wind transport is also much more common than was earlier believed. Gressitt and Yoshimoto (1963) reported that screening of 23 km^3 of air above the Pacific Ocean yielded 1054 insects of 106 families as well as some spiders and mites. One insect was trapped at an altitude of 5700 m. On the basis of this and other studies, they concluded that most dispersal of insects to distant Pacific islands is by air currents, particularly during storms. A number of groups is probably transported directly, others in bits of leaves, sticks, or other material harboring them.

Dispersal via birds is also extremely common and occurs in several ways. Many plants have seeds that are adhesive or have hooks that readily attach themselves to an animal. The importance of this for dispersal of plants to coral cays is emphasized by the fact that of the total flora of six species from Cato Island (287 km northeast of the Queensland mainland in the southwest Coral Sea) three species have clinging seeds. One Tree Island has a vascular flora of 19 species of which six (32%) have seeds that have either hooks or sticky substances covering them. The White-capped Noddy (*A. minutus*), which is common on many of the forested coral cays of the Great Barrier Reef, has been observed on numerous occasions to have the sticky seeds of

Pisonia grandis, in which it nests, clinging to its feathers, in some cases to the extent that its wings become stuck to the body, making flight impossible. I found a Sacred Kingfisher (*Halcyon sanctus*) on One Tree Island that was so covered with *Pisonia* seeds that not only its wings, but its legs as well, were stuck to the body and the bird was completely immobilized.

Some species of plants are dispersed as seeds surviving the passage through a bird's digestive tract, and may be transported from island to island in this manner. Experimental work has indicated that some shore birds retain viable seeds in their digestive tract up to 340 hours and could therefore transport them for several thousand miles (Proctor, 1968). On One Tree Island the ripe berries of *Solanum nigrum* are frequently eaten by the resident populations of Silvereyes (*Z. lateralis*) and Silver Gulls (*Larus novaehollandiae*). Whole seeds occur in the feces. *Solanum nigrum* arrived on the island during my study and subsequently spread from one small group of plants on the beach just above high tide line to cover the entire island and to contribute a large proportion of the herbaceous biomass of the community. Banded Silvereyes from Heron Island have appeared from time to time on One Tree Island. *Solanum nigrum* is present on Heron Island and was almost certainly carried to One Tree Island by one of the two species that eat it. These birds undoubtedly contributed to its rapid spread within the island once it had arrived.

Transport of aquatic organisms in the digestive tract of birds and on the bodies of birds, dragonflies, and dipterans have been observed (Proctor *et al.*, 1967; Revill *et al.*, 1967). Such dispersal is of little importance on coral cays as few have suitable habitats for the transported organisms. However, One Tree Island has a small brackish pond at its center that is frequently visited by nonresident shore birds of a wide variety and occasionally by nonresident dragonflies.

Immigration rates depend on all of the above forms of dispersal and quantitative data are needed not only for overall immigration rate but also for the relative contributions of the different methods of dispersal.

The effort and time required to carry out such studies are immense and they have seldom been attempted. A notable exception is the study of Simberloff and Wilson (1969) in which mangrove cays off the Florida coast were covered with a tent and defaunated by fumigation. The subsequent recolonization by terrestrial–arboreal animals provided a means of assessing immigration rates.

Similar studies are badly needed for coral cays at different distances from a mainland.

VII. Establishment

Survival during transport to an island is not enough to insure success on a coral cay. Establishment is also necessary and depends on ability (1) to survive the rigors of the physical environment of the cay, (2) to find a niche not already occupied by competitors or to eliminate them, and (3) to build up population density before occurrence of the random extinction that is likely to occur in the case of very small populations.

With respect to the first aspect, one of the relevant points is that the species most likely to be transported by flotsam are those that are associated with debris on beaches and hence already adapted to the type of habitat encountered on coral cays. In addition, organisms that live on beaches are likely to be more salt tolerant than others and hence more likely to survive flotsam transport. The same considerations apply to plants whose seeds are transported by flotation.

Finding an appropriate niche may depend very largely on the types of other organisms present, e.g., suitable prey or food plants. In addition, other more subtle factors may be involved. For example, orb-weaving spiders, which are easily wind-transported over long distances because of their habit of producing gossamer "parachutes," would be expected to be one of the common predators on coral cays. This appeared to be true in the Puerto Rico–Virgin Island archipelago. However (Heatwole, 1971), found that on bare sand cays of the Coral Sea, the only spiders were large ground spiders that are almost certainly not wind transported. This is probably because orb-weavers, in the absence of vascular plants, have no suitable place to construct webs and hence cannot capture prey. Vegetated cays contained web-spinning spiders.

Interdependence of species may affect colonization in a variety of ways. Establishment of a species of plant that has a specific, obligate pollinator would require that both it and the appropriate insect reach the island within the life span of the invading propagule. One could therefore predict that such plants would seldom be found on coral cays. Perhaps wind-pollinated species might predominate.

The nature of the reproductive system possessed by a species is also important in colonization by that species. Self-incompatibility would demand that at least two plants of the same species arrive within a relatively short time and this requirement would decrease the probability of permanent establishment. One would therefore expect colonizers of cays to be self-compatible (Baker, 1967). Apomixis among plants and

parthenogenesis among animals bestow an obvious advantage on colonizing species.

It is perhaps dangerous to predict the probability of success of a
given species in being able to find a suitable niche, as insular populations
may show broader ecological amplitude than mainland conspecific populations. For example, Crowell (1962) has shown that Bermuda birds
have a greater range in type of food and in nesting sites than the same
species has on the mainland. He attributed this to the absence of competitors at Bermuda, which permits the species to exploit a broader niche
than is possible in the presence of ecologically similar species. A similar
condition is found in some of the anoline lizards inhabiting coral cays
in the Puerto Rico–Virgin Island archipelago (Levins and Heatwole,
in prep.). It is probable that many species have latent behavioral characteristics that would allow them to expand their niche in the absence of
competition.

Though an insular existence may isolate a species from competitors
temporarily, it is also true that as immigration continues, species will
eventually arrive that overlap in their ecological requirements and competition will occur. Where the competitive advantage lies with whichever
of a species-pair happens to arrive first, a mosaic distribution can be
expected. This has been observed in Pacific ants (Wilson and Taylor,
1967) and in ants of the Puerto Rico–Virgin Island archipelago (Levins
et al., 1973).

Competitive exclusion has almost certainly occurred among ants inhabiting coral cays of the Great Barrier Reef. Green Island (13 km
offshore) and Heron Island (70 km offshore) although widely separated
in latitude, are the only two coral cays in the area known to have *Phei-
dole megacephala*. This is a tramp species originating in Africa but
which is easily transported by humans (Wilson and Taylor, 1967). Both
these islands have tourist resorts on them and a large volume of traffic
with the mainland, and this species has almost certainly reached these
islands via human agency. It is the only species of ant occurring on
these two islands which is very unusual if island size and distance from
the mainland are considered. For example, Erskine Island, a cay only
about 17 km from Heron and about one-third its area, has five species
of ant. It is probable that *P. megacephala* has eliminated the original
ant fauna from both Green and Heron Islands. The species is known for
its competitive interaction in other parts of the world (Wilson and
Taylor, 1967).

On archipelagoes where turnover rates are high and where ecologically
similar species would reach the same islands repeatedly and come into

contact, one would expect that there would be selection for niche divergence. Over long periods of time, the components of such a fauna would become ecologically adjusted and competition would contribute less to extinction rates. Thus, an evolutionary shift in the equilibrium number of species on an island should occur. Data on Pacific island ant faunas support this view (Wilson and Taylor, 1967).

VIII. Coral Cays as Ecosystems

Fosberg (1961a, 1965) has pointed out that coral atolls, including cays, should be considered as ecosystems and has briefly outlined some of the mineral and energy cycles that are involved in their functioning. The insular community, though discrete, does interact with the marine one, and Heatwole (1971) has recently suggested that a coral cay might be more realistically considered a segment of the reef ecosystem rather than a completely separate entity. He found terrestrial insular faunas of up to eight species on some cays in the Coral Sea that were completely devoid of vascular plants; such communities were obviously dependent on external sources for their energy. The following outside origins were identified.

Flotsam (material derived from terrestrial sources such as other islands or a mainland). Almost every island of the more than 200 I have surveyed in various localities has had some organic matter of outside origin on its beaches. Sticks, logs, and coconuts are most common. It was pointed out above that organisms transported by such material contribute to the immigration rate. In addition, the flotsam itself could serve as a significant contribution to the insular food resources. Its relative significance in the energy budget of the island probably varies with island size. On nonvegetated cays for example, there are few, if any, macroorganisms capable of utilizing this food directly and its incorporation into the community via detritus feeders must await its destruction by bacteria and fungi. On larger islands where wood-boring beetles, etc., are present, flotsam can be utilized directly.

Wind may blow some organic materials to a cay but the amount arriving in such a way is probably less than that lost by the same avenue.

Jetsam. Cays in inhabited archipelagoes or near shipping lanes are influenced by the refuse cast from ships or dumped in the sea from nearby islands. On every visit to One Tree island, at least one item of jetsam, which was a potential energy source to the terrestrial community, was found on the beach. Much of this material was in the form of cans, bottles, or jars containing small amounts of food. On the beach the lids quickly rust and make the contents available to the insular fauna.

Marine Carrion and Seaweed. Dead fish, turtles, sea snakes, crabs, jellyfish, mollusks, sponges, marine algae, vascular plants, and occasionally other marine organisms are often found washed up on the beach of cays. It is seldom possible to walk around the entire perimeter of a cay without encountering at least one dead marine organism and thus a rather continuous, though perhaps small, energy source is available to insular animals directly from the sea. For example, on One Tree Island, a number of dead marine animals were encountered on each trip. The importance of this energy source is evident from the size of the earwig population it supported. One Tree beach is composed of coral rubble and earwigs live in the interstices down to the high tide line. The only food source available to the beach earwigs, other than occasional dead birds, is marine carrion. They quickly find any material that washes in. Four tin cans buried to the top in the beach and then sheltered by a piece of coral were baited with sardines and used to trap earwigs. A total of 59 entered the traps during one day and 51 were individually marked and released. The following morning 60 individuals were in the traps, none of which represented a recapture. There must, therefore, be a large population of earwigs on the beach and, although perhaps atypical of cays in general, this does indicate the importance that input of marine carrion can assume.

Transfer Organisms. One of the major, marine-derived energy sources for islands is made available by animals that feed in the sea and subsequently contribute feces and carrion to the terrestrial community. These are called transfer organisms. Intertidal animals may be involved in energy exchange between island and sea, but by far the most important transfer organisms on most coral cays are the sea birds. Their contribution to the organic material on islands is evident from the vast deposits of guano that occur on many islands and that have been mined as a source of commercial fertilizer (Hutchinson, 1950). On some nonvegetated cays, bird guano and carrion serve as the main base of the food web (Heatwole, 1971); on vegetated ones, as well as contributing food for the animal community, guano and carrion provide a source of nitrates and phosphates that influences the vegetation and hence, indirectly, the herbivores and the food web in general.

Bird mortality is frequently high on coral cays. In the Coral Sea, Heatwole (1971) found 0.38 dead birds/m^2 and 1.49 dead birds/m^2 on Southwest Cay, Kenn Reef and North Reef Cay, Frederick Reef,

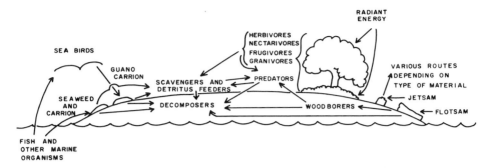

Fig. 4. Diagram of food webs and energy flow in a coral cay ecosystem.

respectively. Although these figures are higher than would be true for most cays, they do indicate the potential importance of this energy source. On North Reef Cay, almost every dead bird contained several adult dermestid beetles and numerous larvae. These insects were also in broken eggs.

Endogenously Produced Energy. On vegetated cays, energy bearing compounds are photosynthetically produced by plants and typical terrestrial food webs can develop.

The relative importance of these various sources of energy input has never been quantitatively assessed. However, it is clear that the ratio of marine-derived to endogenously produced energy decreases with increasing island area. The One Tree study involves a quantitative approach to community structure and function though it is still premature to present detailed results. However, Fig. 4 qualitatively summarizes the types of food web observed there and on a number of other cays on the Great Barrier Reef. The diagram represents the most complex insular food webs. Simpler islands lack some of the steps.

IX. Island Size

Island size is tremendously important in influencing the ecology of a coral cay. Number of species present has been shown to be related to island size by a number of studies (Preston 1962; Levins and Heatwole, 1963; MacArthur and Wilson, 1963, 1967). With respect to the number of plant species present, Whitehead and Jones (1969) have indicated that there are several critical island sizes. Very small cays can support only strand plants, i.e., those salt-tolerant species capable of growing in sand that lacks a freshwater lens. However, if the minimum diameter is 100 m or more, a fresh water lens can form and additional species can inhabit the island. Islands sufficiently large for at least semi-permanent human habitation have exotic plants introduced either intentionally or accidentally and these contribute to a more diverse flora.

X. Conclusion

This chapter has briefly sketched some of the main aspects of insular ecology and the unique features of island communities. The factors influencing numbers and types of organisms on cays are now at least partly understood. However, the functioning of these small communities and the interactions of component species have scarcely been studied. Treatment of islands as ecosystems promises to be one of the most fruitful approaches to insular ecology. Clearly, long-term, detailed studies of individual islands are required.

References

Baker, H. G. (1967). *Evolution* **21**, 853.

Brown, W. C., and Alcala, A. C. (1957). *Copeia* p. 39.

Crowell, K. L. (1962). *Ecology* **43**, 75.

Fosberg, F. R. (1961a). *Atoll Res. Bull.* **81**, 1.

Fosberg, F. R. (1961b). *Atoll Res. Bull.* **82**, 5.

Fosberg, F. R. (1965). In "Man's Place in the Island Ecosystem" (F. R. Fosberg, ed.), pp. 1–6. Bishop Museum Press, Honolulu.

Gillham, M. E. (1961). *J. Ecol.* **49**, 289.

Gillham, M. E. (1963). *Proc. Roy. Soc. Queensl.* **73**, 79.

Gressitt, J. L., and Yoshimoto, C. M. (1963). In "Pacific Basin Biogeography" (J. L. Gressitt, ed.), pp. 283–292. Bishop Museum Press, Honolulu.

Heatwole, H. (1968). *Emu* **68**, 132.

Heatwole, H. (1971). *Ecology* **52**, 363.

Heatwole, H., and Levins, R. (1972). *Ecology* **53**, 112.

Heatwole, H., and Levins, R. (1973). *Ecology* **54**, 1042.

Heatwole, H., and Torres, F. (1967). *Stud. Fauna Curacao Other Carib. Isl.* **24**, 63.

Hindewood, K. A., Keith, K., and Serventy, D. L. (1963). *CSIRO Div. Wildl. Tech. Pap.* **3**, 1.

Hutchinson, G. E. (1950). *Bull. Amer. Mus. Natur. Hist.* **96**, 1.

King, W. (1962). *Quart. J. Fla. Acad. Sci.* **25**, 45.

Levins, R., and Heatwole, H. (1963). *Carib. J. Sci.* **3**, 173.

Levins, R., and Heatwole, H. "The Puerto Rican Bank" (in preparation).

Levins, R., Pressick, M. L., and Heatwole, H. (1973). *Amer. Scient.* **61**, 463.

MacArthur, R. H., and Wilson, E. O. (1963). *Evolution* **17**, 373.

MacArthur, R. H., and Wilson, E. O. (1967). "The Theory of Island Biogeography." Princeton Univ. Press, Princeton, New Jersey.

MacGillivray, W. D. K., and Rodway, F. A. (1931). *Rep. G. Barrier Reef Comm.* 3, 58.

Preston, F. W. (1962). *Ecology* 43, 185 and 410.

Proctor, V. W. (1968). *Science* 160, 321.

Proctor, V. W., Malone, C. R., and DeVlaming, V. L. (1967). *Ecology* 48, 672.

Revill, D. L., Stewart, K. W., and Schlichting, H. E., Jr. (1967). *Ecology* 48, 1023.

Ridley, H. M., (1930). "The Dispersal of Plants Throughout the World." L. Reeve and Co. Ltd., Ashforth, Kent, England.

Simberloff, D. S., and Wilson, E. O. (1969). *Ecology* 50, 278.

Wheeler, W. M. (1916). *Psyche* 28, 180.

Whitehead, D. R., and Jones, C. E. (1969). *Evolution* 23, 171.

Wilson, E. O., and Taylor, R. W. (1967). *Evolution* 21, 1.

AUTHOR INDEX

Numbers in italics refer to the pages on which the complete references are listed.

SUBJECT INDEX

SYSTEMATIC INDEX